Financial Whirlpools

Financial Whirlpools
A Systems Story of the Great Global Recession

Karen L. Higgins

AMSTERDAM • BOSTON • HEIDELBERG • LONDON
NEW YORK • OXFORD • PARIS • SAN DIEGO
SAN FRANCISCO • SINGAPORE • SYDNEY • TOKYO
Academic Press is an imprint of Elsevier

Academic Press is an imprint of Elsevier
The Boulevard, Langford Lane, Kidlington, Oxford, OX5 1GB, UK
225 Wyman Street, Waltham, MA 02451, USA

Notice
No responsibility is assumed by the publisher for any injury and/or damage
to persons or property as a matter of products liability, negligence or otherwise,
or from any use or operation of any methods, products, instructions or ideas
contained in the material herein.

British Library Cataloguing-in-Publication Data
A catalogue record for this book is available from the British Library

Library of Congress Cataloging-in-Publication Data
A catalog record for this book is available from the Library of Congress

ISBN: 978-0-12-405905-4

For information on all Academic Press publications
visit our website at elsevierdirect.com

Typeset by MPS Limited, Chennai, India
www.adi-mps.com

Printed and bound in the United States

13 14 15 16   10 9 8 7 6 5 4 3 2 1

Contents

Part I
Foundations

Part II
The Yin: Human Behaviors

Part III
The Yang: Economic Mechanisms

8. What Goes Up Must Come Down: The Housing Bubble   159

9. On Top of Debt Mountain: High-Risk Loans and Credit   187

Part IV
Yin and Yang: Integration

11. Human Roots Are Deep: Yin Meets Yang

Companion Website for this Book: http://booksite.elsevier.com\9780124059054

Preface

The turmoil that began to build in 2006, hit United States in 2008, and spread to other nations immediately thereafter embodies one of the most challenging economic puzzles in recent history. Early in 2008 after international insurance giant AIG posted billions in loss, the U.S. economy unraveled. In the months that followed, reading the newspaper was like watching a gloomy soap opera; each week brought incredible tales of accounting fraud, losses, bankruptcies, and economic decline. In California, my home state, real estate was faring worse than in many other places. People were worried. As events unfolded, I became intrigued by the complexity and far-reaching effects of what would soon be called the 2008 economic crisis and the 2009 "worst global recession in decades."[1] This perfect storm, as some named it, sparked a passion for viewing problems as the interaction of many parts. Was it feasible to identify the pieces of this puzzle and fit them into a big picture of what had happened and why? Were there system-wide solutions that could reduce the likelihood of a future crisis?

The search for answers required extensive research into specifics of the crisis and into broader areas of economics and finance, psychology, sociology, philosophy, and ethics. To facilitate a deeper understanding, the investigation soon turned to a discipline called *systems thinking*. With this tool one can visualize complex issues in terms of their influences and relationships—a perfect match for this grand challenge.

As I proceeded, it struck me how changes in the social environment had exacerbated the crisis. Innovations born of the Information Age had not only transformed our day-to-day existence in terms of convenience, but also had altered how we interact and how we gather the information that shapes expectations and decisions. This recognition is significant: a nation's economy relies on such social exchange.

Just as telephones "ripped the social fabric and reconnected it"[2] in the early 1900s, personal computers and the internet revolutionized social interaction in the 1970s. Now individuals could share information electronically and forge new communication pathways. By the early 1990s with the World Wide Web and search engines such as Google, connectivity exploded. Access to any information, anywhere, anytime became commonplace. It seemed we had it all. Aside from greater speed and quantity, what more could happen?

1. Roubini, 2009.
2. Gleick, 2011.

Then, in the 2000s, networks outgrew their role as mere connectors of people and led a transformation of everyday life. Social media inventions such as Facebook, YouTube, and the iPhone extended our reach and awareness. Twitter and Facebook, for example, shared on-the-spot updates of terrorist attacks in Mumbai in 2008[3] and helped organize uprisings in Egypt in 2009.[4] Today, we e-shop anywhere day or night in the cocoon of our own homes while seeking others' opinions about what to buy. Our youth are tied by their ears and their thumbs to video games, friends, and strangers across the globe.

These advances are only the tip of a social change iceberg. In this networked milieu where anyone can find facts, opinions, or feelings about nearly anything, the economic crisis took root. Information and emotion-laden rumors raced across the globe in real time, no doubt accelerating the growth of the housing bubble and the spread of mortgage-related investments that activated the crisis.

However, these webs of communication were not the only facilitators of this crisis. Financial innovations added their own connecting threads. Novel types of loans and financial securities tightened links between the failure and success of these products and the fate of borrowers, investors, lenders, and financial institutions. By 2008, the economic world was so intertwined that cause and effect were inseparable; traditional policies would be impotent in propping a crumbling economy. This far-reaching interdependence was a noteworthy factor in the crisis, but when it met with human behaviors in an environment of plenty, disintegration was rapid and encompassing. The world's wealth was drawn into the financial whirlpools of economic excess.

This book uses systems thinking to explore the economic chaos that defined the first decade of this millennium. It begins with activities in the U.S. housing and financial industries and concludes with their effects on the economies of nations across the world. Although it identifies individual components, the book's greater contribution comes from interlocking these pieces to view relationships and movements over time. This bigger picture comes to life step-by-step through many systems diagrams.

The book was written for members of a diverse audience who share the desire to understand and to learn. Those who wonder how the economy works will be drawn to its descriptions, while those who wish to explore the crisis will see the major instigators in their larger context. Economists, social scientists, and policymakers across the globe may be able to use its interpretations to spark fresh thoughts. Those interested in systems behavior will appreciate how these concepts apply to a complex social problem—one whose effects were seemingly sudden and certainly devastating.

---

3. Busari, 2008.
4. Boyd, 2011.

Before we begin, I want to thank those interested and patient people who heartened my enthusiasm for the book and offered insights on various drafts. Kathy Pagel read and reread, commented, edited, and cheered me on. Fresh perspectives from Susan Smith and Dr. Randy Hodson enriched the book. Dr. Susan Rogers and Sherri Gattis gave support and a willing ear at every turn. From Elsevier, Dr. Scott Bentley, Senior Acquisition Editor, and Kathie Paoni, Editorial Project Manager, were paragons of efficiency, patience, and professionalism; Jason Mitchell, Publishing Services Manager, ensured I received all proofs, even during the holidays. Their encouragement and publishing expertise were priceless. And of course, my husband Tim breathed, slept, and ate the subject with me, always constructive in his comments and always sharing my excitement. I am thankful and deeply indebted to you all.

In writing this book, I imagined having a group of readers with me on this journey of discovery, thus I've consistently used "we" and "our" instead of "I" and "my." While this systems story reflects my own interpretation and simplification of the relationships that created the crisis, there are many ways to tell it. If the story piques your curiosity and makes you think about other possibilities, it has done its job. Please join me as an active companion as we explore this challenging puzzle together.

Figures

Tables

Biography

Karen L. Higgins is an adjunct professor of management at the Peter F. Drucker and Masatoshi Ito Graduate School of Management, Claremont Graduate University in California where she teaches Project Management, Ethical Leadership, and Systems Thinking. She is president of Élan Leadership Concepts and a board member for AltaOne Federal Credit Union. During her previous career with the Naval Air Warfare Center, Weapons Division at China Lake, California, she held various engineering and management positions including project manager for Sidewinder missile. While at the Weapons Division, she became a member of the Navy's Senior Executive Service and held the top civilian position of Executive Director and Director for Research and Engineering. She received a B.S. in mathematics and an M.S. in electrical engineering from University of Idaho, and an M.B.A. and Ph.D. in executive management from Claremont Graduate University. She lives with her husband in Southern California.

Dedication

Dedicated to future generations: May your vision be
long and your choices be wise.

Systems Thinking and the Great Global Recession

While the vulnerabilities that created the potential for crisis were years in the making, it was the collapse of the housing bubble—fueled by low interest rates, easy and available credit, scant regulation, and toxic mortgages—that was the spark that ignited a string of events, which led to a full-blown crisis in the fall of 2008.

The Financial Crisis Inquiry Commission[1]

. . . the major problems of our time cannot be understood in isolation. They are systemic problems—interconnected and interdependent.

Fritjof Capra[2]

After economic crisis hit the United States in September 2008 and spread its virus across the world, countless authors have offered interpretations of what happened. From formal investigative committee reports to editorials in local newspapers to theories of consumer behavior, a multitude of books, articles, and videos suggest reasons behind the crisis. In the end, these authors share a desire to understand it—often with the hope of preventing recurrence. Such focus of attention reflects the significance of the crisis; it also reveals a fascination for the relative surprise and swiftness with which it hit.

This book adds to a growing genre, but it uniquely assimilates diverse disciplines of economics, psychology, philosophy, ethics, and management; it presents the economic crisis as an integrated and interactive arrangement of smaller parts. It is not an economics book that will justify, expand, or dispute current economic theory. Nor does it offer a model of mathematical equations and exactness, for some economic factors, particularly those related to human behavior, cannot be explicitly measured or precisely predicted. The book does not mix up a magic potion to cure worldwide economic problems, unemployment, or unethical behaviors. Rather, it is a book about perspective; it intends to replace single factor, cause-and-effect thinking with big-picture views of a national economic crisis that quickly became a recession of global proportion. This perspective clarifies sources and

---

1. Financial Crisis Inquiry Commission, 2011.
2. Capra, 2010.

FIGURE 1   Yin and yang in the economy.

dynamics of the crisis and highlights leveraging actions that might have reduced its sting. As we progress, it should also become apparent that this type of thinking can apply to any complex problem.

Recognizing how much our world has changed over the past two decades underscores the importance of such an integrated viewpoint. We have plunged deeply into the realm of worldwide technological and social connectivity where momentous events bombard us with growing frequency and escalating effects. Just by hearing descriptors of the crisis-fraught economy—uncertain, unpredictable, unforeseen, unstable—we realize that reflecting on isolated events simply doesn't work well. With such a singular approach, we cannot hope to isolate a culprit; the problem is too complicated. Even so, the complexity that razed the financial system was not one of detail, but rather one of dynamics and interaction. In other words, we cannot merely glue together the many pieces to fashion a portrait of the crisis. Instead, we must consider how these pieces worked together over the years—their dynamics.

As we compose this moving picture, two equally important halves of a whole emerge—a yin and yang of complementary economic forces.[3] Shown in Figure 1, Yin represents human behaviors and yang involves mechanisms and policies that keep an economy in motion. We will find that during the crisis, these forces were out of balance; we will discover how human behaviors overwhelmed traditional economic policies and made them impotent.

Organized to highlight these two halves and their interplay, the book has four parts: Foundations, Human Behaviors, Economic Mechanisms, and Integration. Each part builds on previous ones and each chapter progressively expands on an integrated systems perspective. Most chapters include visual cues derived from what is called *systems thinking* to deepen understanding of

---

3. Simpkins and Simpkins, 1999. Yin and yang are part of the Chinese philosophy of Tao and trace to *Tao Te Ching* written by Lao-Tzu around 60 BCE. Yin and yang operate in a "dynamic play of opposites." Yin is softness, femininity, and darkness, while yang characteristics are hardness, masculinity, and brightness. The familiar yin yang symbol of a divided circle is called Taijitu or diagram of ultimate power.

cause and effect, and of relationships and dynamics among elements that generated the crisis. And, as we will soon see, the environment prior to the crisis promoted these interactions in unexpected ways.

The book's first part lays the analytic groundwork. Chapter 1 illustrates systems thinking methodology and explains how to interpret the diagrams in the book. Chapter 2 describes economic fundamentals such as monetary, housing, and lending policies; mortgage loans, securities, and derivatives; supply and demand related to housing prices; and the linear sequence of events that bracketed the crisis in the U.S.

The second part of the book (Chapters 3–7) is dedicated to the human side of the systems picture, the yin. These chapters examine significant human traits and their relationships to the operation of the U.S. economy. Among these traits are values and beliefs that bias decisions and the cultures that contain them; expectations that reflect views of the future; and characteristics such as self-interest, significance, belonging, and pleasure that motivate behaviors. In excess, some of these elements can be unattractive; their potential to cause harm cannot be overstated. And, because these human weaknesses could apply to any one of us under the right circumstances, we will take the time to understand their roots and feel their implications.

The third part of the book (Chapters 8–10) concentrates on economic mechanisms in the United States, the yang. These chapters trace the economy's operation; analyze influential aspects of debt, financial securities, and the housing bubble; and show the roles that each of these played. Although these mechanisms intend to have predictable influence, we know that they only function with human involvement and thus may create unintended outcomes. In these chapters, sprinkles of human expectations and materialistic desires punctuate this uncertainty.

The book's final section (Chapters 11 and 12) incorporates a greater richness of human influence and integrates the yin and yang of the crisis using systems thinking. Here, we visualize the economy's moving parts to understand its precarious balance and to appreciate how these parts became the financial whirlpools that engulfed the economy and characterized its destructive conditions. We then demonstrate the contagion of this crisis into the global economy and investigate future implications and possible actions. However, before continuing this ambitious journey, a few small stories will whet our appetites for what is to come.

* * * * * * *

Cries of shock and disappointment resounded in the New York studio of *Live with Regis and Kelly*. It was September 18, 2009. Boyishly blonde architect and master card-stacker Bryan Berg stood on a tall ladder, holding spare playing cards in his mouth while he gingerly placed one at a time on a growing tower. He was about to capture a new world record for building the tallest card tower in an hour—only a few seconds to go. The audience began counting down at 9 seconds and breathed a sigh of relief just as time ran out. Then the unthinkable happened. The tower came crashing down, spewing cards all over the stage. "Ohhhhhhh" was all that could be heard.[4] No world record for Berg.

More serious emotions filled American International Group's (AIG) corporate offices in New York City just a year earlier. AIG, the world's 18th largest company and major vendor of insurance-like coverage for mortgage-related securities, was a linchpin in the financial industry.[5] As more and more people failed to make payments on their home loans, big financial institutions such as Goldman Sachs and JPMorgan Chase came to collect on the loan default protection they had bought from AIG to cover their mortgage-related securities. On Saturday, September 13, 2008, AIG executives were apprehensive as a team from New York State's insurance department reviewed AIG's books in search of ways to raise money and keep the massive insurer afloat.[6] As the audit continued, the news got worse. AIG, it turned out, had no money to pay the claims and its deteriorating credit prevented it from borrowing the needed funds.

By Sunday, September 14, prospects for recovery were dismal. This financial tower of cards, all built upon home mortgage loans, had hit a limit. However, rather than hundreds of cards splattered across the floor of a TV studio, the fallout from this debacle would spew into corners never imagined. Those affected would number in the millions; dollars lost would be counted in billions; responses would be more poignant than "Ohhhhhhh."

This house of cards analogy has been well-used to describe the instability of an economic structure with a flimsy foundation, particularly as more cards, more weight, and more height are added.[7] In the case of the 2008 economic crisis, millions of people took many years to erect this financial card tower. Just as when a single card is added to the top of an already shaky base, seemingly insignificant decisions and small actions, one-by-one, created a situation that brought the world economy to its knees.

What were these small actions and why didn't we see them coming? Let's eavesdrop on a few fictional conversations to find out. On the surface, events depicted in these conversations didn't appear remotely relevant to the near demise of AIG or to the threatened implosion of the financial industry. They were simply everyday events in everyday lives. However, as we will see, these singular acts were intimately related to the greater economy.

* * * * * * * *

"Jen, we'd better talk," Tom began ominously. He stared out the kitchen window into their tiny yard as his wife talked excitedly about the new homes

---

4. Leo, 2009.
5. This insurance is called a "credit default swap" or CDS. See Chapter 2.
6. O'Harrow and Dennis, 2009.
7. See Faber, 2009; Holhut, 2011.

they had toured. The 2004 school year was nearly over for their two children and they needed to make plans before summer's end.

Tom turned to face his wife and continued, "I know you want to buy the new house with the big yard, but I think we may have to wait. I haven't been getting much overtime at the plant lately and I just don't think we can make it on my salary." Jennifer had desperately wanted to move into the nice neighborhood; the children could play in the nearby park and she would be closer to her part-time job at the day-care center. The timing was right; interest rates were rising, but still reasonable. The price of houses in Middleton Estates where the young couple wanted to buy was increasing every day, so they shouldn't delay.

"Oh no," she groaned with deep disappointment. "I thought you said we could swing it, especially if we don't have to make a big down payment."

Tom sighed and spoke his thoughts aloud. "Well I guess I could check with the bank again. The guys at work were talking about some sort of loan that has unbelievably low monthly payments. I'm not exactly sure what it is, but a few guys already have taken out these loans and didn't have to qualify. Besides houses are getting more expensive—we can always sell if we need to and maybe make some money. I'll drop by the bank on my lunch break tomorrow and see what they say."

"Kimi, can't you do *anything* to increase your commissions?" Jerry scanned his wife's face for a solution. "We really need to pay off our credit cards and remodel this house. I'd love to have a new big screen TV and trade cars."

"Gee Jerry. Competition is tough out there," Kimi answered, hearing the hopefulness in her husband's question. "Well. . . I guess I could start working on subprime loans. My boss is pushing the bank to work this area. It's more risky because borrowers don't have good credit, but we're offering these adjustable mortgage deals that start with low monthly payments they can afford—and now we don't have to do much of a credit check."

Yet she seemed bothered. "I'm a little uncomfortable about what might happen if people can't pay on their loans," she continued. "But they should be okay—if interest rates go up, they can always refinance with the increased equity in their homes. And it's no risk to me—or to the bank. I'll get my commission anyway and the bank can just sell off the loan. Yeah. . . okay—that's just what I'll do. I'll talk to my boss tomorrow. I should be able to up my commissions enough to buy a car. And maybe we can go to the discount store this weekend and take a serious look at some TVs."

"Really, K?! That would be wonderful," Jerry replied, approving of her tentative plan.

"Gene, we've just got to do something—we're running behind our 2004 budget projections and competition is fierce. The stockholders will be upset unless we bring in more money." Peter, CEO of a large investment firm, had stopped at the elevator to talk with Gene, his senior vice president. Budget discussions in the board meeting they had just left aroused his worry about the future.

"Well Pete, there's a lot of money out there, especially with all the foreign investors searching for new places to put their savings," the VP replied. "I heard our competitors are gung-ho selling what they call CDOs—you know, those *collateralized debt obligations.* They're just combining a bunch of MBSs, the *mortgage-backed securities,* into CDOs and selling interests in these CDOs. Remember last year we invested in MBSs from Freddie Mac to boost our bottom line? Freddie Mac has bought home loans from banks for years, combined them into MBSs and sold them to investors like us. Now it's our turn to pool MBSs and sell them as CDOs. Besides, headquarters said we can take on more debt since the government relaxed the rules, so we can invest even more. We could really make some money!"

"Interesting!" Peter's mind was whirring with possibilities. "I've been thinking along these lines too, but I worry about risk. We may be increasing our exposure to subprime loans through our MBSs, especially since that market has expanded. You know, the risk of nonpayment is higher for subprime loans than for the prime loans we give to borrowers with good credit ratings. Subprime borrowers have lousy credit and may not have good jobs. I wonder if investors will buy CDOs that contain subprime loans."

"Well, we do have options," Gene offered. "There's a great computer program we can use to figure out what price to charge to cover our risk—the price of course would be higher for CDOs that contain subprime loans, but the potential returns for our customers would be higher too. Besides, all the mortgages can't possibly go belly-up at the same time—that's the beauty of combining loans from all over the country. We just spread the risk. And we can insure them against default with a *credit default swap* through a big insurance company. I don't think there's much risk to us—we pay a small fee, but it would be worth it. If too many mortgages default, the insurance just pays us for the bad securities. And with real estate prices going up, there's little chance of having to give out much for bad loans anyway. Selling CDOs and covering our risk through a CDS is a great way to make money!"

"Sounds like you've done your homework. Let's go for it! I'll announce it at tomorrow's meeting," Peter laughed. "We're in for a big bonus this year!"

By 2008, conversations like these had spread across the U.S. like millions of cards placed atop a growing tower. Each individual decision added to the financial trends that were measured in trillions of dollars. In 2005 and 2006 more than $6 trillion in mortgage loans were made. Over $1.2 trillion of these were high risk subprime loans, nearly $1 trillion of which were then incorporated in MBS and CDO securities. By late 2006, investors owned $5.8 trillion in MBSs, nearly twice what they held in 2000. And in 2006 alone, over $550 billion CDOs were issued—more than double the amount sold the year before.[8] Risk was spreading like wild fire. Now let's fast forward to early 2008 and listen to conversations as the final cards landed atop this shaky tower.

* * * * * * * *

"I don't know what we're going to do, Sis," Pablo said to his sister with a lump in his throat. "Sue lost her job and the bank is about to foreclose on our house. My salary just can't cover the payments since they went up. When the value of our house increased a few years ago, we refinanced and used some equity to remodel and buy new appliances. We got a terrific deal on an adjustable rate mortgage that had really low monthly payments. We knew the payments might increase after a couple years if interest rates went up, but we figured that was unlikely since rates had been so low for so long. Besides, if our payments went up, we thought we could just sell or refinance again. But interest increased 5 percent— that's a thousand bucks more a month![9] Now, we can't afford the payments. And the price of the house took a nosedive in this market. Now, we owe more than it's worth. We can't pay off our Visa because our house payments are so high, so our credit is in the dumpster and we can't refinance. How can we ever keep it?"

His sister had never seen him so despondent and wondered how she could help. Her finances were stretched thin since she lost most of her nest egg in the stock market downturn a few years ago. Should she tell Pablo to declare bankruptcy? Could they move in with her?

* * * * * * * *

"I knew it was too good to be true! I told you we shouldn't do it!" Kaisha sobbed to her young husband. "We should have waited to buy this house until we both had steady jobs. Since I got laid off, we haven't made our house payments and now they're going to foreclose. We can't even pay our cell phone bills. Where will we live? What will we do?"

"But the bank guy said we couldn't lose," Tyler replied defensively. "They didn't need to check our credit and said we could just pay interest for a while until we got on our feet. My parents own a home, why shouldn't we? Buying was cheaper than renting anyway and the down payment was next to nothing. I thought things would get better."

---

8. MBS and CDO statistics from Gorton, 2008.
9. Median new home price in October 2006 was $250 K; it dropped to $213 K by October 2008 (U.S. Census Bureau, 2011c).

Although these conversations are imaginary, their situations were real—and heartbreaking. Earlier in the decade, credit was easy to get, even for those with poor credit history. Buoyed by the belief that the real estate boom would continue, many felt they could risk a small down payment and pay the invitingly low monthly payments of an adjustable rate mortgage to finance their dreams. After all, this was the land of opportunity. Yet, by early 2008 a quarter of the high risk subprime loans were delinquent;[10] in the first three months alone, "one in every 194 U.S. households received a foreclosure filing."[11] This high rate was more than twice the foreclosures filed in the first quarter of 2007. More cards on the tower. We now advance a few months to September to see what happened next.

Contrary to expectations, far too many mortgages defaulted. Many borrowers could no longer afford their monthly payments, especially when interest rates on their special "affordable" loans increased. Those who had bought and sold the financial securities that contained these bad loans were shocked when their investments faltered.

By early September 2008, defaults reached a critical level. Two significant events were about to take place—two more cards would start the tower shaking. On Sunday, September 7, the government placed Fannie Mae and Freddie Mac—major players in the home mortgage industry—into conservatorship. This action unloaded their $5 trillion home mortgage-related debt onto the shoulders of the U.S. taxpayer.[12] Then on Monday, September 8, Lehman Brothers, the fourth largest investment bank in the United States, began its fatal decline when its stock dropped 15 percent. By Wednesday, it dug its financial hole a little deeper by announcing a nearly $4 billion third quarter loss, most of which involved real estate write-offs.[13] Because it could not convince the U.S. government to pay off the unbelievable $613 billion it owed to 100,000 creditors and because it couldn't find a buyer, on September 15, Lehman Brothers filed the largest bankruptcy in U.S. history.[14]

That same day, the final card hovered. On that day, AIG's credit ratings were again downgraded; they could neither pay nor borrow the $75 billion they owed to companies they had insured.[15] The next day, other U.S. financial institutions began to crumble, rattling nations across the globe. Something must be done to shore up the card tower quickly before it demolished the world's economy, leveling people, businesses, and nations in

---

10. Bernanke, 2008.
11. RealtyTrac, 2008.
12. Jickling, 2008.
13. See McLean and Nocera, 2010.
14. Mamudi, 2008.
15. AIG, 2010; Karnitschnig et al., 2008.

its wake. In a move of last resort, on Tuesday, September 16, 2008, the U.S. government authorized the largest-ever bailout of a private corporation to keep the economy afloat: an $85 billion credit line in exchange for 79 percent ownership of AIG.[16]

However, even with government intervention, repercussions continued over the next several months. By September's end, the five largest investment bank holding companies as well as Fannie Mae and Freddie Mac had been sold, bankrupted, or taken over. With no other recourse, the U.S. government authorized a $700 billion relief program to assist other distressed financial institutions.[17] By November, AIG's total bailout had grown from the original $85 billion to $150 billion;[18] U.S. national debt grew by a trillion dollars.[19] However, this fallout was not confined to the United States. In early October 2008, Iceland teetered on the brink of bankruptcy until the International Monetary Fund provided it with a $10 billion bailout to cover its debts.[20] Later that month, South Korea exposed its vulnerability "to Western market panic" when its government pledged "over $100 billion in loan guarantees and an infusion of $30 billion" to prop its failing banking system.[21] What big consequences emanated from such small beginnings!

Was this outcome a surprise? Statistics expose a whiff of decay before 2008, but its seriousness and magnitude were hidden. By 2008, risky loans and foreclosures in the U.S. reached their peaks. Because record numbers of these failing loans had been put into MBS and CDO securities and then protected by credit default swaps,[22] the financial market strategy to mitigate risk of default backfired. Everyone was hurt and the scope was unparalleled. Let's probe deeper into individual households to find other U.S. trends before the meltdown:

- Personal savings: By 2007, personal savings had decreased to about 2 percent of disposable income,[23] only a quarter of the savings rate in 1992.
- Average debt: By 2007, average credit card debt was around $9900 at an average of 14.7 percent interest.[24] Consumer debt had nearly tripled between 1999 and 2007 to $12 trillion.[25] Total credit card debt hit almost $940 billion in December 2007.[26]

---

16. AIG, 2010.
17. Temple-Raston, 2008; the program was called Troubled Asset Relief Program (TARP).
18. Patalon, 2008.
19. U.S. National Debt, 2008.
20. Stringer, 2009.
21. Fackler, 2008.
22. Chapter 2 has more information on these instruments.
23. Kmitch, 2010.
24. Cardtrak.com, 2007; Chu and Acohido, 2008.
25. FRBNY, 2011b.
26. Federal Reserve Board, March 2009.

- Housing prices: By August 2008, housing prices had already declined 26 percent from their mid-2006 high; they were still dropping.[27]

These facts confirm that Americans were spending more money than they had, dipping into savings meant for their futures, and watching their wealth being sucked into the whirling financial waters. With massive personal turmoil, the U.S. economy was contracting. Annual gross domestic product (GDP) leveled off in 2007 and then began to shrink.[28] In December 2007, the National Bureau of Economic Research officially declared that the U.S. economy was in a recession.

These faceless statistics are hard to digest and don't capture the emotional trauma they represent. But on all fronts the story was consistent: everything was falling except debt, unemployment, and foreclosures. In 2008 alone, millions of Americans lost their jobs and millions lost their homes.[29] Like the ripples from a pebble hitting smooth water, effects of this crisis reached far beyond these losses; reported suicides, broken marriages, and surprise auctions of homes brought America face to face with "a social tragedy alongside an economic one."[30] This "Great Recession," as it was named, became the longest episode of economic decline in the United States since World War II. With its end declared in June 2009, the Great Recession broke the previous 16-month recession record in 1981 to 1982.[31] Yet, the scope of its devastation made this recession different from those past. By March 2008, the economies of many nations around the world were contracting; in January 2009, a Great Global Recession was in full force around the world.[32] It was only in July, August, and September of 2009 that "major advanced nations began to breathe a little easier."[33]

Whose fault was it? How did it happen? For nearly two years following that mid-September day, the U.S. Financial Crisis Inquiry Commission probed every detail to find out.[34] As much as the nation wanted to finger a single cause, the Commission's final report in January 2011 distributed responsibility far and wide. One financial reporter summarized the outcome, tongue-in-cheek: "Twenty months, 700 interviews... and the first

---

27. Standard & Poors/Case-Shiller, 2011.
28. Office of Management and Budget, 2010.
29. In 2008, 3.6 million people lost their jobs (U.S. Bureau of Labor Statistics, 2012a). Foreclosures were filed on 2.3 million properties—81 percent more than 2007 (RealtyTrac, 2009). Foreclosures peaked around 2.9 million in 2010 (RealtyTrac, 2011).
30. Stiglitz, 2010.
31. NBER, 2010.
32. OECD, 2012. Data from this source represent 41 nations including the U.S., European Union, South American countries, Japan, India, Korea, Russian Federation, South Africa, Indonesia, Mexico, Canada, and Turkey.
33. Lewin, 2012.
34. The Financial Crisis Inquiry Commission, 2011.

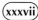

official U.S. government report into the causes of the financial crisis found that—as in *Murder on the Orient Express*—everyone did it."[35] Like the characters in Agatha Christie's novel, all suspects had plunged knives into the economy; all were responsible for its fall.

In addition to finding that it could have been avoided, the official report named eight areas of failure: financial regulation and supervision; risk management and corporate governance; excessive borrowing and risky investments; government response; accountability and ethics; mortgage-lending standards; regulations for over-the-counter derivatives; and credit rating agencies. The Commission highlighted other contributors (e.g., low interest rates and government housing policy) but they found none as significant as those eight.

Supplementing the inquiry committee's work, a U.S. Senate subcommittee conducted a separate investigation and compiled case studies on several major players. Their findings pointed to four roots: "high risk lending by U.S. financial institutions; regulatory failures; high risk, poor quality financial products; and inflated credit ratings."[36] Other economists compared this crisis to those in past centuries and found a simple and common theme: they are all "caused by excesses." Indeed, excesses appeared in consumer spending, in lending by banks, in profit-taking, and in executive bonuses. Some theories suggest that "*monetary* excesses were the main cause" specifically citing that the Federal Reserve kept interest rates too low for too long between 2000 and 2006.[37] A pervasive "moral deficit" marked by "unrelenting pursuit of profits" was another excess that is more difficult to correct.[38]

Although numerous causes were listed in these official reports and in many unofficial accountings, deeper questions remained unanswered: Could we have foretold the crisis? Could it have been prevented? Can we avoid a similar situation in the future? These questions are not trivial. The economic collapse that ravaged the U.S. in 2008 and initiated a global recession is one of the most intricate examples of how events can conspire to create unintended and unexpected consequences.

In this book, we will come to appreciate that regardless of our intent or actions, in a few cases we collide with real limits. For example the price of houses cannot go up forever and people cannot continue borrowing beyond their means. We will also see that the crisis did not begin a month or even a year earlier. Instead, like gears in an old clock, singular events pushed each

35. Braithwaite, 2011.
36. U.S. Senate Permanent Subcommittee on Investigations, 2011; agencies such as Moody's and S&P rate the risk of financial securities. Ratings determine price of these securities.
37. Taylor, 2009.
38. Stiglitz, 2010.

other around and around over many years until everything halted, and then suddenly and vigorously unwound. To appreciate the complexity of this clockwork, we will expand our perspective to consider September 2008 in the context of events that preceded and followed it. We will then apply systems thinking—a discipline especially suited for this type of problem.

Part I

Foundations

Chapter 1

Lines or Circles: The Basics of Systems Thinking

Systems thinking is needed more than ever because we are becoming overwhelmed by complexity. ...by seeing wholes we learn how to foster health.

Senge[1]

There are many ways to solve problems. Our normal mode of thinking causes us to isolate the problem, search for causes, and find solutions. The logic behind this approach follows a straight line: problem→ cause→ solution. Often called event-oriented or linear thinking, this method is highly effective when problems are simple or effects are fairly singular. However, in today's complex world, neither condition is true. Our socioeconomic environment is changing rapidly—often too rapidly for us to see or to understand the implications of important events.

A more effective approach, called systems thinking, views this environment as a group or *system* of elements, and then determines how these elements "interact with each other to function as a whole."[2] This big picture perspective originates in the concept of *holism*, from the Greek word for "whole" or "entire." A holistic or systems perspective means that behaviors cannot be explained by looking only at separate parts or solitary events, but rather by considering how these parts work together.[3] In systems thinking, cause and effect do not always follow a straight line whose end is set apart from its beginning. Instead, actions can be circular; their effects fold back to become a cause. Thus, a solution can actually exacerbate rather than resolve a problem. Another relevant feature of systems thinking is that it considers human actions. British professor Ralph Stacey describes this aspect: "Systems thinking is a holistic way of thinking that respects profound

1. Senge, 2006.
2. Lewis, 1998.
3. Smuts (1926) coined the term *holism* as a "fundamental factor operative towards the creation of wholes in the universe."

3

interconnectedness and. . . puts people, with their different beliefs, purposes, evaluations and conflicts, at the center of its concerns."[4]

With its many interrelated elements and a purpose to promote stability and growth, an economy easily meets the criteria for a system that involves people.[5] Thus the global economic crisis is a perfect candidate for using systems thinking. With these characteristics in mind, we now review the history and fundamentals of systems thinking.

1.1 A BRIEF HISTORY OF SYSTEMS THINKING

In western civilizations, the philosophical roots of systems thinking lie deep in Aristotle's recognition of a whole that is something *besides* the parts.[6] The origin of modern-day systems thinking, however, reaches back to the late 1700s when Thomas Malthus expressed his philosophy on population dynamics.[7] Then in the late 1800s, Herbert Spencer described evolution as the combined development of the physical world, biological organisms, human mind, and human culture.[8] These concepts of *emergent evolution* and *holism* were revived in the 1920s by psychologist C. Lloyd Morgan,[9] statesman Jan Smuts,[10] and others. In the 1930s and 1940s, the holistic perspective reappeared as *systems theory*.[11] During these decades, a group of scholars including Bertalanffy, Boulding, and Ashby[12] created a new paradigm that defined a system as a collection of subsystems and considered that collection to be part of an even larger system.[13] These scientists and engineers shifted academic focus from understanding elements that make up a system to understanding how these elements work together: a holistic view.

This new systems model deviated from the popular reductionist approach that breaks a problem apart and analyzes features of each part. Particularly after Descartes formalized it in the mid-1600s,[14] reductionism was immensely effective. The disciplines of physics, biology, chemistry, and medicine progressed using a reductionist method. Imagine breaking this analytic mold to use synthesis instead—to understand how the whole operated not only by understanding each part but also by recognizing their *interactions*. New insights were possible. Even today on the forefront of

4. Stacey, 2010. See also Jackson, 2000, cited by Stacey.
5. See Meadows (2008) for the definition of a system.
6. Sachs, 2002.
7. Richardson, 1999; see Malthus, 1798.
8. Spencer, 1890.
9. Morgan, 1927.
10. Smuts, 1926.
11. Corning, 1998.
12. Bertalanffy, 1968; Ashby, 1958; Boulding, 1956.
13. Stacey, 2010.
14. Descartes, 2008 (1637).

neurobiology, this same integration, or "linkage of differentiated parts of a system—is at the heart of well-being."[15]

Embraced by diverse disciplines such as biology and engineering, systems thinking became the subject of intense interest in the 1950s and 1960s. From this foundation, researchers and practitioners built three branches of systems theory: general systems theory,[16] cybernetics,[17] and system dynamics.[18] General systems theory and cybernetics regard systems as mechanisms that seek order and stability (homeostasis) or as goal-directed processes that adapt themselves to their environment. Biologists and those in related fields led the way in general systems theory, while engineers explored cybernetics. Engineers also developed system dynamics. This third branch is grounded in concepts of "dynamics and feedback control developed in mathematics, physics, and engineering."[19] Unlike the other branches, system dynamics applies systems theory to national and social problems of large scope and complexity. By modeling organizational and economic behaviors, it showed "how policies, decisions, structure, and delays are interrelated to influence growth and stability."[20]

The distinction between the first two and this third branch is important for our application. Unlike general systems theory or cybernetics, system dynamics recognizes that not all systems reach stability; internal factors may prevent them from attaining specific goals. In this view, a system no longer *regulates* itself. Instead, it *influences* itself; the effects of its actions come back to shape future behaviors. Thus, it can sustain or destroy itself.[21] Because the economy can certainly deviate from a desired goal and because its outputs such as prices or unemployment do influence what happens in the future, this third path of system dynamics is more suited for understanding the 2008 crisis.

1.2 APPLICATION AND RELEVANCE OF SYSTEMS THINKING

Yet, for our purposes, system dynamics in its pure form also has limitations. Often called *hard systems thinking*, system dynamics is quantitative by nature and investigates behavior using engineering equations and computer models,[22] neither of which is easily applied to a problem as complex or as human-centric as the crisis. However, an offshoot of system dynamics, called

---

15. Siegel, 2012.
16. See Bertalanffy, 1968. Concurrently, Bogdanov, a Russian scientist, also explored general systems concepts in the 1920s. See Strijbos, 2010, and Capra, 1996.
17. See Ashby, 1958; Wiener, 1948.
18. MIT professor Jay Forrester founded system dynamics in 1956; see Forrester, 1961.
19. Sterman, 2000.
20. Forrester, 1961.
21. Systems thinking history and branches of thought derived from Stacey, 2010.
22. Jackson, 2000.

soft systems thinking, is appropriate for our analysis. Like system dynamics, this category acknowledges interactions, but unlike system dynamics, it uses data and trends in a *qualitative* manner and does not apply rigorous modeling. Soft systems thinkers promote a systems perspective as a beneficial way to consider interconnections and influences, and to expand individuals' perspective and improving decision-making skills. These goals perfectly complement the book's objectives, thus we will view the economic crisis using soft systems thinking[23] or what we simply refer to as *systems thinking*.

1.3 LINEAR THINKING AND SYSTEMS THINKING

To appreciate the benefits of systems thinking, consider a typical business situation. Suppose a company's goal is to make a profit in a highly competitive industry. Next, suppose that a competitor introduces a popular new product, and suddenly the company's profit decreases. To save money, the company dismisses its customer-support staff. It now believes the problem is solved; lower expenses should increase profit. Figure 1.1 shows that this approach to the problem is linear.[24] It places cause and effect in a straight line without looking for other factors that may indirectly create larger issues.

Alternatively, using systems thinking, the company would expand its investigation to see if the solution ignored critical factors. Figure 1.2 shows

FIGURE 1.1   Linear thinking example.

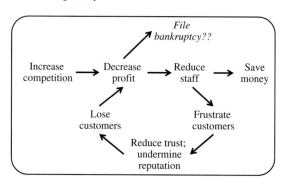

FIGURE 1.2   Systems thinking example.

---

23. See Richmond, 1994.
24. Sterman (2001) refers to this type of thinking as an "event-oriented view of the world" and introduces the notion of dynamic complexity to describe unintended consequences.

that, indeed, it missed important aspects. By reducing service, the company frustrated customers and diminished trust. Lack of trust undermined the company's reputation. This sequence caused customers to leave, which *decreased* rather than *increased* profit—not at all the intent. If the company continues this strategy, perhaps the end result will be bankruptcy. Systems thinking suggests that it should have considered a different solution.

1.4 COMPLEXITY ECONOMICS AND SYSTEMS THINKING

Big picture views are not new to economics. To compensate for the drawbacks of analyzing an economy from its individual components, the discipline of macroeconomics appeared in the early 1900s as a way to understand collective economic behavior. Some economists expanded this view with *complexity theories*. These theories consider how "individual behaviors collectively create an aggregate outcome" and what the reactions are to that outcome. One complexity theory known as *emergence* has been applied to stock market behavior[25] and to business cycle research.[26] This concept has long history; it was recognized in 1875 when Lewes defined "an emergent" as the effect that comes from actions that combine in ways that don't reveal their individuality.[27] Another more recent approach, *agent-based modeling*, assesses actions of individual elements relative to their effects on the larger economic system in which they operate.

These theories regard the economy as a system that is in constant motion. They recognize that "behavior creates pattern; and pattern in turn influences behavior."[28] Financial economist Eric Beinhocker uses the umbrella term *complexity economics* to describe these lines of thinking. He links this "genuinely new approach to economics" to a "long and rich intellectual history" that extends back to the mid-1900s and to notables such as mathematician John von Neumann and economists Herbert Simon and Friedrich Hayek.[29] In fact, parts of modern complexity economics evolved from the same 1950s−60s general systems theory that fostered systems thinking.[30] These applications recognize that individual elements combine to produce unintended patterns of behavior and that these patterns cannot be predicted from their individual elements.[31]

By the 1990s, some theorists touched the systems realm more deeply, adopting "a view of the economy based on positive feedbacks." One technologist describes the effects of societal pressures on behaviors using feedback

---

25. Arthur et al., 1996; Corning, 2002.
26. Gatti et al., 2008.
27. Lewes, 1875.
28. Arthur, 2006; see also Arthur et al., 1997.
29. Beinhocker, 2006.
30. Corning, 1998.
31. Stacey, 1996; this is a definition of emergence.

loops.[32] Experts in system dynamics use nonlinear modeling to better understand aspects of economic behavior.[33] Some suggest that in accepting the idea of feedback, economists "are beginning to portray the economy... as process-dependent, organic and always evolving."[34] By recognizing the tremendous complexity and dynamics of an economy, these theorists are leading the way to view economic events differently.

Although it does not expressly use systems thinking, complexity economics closely parallels its tenets. As we will discover, the feedback concept is a mainstay of systems thinking. Furthermore, complexity economics recognizes that the economy depends on networks of relationships and assumes that large-scale patterns (such as economic health) emerge from microlevel behaviors (such as monetary theory and human expectations) and adapt over time.[35] While complexity economics "is still more of a research program than a single, synthesized theory,"[36] it does provide a niche in economic theory that accommodates systems thinking.

The recent economic crisis exemplifies various types of systems behavior. Certainly single indicators could not have predicted the housing bubble or the subsequent gutting of the financial industry. Parts of the economy, it seems, behaved differently than expected; traditional government interventions were less effective than in the past and repercussions mushroomed beyond all experience. Something else was happening that would require a deeper understanding. So whether we call it systems thinking, emergence theory, or complexity economics, the idea of interdependent and dynamic relationships is a valuable viewpoint from which to discuss the crisis.

1.5 SYSTEMS THINKING CONCEPTS

This book uses four basic systems constructs: loops, lags, limits, and levers. These constructs have roots in system dynamics, but have been adapted for the qualitative application of systems thinking. The first of these, *loops*, emerged from the engineering background of system dynamics founder Jay Forrester, who applied information-feedback theory to management and social topics. Loop behavior is a foundational principle for both system dynamics and systems thinking; loops exist "whenever the environment leads to... action which affects the environment and thereby influences future decisions."[37]

For the study of complex systems, systems thinking also recognizes the importance of a second construct: *lags* or time delays between decision and

32. Schneier, 2012.
33. Sterman, 2000.
34. This and previous quote from Arthur, 1990.
35. See Beinhocker, 2006.
36. Beinhocker, 2006.
37. Forrester, 1961.

action. The third construct, *limits*, is built on the principle that natural systems such as an economy cannot grow unbounded, but have inherent limits. The final construct, *levers*, identifies areas where constructive change would be most effective.

These four—loops, lags, limits, and levers—comprise the systems framework we will use to portray the recent economic crisis in the U.S. and its global implications. The following sections describe these constructs and translate them into the visual language of behavior-over-time graphs (BOTs) and causal loop diagrams (CLDs).

1.6 LOOPS

Like Neapolitan ice cream, systems loops for our purposes come in three flavors: balancing feedback, reinforcing feedback, and reinforcing feed forward. Although each is important for describing a particular phenomenon or relationship, various combinations of the three are required to portray interactions and dynamics in the economic crisis.

1.6.1 Feedback Processes

When we hear the word *feedback* we usually think about someone correcting our behavior or paying us a compliment. If we are receptive, feedback in this sense helps us improve our behavior. However, in systems thinking, feedback is a continuous process rather than a comment; its definition is much broader.

Instead of straight line arrows or linear cause-effect chains, systems thinking uses two types of feedback processes: reinforcing and balancing.[38] "*Reinforcing* (or amplifying) feedback processes are the engines of growth" or "accelerating decline."[39] In other words, reinforcing feedback pushes "a system the way it is going."[40] Alternatively, *balancing* (or stabilizing) feedback tries "to bring things to a desired state (or goal) and keep them there."[41] By itself, balancing feedback is neither good nor bad, "it just means the system resists change."[42] Multiple reinforcing and balancing feedback processes were present in the economic crisis.

1.6.1.1 Reinforcing Feedback

A reinforcing feedback loop can be beneficial, leading to a *virtuous* circle, or detrimental, resulting in a *vicious* circle. Compound interest exemplifies a

---

38. Reinforcing feedback is also called positive feedback and balancing feedback is also called negative feedback. Because this nomenclature (positive and negative) is easily confused with *effects* of the loops we will not use it.
39. Senge, 2006.
40. O'Connor and McDermott, 1997.
41. Anderson and Johnson, 1997.
42. O'Connor and McDermott, 1997.

beneficial reinforcing feedback loop. Putting money into a compounding savings account earns interest. Over time, if we do not withdraw funds, our account grows from the interest earned. That larger balance earns more interest, which in turn earns still more interest and continues to grow until we withdraw our money.[43] Figure 1.3 shows this virtuous circle of saving.

The opposite case of compounding debt becomes the detrimental reinforcing feedback loop or *vicious circle* in Figure 1.4. This situation occurs when a consumer borrows money at some interest rate but does not repay the debt. When interest accrues each month, the debt builds on itself and can become unmanageable. Vicious circles were also prominent in our economic crisis framework.

Reinforcing loops may involve exponential growth, or the "process of doubling and redoubling and redoubling again"[44] as we saw in the compounding interest and compounding debt examples. Alternatively exponential decay is the reverse process of being divided in half again and again. For an economic system, this type of growth or decay can quickly produce astounding and often unexpected effects.

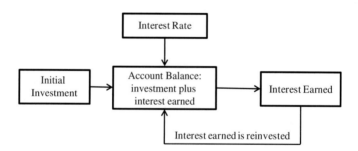

FIGURE 1.3 Compound interest as a beneficial reinforcing feedback loop (virtuous circle).

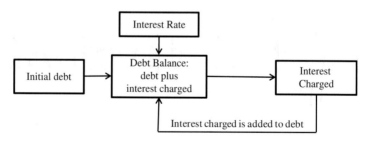

FIGURE 1.4 Compounding debt as a detrimental reinforcing feedback loop (vicious circle).

43. A fixed amount of money invested at 7 percent a year would double in about 10 years.
44. Meadows et al., 2004. Thus, "a quantity grows exponentially when its increase is proportional to what is already there."

1.6.1.2 Balancing Feedback

Balancing feedback has an altogether different nature than reinforcing feedback. Its goal-seeking behavior tries to stabilize a situation or guide it toward a desired outcome. Balancing feedback processes are everywhere in day-to-day life—from steering our cars, to using the thermostat in our homes, to our body healing a cut. In these cases, a desired goal is compared with the actual condition to determine what action will bring us closer to that goal.

Trying to lose weight is an example of a balancing feedback loop. Here we compare our current weight with desired weight; if we weigh too much, we exercise or diet. After a time, we weigh again to determine our next action. Figure 1.5 shows how this feedback/corrective action cycle repeats. If all goes well, we reach our goal.

Meeting organizational goals is a form of balancing feedback that existed during the crisis. As an example, a lending organization will set a goal for its loan officers and then measure their performance against this goal. If agents meet the goal, they are rewarded. If they do not, the company considers other options. These options may be so enticing (big bonuses) or distressing (loss of job) that employees make irrational decisions to meet the goals—sometimes causing unintended consequences. The simple principle here is that the company wants to guide employees toward desired outcomes and employees are motivated to achieve them.

Culture is a more subtle example of balancing feedback. Often without conscious intent, we behave in ways that are consistent with the beliefs and values of the culture in which we live or work. In this case, cultural norms are the goal of a balancing feedback loop; we compare our behaviors to this goal and make decisions that put us more in line with the culture. We will see this type of feedback when we explore human values and beliefs.

1.6.2 Feed-Forward Processes

In a special type of reinforcing loop, the *feed-forward loop,* the anticipation of an outcome determines behavior. In 1848, economist John Stuart Mill identified a feed-forward loop (although he did not call it that) when he found that "a tendency for the price to rise feeds back to produce a still greater tendency for the

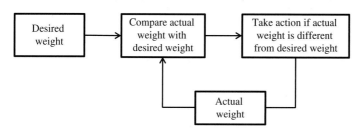

FIGURE 1.5   Dieting as a balancing feedback loop.

price to rise."[45] A hundred years later, sociologist Robert Merton called this same phenomenon a *self-fulfilling prophecy*[46] in which hopes, fears, expectations, and beliefs "lead us to act in ways that fundamentally change the world we observe"[47] and create the very future we had anticipated.[48]

In economics, the feed-forward loop aptly represents speculation on an asset. If for some real or imagined reason people expect its price to rise, they invest in that asset regardless of its worth. Hearing of these investments, others expect prices to rise so they, too, invest and add to the demand. In doing so, they unwittingly create a cycle that reinforces their original expectation of rising prices.

The feed-forward loop is a powerful force. Its presence generated the financial panic of 1893 that became one of the worst depressions in U.S. history.[49] In this case, as concern about the economy increased and confidence decreased, people withdrew their money from banks fearing it would lose value. Rumors circulated. Lines formed in front of the banks as more tried to claim their money. When others heard the rumors and saw the lines, they panicked and ran to pull out their money until the banks' cash reserves were depleted. Banks sought cash everywhere and even recalled loans they had made to businesses. Interest rates soared because the demand for money was perilously high. Businesses went bankrupt, banks failed, and depositors lost everything. Indeed the cycle was self-fulfilling: people did lose their money, but not for the reasons they had imagined. Figure 1.6 shows this self-fulfilling

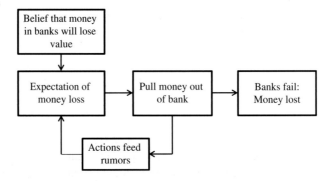

FIGURE 1.6   Expectations form a reinforcing feed-forward loop.

---

45. Richardson, 1999; reference to John Stuart Mill *Principles of political economy* (1848).
46. Merton (1948) referred to it as "a false definition evoking a new behavior which makes the originally false conception come true."
47. Gilovich, 1991; Gilovich references Merton, 1948.
48. O'Connor and McDermott, 1997.
49. Discussion of this period in Akerlof and Shiller, 2009; Lauck, 1907; Kindleberger and Aliber, 2005. (There was a fear that the U.S. would not maintain the gold standard for money. Note that the interest rate for money lent to stockbrokers for overnight transactions at one point reached 74 percent.)

prophecy as a vicious circle. As we will soon see, feed forward reinforcing loops also energized the 2008 crisis.

1.7 LAGS: TIME DELAYS

Understanding lags (time delays) between cause and effect is essential to grasping dynamics in the economy. Because it complicates knowing which actions cause what consequences, a lag between decision and outcome can lead to unpredictability and instability.[50] Lags originate in several ways. For instance, it takes time for a completed action to take effect. We experience this type of lag at Thanksgiving when we don't feel uncomfortably stuffed until 20 minutes after dessert. And in the diet example, it takes time to know how effective our efforts have been. The aftermath of Japan's immense earthquake and tsunami in March 2011 illustrates a more extended lag. In addition to ongoing cleanup of the devastation in Japan, over a year afterward "items ranging in size from a 164-foot shrimping vessel to a soccer ball" finally reached the North American coast.[51]

In some situations, the effect of a decision or action is masked by other events and not recognized until much later. In other situations, if we react before knowing the consequences of our original actions, these reactions may oppose our intent. We witness this type of instability, perhaps with a smile, when we watch student drivers testing their skills in traffic. Until they become used to the delay between pushing the gas pedal and the car accelerating, or hitting the brake and the car stopping, they likely slam on the brakes when the car goes too fast, then floor-board the gas when it goes too slowly. The result is that the car lurches down the road. This type of lag must be considered carefully in the economy, especially when governments enact new policies one after another without considering their long-term effects.

Lags are particularly crucial when determining how a system behaves over time. While some lags are measured in seconds or minutes, the most insidious lags, like those in an economy, are measured in years or even decades. By isolating only a small snapshot (September 16, 2008, for example) we cannot expect to understand what created a situation, when it began, or how events combined to generate unprecedented outcomes. We will identify lags in the events leading up to the economic crisis to better appreciate their enormous consequences.

1.8 LIMITS TO GROWTH

Natural systems, like national economies, operate in an environment where there are limits to the growth they can achieve. In the early 1970s, Forrester

---

50. Sterman, 2001.
51. Thiessen, 2012.

and other systems experts used this concept to model industrial and world issues. Here they found that conditions such as depleted resources, pollution, and crowding could suppress economic growth.[52] These analysts also applied limits to "social necessities" such as education, employment, social stability, and technological progress.[53] System dynamics expert John Sterman describes these limits as the "ecological concept of carrying capacity" of an environment. Every system that initially exhibits exponential growth (growth that builds on itself), he says, will reach its limit or capacity.

Limits in an economic system apply to many elements including availability of money, prices, or even an emotional resource like confidence. As we will see, some limits were bumped during the economic crisis. So what happens when limits are reached or exceeded? When a natural system approaches a limit, it can respond in several ways, two of which are *S-shaped growth* and *overshoot and collapse*.

1.8.1 S-Shaped Growth

In *S-shaped growth*, a quantity grows exponentially at first, but then will gradually "slow and then stop in a smooth accommodation with its limits." This slowing process occurs when the growing entity responds quickly to "accurate, prompt signals telling it where it is with respect to its limits."[54] In the economy, a highly simplistic example of this response may appear when the market for a particular item becomes saturated. First, assume that a company knows there are a limited number of potential buyers for a product. Then suppose that as the product becomes popular, the number of buyers grows quickly. Later, when fewer people are interested, the number of buyers grows slowly. Finally, when all interested consumers have the product, buying stops and the market has smoothly reached its limit.

1.8.2 Overshoot and Collapse

The *overshoot-and-collapse* variant of limits to growth is one of the most complicated system responses. It occurs when "signals or responses are delayed and limits are erodible (irreversibly degraded when exceeded)."[55] In other words, allowing a growth situation to go on for too long causes damage, especially when its effects are slow to appear. In this case, when a system exceeds its limits, its capacity to sustain growth erodes and it suddenly collapses. This response is like "eating your seed corn" to prevent starvation

---

52. Forrester, 1971a, 1971b; Meadows et al., 1972. The international team that studied these phenomena was part of *The Club of Rome*, a group of 30 people from 10 countries who gathered in Rome in 1968 to discuss "the present and future predicament of man."
53. See Meadows et al., 1972.
54. Meadows et al., 2004.
55. Meadows et al., 2004.

in the short term, but causing disaster in the long term when there is no seed to grow food. In this case, the system's capacity to grow food would have eroded.

John Stuart Mill recognized overshoot and collapse in speculative behavior. After an initial price growth, he saw that "when the price greatly exceeds the rationally justified price... Speculators come to think that the price will stop rising, so they start to sell, and indeed the price stops rising and starts to fall."[56] In this case, the "rationally justified price" is the systems limit. Some 160 years later, systems guru Peter Senge formally introduced *limits to growth* as an archetype or fundamental structure of systems thinking. He describes it as a reinforcing growth process that may slow and then "reverse itself to begin an accelerating collapse." Growth, he suggests, is caused by reinforcing feedback and slowing comes from balancing feedback that occurs "as a limit is approached."[57]

Overshoot and collapse can also describe economic events that may occur in the future. For example, when costs arising from various "physical, environmental, and social factors" eventually become too high, "growth in industry can no longer be sustained. ...the positive feedback loop... will reverse direction; the economy will begin to contract."[58] Similar to this prediction, U.S. housing prices during the economic crisis followed an accelerating growth spiral (reinforcing feedback) that reached a limit (balancing feedback), and reversed itself to become a rapidly degenerating spiral (reinforcing feedback) of falling prices. This spiral contributed to contraction of the U.S. economy.

1.9 LEVERS: POINTS OF POWER

It is not sufficient simply to identify the loops, lags, and limits that define a system's dynamic interactions. We must also consider actions that can elicit desired outcomes from that system. Such actions are called *levers*, or small acts applied at critical points to produce large changes. Systems thinker Donella Meadows popularized this idea in the late 1990s when she identified 12 "places to intervene in a system."[59] We will rely on four of her 12 leverage points or "points of power" to analyze the crisis. These four involve actions that: (1) change time delays between cause and effect; (2) improve the ability of balancing loops to limit what is intended; (3) slow or accelerate the growth or reinforcing loops; and (4) influence paradigms such as culture or beliefs. It is naïve to think that a few levers can fix or prevent a situation as large and encompassing as the economic crisis, but understanding the concept of leverage can create insights—which is the book's objective.

---

56. Richardson, 1999; reference to John Stuart Mill *Principles of political economy* (1848).
57. Senge, 2006. (The limits-to-growth archetype initially appeared in the 1990 edition.)
58. Meadows et al., 2004.
59. Meadows, 1999; also see Meadows (2008) for a discussion of leverage points.

1.10 VISUALIZATION TOOLS

We have so far described cause and effect, revealed the complexity of various loop combinations, defined lags and limits, and recognized how levers can identify effective solutions. Now, so that we can visualize what drove the economic crisis, we borrow two tools from system dynamics called *behavior-over-time* graphs and *causal loop diagrams*.[60]

1.10.1 Behavior-over-Time Graphs

For the crisis, it is important to think about how certain factors, such as the price of homes, behave. For example, by considering what happened to housing prices over several years, we can assess reasons for their fluctuation. Our analysis relies on viewing these behaviors with passing time, thus we will use the aptly named tool *behavior-over-time* or BOT graphs.

In systems thinking, identifying trends and influences is more important than determining the exact value of a variable at a particular point in time. BOT graphs describe trends and show behavior of selected factors over some time period (measured in years for the crisis). In the generic graph of Figure 1.7, time falls on the horizontal axis and the factor of interest (such as the price of housing) lies on the vertical axis. A BOT graph may depict the behavior of a single variable such as housing prices or delinquency rates, or it may compare the behavior of different variables. In either case, examining the shape of the curves allows us to identify what types of loops are present. With this information we can then translate BOT representations into causal loop diagrams that show dynamic interactions.

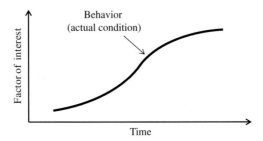

FIGURE 1.7   Generic behavior-over-time graph.

---

60. See Sterman (2000), Anderson and Johnson (1997), and Maani and Cavana (2007) for excellent discussions of CLDs and BOTs. Senge (2006) also has an excellent description of CLDs which he refers to as "circles of causality" or "circle diagrams." Sterman (2000) refers to BOTs as "modes of dynamic behavior."

1.10.2 Causal Loop Diagrams

In its portrayal of feedback structures, system dynamics uses stock-and-flow diagrams to identify specific quantities of an element that accumulate over time (called *stock*) and the *rate* at which a change in these quantities occurs (called *flow*). However, to make "system dynamics accessible to a wider range of people," these complicated quantitative stock-and-flow diagrams evolved into *causal loop diagrams* or the CLDs of systems thinking. Rather than specific quantities and rates, systems thinking CLDs communicate "the essential components and interactions in a system."[61] Figure 1.8 illustrates four important features of CLDs: (1) causal links and link polarity, (2) loop types and loop polarity, (3) feedback and feed-forward loops, and (4) lags or delays.[62]

Causal links are linear; their curved arrows point from cause to effect or from action to consequence. *Link polarity* ("s" or "o") relates the direction of change for a cause to the direction of a change for its effect. For example, an "s" means that cause and effect move in the *same* direction; when cause (such as interest rate) increases, its effect (such as interest earned) also increases, and when cause decreases, effect also decreases. Alternatively an "o" means that they move in *opposite* directions; when cause increases, effect decreases, and vice versa.[63]

Loops are circular combinations of causal links that define reinforcing and balancing feedback and feed-forward processes. They represent the

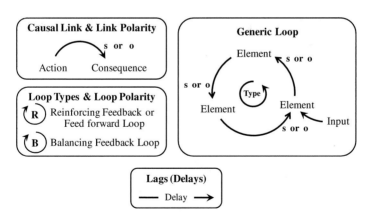

FIGURE 1.8   Features of causal loop diagrams.

61. Quotations and discussion of stock and flow from Richardson, 1986 (editor's comment by J. Sterman).
62. See excellent descriptions of causal loop diagrams in Sterman, 2000; and Anderson and Johnson, 1997.
63. In some CLD notations, "+" replaces "s," and "−" replaces "o."

systems thinking view that "reality is made up of circles" and that "every influence is both cause and effect."[64] These loops link consequence back to originating action. Associated with each loop is its *type*, depicted as an "R" or "B" inside a small circular arrow at the loop's center. "R" indicates a reinforcing loop and "B" designates a balancing loop. When creating a loop, an easy way to tell if it is a balancing type or a reinforcing type is to count the number of causal links that show an "o" polarity. If the number is even (or zero), it is a reinforcing loop. If the number is odd, it is a balancing loop. Similar to link polarity, *loop polarity* is a shorthand way to show the direction in which the reinforcing or balancing loop operates (clockwise or counterclockwise). *Lags* are annotated as a *delay* in a loop or link. With these templates in place, we now describe each loop type (balancing feedback, reinforcing feedback, and reinforcing feed-forward) and two hybrid modes (S-shaped growth and overshoot and collapse) using BOT and CLD visualization tools.[65]

1.10.3 Balancing Feedback Loop

Figure 1.9 describes a factor that approaches its desired goal with passing time. Although the BOT graph on the left shows that the original value of the factor of interest is above the goal, it could also be below the goal. In the balancing feedback CLD on the right, the desired goal is continuously compared with the actual condition. Once the difference or gap between them is determined, some action brings reality closer to the desire and reduces the gap. Note that in this balancing loop, the number of "o"s is odd (one) as predicted.

Figure 1.10 translates the diet example from Figure 1.6 into a balancing feedback CLD. When actual weight exceeds desired weight, the resulting

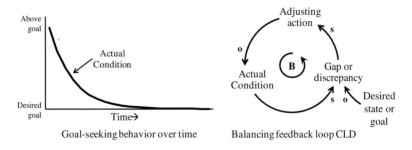

Goal-seeking behavior over time   Balancing feedback loop CLD

FIGURE 1.9   Balancing feedback loop: Goal-seeking behavior.

---

64. Senge, 2006.
65. See Maani and Cavana, 2007; Sterman, 2000.

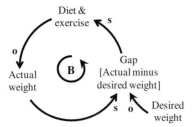

FIGURE 1.10   Balancing feedback loop for losing weight.

gap prompts diet and exercise ("s" arrow) to reduce actual weight ("o" arrow). Weight is measured again and compared with desired weight. When actual weight reaches desired weight (zero gap), the goal has been met. At that point, if diet and exercise decrease ("s" arrow) actual weight may again rise ("o" arrow).

1.10.4 Balancing Feedback Loop with Delays

When delays occur in a balancing feedback loop, the system does not reach its desired goal smoothly but oscillates above and below the goal as shown in Figure 1.11.[66] The novice driver illustrates one form of this behavior by continuously overcorrecting before the car has a chance to respond. Failure to accommodate the delay leads to a jerky oscillation between stop and go. Similar oscillating behavior can appear in the economy particularly when policies change before the full effects of previous policies are known.

1.10.5 Reinforcing Feedback and Feed-Forward Loops

Reinforcing loops are "the engines of growth and collapse."[67] Even their description is recursive: the more change they create, the more change they create. In other words, under some circumstances certain conditions grow or decay more rapidly as time passes. Reinforcing feedback that generates decay instead of growth may lead to collapse. For example, "a drop in stock prices erodes investor confidence which leads to more selling, lower prices, and still lower confidence."[68] Another collapse situation happens when a supervisor's constant harsh criticism about performance demoralizes an employee and causes her performance to diminish further.[69] Figure 1.12 shows exponential growth and collapse derived from reinforcing feedback. Reinforcing *feed-forward* loops have the same CLD representation as

---

66. Sterman, 2000; Anderson and Johnson, 1997.
67. Anderson and Johnson, 1997.
68. Sterman, 2000.
69. Anderson and Johnson, 1997.

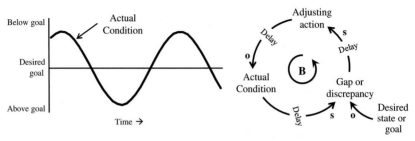

Oscillation: goal-seeking behavior with delays   Balancing feedback loop with delays CLD

FIGURE 1.11   Balancing feedback loop with delays: Oscillating behavior.

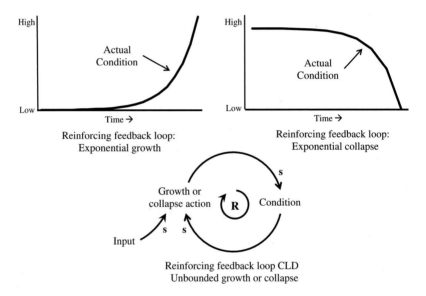

Reinforcing feedback loop: Reinforcing feedback loop:
Exponential growth   Exponential collapse

Reinforcing feedback loop CLD
Unbounded growth or collapse

FIGURE 1.12   Reinforcing feedback loop: Growth and collapse behavior.

feedback loops, except that *expectation* of a condition rather than its *reality* cause growth or collapse.

The feedback loop in Figure 1.13 describes the exponential growth of compound interest from Figure 1.3. When *interest earned* on a *savings account* adds to that account, its *balance* increases, which increases the *interest earned*. Growth in this loop is continuous.

1.10.6 Limits to Growth

A limits-to-growth construct uses one or more balancing feedback loops to reduce the escalating growth or decay of a reinforcing loop. For S-shaped

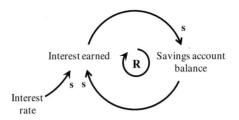

FIGURE 1.13   Reinforcing feedback loop for compound interest.

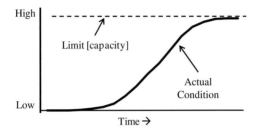

FIGURE 1.14   S-shaped growth behavior.

growth, this escalation may simply slow or stop at a given threshold. For overshoot and collapse, growth may not only stop, but may also reverse to create a degenerative "death" spiral—the collapse side of overshoot and collapse.

1.10.6.1 S-Shaped Growth

Figure 1.14 illustrates S-shaped growth. True to its name, the condition rises rapidly then tapers off at its limit to form the shape of a lazy "S." After a while, behavior bows to the limit and there is little or no growth. As Sterman puts it, growth stops smoothly when the system reaches its "carrying capacity."[70]

This variant of *limits-to-growth* behavior combines a reinforcing loop with a balancing loop that becomes dominant when the system reaches its limit and hits a steady equilibrium. World population is a familiar example of S-shaped growth. In this example, with no limit, population can grow exponentially, as described by a reinforcing loop. When paired with balancing loop B_1 that incorporates a death rate, population growth slows—by how much depends upon average lifetime. If birth and death rate are equal, population remains the same. If death rate exceeds birth rate by a small amount, population declines slowly. If birth rate exceeds death rate, population will

---

70. Sterman, 2000.

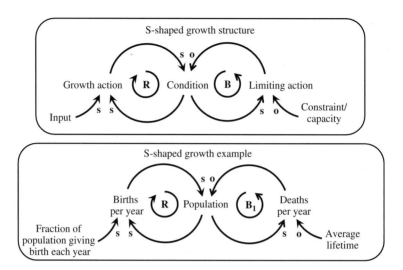

FIGURE 1.15   S-shaped growth CLD and example.

grow more slowly than if there were no death. Figure 1.15 shows an S-shaped causal loop diagram and the population example.[71]

In this example, if death rate exceeds birth rate by a large amount, something else may be happening—perhaps disease or other condition that can lead to overshoot and collapse.

1.10.6.2 Overshoot and Collapse

Overshoot and collapse is a complex behavior in which "a period of rapid growth or collapse followed by a slowdown typically signals a shift in dominance from a reinforcing loop that is driving the structure, to a balancing loop."[72] Unlike the S-shaped curve formed when a balancing loop decreases growth little by little until it reaches its limit, overshoot and collapse involves at least one loop that triggers decay in the reinforcing loop. Soon the system erodes its carrying capacity; it eats its "seed corn." Figure 1.16 shows overshoot and collapse. Like the S-shaped curve, the name of this structure reflects its shape: it overshoots the limit or capacity of the system and then collapses back toward the level at which growth began.

---

71. The classic population CLD represents Malthus' (1798) discussions on geometric population growth and arithmetic growth of subsistence. Various interpretations can be found in Senge, 2006; Meadows et al., 1972; Richardson, 1999; and Sterman, 2000. Senge calls this the "limits-to-growth" archetype for systems thinking. Sterman refers to these archetype behaviors as "interactions of the fundamental modes."
72. Anderson and Johnson, 1997.

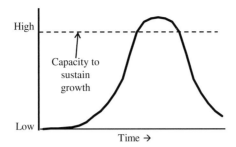

FIGURE 1.16 Overshoot-and-collapse behavior: Erosion of capacity.

Figure 1.17 illustrates an overshoot-and-collapse CLD and a notional example of how it could work.[73] This example adds a second balancing loop B_2 to the earlier population diagram. For this case, suppose that a nation enacts a policy to limit population growth. Suppose also that as *population* grows, the *policy* is more strongly enforced. If policy enforcement strengthens, more families have fewer *children*, thus reducing the number of *births per year*. As the annual *number of births* decreases, *population* decreases. In this case, if the *policy on population* is too severe and death rate exceeds birth rate, the nation's capacity for future population growth will erode, causing the reinforcing loop to reverse from growth to decay in an overshoot-and-collapse condition. Population will decline until something changes one or both balancing loops.

The overshoot-and-collapse type of limits-to-growth is not restricted to population or to natural resources. An economic example appeared in "the dot.com bubble in the global stock market... [in this case] the erodible resource was investor confidence."[74] We will see similar behaviors for housing prices during the crisis.

1.11 SYSTEM BOUNDARIES

Because any system we may define is a small part of a larger network of systems,[75] it is challenging to put a boundary around the system of interest so that it can be studied. One could, for example, include the entire universe and then investigate countless interactions of its subsystems all the way down to DNA.[76] Of course, this is hyperbole; such a system is too large and

---

73. One form of a generic overshoot-and-collapse CLD adapted from Sterman, 2000. See also Senge (2006) for limits to growth archetype and Anderson and Johnson's (1997) description of underinvestment showing erosion.
74. Meadows et al., 2004.
75. Anderson and Johnson, 1997.
76. See Lewis, 1998.

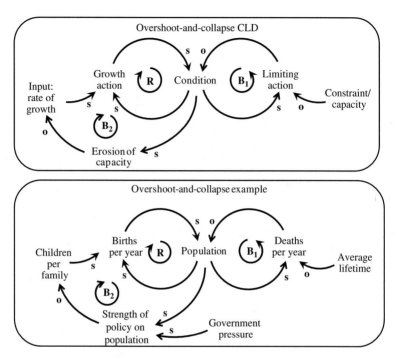

FIGURE 1.17 Overshoot-and-collapse CLD and example: Eroding population. *Source:* The CLD at the top of this figure is adapted from Sterman (2000). *Business Dynamics: Systems Thinking and Modeling for a Complex World.* Irwin McGraw-Hill. Reproduced with permission of The McGraw-Hill Companies.

unwieldy and beyond human ability to conceive. So, we must carefully place boundaries around the investigation. If these are too narrow, we will ignore important influencers; if they are too encompassing, we will be hopelessly mired in complexity.

For the 2008 economic situation, system boundaries involve time and scope. First, events must be understood in the context of their history, or "the infinity of prior events, minute causes, and circumstances that touch it in visible and invisible ways."[77] To capture historical flow we use statistical data between 1994 and 2010 for reasons discussed in Chapter 2, and we recognize the influence of factors that originated much earlier, such as economic policies in the 1970s, 1980s, and early 1990s. Next, to manage complexity, our initial system boundary for scope encompasses levels between individual behaviors and the U.S. economy, as seen in Figure 1.18.

By initially confining scope, we have essentially "closed" the system and excluded elements outside the defined boundary. But we know that a closed

---

77. Brooks, 2011.

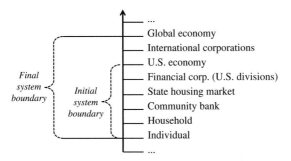

FIGURE 1.18   System boundaries.

approach is unrealistic for an economy. In fact, a basic tenet of general systems theory is that entities such as economic systems are *open systems*.[78] In other words, they interact with their environment. In this case, international economies and other externalities influenced and were influenced by the U.S. economic crisis. Thus our final system boundary, also shown in Figure 1.18, includes these global concerns; we describe this larger system in Chapter 12.

1.12 SYSTEMS THINKING PHILOSOPHY

Before beginning our analysis, we must first set expectations about using systems thinking to describe economic issues. Unlike traditional quantitative models of the economy, the systems thinking approach is a *framework* for understanding influences and relationships over time. By nature, it cannot provide exact solutions or precise predictions about quantifiable economic metrics such as unemployment or debt or gross domestic product. Nor can it precisely predict qualitative human responses to economic events.

However, systems thinking is extremely powerful in visually describing what influences what, especially when cause and effects lie outside our normal patterns of thought. With this framework, we can identify contributors to economic trends and determine where interventions will most likely create beneficial outcomes. We can spot what happens when actions occur in isolation and what might be unintended consequences of these actions. The intent of applying systems thinking to economics, therefore, is to expand our understanding of issues and to open our minds to broader perspectives and more creative ways of handling complex problems.

---

78. In the mid-1900s, Ludwig von Bertalanffy originated open systems theory in biology. He and others applied this theory to other disciplines to create general systems theory. See Weckowicz, 2000; Bertalanffy, 1968.

1.13 SUMMARY

This chapter reviewed history and philosophy of the soft systems thinking approach—the approach that we use to develop an integrated, big-picture view of the recent global economic crisis. Relevant systems thinking constructs include balancing and reinforcing feedback and feed-forward loops, lags or time delays, limits that set bounds for behaviors, and levers that can remedy dysfunction. Many complex behaviors seen during the crisis reflect a combination of these structures. This chapter also introduced tools (causal loop diagrams and behavior-over-time graphs) that translate behaviors into patterns and facilitate visual understanding. These pictorial representations are mainstays in later chapters. Using the loops, lags, limits, and levers of systems thinking, this book sequentially investigates events surrounding the 2008 economic crisis as they pertain to the United States and expands that investigation in the final chapter (Chapter 12) to include the greater global economy.

Chapter 2

As the Gears Turn: Policies, Practices, Markets, and Risk

The forces that hit financial markets in the U.S. in the summer of 2007 seemed like a force of nature, something akin to a hurricane, or an earthquake, something beyond human control.

Gorton[1]

Have you ever used a penny-stamping machine? You put a penny in a slot and for 75¢ you can watch different-sized gears push one another around and around. Finally, your penny falls out the bottom, flattened and stamped with an insignia. If we could somehow view the U.S. economy prior to the crisis, we might see its mechanisms driving one another like gears in the penny machine. Its most significant gears were federal policies, mortgage lending practices, and the housing and financial markets, all of which we discuss in this chapter. And in this case, our squashed penny carried the imprint of risk.

In the years before the 2008 meltdown, the U.S. economy was already roiling. Fueled by speculation in the internet industry, the NASDAQ doubled in 12 months to hit a record high in March 2000. Suddenly by the end of 2000, it had dropped in half when dot-com companies ran out of steam.[2] To counter this stock market crash, aggressive federal policies quieted the economy on one hand, but stimulated a housing boom on the other.[3] By mid-2006, the housing market also faltered; accumulated wealth evaporated like raindrops on hot asphalt. British economist Skidelsky aptly described this crisis as "a global inverted pyramid of household and bank debt" that was built from housing prices. As prices fell, "the debt balloon started to deflate, at first slowly, ultimately with devastating speed."[4]

By 2008, nothing could quell the rising chaos. Home loans were defaulting in droves, financial institutions and individuals were drowning in debt,

1. Gorton, 2008.
2. NYSE, 2011.
3. Kindleberger and Aliber, 2005.
4. Skidelsky, 2009.

Financial Whirlpools.
27

and federal policies were futile. Financial organizations with years of experience and stellar reputations disintegrated as they failed to meet obligations, lost investor confidence, and watched their stocks tumble. Even nonfinancial sectors felt the bind. Auto industry giants GM and Ford had to finance their operations using debt with "sky-high interest rates"; consumers could not get auto loans.[5] Something had pierced the heart of the economy. What had happened? When had we put the penny into the machine?

2.1 TIMELINE

It is difficult to pinpoint a beginning for the economic collapse in the U.S. Some suggest its seeds were planted in the 1960s; they blame "a permissive attitude toward inflation" and a reliance on the financial sector that allowed policymakers to "extend the fruits of economic growth beyond the limits."[6] Some put its roots in the late 1990s when other countries found investing in dot-com technologies appealing.[7] Others believe it started around 2000 when the internet bubble burst and interest rates dropped dramatically.[8] The Federal Reserve Bank of St. Louis was more precise. The crisis, it said, began February 27, 2007 on the day that Freddie Mac would no longer buy "the most risky subprime mortgages and mortgage related securities."[9] Still others thought it officially began in August 2007 when central banks worldwide pushed U.S. dollars into the banking system to provide liquidity.[10]

While these opinions benefit from hindsight, as early as 2000 a few analysts went against popular wisdom that all was going well. These prophets cautioned that in a few years the U.S. housing market would cause a recession.[11] In 2005, others warned that because housing had propped up America's economy for years, there would be "severe consequences" if housing prices declined; they advised U.S. consumers to look overseas to Japan and Germany if they thought prices would continue to rise.[12] For certain, the U.S. economy entered an erratic period in the late 1990s. As the stock market peaked and plunged and interest rates fluctuated, events such as terrorist attacks and gasoline price hikes added uncertainty. So, with such diverse observations, what time period is appropriate for studying the economic crisis?

To trace specific trends, we use data beginning in 1994 before the economy became shaky. And because the crisis didn't happen overnight, we also

---

5. Goldiner, 2008.
6. Krippner, 2011.
7. Rajan, 2010.
8. Soros, 2009.
9. FRBSL, 2011.
10. Soros, 2009.
11. Bezemer, 2009.
12. *The Economist*, 2005.

include policies and events from previous decades. In 1994, housing prices moved with inflation, the stock market was modestly ascending, interest rates had recovered from their highs in the early 1980s, and 5 percent unemployment looked tolerable. December 2010 marks the end of the timeline. By then, although unemployment lingered around 9 percent,[13] housing prices were more stable, federal funds rates were hovering near zero, and annual inflation rested at 1.6 percent.[14] So that we can assess how the U.S. crisis affected the rest of the world, this endpoint also incorporates the global recession that lasted until mid-2009.

Using this timeline, this chapter describes significant federal economic policies and mortgage lending practices, discusses the housing and financial markets, and follows the economy as events swelled toward unavoidable crisis. These discussions highlight trends, yet give enough specifics and background to illustrate intricacies and influences. But don't be disconcerted; the financial details do not intend to make you an economics expert. Instead, appreciate that understanding these complexities is challenging; even the experts were puzzled.

2.2 FEDERAL ECONOMIC POLICIES

To manage the economy, the U.S. government has a toolbox of policies, agencies, and political processes at its disposal. Because housing had a starring role in the economic drama, we focus on tools that affect the housing market. Fiscal policy, for example, is often used to combat recessions by increasing demand for goods (including housing); it advocates government spending or lower taxes so people have more money to spend.[15] Monetary policy influences housing demand more directly by manipulating interest rates that affect home loans. Other tools include specific housing policies. This chapter sets fiscal policy aside since its effects on the housing market are difficult to isolate; it concentrates instead on monetary and housing policies.

2.2.1 Monetary Policy

Founded in 1913, the Federal Reserve System (the Fed) is congressionally mandated to ensure a healthy economy by maintaining maximum employment, stable prices, and a stable financial system.[16] To accomplish these goals, this U.S. central bank determines monetary policy that affects

---

13. U.S. Bureau of Labor Statistics, 2012a.
14. Historical inflation, 2012; federal funds rates from Board of Governors of the Federal Reserve System, Nov 2011a. In 1994, inflation was about 3 percent.
15. Farmer, 2010.
16. Rajan, 2010.

households' inclination to borrow money.[17] In a market economy, "borrowed money, or loaned capital, is a good, and you pay a price to borrow it."[18] Thus, the supply of loanable funds derived from savers and the demand for loans by borrowers can determine market price (interest rates) for these funds. Theoretically, if the market for loans were left alone, interest rates would find their own level. However, this level may not help the economy, particularly if rates spike outrageously with increased demand for loans. So, the Fed intervenes to stabilize the availability and cost of money and credit.[19]

2.2.1.1 Interest Rates

Through monetary policy, the Fed manipulates money supply and the short-term federal funds rate.[20] To gauge success, it watches long-term interest rates such as those for 10-year U.S. treasury notes. These rates incorporate expectations about inflation and about other global factors such as foreign investment in U.S. securities. Traditionally, long-term rates are a better indicator of home mortgage rates than are federal funds rates; they directly affect consumer behavior, which is the Fed's ultimate goal.[21] When monetary policy works well, long-term rates rest above and move in concert with the federal funds short-term rate.

Figure 2.1 tracks short-term and long-term rates from 1994 to 2010. Long-term rates for 10-year treasuries and 30-year fixed rate mortgage (FRM) loans had similar trends; FRM rates rested 1 or 2 percent above 10-year treasuries. After 1997, these long-term rates went up and down with the short-term federal funds rate, but their fluctuations were more moderate, ranging between 1 and 5 percent above the federal funds rate.[22] Abnormally large differences between short-term and long-term rates indicate that forces other than monetary policy are at work. Stated differently, monetary policy has some, but not ultimate influence on the cost of

---

17. Bernanke, 2002. The Fed also has other regulatory, supervisory, and lender-of-last-resort powers.
18. Woods, 2009.
19. Board of Governors of the Federal Reserve System, 2011.
20. FRBNY, 2007; Waring, 2008. Federal funds rate is the short term interest rate that banks charge other banks when lending them money. The Fed does not actually "set" the rate; it sets a desired target. The FMOC (Federal Open Market Committee) encourages this rate by buying U.S. government securities to increase money supply/decrease interest rates or by selling the securities to reduce money supply/increase interest rates.
21. Greenspan (2007) calls this phenomenon "the conundrum" (when monetary policy doesn't play a "leading role in the fall of long-term interest rates"); it has occurred since the mid-1990s.
22. From 1994 to 2010, 30-year FRM rates ranged from 1.25 to 2.35 percent above long-term rates and from 1.32 to 5.01 percent above the federal funds rates. See Freddie Mac (2011b) for 30-year FRMs; Board of Governors of the Federal Reserve System (2011c) for 10-year treasury securities; and Board of Governors of the Federal Reserve System (2011b) for federal funds rates.

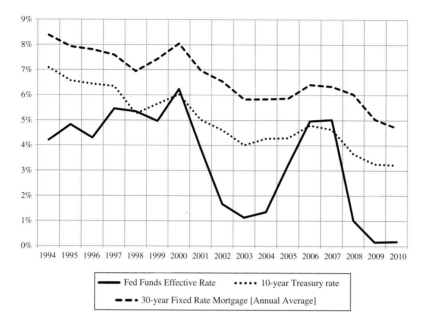

FIGURE 2.1 Interest rate history: Federal funds, 10-year treasury, 30-year fixed rate mortgage.[23]

buying a home and on the tendency of households to save or spend. During the crisis, sizeable divergence or "yield spread" between federal funds and long-term rates suggests that long-term investments were considered risky (particularly from 2002–2005 and from 2008–2010).[24] Monetary policy alone cannot diminish this perception of risk, thus it is not always effective in turning the economy around, especially during uncertain times.

2.2.1.2 Inflation Targets

The Fed's present monetary policy focuses on the greater economy rather than on individual markets. In other words, the Fed does not adjust the federal funds rate simply to control housing prices.[25] Instead, it considers factors like gross domestic product (GDP), unemployment, and inflation before changing the rate.[26] Inflation in particular is the Fed's primary indicator of when to act; it is important to consumers because it reduces their purchasing power.[27]

---

23. Federal funds rate from Board of Governors of the Federal Reserve System, 2011b; 10-year U.S. Treasury Securities rate from Board of Governors of the Federal Reserve System, 2011c; 30-year FRM rates from Freddie Mac, 2011b.
24. Barth et al., 2009b.
25. Some say that monetary policy should consider such bubble behavior (e.g., Morris, 2008).
26. Bernanke, 2002.
27. White, 2008; the Consumer Price Index measures inflation.

Given the Fed's seemingly contradictory goals of maximum sustainable employment and stable prices[28] (low unemployment *and* low inflation), the definition of optimal inflation has been debated for decades. The theory is that low interest rates create deficit spending (people borrow to buy) which stimulates the economy, raises GDP, and lowers unemployment; low rates also increase inflation. Different Fed administrations increase or decrease inflation depending on their philosophies. Although it is not so simple, some even say that the "the whims of policy makers... determine the inflation rate."[29]

Many economists recommend zero inflation to stabilize prices[30] while others believe that zero inflation could reduce GDP by 1 to 3 percent with a corresponding permanent drop in employment.[31] Some suggest using explicit rules, such as the "Taylor rule" to change interest rates.[32] Federal Reserve Chairman Ben Bernanke "argues that positive inflation—by keeping nominal interest rates well above their zero lower bound—preserves the Fed's ability to cut rates if looser monetary policy is needed."[33] There are many opinions about how to use monetary policy; however, all agree "that high inflation rates are disruptive."[34]

While the Fed has no explicit inflation targeting strategy, it does apply a guide to its policies.[35] Current thinking is that low and steady inflation rates are the most reasonable.[36] Accordingly, in early 2011, the Fed aimed at about a 2 percent inflation rate based on long-run economic projections.[37] This low rate, it believes, gives "the economy its best chance of achieving its potential growth rate and thus maximum sustainable employment."[38]

When inflation exceeds the Fed's target, the economy is growing too fast. In this case, the Fed hits the economic brakes (discourages spending, makes saving more attractive, and reduces demand) by increasing federal funds rates. This policy is *contractionary*. Alternatively, if inflation falls below the target, the Fed stimulates economic growth. Low interest rates press the economic gas pedal to encourage spending, increase demand, and

---

28. Theoretically when inflation is high, unemployment is low and vice versa. This inverse relationship is explained by the "Phillips curve" developed in 1958. In the 1990s, the curve lost fidelity and unemployment changed unpredictably. Some economists believe it still holds true in the short term.
29. Hoskins, 2005; see also Taylor, 2009.
30. Hoskins, 2005.
31. Akerlof et al., 1996; Economics Resource Center, 2006.
32. Taylor, 2009; the Taylor rule states that when inflation increases, the Fed should raise the interest rate, but when GDP declines the Fed should lower the rate.
33. White, 2008.
34. Economics Resource Center, 2006.
35. Bernanke, 2003.
36. Akerlof et al., 1996.
37. Nasiripour, 2011.
38. Rajan, 2010.

enhance the value of long-term assets; this *expansionary* policy can also boost inflation. Table 2.1 summarizes expected outcomes of monetary policy. When the Fed reacts to current inflation (column 1) by adjusting the federal funds rate (column 2), various economic factors are affected.

To avoid the novice driver syndrome from Chapter 1, the Fed must know how to drive the economic car. It must consider the magnitude of rate changes *and* the delays in their effects. Tracking these intended increases and decreases can be confusing, but the important point here is that inflation is one signal for when the Fed should press the brake or push the gas pedal.

2.2.1.3 Delays and Other Forces

Intuitively we know that the effects of any policy or action may not be immediate and that hidden factors influence outcomes, thus it is difficult to know whether monetary policy is doing its job. The delay between interest rate change and its effects on the economy is real; the Fed, in fact, sets the rate based on what it *believes* inflation will be in about 2 years. This subjective estimate of the future is not precisely measurable.[39] Some approximate that "the effect of today's monetary policy actions will probably not be felt for at least six to nine months, with the main influence perhaps two or three years in the future."[40]

Additionally, other factors shape long-term rates that influence inflation. Forces inside the U.S. economy include competition, GDP, and money supply.[41] However, factors that directly affect long-term interest rates and overshadow monetary policy are becoming "increasingly global." Former Fed chairman Alan Greenspan believes that since the mid-1990s, global forces have been more potent than monetary policies in bringing long-term interest rates down. The best policies, he suggests, calibrate "monetary policy so that it is consistent with global forces" and require interaction with the world's central banks and financial markets.[42]

For example, Figure 2.1 showed that between 2001 and 2005 short-term rates deviated substantially from long-term rates. And as Figure 2.2 shows, monetary policy did not produce desired changes in inflation or unemployment during some periods. When federal funds rates decreased after 2000, unemployment went up (instead of down); between 1999 and 2005 and again between 2008 and 2009, inflation moved in the same direction as federal funds rates, instead of moving oppositely as desired. Thus, between 1999

---

39. See Rajan, 2010; see also Batini and Haldane (2001) whose research suggests that "an inflation forecast horizon of three to six quarters appears to deliver the best performance."
40. Hoskins, 2005.
41. See Congressional Budget Office, 1982 for discussion of the 1980s recession. Inflation increases when the Fed injects new money into the economy typically by buying bonds with newly created debt (White, 2008).
42. Greenspan, 2007.

TABLE 2.1 The Effects of Contractionary and Expansionary Monetary Policies

	Current Inflation (cause)	Fed Funds Rate	Unemployment	Spending	Loans	Demand for Goods and Services	Housing Prices	Desired Inflation (effect)
Putting on the brakes: Contractionary monetary policy; prevent or curb inflation; slow economic growth	Too high	Up	Up	Down	Down	Down	Down	Down
Pushing the gas pedal: Expansionary monetary policy; increase risk of inflation; encourage economic growth	Too low	Down	Down	Up	Up	Up	Up	Up

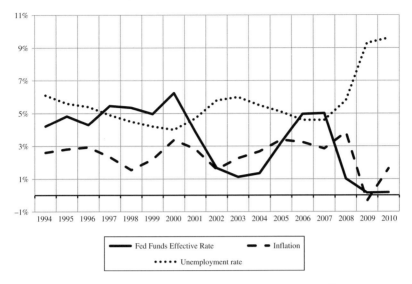

FIGURE 2.2   Statistical history: Inflation, unemployment, and interest rates.[43]

and 2009, even accounting for lag, the effects of monetary policy seemed unpredictable, indicating that other forces were present.

2.2.2 Housing Policies

In addition to monetary policy, a second set of economic policies involves the agency that most influences housing: the Department of Housing and Urban Development (HUD). As part of President Lyndon Johnson's *Great Society*, HUD was chartered in 1965 to strengthen the housing market by enforcing housing related policies and creating opportunities for all to have "quality affordable homes."[44] HUD regulates the Federal Housing Administration (FHA) and the Government National Mortgage Association (GNMA/Ginnie Mae) as well as government sponsored enterprises (GSEs). GSEs include the Federal National Mortgage Association (FNMA/Fannie Mae) and the Federal Home Loan Mortgage Association (FHLMC/Freddie Mac).

The FHA insures home loans made by approved lenders. Fannie Mae, Freddie Mac, and Ginnie Mae expand the secondary mortgage market[45] by purchasing loans from original lenders and reselling them as securities. Ginnie Mae

---

43. Chart derived from Historical Inflation, 2012; federal funds rate from Board of Governors of the Federal Reserve System, 2011b; average annual unemployment from U.S. Bureau of Labor Statistics, 2012a.
44. See *http://portal.hud.gov/portal/page/portal/HUD*
45. "The primary market provides the actual loan to a borrower... the secondary market channels liquidity into the primary market by... purchasing packages of loans from lenders" and reselling them as securities or bonds (Bhattacharya et al., 2001).

promotes "home ownership among families of modest means" by permitting private lenders to sell securities that contain government *guaranteed* loans.[46] Fannie Mae securities contain loans from different parts of the country; Freddie Mac devotes "a share of mortgage financing to low-income and moderate-income families."[47] In other words, these government-affiliated agencies enable more people to buy homes by making resources available for loans.

Presidential administrations guide HUD's policies. The 1977 Community Reinvestment Act (CRA) required "banks to lend in the low-income neighborhoods where they take deposits."[48] In 1992, to invigorate the economy and facilitate the politically popular goal of enabling more Americans to own a home, President George Bush encouraged HUD to open its arms to low-income and minority borrowers; the Federal Housing Enterprise Safety and Soundness Act helped those who could not previously qualify for a mortgage loan.[49] In 1995 President Bill Clinton strengthened enforcement of the CRA, which pressured banks to lend more in low-income neighborhoods and caused opponents to fear "that one day banks would be required to make unsound loans to meet their local credit quotas."[50] Clinton also revised FHA policies in 2000. These policies relaxed qualifications for insured mortgage loans: minimum down payment dropped from 20 percent to 3 percent; insurable mortgage size increased; and premiums for mortgage guarantees were cut in half.[51]

In later years, Presidents Clinton and G.W. Bush expanded HUD's home loan program for low-income housing and for those who could not qualify for conventional loans. Among their expansion policies was the Ownership Society initiative, "aided by the American Dream Downpayment Act of 2003, which subsidized 40,000 low-income households per year to cover down payments and closing costs."[52] By 2004, HUD had boosted Freddie's and Fannie's targets for low income loan types to 56 percent of assets from 42 percent in 1995 and 50 percent in 2000.[53]

Consequently, for over a decade HUD encouraged its agencies to ease credit qualifications and expand the loan market for low-income, less qualified borrowers. At the same time these policies boosted home mortgage lending, the Fed was increasing interest rates to slow the housing boom. In other words, housing policies opposed rather than reinforced monetary policy.[54]

---

46. From agencies such as FHA and Veterans Administration.
47. Information on Ginnie Mae, Fannie Mae, and Freddie Mac from Levinson, 2010.
48. Pressman, 2008.
49. Rajan, 2010.
50. McKinley, 1994.
51. Rajan, 2010; White, 2009.
52. McCoy and Renaurt, 2008.
53. White, 2009; the push to subprime loans began with the Federal Housing Enterprise Safety and Soundness Act in 1992 that reformed regulation of Fannie and Freddie and encouraged low-income and minority home ownership.
54. See Rajan, 2010.

When the Fed put on the brakes, housing policies pushed the gas—the economy was in for a jerky ride. This mixed message resurfaces in Chapter 9.

2.3 HOME MORTGAGE LENDING PRACTICES

Changes to lending practices affected supply and demand for housing. Spurred by reduced interest rates and low-income lending policies, nongovernment lenders increased their mortgage loan goals to enter the game. For example, in 1992 Countrywide began a "House America" program to help low-income and minority borrowers qualify for loans; in 2003, it expanded the program's original $1.25 billion goal to $1 trillion in home loans to be met by 2010.[55] These policies stimulated demand by offering hope for those who had been unable to purchase a home. They also created supply side actions that expanded loan products, modified practices, and incentivized agents to attract this growing customer base.

2.3.1 Lending Strategies

To accomplish the lofty goal of broad access to mortgage credit and to compete in the market, lenders implemented two related strategies: relaxed standards for borrowing and more loans to high-risk borrowers.

2.3.1.1 Relaxed Standards

Most lenders relaxed traditional criteria that rejected loans or limited loan amounts and set loan terms. The Federal Reserve Bank of San Francisco remarked on the prevalence of looser standards, including an "increase in loan-to-value ratios, less stringent debt-to-income requirements, and a willingness on the part of lenders to accept limited or no documentation of borrowers' income and assets."[56] These looser criteria increased risk of default for loans that were larger than was prudent and downplayed borrowers' poor credit.

2.3.1.2 More Loans to Higher-Risk Borrowers

Mortgage lenders use two fundamental loan categories: prime and nonprime. Prime loans are the most desirable with the least risk for lenders; traditionally they were used most often. Prime loans go to credit-worthy applicants who have high credit scores, proof of income, and ability to repay.[57] But to

---

55. Ferrell et al., 2010.
56. FRBSF, 2008.
57. The Fair Isaac Corporation or FICO® score is the most widely used credit rating in the U.S. Scores range from 300 to 850. FICO® scores between 720 and 850, with no past-due bills or defaults, are excellent "prime" credit risks. Scores below 600 indicate high risk (Consumer Federation of America, 2010).

generate business, lenders had to compete in the less familiar area of non-prime loans. So, in addition to relaxing standards, they offered these loans to people who could not meet prime loan criteria.

Within nonprime loans, there are two main options: Alt-A (lower-risk) loans and subprime (higher-risk) loans.[58] Alt-A loans are usually for those who have good credit but need special features, such as tailored payments.[59] However, some Alt-A loans, called "liar loans" or "ninja loans" (**No** Income, **No J**ob, no **A**ssets),[60] require limited or no verification of income or assets.[61] Subprime loans go to those with poor credit histories.[62] Because these borrowers have higher risk of default,[63] subprime loans have higher origination and insurance costs, and interest rates of 2 percent or more above prime rates.[64] Interest rates on subprime loan interest rates are also generally higher than on Alt-A loans.[65]

2.3.2 Types of Loans

Prime and nonprime markets use fixed rate mortgage (FRM) and adjustable rate mortgage (ARM) types of loans. FRM interest rates are based on the prevailing prime rate; they remain the same over the life of the loan. While ARM interest rates may be initially lower than FRM rates, they reset after a given period. This reset rate relates to an index such as the interest rate on 1-year treasury bonds or the London Interbank Offered Rate (LIBOR) and can include some margin amount determined by the lender.[66] Prior to the crisis, to attract borrowers, lenders originated huge numbers of ARMs, some of which offered "teaser" interest rates (as low as 1 percent) for a short time.[67]

For ARMs, borrowers assume the risk that interest may go up. If the Fed raises the rate, and the ARM index increases, borrowers' monthly payments increase. For example, those who took out low-interest ARMs in the mid-2000s saw rates grow to over 7 percent in 15 months; they soon couldn't afford the new payments *or* the fees and penalties to refinance.[68]

---

58. Bar-Gill, 2009.
59. Sengupta, 2010.
60. Soros, 2009.
61. Rosen, 2007.
62. Subprime loans typically have FICO® scores below 620 and may have delinquencies or bankruptcies.
63. FDIC, 2001.
64. Chomsisengphet and Pennington-Cross, 2006; Consumer Federation of America, 2010.
65. FRBSF, 2008.
66. Federal Reserve Board, April 2012.
67. ARMs generally reset after 1–7 years. Other ARM types (interest only, payment options, or teasers) have a 6-month to 7-year term. When these reset, monthly payments increase regardless of current interest rate or, for option ARMS, stay the same but the balance owed rises.
68. der Hovanesian, 2006.

ARMs often include affordability features such as interest-only and pay-ment option loans. For interest-only loans, borrowers pay only interest and no principle for a given period; for payment option loans, monthly payments may be less than the loan's interest, so the balance escalates.[69] Unfortunately, these terms were written in such complicated language that most borrowers weren't inclined to figure them out; they completely trusted their lenders.

Nonprime Alt-A loans historically contain more affordability features than subprime loans. In 2007 for instance, about 28 percent of Alt-A loans compared to 12 percent of subprime loans were interest-only. At the same time, 16 percent of Alt-A loans and almost no subprime loans included pay-ment options.[70] Table 2.2 summarizes loan categories and types.[71]

Although these loan types (particularly ARMs) had been available since the early 1980s, they were rarely used until the early 2000s when growing competition and increasing demand for subprime loans popularized them.[72]

TABLE 2.2 Mortgage Loan Categories and Common Loan Types

	Loan Categories		
	Prime	Nonprime	
	Least risk (e.g., FICO from 720 to 850)	Alt-A (lower risk) with aggressive underwriting	Subprime (higher risk; FICO commonly below 620)
Most Commonly Used Loan Types			
Fixed rate mortgage (FRM)	X	Some	Some
Adjustable rate mortgage (ARM)	Some	X	X
Affordability features	Some	X	Some
Liar loans and NINJA loans		X	
Teaser rates			X

69. Joint Center for Housing Studies, 2008; Ferrell et al., 2010.
70. FRBSF, 2008.
71. Bar-Gill, 2009; Rosen, 2007; Sengupta, 2010; Soros, 2009.
72. Bar-Gill, 2009.

However, it wasn't just competition that encouraged new types. The Fed subtly pressured lenders to expand their offerings. In 2004, Fed chairman Greenspan remarked to a broad audience of lenders that because American consumers could have saved thousands of dollars by using ARMs rather than FRMs, they "might benefit if lenders provided greater mortgage product alternatives to the traditional fixed-rate mortgage." He added that if interest rates had gone up, of course these savings would not have been achieved.[73]

2.4 MARKETS AND HUMAN BEHAVIOR

In competitive markets such as the financial and housing markets, "there are many buyers and sellers of the same good or service... and no individual's actions have a noticeable effect" on prices.[74] Prices in a market economy influence the individual buying and selling decisions of its participants.[75] Implied in these decisions are assumptions about human behavior and theories about how individuals make choices. Two contrasting views portray human decision making. The first, often called rational choice theory, has roots in sociology and psychology. Applied to economics, this theory assumes that individuals are fully informed of all circumstances and make decisions as rational, self-interested entities who desire wealth, avoid unnecessary work, and maximize their own well-being. The alternate view assumes instead that individuals have imperfect knowledge or what Simon describes as "approximate" or "bounded rationality"[76] that at times can even be irrational.[77] Chapter 3 describes these theories in more detail.

Our systems interpretation of the housing and financial markets merges both views. It begins with a structure that incorporates simplistic rational human responses to show how supply and demand would ideally behave and then integrates psychological traits that involve expectations, emotional sides of self-interest, rationalization, and lack of information.

2.5 HOUSING MARKET

Principles of supply and demand regulate the housing market. Demand applies to consumers who want to buy a house and are looking for a good

73. Kirchhoff and Bagenbaugh (2004) describe Greenspan's speech to the Credit Union National Association.
74. Henderson, 2010. This old reference (1922) describes supply and demand. See also Krugman and Wells, 2010.
75. Market economy contrasts with a "command economy" in which some central authority makes decisions about national production and consumption.
76. Simon, 1955; Simon references "bounded rationality" in *Models of Bounded Rationality* published in 1982 by The MIT Press, Cambridge, MA.
77. See Slovic, 2009; Ariely, 2009.

deal. While lower prices encourage them to buy, prices that are too high cause them to avoid buying and use their money elsewhere. Thus, quantity demanded rises when price goes down and vice versa. Supply applies to sellers who are looking to make a profit. For example, at higher prices, more homeowners and builders will want to sell houses to make money; in contrast, they will want to sell fewer houses when prices are low. In other words, quantity supplied increases when price increases; conversely quantity supplied decreases when price decreases.

In theory, a market economy experiences this see-saw behavior as part of the equilibrium principle. At equilibrium, the quantity supplied by producers equals the quantity demanded by consumers and both parties are satisfied with a given price (see the Appendix for a thorough discussion). Microeconomic theory offers alternate views about whether markets ever experience exact equilibrium or whether they are always in a state of flux. The latter view recognizes time delays involved in changes to supply and demand,[78] the limited ability of participants to make rational decisions, and the incomplete availability of information. We incorporate this dynamic view into our systems perspective, and assume that supply and demand are constantly moving but that they *tend toward* an equilibrium state.

Supply and demand interactions are the foundation for housing market operation. Under *normal* conditions, although average housing prices fluctuate with changes in supply or demand, they seek equilibrium. During the economic crisis, however, conditions were anything but normal. Rather than moving toward a stable equilibrium price, housing prices kept increasing and then suddenly dropped. This behavior reflected *shifts* in demand and/or supply that altered the equilibrium price and created a housing bubble. The Appendix illustrates how such shifts alter equilibrium price in systems thinking terms; Chapter 8 relates shifts in the demand for houses to the housing bubble.

Near the beginning of our timeline, federal economic policies and lending practices described earlier increased demand and prices for homes. Between 2000 and 2005, new house sales grew 46 percent to an all-time high;[79] housing prices increased nearly 87 percent in the same 5 years.[80] The financial market was eager to profit from the rising demand for houses and the subsequent increase in home loans.

---

78. See Beinhocker's (2006) discussion on traditional economics theory of supply and demand, and "the law of one price." He references Sterman's (2000) computer models of supply and demand which, unlike traditional theory, assume that changes in supply or demand are not instantaneous but instead are in a disequilibrium state created by time delays.

79. U.S. Census Bureau, 2011a.

80. Standard & Poors/Case-Shiller, 2011.

2.6 FINANCIAL MARKET

For our purposes, the financial market includes the capital market where entities raise funds in the form of debt (bonds) or equity (stocks), and the derivatives market where risk is bought and sold as hedge funds or credit swaps. To understand why this market expanded during the crisis, we first consider the *Efficient Markets Hypothesis* that underlies its operation. In the 1970s, finance professor Eugene Fama proposed that prices in financial markets "fully reflect all available .information."[81] This hypothesis soon drove decision-making for buying and selling stocks and securities. Although the NASDAQ boom and bust in 2000 contradicted it, the theory was so ingrained that the financial market continued to rely on it. Two aspects of it relate to the crisis: it suggests that financial markets "are sufficiently well-developed to encompass all economically relevant sources of risk" and it proposes that "there is no need to worry about imbalances in savings and consumption."[82] Thus, during the crisis, buyers and sellers of securities believed that prices appropriately accounted for risk and that taking on debt to make investments was sensible; they felt secure about investing. (As we will soon see, however, prices did not fully account for risk and contradicted this foundational theory.)

While federal policies promoted the rapid increase in demand for home loans, the underlying confidence about risk encouraged financial institutions to buy these loans, restructure them into securities, and sell them in the financial market. Lenders who sold the loans could then use the proceeds to make more loans. Then, as investors' desire for mortgage-related securities grew, the number of securities mushroomed and extended the reach of mortgage loans and all their potential risk deep into the financial market. Table 2.3 summarizes three financial market activities that relate to mortgage loans: securitization, structuring, and derivatives.[83]

In addition to these innovative financial instruments and the assumption of complete information on risk, a significant change in banking legislation tightly linked mortgage loans with financial securities. In 1999, the firewall between commercial and financial banking was eliminated when the Gramm−Leach−Bliley Act repealed the Glass−Steagall Act.[84] As a result, financial entities could use depositors' FDIC-insured money rather than their

---

81. Fama, 1970.
82. Quiggin, 2010.
83. See Davidson and Sanders (2009) for descriptions.
84. Gramm, 1999. Commercial banks grant credit and holding deposits; investment banks can use credit to invest in securities. In 1933, President Roosevelt created the Federal Deposit Insurance Corporation (FDIC) to maintain stability in the U.S. banking system and passed the Glass−Steagall Act that ensured commercial banking and investment banking could not be done by the same entity. The Gramm−Leach−Bliley Act removed this safety net, claiming the old legislation did not adapt to the new world; this act intended to encourage competition, reduce financial fees, and allow the financial sector to offer new, better, cheaper products.

TABLE 2.3 Financial Market Activities Involving Mortgage Loans

Financial Process Involving Mortgage-Related Assets	Definition	Related Product Names
Securitization	The process of converting individual loans into securities that can be traded	Mortgage-backed securities (MBS)
Structuring	The process of pooling a collection of one kind of security (such as MBSs) and then segmenting or dividing cash flows (also called tranching) from this pool to make another type of security (such as CDOs); these secondary securities are then sold according to the risk of their underlying assets	Collateralized debt obligation (CDO); CDO-squared; synthetic CDO
Derivatives	Financial instruments that transfer risk on given assets from one party to another and whose value is derived from these underlying assets	Credit default swaps (CDS)

own resources to make risky investments, in essence they would keep "their gains when their gambles are correct and pass their losses onto taxpayers when their gambles turn sour."[85] This deregulation has been linked to excessive risk-taking, conflicts of interest, and extensive damage from subprime loans.

2.6.1 Securitization: Mortgage-Backed Securities

The number of mortgage loans increased with the rising demand for houses. But rather than keep the loans on their books as they had in the past, lenders sold more of them to third parties. Thus they made a profit, reduced risk exposure, and used the money from sales to make new loans. The third parties bundled the mortgages they purchased into pools that typically contained similar loan types and sold payment rights of the mortgages as *mortgage-backed securities* using a process called "securitization."[86]

---

85. Lal, 2010.
86. Rosen, 2007; Lewis Ranieri coined the term *securitization* when Salomon Brothers and Bank of America introduced the first private (nonagency) mortgage-backed securities in 1977 (McNamee, 2004).

Securitization of home mortgages (bundling individual loans into an income producing security) traces back to the "early 1970s when Ginnie Mae pooled mortgage loans and sold single-class, mortgage-backed securities against the pool."[87] These securities were called pass-throughs or "undivided interests or participations" in a particular pool.[88] In 1983, nonagency (private) firms augmented these pass-throughs with a new security called a *collateralized mortgage obligation* (CMO).[89] CMOs sliced mortgage pools into "three segments, with different bonds for each segment."[90] Each bond was rated according to risk and sold to investors whose risk appetite matched the risk rating.[91] Also in the early 1980s, Freddie Mac and Fannie Mae began to securitize *conforming mortgages*, that is, small to medium-sized, 15 or 30-year fixed rate loans that meet certain criteria.[92] Because these three agencies (Ginnie, Freddie, and Fannie) had ties to the federal government and were prevented from buying high-risk loans, they could guarantee repayment of the loans.[93]

In the early 2000s, securitization grew popular as *non-agency* companies issued more MBSs.[94] Between 2003 and 2005, nonagencies more than doubled their issuance of these securities.[95] Instead of containing only conforming mortgages, nonagency or private label MBSs also contain subprime and Alt-A loans[96] and have no guarantees.

2.6.2 Structuring: Collateralized Debt Obligations

Buying and selling mortgage-related securities soon extended beyond MBSs. After the CMO market failed in 1994,[97] more conservative mortgage-related securities appeared; these securities drew rating agencies into the mix to "improve geographic diversity" and to "estimate default risk" with

---

87. Vallee, 2006.
88. Lowell, 2001.
89. Financial guru Larry Fink invented CMOs in 1983.
90. Morris, 2008.
91. McLean and Nocera, 2010.
92. Rosen, 2007; borrower quality and loan-to-value-ratios were among these criteria.
93. Fannie and Freddie could not "buy loans with original loan-to-value ratios greater than 80 percent without a credit enhancement" (see Lockhart, 2009). The U.S. government backs Ginnie Mae's guarantee; as government sponsored entities, Fannie Mae and Freddie Mac mortgages are guaranteed by "emergency drawing rights on the U.S. Treasury" (Lowell, 2001).
94. Top 10 nonagencies issued about 60 percent of total MBS originations in 2006: JPMorgan Chase, New Century, IndyMac, Goldman Sachs, Wells Fargo, Bear Stearns, Residential Funding, Lehman, Washington Mutual, and Countrywide. Six were out of business by 2009 (Davidson and Sanders, 2009).
95. Vallee, 2006.
96. Rosen, 2007.
97. Factors causing failure included "pushing tranching technology to an extreme" (Morris, 2008) and increased federal funds rate.

proprietary models.[98] By 1996, companies were experimenting with other mortgage-related securities.

Recognizing potential profit, companies such as Merrill Lynch and Goldman Sachs bought and pooled MBSs, structured the pools as collections of bonds (also called segments or tranches) called *collateralized debt obligations* (CDO), and sold the CDOs to large investors.[99] By the early 2000s, the influx of new mortgages and their securitization into MBSs accelerated the market for CDOs that contained MBSs.

Unlike MBSs, CDOs use bonds instead of loans as their underlying collateral.[100] The structuring process for CDOs combines and segments MBSs into bonds that are rated and sold according to risk. After CDOs are divided into risk segments, some bonds could be rated more highly relative to the total pool of MBSs in the CDO. Many earn a premier triple-A rating even though their underlying MBSs include lower-rated triple-B junk bonds. One justification for this rating upgrade is that higher-risk bonds with higher potential returns act as a buffer for lower-risk, higher-quality bonds; in case of default, high-risk bonds shoulder the first losses.[101] Another rationale is that the combination of so many securities could reap the benefits of diversification—different risks, different lenders, and different geographic areas.[102]

By selling CDOs, financial institutions expanded product lines and spread the risk of default for their underlying mortgage assets. Because CDOs offered better rates of return than corporate bonds, growing numbers of foreign investors with ready assets snapped them up.[103] This structuring process attracted "vast classes of investors: pension funds for the senior tranches, and hedge funds for the risky assets."[104]

However, the process didn't end there either. Institutions such as Goldman Sachs created the "CDO-squared" (a "CDO of CDOs").[105] These instruments took hard-to-sell, highest risk segments of the original CDOs[106] and repeated the structuring process, again segmenting them as new bonds with new ratings.[107] Now the *best of the worst* could be readily sold as highly rated securities to other financial firms like Morgan Stanley.

And where did the *worst of the worst* go? Many were bought by unregulated hedge funds that "promise extraordinary returns." Hedge funds' "appetite for the riskiest positions has made them a major source of liquidity in the

98. Morris, 2008.
99. See Shenn, 2007; this process is referred to as *resecuritization* (Rosen, 2007).
100. Davidson and Sanders, 2009.
101. See Rosen, 2007.
102. See Davidson and Sanders, 2009.
103. Gethard, 2010.
104. Cohen, June 2008.
105. Taibbi (2011) discusses CDO-squareds.
106. Highest risk bonds were called "lower seniority."
107. Barnett-Hart, 2009.

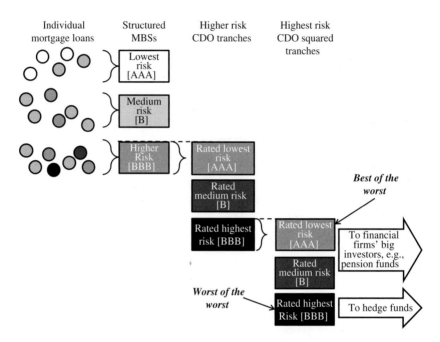

FIGURE 2.3   Process to segment groups of MBSs into CDO and CDO-squared securities.

CDO and credit default swap markets"; in 2007 hedge funds accounted for about 60 percent of all CDS trading and a third of CDO trading.[108] Figure 2.3 illustrates how CDOs and CDO-squared securities could be sold with high ratings. Note that the rating of the underlying mortgages remains the same.

2.6.3 Derivatives: Credit Default Swaps

Derivatives have no inherent worth; their value is *derived* from their underlying mortgage loan assets. *Credit default swaps* (CDSs) were the primary type of derivatives used during the crisis and are loosely described as a type of insurance that pays if people default on their loans. As their CDO portfolios grew, investors sought to reduce risk of default on the loans underlying the CDOs and purchased CDS derivatives from financial institutions. These CDSs "are not traded on exchanges; they instead are private deals arranged for a fee"[109] in unregulated over-the-counter (OTC) trading.

   The CDS market reached significant levels by mid-2005.[110] By then the securities market was even more complex; CDSs were grouped and sold as

---

108. Morris, 2008.
109. Morris, 2008.
110. Davidson and Sanders, 2009. CDSs were first used by JPMorgan in 1994 (McLean and Nocera, 2010). Another derivative product, the ABX Index, is a series of CDSs that insure subprime mortgages. Investors trade on this index without owning the securities.

synthetic CDOs. Here, a company would buy CDSs to cover potential losses on their CDOs, then pool this risk coverage and resell it as segments (tranches) of a synthetic CDO.[111] Whew! While keeping these acronyms and processes straight is difficult enough, the securities market was even harder to understand. Who could possibly understand the risk?

2.7 RISK

By early 2006, the economy was abuzz. Housing prices were rising; banks were making money selling loans; financial firms were trading securities; CDS sellers were reaping premiums; and hedge fund owners were swimming in their returns. Everyone, it seemed, was making money while washing their hands of risk.

Yet, although concealed, risk was migrating along the financial market gravy train. Securitization put mortgage loan originators at arm's length from defaults and obscured the risk for MBS and CDO buyers. Securities were often underpriced. Companies were unaware or deliberately understated risk, and rating agencies inaccurately assessed it as we will discover in Chapter 10. Attempts to determine actual level and cost of risk failed. For example, to gauge their CDS risk, AIG used expensive computer models; unfortunately, these models inadequately accounted for a housing market decline and for the complicated terms of securities. Thus CDO and CDS prices ignored the possibility of massive defaults.[112]

Two government policies also affected risk: deregulation of the sale of derivatives and a change in the net capital rule. In the first case, holding companies and investment banks could buy and sell derivatives outside federal regulation. Although debate heated up in 1998 over lack of regulation, in December 2000 Congress formally deregulated and eliminated oversight of the OTC derivatives market.[113] While this market grew rapidly after the 1980s, after deregulation, MBS, CDO, and CDS sales exploded. Lack of oversight introduced more economic risk.[114]

The second policy was enacted in 2004. Motivated by industry complaints of excessive regulation in the face of growing overseas competition, the Securities and Exchange Commission relaxed the *net capital rule* that limits the amount of debt a company can take on. To improve competitiveness, large companies were trusted to govern themselves through "self-preservation and responsibility." They could now go beyond the prescribed

---

111. Münchau, 2010.
112. AIG commissioned "computer models to gauge risk for more than $400 billion complicated credit default swaps... Unfortunately... [the models] did not anticipate how market forces and contract terms could turn swaps into huge financial liabilities" (Ferrell et al., 2010). See O'Harrow and Dennis, 2009; Salmon, 2009.
113. Congress passed the Commodity Futures Modernization Act (DFMA) in December 2000.
114. The Financial Crisis Inquiry Commission, 2011.

$12 debt to $1 equity ratio under the old rules, and simply assume responsibility for losses. This exemption released billions of dollars that these companies had held in reserve to cushion against loss, and allowed them to invest billions in seemingly profitable CDOs or derivatives.[115]

Before long companies' actual debt ratios rose sharply; Merrill Lynch, for example, went as high as 40 to 1. For every $1 they had in assets, they took on $40 of debt to make investments and could spend some of the reserve they had previously set aside for potential loss.[116] Of course, if their investments lost value they couldn't cover their losses. The financial industry had gulped down risks like candy pills; soon its stomach would rumble.

2.8 SYSTEMS INTERPRETATION

Figure 2.4 traces the linear sequence of events in the U.S. This path flows from federal policies and lending practices to activities in the housing and financial markets and leads us to the culmination of a crisis that had fermented for over a decade. In this diagram, imagine that risk flows with the arrows.

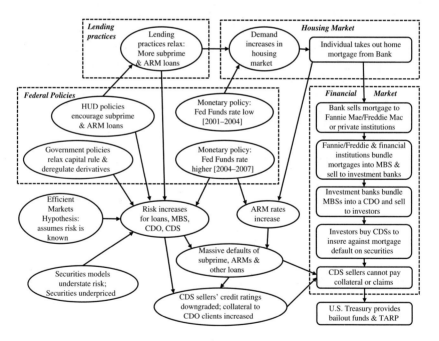

FIGURE 2.4   Linear event diagram of the economic crisis in the U.S.

115. Labaton, 2008; ratios measure debt-to-total-assets.
116. Satow, 2008.

By this book's end, the depiction shown in Figure 2.4 will have evolved into a systems diagram that shows dynamics and interdependencies. This section begins the evolution by introducing systems interpretations of monetary policy, supply and demand, and a fundamental relationship between the housing and financial markets. When viewing these diagrams, recall from Chapter 1 that "s" arrows mean the factors move in the *same* direction: when one increases, so does the other and when one decreases so does the other. The "o" arrows say the factors move *opposite* one another: when one increases, the other decreases and vice versa.

2.8.1 Balancing Loop for Monetary Policy

The balancing feedback loop $B_{monetary}$ in Figure 2.5 is a highly simplified account of how monetary policy uses interest rates to keep inflation at a desired level.

Inputs to this loop are *desired inflation* and *other economic factors* such as gross domestic product. The difference or *inflation gap* between *actual* and *desired inflation* tells the Fed whether to adjust the *federal funds rate*.[117] If *actual inflation* exceeds *desired*, a positive gap prompts the Fed to raise the *federal funds rate*, which should reduce *actual inflation*. Conversely, when *actual* inflation drops below *desired*, a negative *gap* signals the Fed to decrease the *rate*, thus increasing *inflation*. Ideally, in both cases, once rates are adjusted, inflation changes after a delay and feeds back into the loop to continue the balancing cycle.[118]

2.8.2 Balancing Loops for Housing Supply and Demand

Figure 2.6 describes the relationship between housing supply and demand as two connected balancing loops that attempt to maintain an *equilibrium*

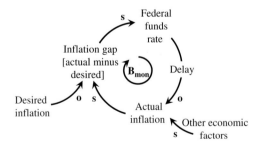

FIGURE 2.5   Balancing loop for monetary policy.

---

117. The Fed's process of altering interest rates is simplified here.
118. Anderson and Johnson, 1997.

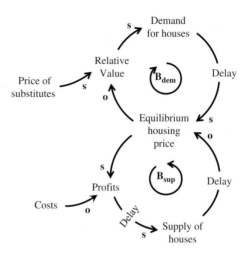

FIGURE 2.6 Balancing loops for housing supply and demand. *Source:* Adapted from Sterman (2000). Reproduced with permission of The McGraw-Hill Companies.

housing price. The B$_{demand}$ loop shows that increased *demand for houses* pushes *housing price* up and the B$_{supply}$ loop shows that increased *supply* pushes it down. Higher *price* reduces the *relative value* of a house (compared with the price of substitutes) which decreases *demand*; it also increases *profits* to suppliers relative to building and other costs, which drives *supply* up. The diagram reflects how the dynamic movement of housing supply and demand pushes housing price *toward equilibrium* and includes relevant delays. The Appendix discusses the generic form of this diagram in detail.

2.8.3 Influence of the Housing Market on Securities and Derivatives

Figure 2.4 showed that federal policies and lending practices supporting the government's goals for home ownership increased demand for houses.[119] More demand generated a housing boom and the industries associated with houses escalated.[120] But more demand for houses by higher-risk borrowers also meant that more high-risk mortgages spread into the financial market

---

119. Home ownership increased from 62 percent of households in 1994, to 69 percent in 2004. See Rajan, 2010; Zandi, 2009; U.S. Census Bureau, 2012b. Data show highest home ownership growth from about 43 percent in 1940 to over 60 percent in 1960, spurred by no-down payment VA mortgages after WWII and expansion of highways.

120. Morris, 2008; by mid-2005, half of U.S. GDP growth "was housing-related, either directly through home-building and housing-related purchases, like new furniture, or indirectly, by spending refinancing cash flows."

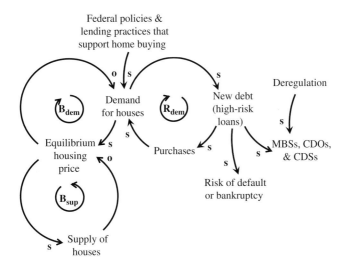

FIGURE 2.7   The housing market encourages the sale of securities and derivatives.

through securitization. These policies and practices had rapidly propelled the economy into the land of rising housing prices and growing risk. To illustrate how the housing market influenced the sale of securities and derivatives, Figure 2.7 adds a reinforcing loop R_{demand} to the interaction of supply and demand for houses from Figure 2.6. Together these loops operate like the gears of the penny-stamping machine to heighten the risk of default and bankruptcy and increase the sale of MBSs, CDOs, and CDSs. These same loops appear in later systems diagrams. Note that this depiction deletes relative value and price of substitutes from the demand loop, and profit and cost from the supply loop since these factors are not the focus of this analysis and can be assumed.

From Figure 2.7, *federal policies and lending practices that support home buying* heightened *demand for houses* because loans were readily available; increased *demand* raised *housing prices*. Rising *prices* tagged housing as an excellent investment, further increasing demand and encouraging more people to take out *new debt* to *purchase* a home. When new debt increased, high-risk loans increased, *risk of default or bankruptcy* escalated, and more *high-risk loans* were structured into potentially profitable *MBSs, CDOs*, and *CDSs. Deregulation* in the financial industry facilitated the sales of these new securities and derivatives. Although this diagram is a simplistic interpretation of more complex interactions, it shows that the two markets are critically connected through new debt, specifically high-risk loans. Eventually risk became reality; massive defaults and bankruptcies destroyed the whole operation.

2.8.4 Candidate Leverage Points

One way to counter these risk-producing loops is to redefine the policies and practices that fed them *before* they can generate a crisis. Earlier and more tempered changes to monetary policy could have kept interest rates up and discouraged some high-risk borrowers from taking out loans. Federal housing policies could have modulated the enthusiastic response of the housing and financial industries. Lending agencies could have tightened their practices by revising criteria for subprime and ARM loans, by increasing high-risk loan rates, and by eliminating the all-too-tempting high risk mortgage types. Finally, financial institutions could have reduced the irrational attraction to securities by making certain their prices reflected *risk* (thus supporting the efficient markets hypothesis).

2.8.5 Current Activities

We've seen policies and practices that stimulated the crisis and suggested leverage points for applying pressure when the clouds were gathering. However, in reality, actions came too late to prevent the damage. All that could be done was to try to stop or reverse the worst of it. One action involved monetary policy; the Fed drastically dropped federal funds rates in 2008 and 2009 until they were nearly zero. The government also enacted the Dodd–Frank Act in July 2010 to protect consumers and reform Wall Street. Although it was still being debated in late 2012, a subset of this act, the Volcker Rule, intends to reduce the risk created by the repeal of the Glass–Steagall Act and again "bans banks from speculating with their own money"; traditional banks would no longer be allowed to trade in financial instruments for profit.[121] This rule reduces conflicts of interest between lenders and securities buyers or sellers, and between the housing and securities markets.

In a third action, banks changed lending policies, not so much from a desire to improve the economy, but more from a desire to survive. After 2008, banks became "stingy" with credit "due to past lending mistakes" and the fear that inflation could wipe out profits when loans are repaid, especially while interest rates are so low.[122] Tightened credit slowed the economy down—less buying, more unemployment.

2.8.6 Cautions

While these actions are reasonable, later chapters reveal that they are not enough to prevent a future crisis or to fully recover from the current one.

---

121. Goldfarb and Schneider, Feb 28, 2012. The Dodd–Frank Act is also called the "Wall Street Reform and Consumer Protection Act."
122. Tamny, 2009.

Furthermore, we cannot simply make a "to-do" list. Just as individual parts work together to create the whole, so are these actions pieces of a larger solution. Taken individually, they may do little to alleviate the crisis, and, as in the case of stingy credit, they may exacerbate the economy's woes.

2.9 SUMMARY

This chapter reviewed how federal policies, lending practices, and the housing and financial markets operated between 1994 and 2010, and recognized that policies from earlier decades had already set the stage for crisis. It first presented events as a linear sequence and explored economic mechanisms that operated like the gears of a penny-stamping machine, leaving their deep imprint of risk. New policies and practices, new loan types, and innovative securities encouraged home buying. Together they played off Americans' desire to own a home and off external investors' thirst for high returns in the financial market. In this chapter, we related supply and demand to the housing market; saw how the Fed used monetary policies and how government policies affected behaviors; watched risky mortgages migrate from the housing market into the financial market; and recognized how assumptions about financial market operation created false confidence. Eventually, all these factors (policies, practices, markets, and risk) coalesced into massive loan defaults that threw the economy into a tailspin.

Independently, each event seems benign. Loans were made one by one; securities were sold one by one. Jointly however, they tied the whole global financial industry together with the rotting thread of risky loans. Further compromising this perilous state was the undervaluation or even disregard for risk. This chapter noted three factors that intensified risk.

First, *federal economic policies* encouraged home ownership for high-risk consumers, removed regulation on financial derivatives, and allowed more corporate debt. These policies sometimes operated counter to monetary policy. During some periods, the Fed raised interest rates to slow the economy at the exact time that housing policies further encouraged its growth. Second, by tempting financial institutions' pursuit of profitability and consumers' desires to own homes, revised lending practices with lax qualifications pushed high risk subprime loans (and the likelihood of default) to unprecedented levels. Finally, migration of mortgage loans from the housing market to the financial market through securitization, structuring, and derivatives shifted risk to investors whose holdings spanned the globe.

These specifics evolved into three systems thinking representations. First, a balancing loop, whose goal was a target inflation rate, described monetary policy. Second, supply and demand for houses became two balancing loops that seek equilibrium price. Third, a reinforcing loop tied high-risk debt to the supply and demand balancing loops for houses. Energized by federal policies, lending practices, deregulation, and assumptions about risk, this last subsystem of loops generated risk as it stimulated price growth in the housing market and encouraged security and derivative sales in the financial market. Although four leverage areas (monetary policies, housing policies, lending practices, and securities risk assessment) could dampen the effects of the loops, these levers cannot be considered individually; they must be woven into a complete picture of interactive cause and effect.

Even considering these mechanisms, we have yet to identify the main catalyst of the crisis. Although less tangible, one factor affects all these loops and indeed the entire economic system. And what is that factor? It is the human element, the Yin in our philosophical metaphor, which appears in Part II.

The Yin: Human Behaviors

Chapter 3

Where Can I Buy One? Humans and the Economy

We will never really understand important economic events unless we confront the fact that their causes are largely mental in nature... the current crisis... was caused precisely by our changing confidence, temptations, envy, resentment, and illusion— and especially by changing stories about the nature of the economy.

Akerlof and Shiller[1]

In the late 1980s, the television show *Star Trek: The Next Generation* introduced the Borg. These part human, part artificial beings are implanted with bio-chips that link their brains to a collective consciousness.[2] With thousands of voices in their heads, they are always aware of one another's thoughts and do not need to communicate directly; they just know what the whole is thinking. Perhaps without too big a leap of fancy, one can compare a nation's economy to this Borg collective, sans bio-chips.

An economy has highly mechanistic protocols that define markets, reflect prices, and value goods and services. Instead of seeking out technology like the Borg, an economy pursues wealth. However, the goals of an economy extend beyond its classic definition, beyond the productive management of resources. Far more valuable than the statistics it generates, the economy of any nation is a social system that enables individuals to survive and flourish, or forces them to strive and flounder. Within this social system sit human beings. An economy's impersonal workings are brought to life by highly personal interactions, behaviors, and responses. In his comprehensive research on the market economy, Lane agrees with this duality, acknowledging that "the economic system cannot be studied in isolation of the social system."[3]

So imagine that the economy *is* like that giant Borg collective whose aggregate thoughts set expectations, reflect cultural values, and influence behaviors within an economic framework. Imagine how difficult it would be

---

1. Akerlof and Shiller, 2009.
2. Retrieved from *www.startrek.com/database_article/borg*.
3. Lane, 1995.

to move that collective one way or the other from the outside. Then, imagine the challenges this organic social system poses as it adapts to changes in its environment—oftentimes with unpredictable outcomes. All these difficulties are evident in America's market economy where aggregate behaviors create supply and demand. And herein grow the seedlings of the economic crisis. Behind the performance of an economy, behind its complexity and unpredictability are human beings with all their preferences, strengths, feelings, and foibles.

Humanness, as revealed in behaviors, seeped into every crevice of the global economy during the crisis and could not be smoothed over with policies or formulas. Notably, five types of behavior weighed heavily on housing-related industries in the U.S. and threatened the global financial system. These behaviors involved decisions and actions in the buying or selling of products related to mortgages and to financial securities. They rattled the very core of economies across the world.

Two of the five behaviors involve consumer buying. I call these buying behaviors *persistent buying* and *unrealistic buying* of homes and things. Antecedents of these buying behaviors trace back to values and beliefs in the American culture and to expectations that depend on human nature and the economic environment. Three other behaviors—*unethical acts, risk-taking*, and *self-interested reward seeking*—spring from norms in the cultures of corporations that were most prominent in the crisis. Unethical acts expose a seedy side of people that is intimately related to human nature and abetted by values, beliefs, and circumstances. Risk-taking and reward-seeking behaviors during the crisis lacked concern for consequences and cared not about the welfare of others.

This chapter lays the foundation for understanding why individuals behaved as they did during the crisis and why events seemed unpredictable. Chapters 4, 5, and 6 expand these behaviors and identify how they created situations that could not be halted by ordinary means. Before studying the details in these later chapters, we will first explore the history of human psychology in economics, and then discuss the role of values and beliefs, of expectations, and of human nature in the economy, specifically as they relate to the economic crisis.

3.1 HISTORY OF HUMAN PSYCHOLOGY IN ECONOMIC THEORY

In the study of the human mind and its mental states, psychology deals with emotions and behaviors that have been painted with the broad brush of values and beliefs. Psychology informs our understanding of the world as a whole. We use it to manage teams and lead organizations; we use it in neuroscience, in medicine, and in other scientific fields; we even use it in sports. It surfaces in areas that touch humans, including economic theory. In the evolution of economic theory, however, the importance of psychology has alternately waxed and waned.

For centuries, human knowledge in the natural sciences advanced by favoring reason, logic, and scientific truth over the highly personal human values, beliefs, and emotions. This approach is embodied in what we know as the scientific method, with a history that stretches back millennia. It requires empirical data and measurable evidence, and breaks the whole into discrete parts that are explained by laws and equations. Notably, since the seventeenth century when René Descartes clearly described this rational and deductive method,[4] we have made unimagined progress. In areas such as physics, chemistry, and biology, it replaced guesswork and intuition with rigor and brought about incredible results.[5] We have only to consider today's computer technology and medical advances to see its imprint.

In the 1700s—the early days of modern economics—even as the scientific method tipped the scales toward rationalism in the natural sciences, attention to human emotion still prevailed in the study of the economy. A pioneer in this field, Adam Smith, described not only the mechanics of an economy, but also the criticality of basic human drives like "moral sentiments," the "desire to be worthy of admiration," and "self-interest."[6] Two centuries later in the early and mid-1900s, theories that support rational decision making and those that favor more emotionally tinted behavior shared prominence in economic theory.

The first theory of human decision-making behavior, called *rational choice theory*, has been around for a long time. Relative to the economy, it assumes that rational, self-interested individuals have all the information they need to make decisions and that their decisions will be logically guided by a desire to increase their wealth, avoid unnecessary work, and maximize their own well-being. British political economist John Stuart Mill embedded this theory in his 1836 work[7] and British economist Lionel Robbins included it as *homo economicus* (economic man) in his writings 100 years later.[8]

Criticism of the rational choice theory surfaced in the early to mid-twentieth century. Economists such as Herbert Simon, Thorstein Veblen, John Maynard Keynes, and Friedrich Hayek believed that in the midst of uncertainty, actions in an economy are "guided by imagination as well as reason."[9]

4. Descartes, 2008/1637.
5. Brooks, 2011.
6. See Smith, 1937, 2004. Smith was dubbed the "father of modern economics."
7. Mill, 1836.
8. Robbins, 1932.
9. Brooks, 2011.

Keynes appreciated that reason as well as "animal spirits" govern economic activity.[10] Even as he researched statistical probabilities and fiscal policies, Keynes argued that because it deals with values, expectations, and psychological uncertainties, "economics is a moral science" which cannot capture reality in universal, mathematical laws.[11] These concepts broke new ground for what would become behavioral economics.

Then, late in the twentieth century, human traits took a back seat to logic and reason. With its tremendous success in the natural sciences, the scientific method spilled over into the social sciences, most notably into the field of economics.[12] This approach produced tools and models to replicate how the economy works. Soon economists were discounting individual emotions and behaviors in favor of reason, technical factors, government actions, or monetary policies.[13] However, without the human dimension, the models-and-numbers approach fell flat. This "obsession with quantification" without understanding personalities and culture has been linked to great failures and misjudgments about many world events, including the Vietnam war and the failed "expansion of lending by the World Bank" during former Secretary of Defense Robert McNamara's tenure.[14]

Now in the twenty-first century, the trend is changing. Although many of the economic policies intended to contain the U.S. crisis still assumed super-rational, ideal, and predictable human behavior and "played a role in the Federal Reserve's failure,"[15] we are again recognizing that humanness does matter. Two disciplines, behavioral economics and neuroeconomics, have reframed the role of human psychology in economic theory and can contribute to our understanding of what happened.

3.1.1 Behavioral Economics

In the 1940s one specialty area of psychology, social psychology,[16] crossed into economic territory. And by the 1950s, various scholars challenged the traditional theory of the perfect rationality that economists had assumed about individuals' decision-making behaviors. For example, Simon suggested that individuals have only "approximate rationality" or "bounded rationality"

10. Akerlof and Shiller, 2009; Keynes is one of the founders of macroeconomics.
11. Brooks, 2011; Keynes citation from Skidelsky, 2009.
12. Brooks, 2011.
13. See Brooks, 2011; Akerlof and Shiller, 2009.
14. Kay, 2011. McNamara was a former "Whiz Kid" from RAND whose rational, numbers-focused approach succeeded in planning logistics for the U.S. Armed Forces during the Vietnam War. He became U.S. Secretary of Defense in the 1960 s and then president of the World Bank.
15. Stiglitz, 2010.
16. Social psychology grew from Lewin and others' research on group dynamics; see Lewin, 1947.

with which they make decisions.[17] In the 1960s, economics and psychology formally merged when psychologists Katona, Tversky, and Kahneman applied principles such as expectation, risk, and uncertainty to macroeconomics.[18] By the 1970s, psychology exposed "a far more complicated portrayal of decision making" that can at times be irrational.[19] Evolution of this marriage of psychology and economics continued through the 1980s to change the way economists view decision making; it matured into the behavioral economics we know today. In the 1990s, behavioral economists such as Thaler, Shiller, Ariely, and Akerlof expanded earlier insights, recognizing that emotions, too, affect rational decision making and that unconscious beliefs or intuitions influence choices.[20] This recognition now helps us explain behaviors such as asset bubbles and speculation.

3.1.2 Neuroeconomics

Neuroeconomics, a field that has emerged in the last decade, blends psychology, neuroscience, and economics into models of decision making, rewards, risks, and uncertainties.[21] Neuroeconomics penetrates the human being more deeply than behavioral economics; it delves into the physical structure and functions of the brain itself. Findings in this field suggest that feelings such as anxiety, fear, or even happiness can "color our view of all things at the moment."[22] Here, economic decisions in the presence of strong emotions may not reflect good choices and could even be harmful. In Section 3.4, we apply these physiological views to understand the role of human nature in market-related behaviors and in the unethical behaviors that dominated the crisis.

* * * * * * * *

Today, we are fortunate to access thinking that integrates human characteristics with economics. We recognize that a nation's economy *does* have predictable parts that can be aggregated into equations and trends by following the scientific method. However, just like the human collective it embodies, sometimes an economy is unpredictable. Making sense of this uncertainty requires insights into human behavior. Because the social system behind a nation's economy contains institutions and policies as well as human beings, it requires a subtle balance between mechanics and

---

17. Simon, 1955; Simon references "bounded rationality" in *Models of Bounded Rationality* published in 1982.
18. See Katona, 1960. Katona devised the precursor of the "University of Michigan Consumer Sentiment Index"; see also Tversky and Kahneman, 2008.
19. Slovic, 2009; see also Ariely, 2009.
20. Brooks, 2011.
21. McCabe, 2003.
22. Belsky and Gilovich, 2010.

organics—and an understanding of that Borg-like combination. Let us now consider what role values and beliefs, expectations, and human nature played in the economic crisis drama.

3.2 THE ROLE OF VALUES AND BELIEFS IN ECONOMICS

Values are central to our individual characters; they make us who we are. They express what Rokeach calls ideal ways to behave, or ideal terminal goals.[23] Beliefs are less abstract than values and reflect what we hold to be true about ourselves and our world. Beliefs tell us that something is good or bad, true or false; they tell us that "something is real."[24] They can be spiritually uplifting or can diminish our self-esteem. When we believe, we trust and we place confidence in an idea, condition, person, or thing. Beliefs and values are critical human processes that bring order and establish patterns[25] in an uncertain and often ambiguous world. They guide what we think. They dictate how we make decisions and take actions. They color how we feel about these decisions and actions and help us justify them later.

For the economic crisis, decisions about buying—buying homes and buying "things"—have emotional roots embedded in what we believe and what we value. For example, if we believe that owning a home is a symbol of worth, we will want to buy one to feel important and significant, even if it means borrowing beyond our means. Or if we believe that a particular "thing" will bring us happiness, we will get in line to buy it even if we have to use an already over-extended credit card.

Where do we get values and beliefs like the ones in these examples? While many of our beliefs come directly from our values,[26] both have diverse origins: parents, religion, education, observation, experience, and interaction with others; they are even influenced by "what we think others believe."[27] Behavioral scientists suggest that for all individuals, "some values are selected biologically... some are the by-product of the physical and institutional environments, and the rest are the by-product of personal history."[28]

Relative to environmental sources, we grow up in an ocean of values and beliefs: social norms, customs, and patterns of shared assumptions—all elements of a national or organizational culture.[29] Holding a script of norms,

---

23. Rokeach, 1989.
24. Williams, 1965.
25. Gilovich, 1991.
26. Bem, 1970.
27. Gilovich, 1991.
28. Hechter, 1993.
29. Schein, 2010.

habits, and beliefs, culture is like a little director sitting on our shoulders, whispering "implicit and often unnoticed messages about how to feel, how to respond, how to divine meaning."[30] Thus, values and beliefs for citizens of any nation or for employees of any organization are concentrated in their cultures. As we will see in the Chapter 4, the American culture and the cultures of various corporations, with their strong values and beliefs and their potent effects on behavior, played crucial roles in the U.S. economic crisis.

3.3 THE ROLE OF EXPECTATIONS IN ECONOMICS

Human expectations have greater power than we may think. They are described as "notions about what will happen" to the person who has the expectation, or to the society or economy of which he or she is part. Because they also influence a "demand for certain goods",[31] expectations are important to economics, as John Maynard Keynes believed when he introduced them into mainstream economic theory in the 1930s.[32]

Since the 1960s when psychologist George Katona and others blended economics and psychology into its own discipline, we have acknowledged that individual motives, attitudes, and expectations are potent enough to change the behavior of collectives and can "thereby influence the entire economy."[33] A fundamental tenet of behavioral economics today is built on the power of expectations where perceptions are colored by what the mind thinks will happen.[34] Through expectations, individuals can sway a group's behavior more easily than they can alter that group's values. Often expectations are fueled by media, gossip, or just "gut feeling" rather than by rational analysis or clear knowledge of what the future holds. Expectations may be transitory but they are indeed powerful.

After the 2000 dot-com crash and the 2008 economic collapse in the U.S., we abruptly awakened "to the reality that psychology and irrational behavior play a much larger role in the economy's functioning than rational economists... had been willing to admit."[35] In particular, expectations create irrational behavior, often fueling speculative bubbles in the stock market or in real estate by pushing the price of stock or property far beyond its underlying value. We discuss expectations and their influence on consumers' unrealistic buying behaviors in Chapter 5.

---

30. Brooks, 2011; see also Scruton, 2007.
31. Katona, 1960.
32. Skidelsky, 2009.
33. Katona, 1960.
34. Brooks, 2011.
35. Ariely, 2009.

3.4 THE ROLE OF HUMAN NATURE IN ECONOMICS

Although its specific definitions vary, human nature integrates characteristic ways of feeling, thinking, or acting that come naturally to human beings. Philosophy professor Leslie Stevenson aptly observes that "rival beliefs about human nature are typically embodied in different individual ways of life, and in political and economic systems."[36] Regardless of whether we consider psychological, philosophical, religious, ethical, emotional, motivational, or even neurobiological perspectives, we can safely say that human nature has many facets, some of which are expressed as inclinations, instincts, and drives that dictate behavior. It includes simple needs for procreation, security, significance, achievement, and belonging; a moral sense of right and wrong; and even a more complex drive to realize our full potential, to learn, to create, and to find meaning in our lives.

Just as values, beliefs, and expectations excite behaviors that affect the economy, so does human nature. Human nature is the clay from which external values and beliefs sculpt the whole person, ultimately influencing behaviors. Depending on the strength of these influences—whether from the environment or from culture—they can mold human nature to foster dysfunctional and unethical behaviors. Characteristics such as greed or pride—negative aspects of self-interest—frequently emerge in economic settings, particularly if these situations involve money or power.

Many examples of self-interested unethical behaviors have made the news over the past decade. Enron, whose focus was on "how much money could be made for many executives,"[37] displayed a blatant lack of integrity in its accounting practices and brought the company and many of its employees to ruin; Bernie Madoff used a Ponzi scheme to bilk investors out of billions; Goldman Sachs made $1 billion by ensuring that high-risk mortgage-backed securities went into the CDOs they sold to investors, and then betting "against the CDO so it would profit if the CDO lost value."[38]

We will learn in Chapter 6 that unethical behaviors derived from human nature and influenced by values and norms present at the time of the crisis contributed to economic calamity. Mortgage frauds, disreputable lending, and irresponsible buying and selling of securities amplified the woes of the already weakened mortgage-related and financial industries.

3.5 SUMMARY

This chapter introduced the human mechanics that set the economic crisis into motion, spread and deepened its effects, and prolonged its life. In it we learned that economic theory has evolved over the years, alternately

---

36. Stevenson and Haberman, 1998.
37. Ferrell et al., 2010.
38. Goldstein, 2010b.

embracing and ignoring the realities of human influences. Today, particularly after the crisis in the U.S. rippled across the world, economic theory is more fully incorporating human characteristics to achieve a better understanding of the socioeconomic system in which the crisis took root. In considering various aspects of humanness, we suggested that humans' values and cultural beliefs can drive *persistent buying* of homes and things. We related that expectations of what may happen in the future greatly sway consumer buying, and may influence a more irrational type of consumer behavior that we called *unrealistic buying*. Finally, human nature, particularly when external factors aid its more negative aspects, can lead to greed, risk-taking, and self-interested reward-seeking that cause irresponsible, fraudulent, or dishonest acts. Simply put, human behaviors manipulate economic decision making.

The highlights in this chapter merely summarize what will follow. In later chapters we investigate factors that influence human characteristics and describe how and why these characteristics affect behaviors and economic decision making. Then, using systems thinking, these chapters illustrate relationships and identify candidate leverage points in which small actions can have large effects on behaviors and decisions. Chapter 12 combines the strongest of these candidates into a comprehensive action program that addresses both positive and negative aspects of human behaviors.

Chapter 4

Who Are You Anyway? Values, Beliefs, Norms, and Behaviors

One interviewee replied to attempts to get him to justify why honesty was good and lying bad:... "I don't know. It just is. It's just so basic... It's part of me. I don't know where it came from, but it's very important."

Bellah et al.[1]

Standard economic theory assumes that we are born with fully formed preferences. But we are shaped by what happens around us, including, and perhaps most importantly, by the economy.

Stiglitz[2]

How do you define yourself? Is your identity established by what you do, what you have, or what you think? In my MBA course on ethical leadership, students write a three-page paper with the title "Who I am and what I believe." For some, this paper is difficult—how in the world can you define yourself in three pages? One way to approach it, I tell them, is to consider the questions: What characteristics make you uniquely "you"? What inside of you cannot be compromised and is not for sale? What are your core beliefs and values?

Indeed, these questions seek out the essence of who we are; our values and beliefs characterize many of our unique qualities and frame our identity. These values and beliefs, whether about self, about others, or about the world around us, are so deeply ingrained that we may be unaware of their influence. Often we have no explanation for them other than "because" or "it's just how I feel." These intrinsic qualities are the fount of contentment, dissatisfaction, guilt—and behavior.

What are these values and beliefs and where do they come from? Values reflect preferences and ideals that shape many of our beliefs. They dictate our biases and mold our likes and dislikes—what we cherish and what we

---

1. Bellah et al., 1996.
2. Stiglitz, 2010.

discount. Moral values define our sense of right and wrong. Stacey suggests they give "life meaning and purpose."[3] Another theory proposes that, within a cultural context, values increase fitness for survival.[4] They help us adapt successfully to new situations.

Chapter 3 described many sources of values and beliefs. Sociology professor Michael Hechter enumerates their more generic origins from the value producing mechanisms of biology, environment, social institutions, and membership in specific groups.[5] Biological or innate values that come with human nature include traits that influence our tendencies toward self-interest and social interest. We discuss these moral-based values more fully in Chapter 7 and Chapter 11 when ethics appear in our systems story. This chapter focuses on social groups and how the values we derive from them affect our material cravings and buying behaviors.

We grow up as a part of various social collectives. From family units to schools, sports teams, and religious organizations, from our workplace to the country we call home, we are exposed to value-based ways of thinking. Each of these groups contains patterns of shared assumptions called culture. Management professor Edgar Schein's formal definition of culture can help us understand its influence; cultures contain: (a) espoused values, or "publicly announced principles and values"; (b) shared meanings or the "understandings that are created by group members as they interact"; and (c) group norms or "implicit standards and values that evolve" from interaction with others.[6]

For nations, shared beliefs and norms that dictate "how things are done in this country," and shared values that rouse national pride have evolved into durable cultures. For corporations, shared beliefs and norms tell employees "this is how we do business around here," and provide "criteria for what *ought* to be done, what is *right*";[7] shared values reflect how to treat others and what behaviors are rewarded. An important characteristic of a corporate culture is that, because it is more contained than its national counterpart, organizational leaders directly influence its content. Concentrating on the U.S. economic crisis, this chapter investigates how the American culture molded consumers' persistent buying behaviors and how corporate cultures promoted short-term reward-centric, risk-seeking, and unethical behaviors that translated into high-risk loans and securities.

3. Stacey, 2010.
4. Michod, 1993.
5. Hechter, 1993.
6. Schein, 2010.
7. Stacey, 2010.

4.1 AMERICAN CULTURE

Like cultures in general, America's culture has passed from generation to generation through ideals, policies, censures, approvals, and emotions. Although environments evolve and generations disagree on details, analysts conclude that even in the presence of tremendous change, the distinctive features of national cultures endure.[8] Values in the American culture originate from the Declaration of Independence which endows Americans with certain rights including "Life, Liberty, and the pursuit of Happiness." From these roots, America's culture fostered strong beliefs that eventually affected buying behaviors—specifically the "persistent buying of homes and things" that contributed to the 2008 meltdown. Figure 4.1 maps how this culture accomplished such unintended influence.

4.1.1 Value Patterns

In his influential work in the 1950s, sociologist Robin Williams identified 15 value patterns of desirable qualities in America's culture that hold

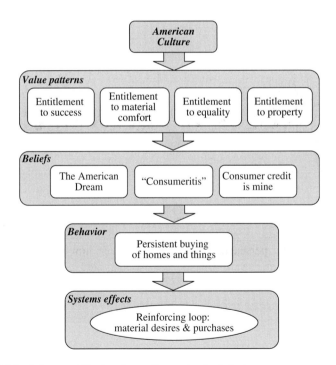

FIGURE 4.1   Influence of the American culture on buying behaviors.

8. Trice and Beyer, 1993.

true yet today.[9] These patterns have nurtured a nation that reveres human life (ranking 4th in human development); maintains a high standard of living (ranking 13th in quality of life); and fosters innovation (placing 1st or 2nd in patent applications since the late 1800s).[10] Four of these 15 value patterns are germane to our discussions: achievement and success; material comfort; equality; and property rights. When at their most positive, these four shaped a strong nation and helped Americans become responsible citizens. However, on their downside, these values became entitlements and promoted buying behaviors that fueled the economic crisis.[11] Of course, not all Americans exhibited less-than-constructive behaviors, but the many who did were enough to affect the economy.

4.1.1.1 Entitlement to Success

The first cultural value pattern celebrates personal achievement and success. Federal Reserve chairman Ben Bernanke expanded on this "bedrock American principle" stating that all should have an opportunity to succeed based on "their own effort, skill, and ingenuity."[12] His comments are mirrored in a 2009 survey showing that over 60 percent of Americans think people should be rewarded for their diligence and skill.[13] Americans believe they can get ahead if they work hard enough and have the right proficiencies.

The shadow side of this value places *results* or *rewards* above personal excellence and achievement. In fact, since the 1940s, achievement has been de-emphasized and success has become more important.[14] By holding success and rewards for success *above* achievement, an attitude of entitlement *regardless* of efforts emerges. Beyond entitlement, it also seems that *what* we buy with these rewards matters. Evidence shows that "how one spends his income, rather than what he did to earn it appears increasingly to be a mark of 'achievement'."[15] Although hard work and skill matter to Americans, success or a show of success may matter more. This shift from means to end suggests that Americans value what one *has* more than how *well* one does or how *hard* one works. For some, it translates into a bias toward *appearance* of economic success rather than *actual* success.

---

9. Williams, 1965.

10. Human development index from United Nations Development Programme, 2010; Quality-of-life index from Economist Intelligence Unit, 2005; patent application statistics from WIPO, 2010.

11. Except where otherwise noted, discussions and quotations on American values and value clusters from Williams (1965) and from Trice and Beyer (1993).

12. Bernanke, 2007.

13. Sawhill and Morton, 2009.

14. Trice and Beyer, 1993.

15. Williams, 1965.

Basic human motivations reinforce the cultural partiality toward success in others' eyes, making it all the more noteworthy. Many motivation theories, for example, share the premise that humans are driven to achieve, excel, and succeed—not only to increase self-esteem and confidence, but also to attain intangibles such as social status, appreciation, and respect.[16] In its less favorable form, pure success-focus can create circumstances in which individuals use any means to appear successful. Implications for the economic crisis are many: individuals purchase trappings (big houses or new cars) that they cannot afford; mortgage loan officers boost commissions by pushing loans to those who cannot make the payments; financial managers and executives increase bonuses and social status by selling risky securities without adequate cautions.

4.1.1.2 Entitlement to Material Comfort

In this second value pattern, Williams noted that American culture places more value on the "*external world* of things and events... rather than in the inner experience of meaning and affect."[17] In a country with one of the highest standards of living in the world, Americans have acclimated to the external world of *material comfort* and hold it in high regard.

At their most damaging, values that incorporate material comfort create a cycle of ever-increasing desires. The cycle begins as soon as desires are satisfied and individuals come to believe that fulfilled desires are rights to which they have a moral claim.[18] Thus, as old desires become entitlements, new ones surface. One explanation of this psychological phenomenon, the "hedonic treadmill," points to humans' innate adaptability. Once on this treadmill, behavioral economist Dan Ariely says, "we look forward to the things that will make us happy, but we don't realize how short-lived this happiness will be, and when adaptation hits we look for the next new thing. 'This time,' we tell ourselves, 'this thing will really make me happy for a long time'."[19] And when it doesn't, we climb back on the treadmill, still searching.

Recent studies find that materialistic behavior has increased over the past generation, prompted by a growing confidence in capitalism.[20] We are a nation addicted to material goods and comforts, and to the temporary psychological highs they bring. While materialism easily becomes entitlement in a society used to elevated levels of "things," it also draws our attention inward. In a compelling discussion of recent shifts in American culture, psychologists

---

16. Theories such as Maslow's (1970) hierarchy of needs; McClelland's (1962) acquired needs; the four drives theory of Lawrence and Nohria (2002).
17. Williams, 1965.
18. Williams, 1965.
19. Ariely, 2010.
20. Shiller, 2005.

Twenge and Campbell found that a move away from "the greater good of the 1960s" and toward a focus on the individual began in the 1970s, became epidemic by the 1990s, and is now embedded as a cultural value. This self-focus, they suggest, has indeed promoted entitlement: "many people in the United States today are simply oblivious to others' needs, or worse, think that others' needs are just not as important as their own needs... [and believe that] one deserves special treatment, success, and more material things."[21] These entitled, materialistic, and self-interested tendencies clearly displayed themselves in the economic crisis; they drove individuals deeply into debt and put them on the hedonic treadmill so they could satisfy their desire for *more*.

4.1.1.3 Entitlement to Equality

At its most basic, *equality* implied by the U.S. Constitution means that the government guarantees the rule of law, security, and certain human rights, such as the right to liberty, *equally* to all people. The word *equality*, however, didn't appear until the Fourteenth Amendment in 1868 protected these rights for former slaves. Since that time, equality has assumed many value-laden interpretations including "an equal right to fundamental opportunities."[22] Federal Reserve chairman Bernanke reiterated this constitutional value, stating that opportunity for economic well-being should be widely and equally distributed, and that individual economic outcomes should be linked to individual contributions.[23] Two manifestations of the equality value pattern are particularly relevant: the general desire for equal socioeconomic status[24] and the specific desire for equal income.[25]

This deep and abiding value of "equal rights to opportunity" in the American culture prompts beliefs in the desirability and likelihood of upward mobility in income and social class. Many Americans are optimistic about their chances and their children's chances of increasing social status; a 2005 poll found that 40 percent "believed the chance of moving from one class to another had risen over the last 30 years."[26] However, their optimism squarely confronts a reality in which neither status nor income mobility is present.

---

21. Twenge and Campbell, 2009.
22. Williams, 1965.
23. Bernanke, 2007.
24. Income, occupational prestige, education level, and wealth are common discriminators of social class. See Beeghley, 2004; Gilbert, 2003; Thompson and Hickey, 2008. Social classes are lower, working, lower middle, upper middle, and upper class (Thompson and Hickey, 2008). About 20 percent of people are upper and upper middle class; 44 percent are working or lower class. Income levels and education vary substantially.
25. A different phenomenon emerged after the crisis and in the midst of a long recession. In 2011 survey results, financial security was more important to Americans than upward mobility; see Mellman Group, 2011.
26. Scott and Leonhardt, 2005.

Research confirms that mobility in America is lower than most people believe. For some, in fact, intergenerational mobility (how children compare with their parents) has decreased; in 2004 men in their thirties had about "12 percent less income than their fathers' generation at the same age."[27]

The income gap has been widening for nearly three decades.[28] Certainly the immense incomes of CEOs are part of income inequity, but most people do not aspire to this top echelon where a typical CEO makes more in an hour than a minimum-wage worker makes in a month.[29] A better way to regard income inequality in America is to compare the poorest 20 percent of Americans with the richest 20 percent. In the quarter century between 1979 and 2004, after-tax income rose 9 percent for the poorest and 69 percent for the richest.[30] The Census Bureau's income inequality ratio recognizes this growth trend.[31] Although some cite discrepancies in these reports,[32] there is sufficient rationale to believe that income inequality is increasing. What matters here is not statistical precision, but rather the perception that income inequality not only exists, but is growing.

So how do these statistics and perceptions apply to the economic crisis? First, for some Americans, equality has evolved from a right to equal *opportunity* into an entitlement to equal *income* and equal ability to *acquire material things*. Second, when this social desire for equal living conditions confronts stagnant social status and income inequality, tension grows. In an environment where probability of a substantial jump in income is low, people use methods other than their own intelligence, skills, education, or hard work to resolve this tension. Prior to the crisis, many aimed to *appear* more equal by buying the trappings. With cheaper goods, it has in fact become "harder to read position in possessions"; the middle class today is living as well as the upper class did 50 years ago.[33] Easy access to credit fueled this possessions creep; it removed barriers that prevented people from buying things that make them seem more equal.

For the economic crisis in the U.S., buying a home was a significant way to display or to feel equality. Contemporary economists believe that income inequality pressured politicians to increase access to low-cost housing and encourage high-risk loans. This remedy for inequality is certainly more

---

27. Sawhill and Morton, 2009. Studies also find that upward mobility in other industrialized countries, such as Denmark or Canada, is two to three times that in the U.S. (see Sawhill and Morton, 2008).
28. Johnston, 2007; see also Stiglitz, 2011.
29. Sawhill and Morton, 2009.
30. Sawhill and Morton, 2009.
31. U.S. Census Bureau, 2011f. The Census Bureau uses the Gini index (index of income concentration). High numbers mean greater income inequity. It had grown to 0.466 in 2008.
32. See for example Reynolds, 2007.
33. Scott and Leonhardt, 2005.

politically expedient than funding education or reducing unemployment.[34] Voters are attracted to the promise of an ability to buy the frills of a higher social class.

4.1.1.4 Entitlement to Property

The final value pattern, *property rights*, is particularly relevant to the crisis. Derived from the Declaration of Independence, this highly cherished value emphasizes "unalienable rights," which for Americans include property rights.[35] Some suggest that Americans' admiration for private property actually fueled real estate market booms. For example, Shiller notes that capitalism "seems to be evolving into an even more extreme ideal where the value of our private property has a greater influence on our lives."[36] Others offer that the government used the rationale of expanding home ownership into low and middle-income households to grow the economy.[37] These policies reshaped the cultural value of a *right* to own property into an *entitlement* to own a home. Such beliefs made individuals vulnerable to any solution that could help, including subprime home loans they couldn't afford.

* * * * *

We have deeply scrutinized American culture because it so strongly molds our economy. Human desires for social status, respect, rewards, equality, and significance helped to create and strengthen these cultural values. Now we will discover how the four value patterns of entitlement—to success, material comfort, equality, and private property—coalesced into three cultural beliefs that Americans hold to be true. These beliefs shape buying behavior as powerfully as any other factors.

4.1.2 Beliefs

The first belief involves the *American Dream*. The second recognizes Calder's description of America's "culture of consumption."[38] I call it *consumeritis* or the inflamed belief that consumption will satisfy all desires. The third suggests that consumer credit is a sort of *possession* that individuals can use whenever they want, to buy whatever they want.

---

34. Rajan, 2010.
35. Locke, 2004; property rights in the Declaration of Independence were inspired by English philosopher John Locke's proposal that it is one's right to own property earned through one's labor.
36. Shiller, 2005.
37. Rajan, 2010.
38. Calder, 1999.

4.1.2.1 The American Dream

James Truslow Adams first coined the term "the American Dream" in 1931, defining it as "that dream of a land in which life should be better and richer and fuller for every man, with opportunity for each according to his ability or achievement.... a dream of being able to grow to fullest development."[39] The very potential of this dream makes "our way of life attractive and magnetic to people in other lands."[40]

The American Dream has become synonymous with the goals of creating personal wealth and owning property. Ideally, achieving these goals not only makes us financially secure, but also establishes our worth and equality and fulfills our desire for material comfort. Today, these goals include owning a home. But wait. The original American Dream said nothing about owning a home; it just offered opportunity and hope. When did home ownership steal its way into the heart of the dream?

Ironically similar to government policies for low-income families in the 1990s, the government promoted home ownership to returning WWII veterans, offering them low-interest home loans with no money down. Speculating on the future, one entrepreneur, William Levitt, began building homes in the state of New York; now it was possible for many nonwealthy citizens to be proud home owners. As Levitt's idea spread, home ownership embedded itself into the American Dream; the 45 percent of households that owned homes in 1940 grew to 62 percent in 1960 where it remained until the 1990s.[41]

After Levitt's time, this home ownership idea planted roots in the American Dream. In a 2009 economic mobility poll, 60 percent of those surveyed felt that "owning a house" is a significant part of the American Dream,[42] yet in an earlier 2006 poll, most believed that it is impossible to reach that dream.[43] Optimism fizzled more after the crisis: in 2008, about half of those surveyed believed they had achieved the American Dream while in 2011, less than a third did.[44] Thus before housing prices fell in 2006, the confident belief that one can achieve the American Dream and is entitled to own a home invigorated excessive home buying. This belief was motivated by the desire to have at least an *appearance* of success and equality.

---

39. Adams, 1931.
40. Kamp, 2009.
41. Parts of this discussion can be found in Kamp, 2009.
42. Economic Mobility Project, 2009; the importance of owning a home nearly matched other aspects of the American culture such as "succeed regardless" and having your children be "better off financially than you are."
43. CNN.com, 2006; 60 percent of those without a college degree and 38 percent of college graduates believe it is impossible to reach the American Dream.
44. Mellman Group, 2011; the percentage of those surveyed who believed they had achieved the American Dream was 55 percent in 2008 and 31 percent in 2011.

4.1.2.2 Consumeritis

The second of the two culture-related beliefs that significantly influence
economic behavior, *consumeritis*, dovetails nicely with the American
Dream. Of course, buying goods is not done merely to satisfy physical
needs; it is also a mental and emotional act. Material goods have become
a part of one's personal identity, even more, some say, than one's work
roles.[45] They are symbols of success or equality for others to see and are
even "therapeutic remedies for the problems that ail us."[46] American's
belief that material goods will change their identity or satisfy all desires
has induced a behavior of what I call *persistent buying*. We have only to
note all the Macys, Starbucks, and Targets to recognize that buying is a
national pastime. Some even say that "the freedom to shop has become...
a political right."[47]

Although more intense, this behavior is not new in America. In 1899,
economist Thorstein Veblen "coined the term *conspicuous consumption* to
characterize the enthusiasm with which Americans pursued material comforts
and ostentation."[48] Veblen remarked at that time that "unproductive consumption of goods is honourable, primarily as a mark of prowess and a per-
quisite of human dignity."[49] This consumption ideal was further embedded
into American culture after WWII when "mass consumption was extensively
reshaping the nation." In fact it evolved from a "personal indulgence" into
"a civic responsibility."[50] At the time, with a motive to bring America out of
a deepening recession, President Eisenhower portrayed the ideal citizen as
one who "simultaneously fulfilled personal desire and civic obligation by
consuming."[51]

Furthermore, surrounded by personal motivations and culturally-driven
beliefs of entitlement to material comfort, equality, property, and success,
Americans are subconsciously primed to consume. Influenced by the need
for approval and by culturally conceived ideals,[52] they are tempted by mass
advertising "to go beyond the bounds of prudence."[53] Attractive images of
thin beautiful people living the good life encourage emotion-based
consumption.

Human motivations for equality and success, a desire to gain approval,
and a consumption-oriented, entitlement-rich culture enhance Americans'
belief that buying brings satisfaction. Consumeritis with its *persistent buying*

---

45. Bocock, 1997.
46. Calder, 1999.
47. Galbraith, 2008.
48. Trice and Beyer, 1993; Veblen, 1931.
49. Veblen, 1931.
50. Cohen, 2004; quotation from *Life* magazine May 5, 1947.
51. Cohen, 2004.
52. Bocock, 1997.
53. Lane, 1995.

behavior merges with the American Dream and its *home buying* behavior: Americans are caught up in buying houses and things. With a voracious appetite for material goods and for homes, Americans want to have it all— now. Although all this buying is a commanding force, it is expensive. Many cannot afford it. So, just how can they buy? Media headlines tell us that the answer to this question is not with savings or current income: it is with consumer credit.

4.1.2.3 Consumer Credit is Mine

The third cultural belief, that we are entitled to credit, facilitates the other two buying-focused beliefs. While cultural values have changed little over the years, how Americans live these values has blurred around the edges. For example, early in America's history, thrift was a core value and a "mainspring for national prosperity." Since WWII, however, people view debt differently. Thrift has become almost "un-American."[54] Shiller calls the U.S. an "ownership society," noting that saving for the future seems irrelevant when people can just buy and hold their assets, and watch them increase in value.[55]

Economists remark that "the American icons of the shopping mall and the credit card are suggestive of our lax attitudes toward saving."[56] Statistics on saving support this perception. The ratio of personal saving to disposable income averaged 9 percent in the 1980s, dropped to about 5 percent in the 1990s, and bottomed out near zero in 2005. Some suggest that the decline comes from people acclimating to prolonged rises in housing and stock prices, and to low interest rates.[57] Now, rather than save to purchase a home or buy things, Americans borrow. Debt is a no longer a dirty word; it is necessary, acceptable, and *it is mine* to use whenever I want. Yet at the same time that saving decreased, Americans actually increased their wealth: their homes appreciated in value.

This have-your-cake-and-eat-it-too phenomenon, that is, spend liberally while growing your nest egg, apparently caught on because debt has soared in the past decade. However, using debt to fund living expenses is not a newcomer to the American economy. As Calder reminds us, since the 1920s consumer credit has facilitated this "culture of consumption" in pursuit of the American Dream.[58] Still, the *amount* of debt relative to income *is* new. In the mid-1980s, household debt represented 65 percent of annual disposable

---

54. Calder, 1999; Calder cites J. K. Galbraith (1958), *The Affluent Society* Boston: Houghton Mifflin and W. H. Whyte, Jr. (1956, March). Budgetism: Opiate of the middle class. *Fortune*.
55. Shiller, 2005; the phrase "ownership society" is attributed to George W. Bush.
56. Akerlof and Shiller, 2009.
57. Statistics from Lansing, 2005; Glick and Lansing, 2009.
58. Calder, 1999.

income; by 2007, it reached 133 percent.[59] Americans were in over their heads. For every $3 the average household had in disposable income, they had $4 of debt. "The story of consumer credit since 1940," says Calder, "can be summed up in a single word: *more*."[60] America has become a nation where saving is passé and where it is okay to borrow to buy beyond your ability, especially if it gives you an appearance of success. *More* always seems better.

With this belief about debt, material desires can be managed if credit is available. So, let us move from the buying side of the economy to a second belief system that affected the credit and investment side. Although its influence is narrower, this cultural belief system guided behaviors in lending organizations and financial firms that were closely associated with the crisis.

4.2 CORPORATE CULTURES

The workplace has an immense bearing on behavior, simply because we spend many waking hours at work and because our jobs are our livelihoods. Just as a national culture shapes behavior of its citizens, so do corporate cultures establish norms for employees. In particular, these cultural norms tell employees what type of behavior is expected and how to succeed. Corporate cultures often differ significantly from one another. Examples of positive cultures include those that embody trust, empathy, and efficacy, and whose climates inspire traits of respect, openness, and confidence.[61] These cultural attributes can lead to competitive advantage for an organization and to positive development and moral growth for individual employees. In contrast, the cultural norms in other organizations can produce seedy and often unethical behaviors that result in short-term benefits and long-term damage.

A familiar example illustrates this dark side of corporate culture and shows the power that such cultures have over individuals. Enron, the energy company that went bankrupt in 2001, had a corporate culture gone awry; its "arrogant or prideful" culture contributed to extensive losses and eventually sent some to jail. Some say it focused "on how much money could be made for many executives" and encouraged "risky behavior, if not breaking the rules."[62] More relevant to the crisis, recent comments about the culture at Goldman Sachs created quite a commotion. In a public letter of resignation, an executive director described the deteriorating culture as "toxic and destructive," and as one in which employees refer to clients as "muppets" and callously talk about ripping them off.[63]

59. Glick and Lansing, 2009; this debt to personal disposable income (annual) is called "household leverage."
60. Calder, 1999.
61. Higgins and Rogers, 2012.
62. For Enron culture discussion see Ferrell et al. (2010).
63. Rizzo, 2012.

Leaders have extensive influence on the cultural climate that surrounds their employees. In fact, research shows that "people tend to behave in accordance with the expectations of those who are significant to them"[64] and that "subordinates, more often than not, appear to do what they believe they are expected to do."[65] Given their roles, leaders *do* instill cultural values, even if those values are dysfunctional or unethical, as many were during the crisis.

Tied to leaders' influence on culture, some researchers implicate failed leadership as a root cause of the crisis. One study concluded that better leadership would have made a difference not only in financial organizations at the center of action, but also in organizations that invested in risky securities.[66] The study described leadership failures in three broad areas: (1) lack of competence, particularly failure to create structures, systems, and processes that handle risk; (2) negative characteristics including lack of ethics, greed, narcissism, hedonism, overconfidence, collective hubris, and hyper-competitiveness that led to irresponsible risk-taking; and (3) failure to do "the real, gritty, hard work of leadership" and to accept "their responsibilities to the communities and societies within which they operated." Others suggest that "in a scramble to make money for themselves," leaders in these firms failed to protect clients' long-term investments.[67]

From these insights, we can categorize five leader characteristics that most likely affected the crisis. As we will see in examples that follow, leaders were: closed to the constructive dissent that encourages discussion of risk, consequences, and the wisdom of aggressive strategies; overconfident about the future, prideful, and incompetent in assessing risk and repercussions; lacking integrity with a low sense of social interest; unreasonably tolerant of risk; and oriented toward short-term results and rewards.

Figure 4.2 shows how these characteristics influence cultural beliefs and norms. Derived from these characteristics, six cultural attributes seem most relevant for the crisis: entitlement; risk-seeking overconfidence; hubris; ethical complaisance; rewards for short-term performance; and organizational silence that stifles bad news. Cultural beliefs and norms like these facilitated the glut of high-risk loans and securities; they fostered greedy and unethical acts, risk-taking, and excessive self-interest to gain individual rewards. In addition to culture, temptations and opportunities in the economic environment further nurtured dysfunction. Chapters 6 and 7 explore these aspects in more detail.

---

64. Latham, 2007.
65. Livingston, 2003.
66. Gandz et al., 2010; this study documented nine months of discussions with business thought leaders worldwide beginning September 2009.
67. George, 2008.

Several examples illustrate this model (Figure 4.2) and identify leader characteristics and cultural beliefs that led to excessive behaviors. These characteristics and cultural beliefs were evident in the big financial organizations that were intimately involved in the crisis. For example, some say that the drive and confidence of CEO Dick Fuld "permeated the culture of Lehman."[68] With greater candor, others suggest that he wore his "undisguised, naked greed... like a misplaced badge of courage," "secluded himself in his palatial offices" to nurse his ambitions, and was subject to "rages, threats, and vengeance," all of which created an environment of fear and secrecy.[69] Merrill Lynch's CEO Stanley O'Neal had a "burning ambition" to change the company; "he wanted to transform its 'mother Merrill' culture, which he viewed as bloated and soft... and pushed Merrill to take more risks and bigger risks—Goldman Sachs-like risks."[70] Countrywide's CEO Angelo Mozilo "created a corporate culture focused on low-documentation and subprime mortgages"; he emphasized short-term commissions "with little concern for stakeholders."[71] Analysts say that in the big financial companies "there's still a deeply ingrained culture of entitlement"[72] making people feel they deserve whatever they want, regardless of how they get it.

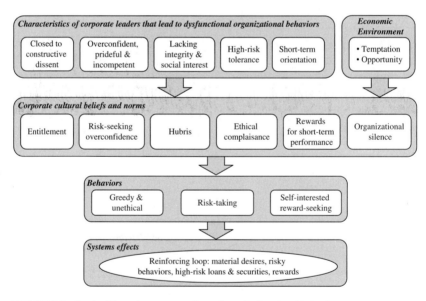

FIGURE 4.2   Leadership and corporate culture shape dysfunctional behaviors.

68. Plumb and Wilchins, 2008.
69. McDonald, 2009.
70. McLean and Nocera, 2010; O'Neal became CEO in 2002.
71. Ferrell et al., 2010.
72. Associated Press, 2009.

Cultural norms and leader characteristics created the perfect climate for bad conduct. The blending of two cultures—one national and one corporate—promoted complementary behaviors that affected supply and demand for housing and for home-related loans and securities. Consumers wanted to buy so urgently and lenders and financial agents wanted to sell so desperately that none cared about reason or risk: a perfect recipe for short-term benefit and long-term disaster.

4.3 SYSTEMS THINKING INTERPRETATION

When individuals' innate materialistic desires, their human need for status and significance in others' eyes, and their tendencies toward self-interest are supported by cultural values that promote entitlement, consumption, and risk, the potential for economic crisis intensifies. In systems thinking terms, we show the tremendous influence of the American culture and corporate cultures on buying and selling behaviors. Note that although culture can be a balancing loop that brings behaviors in line with its inherent norms (see Chapter 1), for simplicity, our systems depictions show it as an influencing factor only.

The reinforcing loop R_{desire} in Figure 4.3 illustrates how values of entitlement to success, material comfort, equality, and property in the *American culture*, join with the *self-interest* traits of human nature to increase *material desires*. Hoping to satisfy these desires, consumers increase *new debt* to make *purchases*. As we continue around the loop, *persistent buying* raises aspirations for possessions. In accumulating more and more possessions, consumers step on the hedonistic treadmill described earlier; the more that people have, the more they want—*material desires* continue to increase. This basic reinforcing loop appears in later systems diagrams. Chapter 7 describes several significant human traits that support self-interest.

This loop has a beneficial by-product. Because credit (credit cards, refinancing, or new home loans) rather than savings or income facilitated

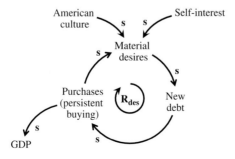

FIGURE 4.3   Material desires reinforcing loop.

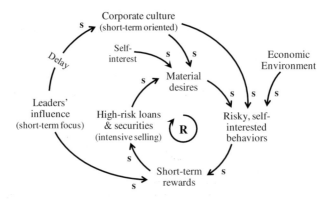

FIGURE 4.4 Reinforcing loop for corporate culture, rewards, and high-risk loans and securities.

purchases, "personal consumption expenditures... [grew] faster than disposable income."[73] More *purchases* increased *gross domestic product (GDP)*. However, because this inflated GDP was built from risky debt, it flattened when the economy crashed. GDP and other indicators of economic health appear in Chapter 12.

A similar reinforcing loop shows how a short-term oriented *corporate culture* and the temptations and opportunities in the *economic environment* influence the selling of *high-risk loans and securities*. In Figure 4.4, *leaders* with a short-term focus have two effects. First, over time they shape *corporate cultures* and second, they establish *short-term rewards* to incentivize employee behavior. *Corporate cultural* norms that are short-term oriented encourage both *material desires* and *risky self-interested behaviors*. These risk-taking behaviors are rewarded with *short-term rewards* and engender more intensive selling of *high-risk loans and securities*. This pattern further inflames *material desires* to complete the reinforcing loop. Although not shown, consistent use of short-term rewards can become a cultural norm. When they grow strong, these norms are difficult to change. Relationships among material desires, short-term rewards, and culture in this reinforcing loop will appear in later systems diagrams. An important point to remember here is culture's influence on material desires.

4.3.1 Candidate Leverage Points

In reality, neither persistent buying of houses and things nor intensive selling of high-risk loans and securities is sustainable. In the U.S. economic crisis, both buying and selling ended abruptly and unfavorably. However, before

---

73. Glick and Lansing, 2009.

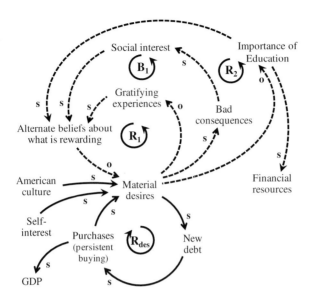

FIGURE 4.5   Alternate beliefs reduce material desires.

the economy reached crisis levels, intervention could have been applied as balancing loops in at least two areas. The following paragraphs illustrate systems interpretations of these leverage points.

4.3.1.1 Alternate Beliefs

Although somewhat difficult to implement—and perhaps idealistic—the first leverage point controls excesses in the R_{desire} loop by diluting Americans' cultural reverence of materialism and replacing *material desires* with *alternate beliefs about what is rewarding*. In Figure 4.5, *alternate beliefs* that incorporate *gratifying experiences, social interest,* or *education* can mute cultural entitlement and dependence on consumption. Three loops (R_1, R_2, and B_1) illustrate the effects of such beliefs on *material desires* and ultimately on *purchases* that are funded by *new debt*. The final leverage points discussed in Chapter 12 include insights derived from these loops.

One alternative belief might be that "experiences create inner happiness." The theory behind this belief relies on the adaptive nature of humans. When we are continuously exposed to a condition or environment, we become used to it and then seek out something different to make us happy. Ariely suggests that by investing in transient experiences such as travel or concerts rather than in things that will blend into our environment, we can harness our adaptive nature, "maximize our overall satisfaction in life,"[74] and jump off that

---

74. Ariely, 2010.

hedonic treadmill. Thus in loop R_1, *gratifying experiences* counteract the cultural and human propensity to believe that only material possessions will make us happy. Over time, *gratifying experiences* diminish *material desires*.

Another belief involves *social interest*. Although prevalent cultural values focus on improving one's own image, one's own circumstances, or one's own happiness, humans are more than engines of self-interest. As social creatures, we also have other-directed orientations. Philosophers observe that by nature, man will consider the needs of others[75] (within limits). The premise here is that when we express a *social interest* and involve ourselves with others, *material desires* wane. By opening our eyes to the consequences of our actions on others, we invoke other-focused motives and may find it satisfying to help them. In this case, beliefs that emphasize responsibility to the larger society could include "If I buy and borrow more than I can afford, I will hurt someone." Here balancing loop B_1 counters *material desires* by considering potentially *bad consequences*. Chapter 11 expands these relationships.

Another alternative belief centers on *education*. Reinforcing loop R_2 shows the effects of the *importance of education* on *material desires*. Through *education*, this loop also increases *financial resources*. Data confirm this relationship. For example, median annual income for workers without high school or college is about $6000 less than U.S. median income, whereas for those with college degrees it is above $10,000 more.[76] By tackling income inequality,[77] education also improves our sought-after social status.

Statistics on education, however, ignore these factors. Although a greater percentage of people hold college degrees today than in 1994, the education path is less used.[78] One economist suggests that higher education seems out of favor in America because "there might be a natural limit to how much education a population can absorb."[79] Another possibility is that individuals, debt-ridden from student loans, cannot get a job in their field.[80] Regardless of the reason, education is not a preferred solution to remedy income inequality.

75. Niebuhr, 1960.
76. U.S. Census Bureau, 2011d; 40 percent of workers between 21 and 64 have no high school and/or no college degree; 26 percent have at least a college degree; the rest have "some college" and earn near the median income.
77. Bernanke, 2007.
78. Digest of Education Statistics (2011) shows an increasing percentage of college educated persons. In 1994, 22.2 percent of those ≥ age 25 held bachelor's or higher degrees; in 2009 it was 29.5 percent. However, the *rate* of increase has dropped. From 1994 to 1999, the percentage of degreed persons increased 13.5 percent; from 1999 to 2004, it increased 9.9 percent; and from 2004 to 2009, it increased only 6.5 percent.
79. Rajan, 2010.
80. Samuelson, 2012.

There is another caution for this path. While education improves equality of income and status, the temptation of the hedonic treadmill remains. Simply put, people with higher incomes and status desire more expensive things. As an example, in today's world of the elite, when the wealthy socialize with the *very* wealthy, those with less money feel compelled to "keep up with their richer brethren" and find themselves "spending more and borrowing heavily."[81]

Thus the greater power of this lever does not come from an increased income that enables more *purchases*; it is derived from the *rewarding* experience of getting an *education* and its potential for creating job and life satisfaction. These intrinsic rewards could temper *material desires* and create a more permanent avenue for happiness. Furthermore, doing well in school has broader long-term benefits for nations. It is a "powerful predictor for the wealth and social outcomes that countries will reap in the long run."[82] Of course education takes desire, time, energy, money, and opportunity—and in the short-term creates more debt.

4.3.1.2 Leaders' Influence on Corporate Culture

The second leverage area attends to the reinforcing loop around risky behaviors and high-risk loans and securities. Since leaders greatly affect culture, leverage here changes *leaders' influence* and proposes to transform *corporate cultural* norms that promote *short-term rewards* and produce *risky self-interested behaviors*. As for all individuals, leaders' values mature in a crucible of biology, experience, and environment. At best, they take time to change. One approach is simply to replace a mismatched leader with someone whose values and behaviors align with what is desired. Barring this wholesale substitution, an organization could reinforce desired values and alter goals and rewards to develop existing *leaders' focus on the long-term*.

Figure 4.6 shows both possibilities. Replacing the leader can immediately change *leaders' influence* to reflect a long-term focus. For the second possibility, we introduce balancing loop B_2 to define desired *long-term goals and values* and provide *long-term oriented rewards* that alter leaders' behaviors. To gain these *rewards*, leaders must care about the long term effects of their decisions. These leaders diminish the short-term orientation of their *corporate culture* and reduce the use of *short-term rewards* for employees which ultimately lessens employees' *risky self-interested behaviors*. The final leverage points in Chapter 12 use the concept of corporate purpose to realize these powerful behavior-changing influences.

---

81. Frank, 2007.
82. Friedman, 2012; this source also referenced a study that correlated performance on a high school international assessment exam with total earnings on natural resources as a percentage of GDP.

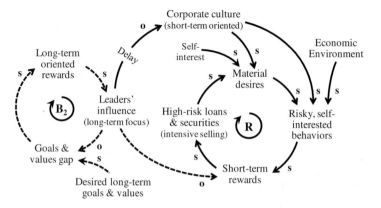

FIGURE 4.6   Changes in leadership goals and values affect corporate culture.

4.3.2 Current Activities

One leveraging action relies on bad consequences to change beliefs and reduce material desires. These consequences could involve bankruptcies and foreclosures that result from excessive debt. A recent decline in credit card debt indicates that we may be witnessing this very phenomenon. Consumers are spending more cautiously, just wanting to get out of debt.[83] Credit card debt, for example, dropped about $150 billion (over 15 percent) between 2008 and 2010; it continued to decrease until the end of 2011.[84] Some lenders have also assimilated lessons from bad consequences and have eliminated credit to high-risk consumers. Other current activities that incorporate our leverage points include the current administration's policies to encourage education and reduce student costs.[85]

4.4 SUMMARY

By exploring the effects of values and beliefs on behavior, this chapter touches a human nerve in the economic crisis. It proposes that intense desires for more—more happiness, more success, more respect, more equality, or more things—were magnified by the American culture and by corporate cultures in the case of those who worked for institutions involved in lending or in buying or selling securities.

Under normal circumstances, these boundless desires are held at bay by limited resources and by self-discipline. For the crisis, easily available

83. Simon, 2011.
84. Federal Reserve Board, 2012; revolving credit dropped from $1010B at the end of 2008 to $857B at the end of 2010; by April 2012 it was $862B.
85. Wolf, 2012.

credit made resources abundant. This ready credit was like visiting an all-you-can-eat buffet, with the added twist that the waiters make a commission every time you fill your plate. So with the resource limit barrier down, self-discipline was the lone soldier to prevent overindulgence.

Now enter the American culture. Could Americans rely on its guidance to strengthen self-discipline? Apparently they could not. Even prior to the crash, some of the steeped-in values that made America great also displayed their dark sides. Through human tendencies to adapt and take things for granted, people translated these values from privileges into entitlements. It was no longer a privilege to own a home or to buy material goods *based on* what you could afford; it was your right, *regardless of* what you could afford. The latest gadget or material comfort became passé once we got used to it. Jaded attitudes pressed us to replace one thing with some other thing that might satisfy our deep-seated need for happiness or conjure up an image of success in others' eyes. In this milieu, a search for happiness translated into material desires that were pursued regardless of cost. These relationships defined the material desires reinforcing loop R_{desire}.

What about the power of corporate cultures in crisis-related industries? Could they curb self-interest on the selling side of the economic equation? Again, they apparently could not. In fact, rather than inspire moral growth or contain these behaviors, these cultures emboldened dysfunctional acts. Strong values and beliefs, particularly by leaders who influenced culture, created a self-gratifying climate of risk and entitlement, overconfidence and hubris, ethical complaisance, intolerance for negative feedback, and encouragement of short-term performance.

As a result, with a limitless buffet, weakened self-discipline, and cultures that abetted dysfunctional behaviors, we bought and sold ourselves sick with no thought for others, for society, or for the future. Persistent buying entered a vicious circle. Intensive selling spurred by massive short-term rewards flooded the market with high-risk loans and securities. However, as we know, nothing can continue forever. Inevitable repercussions replaced resource limits, self-discipline, integrity, and responsibility. The tower of cards tumbled; defaults, bankruptcies, and foreclosures took over. The system fell hard.

What could have stabilized this buying and selling? Using a systems view, two candidate leverage points could possibly have subdued the culturally induced reinforcing loops that increased material desires, purchases, and risky loans and securities. The first point of intervention involves modulating beliefs about what is rewarding. Three alternatives counteracted the negative aspects of the American culture. If these new beliefs are strengthened by governmental and organizational policies and by media attention, they could eventually become part of the culture and change the ways in which Americans seek success and happiness. One alternative suggests that individuals, institutions, and government alike can learn from bad consequences, thus enhancing responsibility and an interest in society to reduce entitlement and the longing for more. Another would have us focus on ways other than materialistic buying to achieve happiness, including gratifying experiences that are more transient in nature. A final belief tapped education to diminish materialistic desires. Additional education provides higher income and higher status, thus reducing the sting of inequality and increasing one's ability to make purchases; but more importantly, it can be a fulfilling substitute for material goods and have a long-term effect on a nation's economy.

The second leverage point involves altering leaders' influence on corporate cultures and on short-term rewards for employees. One aggressive action replaces leaders whose behaviors shape a short-term, dysfunctional environment with leaders whose behaviors are opposite. A preferred approach, however, is to modify a corporation's goals and the rewards given to leaders to elicit long-term oriented behavior. In either case, over time, corporate cultures could evolve to create beneficial long-term outcomes.

This chapter proposed actions that detour us around the spiral of persistent buying, intensive selling, and risky corporate behavior. However, its goal is not to present a panacea that makes everything better, or to offer ways of achieving the much-sought-after human happiness. Rather, the chapter intends to make us ponder the strength of the values and beliefs of human actors in an economy, especially when they are reinforced by the cultures of our nations and our organizations. We continue our discussion of human elements and their effects on buying behaviors in the next chapter.

Chapter 5

Visions of Grandeur: Expectations and Behaviors

Expectations are more than the mere anticipation of a boost from a fizzy Coke.... although expectations can make us look foolish from time to time, they are also very powerful and useful.... expectations can influence nearly every aspect of our life.

Ariely[1]

Even as a young blacksmith's apprentice, Pip, the orphan boy in Charles Dickens' *Great Expectations,* longs to improve his lot in life. He wholeheartedly believes it is possible to raise his social class and become wealthy. Pip's great expectations about a rosy future become reality when a rich benefactor brings him to London to become a gentleman of means. Although in real life we don't all have a rich benefactor, we humans do share the desire to better ourselves. We, too, have great expectations for wealth, happiness, and success.

Expectations, however, are more than desires and daydreams. Through the lens of environment, our perceptions of the present world become beliefs and expectations about the future world. These beliefs then translate into behaviors and actions that we think will bring us closer to our deepest desires.[2] Expectations shaped from beliefs about the future operate differently than the cultural beliefs and values we discussed in Chapter 4. Cultures, such as the relatively stable American culture and the more malleable corporate cultures, comprise an external collective that sets norms for behavior. However, although they are somewhat affected by cultural surroundings expectations come from inside; they develop from what we think might happen based on past experience and our own views of the world.

1. Ariely, 2009.
2. Deci, 1980.

5.1 EXPECTATIONS AND THE ECONOMIC ENVIRONMENT

Are expectations important in the economy? Definitely. In discussing behavioral economics, Chapter 3 noted that expectations are a significant factor in a market economy. In fact, the Fed purposely uses the "expectations hypothesis" when it sets monetary policy; if it sets a low short term rate and "the market believes it will be held low for a sustained period, the Fed can influence expectations" about future interest rates.[3] More notably, the expectation that low interest rates would continue was one reason that borrowers barely blinked when they signed up for adjustable rate mortgages. Another simple example illustrates the sway of expectations. If individuals hear about a cold front in California, they may expect a future shortage of oranges and buy more than usual. When many shoppers with similar expectations buy oranges, they force a shortage and the price of oranges increases regardless of whether or not there was a frost. During the crisis, such beliefs about the future created expectations about housing prices that resulted in irrational behavior, as we will soon see.

Expectations form in many ways. Economist John Maynard Keynes notes that an expectation may not depend on the "most probable forecast we can make" but in fact is biased by environment.[4] Psychologist Edward Deci believes that "expectations are learned" and may not represent reality at all.[5] Others conclude that numerous factors create expectations, including economic policies, social interactions, implied market promises, and even personality traits such as optimism or pessimism.[6] From these theories, we deduce that certain aspects of the economic environment have a primary role in shaping expectations. In this social milieu, individuals conduct business, plan for their future, and seek happiness and well-being. Expectations grow from experience and from interpreting environmental cues.

Yet we do have predispositions about what we will believe. We are pattern-seekers who need to make sense of the world; we do so by making inferences from what we already know. Psychology tells us that "the brain cannot start from scratch at every new situation. It must build on what it has seen before."[7] For this reason, the more familiar we are with a situation or the longer we are exposed to a certain condition, the more we adapt to that situation or condition, become used to the patterns within it, and expect that it will continue. Because forming expectations is often unconscious, we may be unaware of how our expectations come into being or how to let them go. In her classic work on the psychology of expectations, Clara Hitchcock explains, "expectation is in its beginning non-rational.... if someone points

---

3. Rajan, 2010.
4. Keynes, 1964.
5. Deci, 1980.
6. See Katona, 1960; Lane, 1995.
7. Ariely, 2009.

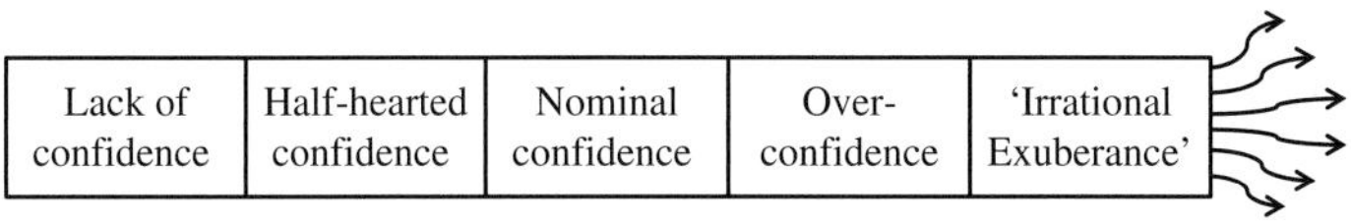

Lack of confidence	Half-hearted confidence	Nominal confidence	Over-confidence	'Irrational Exuberance'

FIGURE 5.1   Continuum of confidence for expectations.

out the irrationality of a certain anticipation, we are not always able to give it up at once."[8]

And we have another predisposition concerning the content of our expectations. Just as Scarlett O'Hara in the novel *Gone With the Wind* believed that "tomorrow's another day," we too tend to expect a better future.[9] Apart from fiction, expectations in an economic context are very real. Lane suggests that expectations escalate not only from promises made by the market, but also "because the modern human psyche is disposed to expect the self to be favored."[10] Unless we are despondent, we humans expect more, expect what we have seen before, and expect that times will get better.

5.1.1 Confidence Levels

Keynes states that expectation also "depends on the *confidence*" with which we forecast our future.[11] Other economists discuss expectations in terms of what I call a *continuum of confidence*. This continuum ranges from complete lack of confidence to a most energetic form of "irrational exuberance"[12] as shown in Figure 5.1. Distinctions between confidence levels tell us how rational a person's decision making might be. Level of confidence reveals whether we will act on an expectation and how quickly that expectation will spread to others. Relative to systems thinking, I suggest that the higher the confidence level for an expected future, the greater the likelihood that reinforcing loops are involved; these loops tend to perpetuate the expectations to which they are attached.

At the far left of this continuum is *lack of confidence* where individuals may not act even when they see others around them behaving in certain ways. *Half-hearted confidence* is more a wait-and-see state, where consumers might dip their toes in the economic waters to see what happens. Expectations at a *nominal confidence* level reveal what an individual believes could happen, such as "housing prices will go up," or "real estate is

---

8. Hitchcock, 1903.
9. In Margaret Mitchell's 1936 book *Gone with the Wind*, heroine Scarlett O'Hara used optimism whenever she faced a challenge, "I won't think of it now. I can't stand it if I do. I'll think of it tomorrow at Tara. Tomorrow's another day."
10. Lane, 1995.
11. Keynes, 1964.
12. Shiller, 2005.

a good long-term investment." Even at this level, decision making is not necessarily rational; in good times when people are trusting and confident, they relax their suspicions.[13]

Overconfidence indicates that the individual is highly certain of an outcome, but that the basis of this confidence is weak or unfounded. Columnist David Brooks observes that "the human mind is an overconfidence machine."[14] Shiller echoes this thought, suggesting that humans have a tendency "toward overconfidence" in their beliefs, and that they will act on "stories or reasons that one might think they should have little confidence in."[15]

Overconfidence also grows from assumptions that people make when they want to explain something they don't understand. They look for familiar patterns and presume "that future patterns will resemble past ones, often without sufficient consideration of the reasons for the pattern or the probability of the pattern repeating itself."[16] Overconfident individuals are likely to act with little analysis or consideration of outcomes. Economic repercussions at this level mean that rational decisions, whether they involve selling, buying, or borrowing, may happen only by accident rather than by analysis.

Finally, *irrational exuberance*, a term first used in 1996 by former Federal Reserve Board chairman Alan Greenspan, is "more like the kind of bad judgment we all remember having made at some point in our lives when our enthusiasm got the best of us."[17] At this level, strong emotions blot out rational thinking—oftentimes entirely. Irrational exuberance rouses an unchecked "person-to-person contagion."[18] Excitement itself creates a fertile environment for fish tales that exaggerate reality. The mere effects of irrational exuberance are "amplified by a feedback loop, a speculative bubble" in which price, rather than underlying value, increases the exuberance.[19] Energy bursts out this end of the continuum with behavior that cannot possibly be justified.

If we apply what Akerlof and Shiller call a confidence multiplier[20] to low levels of confidence, we find that confidence feeds off itself to generate even greater levels of confidence, perhaps at times turning half-heartedness into irrational exuberance. This multiplier is a form of the basic feed-forward loop from Chapter 1. The more confidence one has about an expectation, the

---

13. Akerlof and Shiller, 2009.
14. Brooks, 2011.
15. Shiller, 2005.
16. Shiller, 2005.
17. Shiller, 2005.
18. Akerlof and Shiller, 2009.
19. Shiller, 2005.
20. Akerlof and Shiller, 2009; Akerlof and Shiller combine economic multiplier theories of Keynes and Hicks with research on the effects of confidence levels. From this combination, they define a concept called the "confidence multiplier."

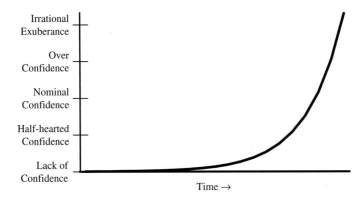

FIGURE 5.2   Increasing confidence level of expectations over time.

more probable that he or she will act on that expectation. Each individual action increases others' confidence and causes them to act similarly. In the aggregate, these actions make the expectation a reality, which boosts confidence. The cycle continues; each round multiplies both the level of confidence and the actions that result from that confidence. Eventually it becomes an infectious self-fulfilling prophecy.

Figure 5.2 uses a behavior-over-time chart to visualize this rapidly increasing and contagious confidence, for example, in an environment of continuously rising housing prices. This type of exponential growth indicates that a reinforcing loop is present.

5.1.2 Effects of the Environment on Expectations

Figure 5.3 illustrates how the economic environment might influence expectations and multiply confidence levels. In certain environments, the confidence with which one holds an expectation may intensify to the point where individuals buy things whether they need them or not, and regardless of whether they can afford them. These dynamics create a reinforcing loop between expectations and demand, with each stimulating the other.

The economic environment in the U.S. prior to 2008 created a mix of very real, but misplaced expectations that caused unrealistic buying and irrational decision making. Six particular expectations widely applied to consumers. Mortgage lenders and sellers of mortgage-related securities held a seventh expectation. Although most expectations were at low to medium confidence levels, some reached the high pitch of irrational exuberance, at which point better judgment was simply suspended. To understand how these seven expectations evolved, let's review prevailing conditions in the U.S. a few years before the crisis.

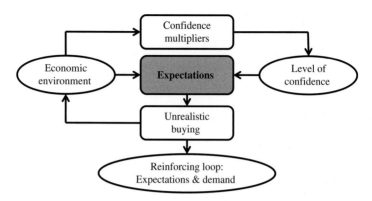

FIGURE 5.3   Expectations influence buying behavior.

5.1.3 Environment before the Crisis

The economic environment that existed in 2004—just before the massive bankruptcies and foreclosures—provides a perfect snapshot of conditions that shaped expectations. A person in 2004 would have been used to an environment in which:

- *Interest rates for housing were moderate to low.* In mid-2001, federal funds rates fell below 4 percent and 1-year ARMs dipped below 6 percent; the next three years into 2004, federal funds rates rested well below 2 percent and 1-year ARMs were under 4½ percent.[21]
- *Housing prices had been going up "forever."* Average U.S. housing prices have climbed steadily since the 1940s. This trend spans generations and was a fact of life before many borrowers were even born. The trend was more pronounced in the seven years prior to 2004 when average housing prices increased between 7 and 15 percent a year.[22] Media coverage about the housing market was frequent, so these conditions were well known.
- *Nonprime loans were gaining popularity.* The use of nonprime mortgage loans for those who could never before qualify had been increasing since 2000. By 2004, subprime loan originations accounted for nearly a fifth of all loans and were on the upswing.[23] In addition, more people were using interest-only and payment option loans,[24] and the number of ARM

---

21. Federal funds rates from Board of Governors of the Federal Reserve System, 2011b; 1-year ARM rates from Freddie Mac, 2011c.
22. Standard and Poors/Case-Shiller, 2011.
23. Subprime loan origination data from Joint Center for Housing Studies, 2008; subprime loans accounted for over 18 percent of all loans in 2004.
24. By 2005, 10 times more people were using special loans than they were in 2003; Joint Center for Housing Studies, 2008.

originations grew from 21,000 in 1995 to over 644,000 in 2003.[25] These loan types became accepted and even commonplace.

- *New home sales were on a steep incline.* In 2004, the number of new houses sold per year was over 80 percent more than a decade earlier; much of this growth had occurred since 2000.[26] New housing tracts, construction sites, and realtors proliferated.

- *Unemployment was reasonable and stable.* By 2004, unemployment had rested below 6 percent for a decade.[27] Average incomes grew 2 to 4 percent a year between 1994 and 2000, dipped slightly then stayed about even from 2002 to 2004.[28] This stability allowed people to concentrate on today and not worry about tomorrow.

- *The flood gates to increase home sales were open.* By 2004, both the federal government and well-known banks had expanded their loan policies for low-income households. Between 1992 and 2000, HUD increased Fannie Mae and Freddie Mac's low-income loan targets from 42 to 50 percent.[29] Targets for borrowers with even lower income climbed from 12 to 20 percent between 1996 and 2000.[30] The government set other lofty goals for home ownership. On national TV in 2002, President Bush unveiled an initiative to help "5.5 million minority families buy homes before the end of the decade."[31] Big banks got on the bandwagon; for example, in 2003 Countrywide announced the second stage of its "We House America" program.[32]

5.1.4 Expectations before the Crisis

All these environmental factors fused into a set of expectations for the future. Unconfined, these expectations were shared by thousands upon thousands of people whose backgrounds and objectives were just as diverse as their numbers were large. Borrowers from every social stratum, realtors and financiers, politicians, and media representatives all held these expectations. Most significant among the expectations were the following.

---

25. Chomsisengphet and Pennington-Cross, 2006.
26. U.S. Census Bureau, 2011b; 2004 showed about 30 percent more new houses sold than sold in 2000.
27. U.S. Bureau of Labor Statistics, 2012a.
28. U.S. Census Bureau, 2011e; average per capita income from the "current population survey" was expressed in 2009 dollars, adjusted for inflation.
29. White, 2009.
30. Roberts, 2008a; low-income borrowers are those whose incomes were less than 50 percent of their area's median income; those with even lower income were borrowers with less than 60 percent of their area's median income.
31. McLean, 2005.
32. Ferrell, et al., 2010.

5.1.4.1 Expectation One: Current Economic Conditions Will Continue Indefinitely

As Keynes suggested, it is our usual practice as human beings to project the current situation into the future, and to alter it only if we have definite reasons to expect something different.[33] This propensity to expect what we are used to revealed itself in the years prior to 2006 before housing prices dropped. From decades of history and recent policies, people saw housing prices continuously go up. Long experience and observation turned into what behavioral economists call an *anchor,* or a foundational situation that people feel they know and understand.[34] The strong expectation that *housing prices will continue to rise* developed relative to this anchor of price growth. Conventional wisdoms provided more fodder: "Housing prices never, or rarely, go down. Housing is always a good investment, isn't it? It's an inflation hedge and it's an investment that you get to use every day, plus you get a great tax break. And the home, after all, is a big part of the American dream."[35] In fact, people's expectation that housing prices would only go up went beyond a mere belief; it blossomed into a "strong intuitive feeling." This intuition enhanced "the contagion of the argument for ever-increasing home prices" and created stories about real estate booms that spread rapidly by word-of-mouth.[36]

The expectation about rising housing prices combined with memories of the stock market crash in 2000 cemented the conviction that real estate was a better investment.[37] Survey data taken in 2003 and 2004 in four major cities corroborates this belief; depending on the city, 75 to 90 percent of those surveyed agreed that real estate was the best long-term investment.[38] During this period, the thought that "homes and apartments were spectacular investments gained a stronghold on the public imagination. ... Not only did prices go up, but there was palpable excitement about real estate investments."[39]

Added to these convictions about housing prices and real estate was the belief that government and banks would continue their low interest rates and supportive home buying policies for low-income households. Subprime and ARM loans appeared to be good deals—as evidenced by their climbing

33. Keynes, 1964.
34. See Shiller (2005) for a discussion of "psychological anchors." These include numbers-based anchors which people use as indications of whether it is a good time to buy, and moral anchors that compel people to compare the strength of their argument for investing to increase wealth against their need to spend money now.
35. Thornton, 2004.
36. Akerlof and Shiller, 2009.
37. Shiller, 2005.
38. Shiller, 2005; confidence study was done by Karl Case and Robert Shiller in Boston, Los Angeles, Milwaukee, and San Francisco.
39. Akerlof and Shiller, 2009.

numbers. After all, if interest rates stayed low and housing prices continued to rise, people with ARMs wouldn't have to worry that their payments would go up. Besides, everyone felt certain that they could sell their homes for more than they paid.

This period of relative prosperity acted as "a drug induced stupor that causes us to take risks that we know we should avoid."[40] All these factors compounded the perception that housing was a safe way to increase wealth, and solidified the expectation that the environment of economic growth would thrive far into the future.

5.1.4.2 Expectation Two: Housing Prices are Rising so I'd Better Buy Now

Confidence that "housing prices would only increase" grew to irrational exuberance. Fast-rising prices reinforced "the belief in an ever-upward trend of home prices" and the proliferation of media articles discussing houses as investments fueled this belief.[41] At this point, emotions entered the picture, which, as neuroscientist Antonio Damasio describes, can induce feelings that ultimately translate into behaviors.[42] Emotions involved here were the excitement of anticipation and an anxiety bordering on fear. People were excited by the possibility that they could really make money in the housing market. They also feared that if they didn't hurry up and buy, the opportunity would disappear and they would fall behind everyone else—housing prices might rise beyond their means. Rapid escalation of housing prices intensified these emotions. In the decade prior to 2004, average real home prices grew 16 percent; in 2004 they were still climbing.[43]

As a result "people began to buy housing as if this were their last chance ever." Speculators took advantage of this fervor believing that people were willing to buy "at almost any price."[44] By 2004, their frenzies pressed people into homes beyond their means and larger than previous norms,[45] for Americans have a grand "love of bigness."[46] Now people were willing to buy big homes priced at more than four times their annual income, whereas just the decade before, home prices had been only three times annual income.[47] Anxiety and excitement fashioned a reinforcing loop that triggered

---

40. Dubner, 2009.
41. Akerlof and Shiller, 2009.
42. Damasio, 1999.
43. Joint Center for Housing Studies (2010) in 2009 dollars adjusted for inflation; average housing prices rose from about $207,000 to $240,000.
44. Akerlof and Shiller, 2009.
45. The size of an average new home had been growing for decades, but from 1994 to 2004, that average grew by 200 square feet to 2140 square feet. See Joint Center for Housing Studies, 2010.
46. Williams, 1965.
47. Joint Center for Housing Studies, 2007; also see Joint Center for Housing Studies, 2011.

greater anxiety and more excitement for borrowers, lenders, and builders as their expectations moved farther right on the continuum of confidence. Home buying reached feverish levels, as evidenced by the five-fold growth of mortgage originations between 1994 and 2003.[48]

5.1.4.3 Expectation Three: My Financial Security is Permanent, so I Can Afford to Spend Money

During the decade before 2004, household net wealth had grown for all but the bottom 10 percent of the population. Since 1995, net wealth jumped between 27 and 86 percent for 7 out of every 10 households. Home equity naturally accounted for a large part of this increase.[49] Real wealth was accumulating and people exhibited the largesse that comes from feeling secure.

This sense of financial security translates into a phenomenon called the *wealth effect*, which causes people to spend money. The wealth effect is normally attributed to owning stock in a bull market, but researchers investigated the possibility of a wealth effect in the housing market.[50] Empirical evidence indicates that there was no such effect before 1980, but by the mid-2000s the housing wealth effect was indeed present—and robust. Using a statistical crosscheck, others corroborate that between 2001 and 2006, the high growth of housing wealth in the presence of high consumer spending could be partially attributed to a wealth effect.[51] Some believed that this wealth effect caused a 6 to 7 percent increase in overall spending habits.[52]

The feeling of security translated to other areas as well. In the past, people extracted equity primarily when they moved and sold their homes, but in this case some felt so secure that they refinanced their homes to "take equity out and spend it to increase their standard of living."[53] The amount of home equity cashed out by refinancing in 2004 was over 10 times that in 1995.[54] In the subprime market alone, in 2003 over 560,000 loans (nearly 35 percent) were cash-out refinances.[55] Indeed, cash-out refinancing was a popular way to buy things.

---

48. Mortgage Statistics, 2009; originations were $200B in 4th Q 1994 and $1T in 3rd Q 2003.
49. Joint Center for Housing Studies, 2007; median wealth in 2004 dollars, adjusted for inflation.
50. See Campbell and Cocco, 2004; Jelveh, 2008; Muellbauer, 2007; Tseng, 2011; Shiller, 2005.
51. Jelvah, 2008.
52. Muellbauer, 2007.
53. Thornton, 2004.
54. Joint Center for Housing Studies, 2007; home equity cashed out to spend reached annual levels of $161 and $152 billion in 2003 and 2004 from $15 billion in 1995.
55. Chomsisengphet and Pennington-Cross, 2006; compare these statistics with 250,000 refinance loans with no cash-out, and 820,000 regular home purchase subprime loans.

5.1.4.4 Expectation Four: Because Others are Doing it, it Must Be Good, so I Will Do it Too

Three concepts describe this "me-too" expectation. The first is *herd behavior* that results from what is called information cascade. Next *critical mass* triggers individual behaviors when high numbers of people are behaving in certain ways. The final concept relates to *conformity* that comes from uncertainty. Although these concepts differ in some ways, they all lead to the same result: people will do something because others are doing it.

Even when they know that they are only following someone else's lead, people still exhibit herd behavior and follow others. Oftentimes, herd behavior occurs when false or misleading information is proliferated through rumors or when people "decide to ignore their private information and focus instead on the actions of others, even if that action conflicts with their own knowledge or instincts."[56] The more people discuss rumors or misconceptions, the more others listen to the rumors and tell their acquaintances. This gossip continues until "one focus of attention leads to... another, and then another,"[57] resulting in an information cascade that causes people to automatically believe what they are hearing, and to follow everyone else in the herd without asking why. News media have a fundamental role in spreading information that is valued more for its sensational appeal than for its accuracy.[58] Even rational people behave irrationally and become part of the herd "when they take into account the judgments of others."[59]

In addition to herd behavior created by information cascades, we find the related phenomenon of *critical mass* in an economy. An economy is essentially a "*system of interaction* between individuals and their environment"— an environment that includes other people. Because our choices are often constrained or somehow relate to others' actions, we end up with "behavior that depends on what others are doing." In this type of interactive relationship, individual behaviors are influenced by how many other people are behaving in a certain way or how energetically they are acting.[60] When the number and energy levels in pursuing these activities are high, we have *critical mass* in which a given behavior becomes self-sustaining—everybody does it because everybody is doing it. In an economic context, we might find that when individuals see so many others excitedly buying houses, they join in, inadvertently encouraging others to follow. During the crisis, house buying hit critical mass and many simply did what others were doing.

A third concept that explains the "me-too" expectation is *conformity*. Conformity in this sense originates from uncertainty: when we don't know

---

56. Belsky and Gilovich, 2010.
57. Shiller, 2005.
58. Shiller, 2005.
59. Shiller, 2005.
60. See Schelling (2006) for this discussion on critical mass.

what to do, we do what others do. Applied to the economic environment, conformity allows "the judgment of others to steer you into unwise investments, or out of sound ones."[61] It leads back to herd behavior: "The more uncertain people are and the higher the stakes, the more vulnerable they are to the sort of cue-taking that leads to herd behavior."[61] Although the causes are related, this time herd behavior results from insecurity rather than from cascades of misleading or incomplete information.

5.1.4.5 Expectation Five: My Success Will Continue because I'm Good and I'm Lucky

The human brain is a wonderful orchestrator of adaptation and illusion. We love to believe that we have control of our lives and that we are highly competent beings. When circumstances reinforce these ideals, our brain allows us to take the credit, even when it doesn't really make sense. Because the "conscious level gives itself credit for things it really didn't do and confabulates tales to create the illusion it controls things. . . . People get intoxicated by their own good luck." In these circumstances, we tend to discount risk and overestimate our abilities to explain why we make certain decisions.[62] We really *do* believe we're good!

Overconfidence that a particular expectation holds true, especially when speculation is involved, may also come from what psychologists call "magical thinking." Here, "people have occasional feelings that certain actions will make them lucky even if they know logically that the actions cannot have an effect on their fortunes."[63] Like winning a dollar when we bet on lotto numbers that include our birthday, we not only believe we're good—we believe we're lucky too! Thus, people tend to believe that *their* investment in a house will be a grand success.

5.1.4.6 Expectation Six: I'll Be Able to Manage My Loan Payments Even Better in the Future

When individuals took out ARMs with teaser rates or loans with low initial monthly payments, they made assumptions about the long term or ignored it altogether. The allure of affordable payments made "optimistic borrowers underestimate the future cost[s]. . . . They overestimate their future income. They expect to have unrealistically attractive refinance options."[64] Evidence of these expectations appeared when subprime borrowing went from 8 percent of all mortgage originations in 2003 to nearly 20 percent in 2005 and in 2006,[65] at a time when interest rates were already rising.

---

61. Belsky and Gilovich, 2010.
62. Brooks, 2011.
63. Shiller, 2005.
64. Bar-Gill, 2009.
65. Joint Center for Housing Studies, 2008.

5.1.4.7 Expectation Seven (for mortgage lenders and sellers of mortgage-related securities): Borrowers Will Not Default on Home Loans

This expectation trails back to our small-town beginnings when contracts relied on handshakes and everyone expected that everyone else would live up to their promises. In such communities there were few secrets. Reneging on a promise tarnished reputations and caused people to stop doing business with you—a definite deterrent to not paying off a debt. Today in an environment where contracts are formal and you may never see the people you are dealing with, deterrents must be spelled out. In years past, written loan contracts with penalty clauses and foreclosure conditions were enough to ensure repayment in all but the worst circumstances. The validity of this assumption for home loans was still evident prior to 2004. Between 1998 and 2004, for example, delinquency rates for prime loans hovered around 2.5 percent of all mortgages; foreclosures were below 0.2 percent.[66]

This favorable history with prime loans anchored the expectation that all loans would be repaid. Even during the ascent of the housing market, banks assumed that people would try hard not to over-borrow because the last thing they wanted to lose was their home. And, as they had in the past, lenders included penalties and fines in mortgage contracts "in case people decided to walk out on their mortgages."[67]

Lenders and securities buyers and sellers were blinded by the same expectations that controlled the rest of the economy and failed to recognize that borrowers could be overburdened if interest rates went up and housing prices dropped.[68] Moreover, the financial industry was subconsciously operating under the efficient markets hypothesis (see Chapter 2) and assumed that securities' prices incorporated all information, particularly about risk. They hadn't anticipated such extensive use of subprime, affordable option, and ARM loans.

* * * * * * * *

The first six expectations generated *unrealistic buying* behaviors in much of the population, particularly when it came to buying houses or buying things. Augmented by emotion and encouraged by others' behaviors, the confidence level about these expectations in some cases approached irrational exuberance. Buying decisions had little regard for fact or future consequences. Demand for houses grew right alongside this escalation of confidence. Then with the assumption that few would default on their home loans, the seventh expectation downplayed the hazards of risky loans and

---

66. Dunne and Meyer, 2007; delinquency rates measure past due mortgage payments at a given point in time; foreclosure rates represent loans that entered foreclosure during the quarter.
67. Ariely, 2009.
68. Negative equity occurs when borrowers owe more than their houses are worth.

accelerated the use of high-risk loans to finance *unrealistic buying* and *selling* of homes. As we will see in a later chapter, the growth of these loans sparked frenzied selling and buying of mortgage-related securities in the financial market. With so much emotion involved, participants in these markets must have been rationalizing rather than thinking rationally. As we know, these expectations had many repercussions; they eventually devastated the economy.

5.2 SYSTEMS THINKING INTERPRETATION

To illustrate the pre-crisis conditions that we described above, let's consider the expectation that "housing prices will continue to rise." Two reinforcing loops describe the dynamics associated with this expectation. First, a new reinforcing feed-forward loop perfectly portrays how expectations about housing prices operate as a self-fulfilling prophecy. Then, when we add the demand reinforcing feedback loop R_{demand} from Chapter 2, we will appreciate how expectation influences the growth of high risk home loans.

5.2.1 Expectation Reinforcing Feed-Forward Loop

Policies and practices that encouraged home buying bolstered confidence about investing in a home and fueled the expectation that housing prices would continue upward. For some, particularly those whose credit had earlier prevented their buying a home, half-hearted confidence blossomed into overconfidence and finally into irrational exuberance as they saw others succeed. The swell of confidence strengthened and spread throughout the economy in the form of increased demand for houses. With higher demand, housing prices soared—not from the intrinsic value of a home, but from the belief that it would be more valuable in the future.

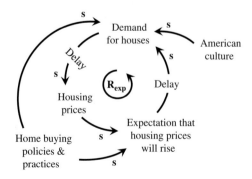

FIGURE 5.4   Expectation reinforcing feed-forward loop.

In systems language, the new feed-forward reinforcing loop $R_{expectation}$ in Figure 5.4 demonstrates how this expectation affects consumer behavior and housing prices. First, note that norms of persistent buying in the *American culture* fuel *demand for houses*. *Policies and practices* that support home buying strengthen both *demand* and confidence in the *expectation that housing prices will rise*. When more people share this expectation, and confidence rises, the *demand for houses* grows and unrealistic buying takes over. Over time, higher *demand for houses* raises *housing prices*. The critical link in this self-fulfilling prophecy is that a rise in actual *housing prices* feeds the *expectation* that they will rise. However, if expectations somehow change to the belief that prices will fall, *demand for houses* will also decrease and *housing prices* will drop as quickly as they grew.

While this systems interpretation concentrated on one expectation, the first six expectations created emotional tensions that urged people to hurry up and reassured them that buying was okay.

5.2.2 Demand Reinforcing Feedback Loop

As high expectations drove demand upward, many people relied on high-risk loans so they could satisfy their voracious appetite for homes. To show how high-risk loans grow with demand for houses, Figure 5.5 adds the reinforcing feedback loop R_{demand} from Chapter 2 to the expectations feed-forward loop $R_{expectation}$. In this evolving depiction, low *interest rates* join with an *American culture* of entitlement and with supportive *home buying policies and practices* to increase the *demand for houses*. Growing *demand* requires more *high-risk loans*. More *loans* mean more *purchases* which in turn push up *demand for houses*. Increased *demand* then enters the $R_{expectation}$ loop to raise *housing prices*. As *housing prices* increase, *expectation* grows. Now we can recognize the combined power of high-risk loans and expectations;

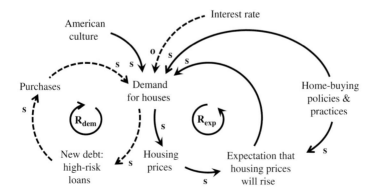

FIGURE 5.5 Demand reinforcing feedback loop.

both influence demand and both keep the two loops going. The more important feature in this diagram is that demand is at the epicenter and fuels both loops.

We will witness the power of both reinforcing loops in subsequent chapters when we expand our systems picture. Another far-reaching effect not shown in the diagram is blindness to risk. People who felt secure and expected good conditions to continue believed they could borrow and spend money to gain happiness. In flurry of activity, *unrealistic* and *persistent* buying fed on itself without regard for the risk of consequences or the wisdom of choices. We discuss risk extensively in later chapters.

5.2.3 Candidate Leverage Points

By 2003, the demand and expectation reinforcing loops in Figure 5.5 were operating full force. Expectations, loans, demand, and housing prices seemed out of control. Before this unrealistic growth caused so much damage, could it have been dampened? Let us explore candidate leverage points to find out.

As we learned earlier, reinforcing loops for natural systems do not continue forever. The expectation and demand loops are no exception. Two candidate leverage points might have tempered the growth created by these loops. The first influences demand; the second alters expectations more directly.

5.2.3.1 Demand Leverage

Because demand for houses affects both housing prices and high-risk loans in our systems depiction, we can multiply our leveraging efforts by somehow altering that demand. A change to economic policies and banking practices is an excellent place to start. Home-buying policies and practices had promoted easy financing for high-risk borrowers since the early 1990s. However, if government agencies had modulated their own exuberant encouragement of home ownership for a high-risk audience, or if lenders had maintained stringent loan qualifications or had not pushed ARMs and low payment option loans so intensely, demand may not have grown so high.

A second feasible action relies on the Fed's monetary policy. To demonstrate this action, we can consider what happened when the Fed did reduce the federal funds rate in 2000 to stimulate the economy. At that time, lower interest rates joined with supportive policies and practices and increased both demand for houses and high-risk loans. Figure 5.6 shows that the total number of mortgage loan originations sharply ascended soon after this expansionary monetary policy went into effect. Then to slow the economy, after 2003 the Fed began to increase the federal funds rate. With higher interest rates, people were less inclined to take out loans. Although we can see a downward

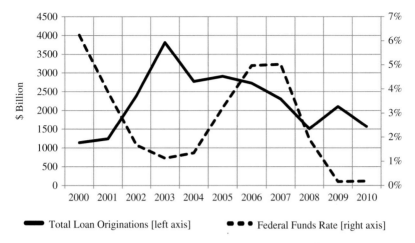

━━ Total Loan Originations [left axis]   ● ● ● Federal Funds Rate [right axis]

FIGURE 5.6   Interest rate and mortgage loan originations (2000–2010).[69]

trend in loan originations in Figure 5.6, we must be careful in drawing conclusions here; interest rate was not the only factor affecting demand and high-risk loans. We will learn in Chapter 8 that after 2003 other forces counteracted some effects of monetary policy.

This historic account of the relationship between interest rates and mortgage loan originations implies that a more conservative monetary policy may have eased the out-of-control growth of demand and high risk home loans. In other words, not allowing interest rates to drop so low so rapidly may have slowed the reinforcing loops.

5.2.3.2 Expectations Leverage

A second leverage point lies with expectations. Earlier we noted that expectations directly and indirectly powered both reinforcing loops. Thus, they are a potent lever with which to change the system. To alter expectations, however, one must touch beliefs, so this lever is not easy to apply. Still, some actions could have modulated expectations prior to the crisis and thus may have kept demand at more realistic levels.

The leverage to dampen demand that we recommended earlier (change home-buying policies and practices) has the dual benefit of bringing expectations about housing prices more in line with reality. In addition, the government and other financial organizations could have helped dispel irrational beliefs about the permanence of current economic conditions and about the wisdom of following the herd. If more facts had been available about

69. Loan originations from the U.S. Census Bureau, 2012a; federal funds rate from Board of Governors of the Federal Reserve System, 2011b.

possible risks and about the fantasy of housing prices rising forever, some may have listened—that is unless they had already become irrationally exuberant.

However, these leveraging actions pale compared with what actually happened to change expectations. After the Fed increased interest rates beginning in 2004, many ARMs were due to reset. Monthly payments for a large number of ARM loans grew so high that borrowers could no longer afford the payments when the terms of their loans changed. In addition, the struggles of those who had borrowed beyond their means began to surface. As more and more home loans went into default and foreclosure and as housing prices began to decline, consumers realized that buying a home wasn't such a good idea. Expectations about rising housing prices were affected by these realities. Somewhere along the line, optimistic expectations had become expectations that housing prices would fall. As we will see in Chapter 9 (as illustrated in Figure 9.16), these altered expectations were one reason that the virtuous circles for high-risk home loans and prices for houses became vicious circles. Unfortunately, pessimistic expectations grew so strong that when the Fed slashed interest rates in 2006 to stimulate the economy, the hoped-for rise in demand and prices for houses did not materialize.

5.2.4 Current Activities

After the crisis, various actions touched the two leverage points of demand and expectations. For example, in 2012 interest rates were still at their 2009 record low levels and the Fed promised to keep them low until late 2014.[70] In theory, low interest rates should encourage demand and the knowledge that rates will remain low should shape people's expectations so they can be confident about borrowing money. However, these actions have had little effect on the gloomy expectations about housing prices or on the U.S. economy.

Another recent action demonstrates the imprecision of shaping expectations and the potential for unintended consequences. Government policies to mitigate the unemployment resulting from the crisis played a role in shaping expectations about economic recovery and the desirability of buying a home. In 2009 and again in 2011, Congress authorized "full federal financing of the Extended Benefits program" to provide additional weeks of unemployment compensation to eligible unemployed workers.[71] While these actions may have encouraged optimism about the economy, they also could have had detrimental effects, reminding people about the extent of unemployment and that they should be holding on to their money in case they, too, lose their

---

70. Piovano, 2012.
71. GAO, 2012.

jobs. Thus, while expectations form an exceptionally powerful lever, they are also extremely difficult to manipulate and to predict. Although awareness can be helpful when determining actions, policymakers should consider unintended consequences.

5.3 SUMMARY

In this chapter, we described how environment, experience, and the human need to make sense of the world and reduce uncertainty shape expectations about the future. We also noted how the confidence with which individuals hold these expectations is influenced by emotion and by what others are doing. The greater the confidence, the more inclined individuals are to make irrational decisions. A *continuum of confidence* that ranged from complete lack of confidence to "irrational exuberance" illustrated the changing intensity of this confidence. Both the content and the intensity of expectations determine what actions they encourage.

In the case of the economic crisis in the United States, we identified six environmental factors occurring between 1994 and 2004 that affected both the substance and confidence level of individuals' expectations and motivated crisis-related behaviors:

1. Interest rates for housing were moderate to low.
2. Housing prices had been going up "forever."
3. Nonprime loans were gaining popularity.
4. New home sales were on a steep incline.
5. Unemployment was reasonable and stable.
6. The flood gates to increase home sales were open.

From these environmental factors, we then proposed the following seven expectations that most likely existed during the crisis:

1. Current economic conditions will continue indefinitely.
2. Housing prices are rising so I'd better buy now.
3. My financial security is permanent, so I can afford to spend money.
4. Because others are doing it, it must be good, so I will do it too.
5. My success will continue because I'm good and I'm lucky.
6. I'll be able to afford my loan payments even better in the future.
7. Borrowers will not default on home loans.

Home buyers and those involved in buying and selling mortgage loan-related products held these expectations with growing levels of confidence which made them behave in ways ranging from fairly rational to completely irrational. High levels of confidence in unrealistic expectations pushed them to do what others were doing—to follow the herd. These expectations became contagious and self-reinforcing and often drove unrealistic buying and selling of homes, high-risk home loans, and mortgage-related securities.

Additionally, because they were not supported by fact or reason, they eventually caused the economic tower of cards to tumble.

In this chapter we identified two candidate leverage points where actions could have been applied prior to the crisis. First, to diminish unrealistic demand, we proposed tempering the Fed's manipulation of interest rates, and modifying home-buying policies and practices to be less supportive of high-risk borrowers. Second, while difficult to implement, actions to shape expectations should be considered. Here, changes to home-buying policies and practices could diminish the expectation about rising housing prices. We also alluded to default and foreclosure conditions that most probably contributed to a turnaround of expectations. (In Chapter 9 we describe how this reversal occurred.) This chapter emphasizes that we should not underestimate the power of individual expectations and the behaviors they cause, and that we must understand the bigger picture so that the prescribed medicine doesn't kill the patient.

Chapter 6

A Crisis of Human Proportions: Ethics and Behaviors

When Sheila Smith got a look at what she thought was her dream home, she didn't hesitate to take it. . . . It wasn't long before the dream became a nightmare. . . . Although Smith and her husband were "viable citizens with good credit," they were quickly steered into an expensive subprime loan with ballooning payments and hidden fees that they couldn't keep up with. Their home's builder was indicted and the mortgage broker was quickly revealed to be collaborating with the builder to, as Smith put it, "unload crappy homes for pretty quick money."

Bosworth[1]

The truth is that many of us in the industry were deeply distressed by the growing practice of pushing high risk loans on borrowers who had no reasonable expectation of being able to repay the mortgage. . . . The broken trust that resulted has damaged borrower confidence.

Stern[2]

Authorities are still uncovering the foul-tasting remnants of unethical behaviors that filled the years prior to the economic crisis. When the most flagrant instances were discovered, various regulations emerged to discourage poor behaviors such as bankruptcy abuse[3] and to require more transparency

---

1. Bosworth, 2008.
2. Stern, 2008; Scott Stern is CEO, Lenders One.
3. Sahadi, 2005. The Bankruptcy Abuse Prevention and Consumer Protection Act of 2005 made "fresh start" or Chapter 7 bankruptcy more difficult. Attorneys' fees doubled to account for increased liability required by the law. Fewer people could wipe out debts they could afford to pay, forcing more to file Chapter 13 bankruptcy that put the person on a repayment plan and required credit counseling.

from mortgage lenders.[4] But the consequences of corrupt conduct cannot be cured overnight with laws and regulations; these consequences carry long tails of damage that may not be sorted out for decades. Patterns of grave harm were extensive and wrong-doings were systemic, and thus we examine unethical behavior in our systems look at the crisis.

While our first reaction to these behaviors may be disgust or anger, we must remember that not everyone was dishonest or unethical. Some were trustworthy and honest; others were merely ignorant, naïve, or unaware. We will set judgment aside and focus on our goal of viewing the bigger economic picture. To portray the moral climate prior to the crisis, this chapter considers the most common unethical behaviors. Chapter 7 explores the origins and broad effects of these behaviors.

As we might infer from nicknames of the economic crisis—real estate mess, mortgage meltdown, subprime crisis—unethical behaviors involved mortgage loans. From individuals to huge corporations, immoral acts appeared at all levels of human transaction. Four types are most significant: mortgage fraud; disreputable lending; shady corporate strategy; and deceitful dealings by securities agents. Figure 6.1 illustrates levels and types of unethical behaviors.

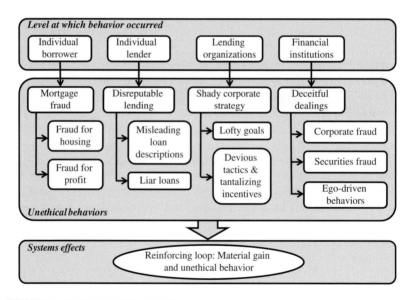

FIGURE 6.1   Levels and types of unethical behavior.

---

4. Department of Corporations, 2009. Called the SAFE Act, the Secure and Fair Enforcement for Mortgage Licensing Act of 2008 requires uniformity of application and reporting processes for loan originators, supervision and licensing, accountability, consumer protection and anti-fraud, and helps prevent foreclosure. It facilitates "responsible behavior in the subprime mortgage market" and establishes "a means by which residential mortgage loan originators would... be required to act in the best interests of the consumer."

6.1 MORTGAGE FRAUD

Evidence of widespread *mortgage fraud* appeared as early as 2004 when the FBI warned of a "mortgage fraud epidemic."[5] Indeed, at the 2006 peak of loan fraud, an estimated $27 billion in fraudulent loans were originated.[6] Growing numbers of suspicious activity reports confirmed this warning; the FBI received 36 percent more reports in 2008 than in 2007.[7] They explained reasons behind the fraud: "People want their home's equity to be greater than the mortgage loan on the home, and with housing booms going on throughout the U.S., there are people who try to capitalize on the situation, and make an easy profit."[8] Several mortgage fraud schemes are typical at the individual borrower level. Two types involve loan origination: fraud for housing and fraud for profit.[9]

6.1.1 Fraud for Housing

Fraud for housing involves illegal actions of borrowers whose motive is to own a house under false pretenses.[10] In these cases, buyers lie to the lender about their income, employment, or other personal details to appear creditworthy and qualify for a mortgage loan. This fraud normally occurs with single loans. For example, Freddie Mac cites an Alaskan woman who stated that she had a job on her loan application and even showed a fake paystub when in fact she had been fired for stealing.[11]

6.1.2 Fraud for Profit

Fraud for profit generally involves home buyers and housing industry insiders such as builders, appraisers, and title company employees who collude with buyers. Illegal actions here often entail kickbacks to these insiders to inflate the value of the house or to ensure that the loan will go through. Of course, making money is the primary motive for this fraud and ways to commit it are plentiful and creative. Some tactics involve falsely inflating the property's value or obtaining loans with fictitious information.[12]

---

5. Frieden, 2004.

6. Swanson, 2011. The FBI uses CoreLogic estimates for these numbers. $12 to $15 billion loan origination frauds still occurred in 2009 and 2010.

7. U.S. Department of Justice, 2008; the FBI received 61,173 suspicious activity reports in 2008.

8. U.S. Department of Justice, 2008; mortgage fraud involves "misstatement, misrepresentation, or omission relating to the property or potential mortgage relied on by an underwriter or lender to fund, purchase, or insure a loan."

9. The FBI investigates these two types. See U.S. Department of Justice, 2008.

10. U.S. Department of Justice, 2008.

11. Freddie Mac, 2011a.

12. U.S. Department of Justice, 2008.

Speculation and property "flipping" activities are easy marks for this type of fraud. Both involve using a loan to buy property at a low price and selling when the price increases. Making money this way generally works well for everyone—except when speculators who are looking to make a quick buck are "all too willing to default on their loans" if prices drop.[13] In the case of illegal property flipping, buyers purchase property, collude with appraisers to falsely inflate its value, and sell it at a profit. Inflated properties are "repurchased several times for a higher price by associates of the 'flipper.' After several sham sales, the properties are foreclosed on by victim lenders."[14]

The complete list of mortgage fraud for profit schemes is long and dismal. In most cases, home buyers mislead lenders into believing they can afford the loan. For example, using a "silent second," the buyer borrows from the seller to cover a down payment but doesn't tell the lender about this second mortgage. A straw borrower scheme involves using another person's name and credit history with their permission, often paying them a fee. Fictitious or stolen identity fraud occurs when the borrower uses another person's information without his knowledge. Appraisal tweaking is also common. Borrowers and appraisers collude to make a profit. Some overstate the property's value to increase the loan amount and spend the excess money elsewhere; others understate its value to get a good deal when buying a foreclosure.[15]

Another unethical, but not necessarily illegal activity, involves walking away from a mortgage. Here, an individual purchases a home intending to live in it for a while without making payments and then declares bankruptcy. Walking away becomes illegal with a tactic called *buy and bail*. In this case, before walking away from their existing home, individuals finance a new home. Once they secure a loan for the new home with their good credit rating, they intentionally default on their existing loan. Many justified this behavior because "they believe they were duped when they bought their existing home."[16]

Some instances of fraud were so elaborate that they bear repeating. For example, one Texan purchased 211 homes from builders, transferred the deeds to fictitious names similar to the builders' names, colluded with appraisers to inflate the homes' values, and then sold the homes at overblown prices to out-of-state investors, who believed they were purchasing homes from builders at fairly appraised values.[17] Often investors, anxious to make a buck, bought them sight unseen.

---

13. Retsinas and Belsky, 2008.
14. U.S. Department of Justice, 2008.
15. See U.S. Department of Justice, 2008; Christie, 2008.
16. Weintraub, 2011.
17. U.S. Department of Justice, 2008.

6.2 DISREPUTABLE LENDING

While each of the above fraudulent activities involved some sort of borrower dishonesty, not all the blame falls on borrowers. Lenders, too, were deceitful, and exhibited various *disreputable lending* practices, including misleading borrowers about the terms of the loans and lying or encouraging lying on borrowers' loan applications. Individual loan officers used these dishonest tactics to increase their bonuses or to otherwise profit.

6.2.1 Misleading Loan Descriptions

In this category, lenders promoted adjustable rate mortgages with teaser rates "to suck in clueless buyers"[18] or talked otherwise creditworthy borrowers into expensive subprime mortgages when they qualified for less costly prime loans. Some lenders were in cahoots with an appraiser friend to overvalue a home so they could inflate the loan amount and increase their sales-based bonuses. Another lender tactic was hiding mark-ups or premiums on loan products.[19] Because borrowers were uninformed and unsophisticated, they relied on agents as trusted experts.

6.2.2 Liar Loans

Lying on loan applications, or so-called *liar loans*, involved collusion of buyer and lender who would omit financial information altogether, or over-state income and assets to increase the size of a mortgage. Lenders might tell borrowers how to falsify their loan applications or have them sign blank applications which the lenders would fill in later. Some borrowers who obtained liar loans from Countrywide Financial and subsequently struggled to make payments eventually accused Countrywide of "*predatory lending*, saying the company misled them."[20]

Computers facilitated these liar loans and put lenders at arm's length from loan specifics. After the 1980s, automation replaced the manual under-writing of loans that required "personal experience, intuition, and strict underwriting standards." Traditional requirements relaxed when companies relied on computer software to analyze loan trends. Without conditions such as a large down payment, several months of expenses in a savings account, or years of continuous employment, lenders could now make loans to those who were previously unqualified.[21] Although the transition to automation was not itself unethical, it allowed lenders to take advantage of predefined formulas and diminished their accountability. Former Countrywide brokers

18. Roberts, 2008b.
19. Belsky et al., 2008.
20. Ferrell et al., 2010.
21. Discussion of loan automation from McCoy and Renuart, 2008.

told stories about how "officials thought nothing of changing the applicant's information to secure a loan." Often they would leave out the salary because it was not high enough, and then allow a computer program to fill it in based on the applicant's job title. One broker said that they would just change an applicant's title to manager, and the computer would assume his salary was $100,000 so the loan would go through.[22]

* * * * * * * *

Rather than blaming either borrowers or lenders, we must recognize that each side propped up the other. If borrowers hadn't taken part in falsifying their loan applications or hadn't created a demand for affordable loans, lenders would have had fewer customers and would have offered more straightforward loan types. On the other hand, if lenders hadn't pushed complex loans, borrowers would not have purchased them. At any rate, lying, cheating, and deceit were at the crux of acts that allowed both borrowers and lenders to benefit—and eventually to suffer.

6.3 SHADY CORPORATE STRATEGY

To serve their customers, maintain profitability, and increase the price of their shares, corporations devise strategies to distinguish themselves from competitors. If too many players enter the field, the competitive environment can become cutthroat, opening the door to underhanded and devious tactics. Soon companies view these tactics as accepted ways of doing business to the point that they become cultural norms. When this situation occurred in the mortgage lending industry, mortgage frauds and disreputable lending activities of individual borrowers and lenders were small potatoes in comparison. Singular acts like these were magnified in corporate strategies, goals, and tactics that encouraged unethical behavior on a grand scale.

6.3.1 Lofty Goals

Clear and compelling goals are some of the most powerful tools that a CEO can use to achieve the company's strategy. When goals are paired with incentives, they become doubly effective. However, if the goals become so appealing and the incentives so enticing, and if the corporation does not set strong moral thresholds, human behavior lowers itself onto immoral ground. These circumstances exactly describe what happened in some companies when a glut of mortgage-related businesses intensified the competitive scene.

One corporation, Countrywide Financial, vividly illustrates unethical behavior that began with corporate goals. In 2004, as the largest home mortgage originator and second largest originator of affordability loans,

---

22. Morgenson and Rosner, 2011.

Countrywide was the "biggest player on the field," and set the standard for other companies.[23] Angelo Mozilo, founder and CEO of Countrywide,[24] initially operated his company in a traditional manner. By providing standard mortgages to people with good credit, then selling these loans to Fannie Mae and Freddie Mac, Countrywide grew at an astonishing rate, almost tripling its market share to over 52 percent between 1989 and 1992.[25]

Over time, Countrywide set goals to put more low-income and minority buyers into homes. As noted in Chapter 2, in 1992 Countrywide's "House America" program committed to a $1.25 billion goal for these high-risk loan types. Success encouraged it to raise this loan commitment to $80 billion in 1999, to $100 billion in 2001, and finally to $1 trillion in 2003, a target the company hoped to meet by 2010.[26] A trillion dollars is a lot of loans! How could Countrywide possibly meet the goal? The answer: devious tactics and tantalizing incentives.

6.3.2 Devious Tactics and Tantalizing Incentives

Like in any sport, winning strategies are accomplished through effective tactics—and sometimes with a bit of pushing and shoving. Countrywide's tactics began mildly enough, then intensified to accommodate extreme competition. The son of an Italian immigrant, Countrywide's CEO Mozilo strongly believed that his "House America" strategy would allow immigrants and minorities to buy homes. But by the mid-1990s, he found it increasingly difficult to compete. With his goals in jeopardy,[27] he turned up the heat.

In 1995 Mozilo established a subprime loan business. Besides lending to those with poor credit, Countrywide offered various loan products that would appeal to low-income borrowers. Various affordability loans helped the company increase market share and make huge profits, "mainly from regular people who had to pay commissions on loans that they should not have been eligible for in the first place. The company was like a drug dealer, hooking people on something they desperately wanted, with no way out once they were addicted."[28]

Countrywide then used its incentive system to encourage sales people to "move borrowers into the subprime category, even if their financial position meant that they belonged higher up the loan spectrum." Computer software helped sales representatives push for pricier loans because it ignored some of the borrowers' assets. The reason? Subprimes were money-makers. Sales commissions on subprime loans were half a percent of the loan's value while

23. Morgenson and Fabrikant, 2007; Tasini, 2009.
24. Mozilo and Loeb started Countrywide in 1969.
25. McLean and Nocera, 2010.
26. Ferrell et al., 2010; McLean and Nocera, 2010.
27. McLean and Nocera, 2010.
28. Tasini, 2009.

commissions for higher-quality loans were less than a quarter percent. Corporate profits on subprime loans were rewarding as well, especially "when the subprime machine was really cranking." In 2004, for example, subprime profits reached over 3.5 percent, nearly four times that for prime loans.[29]

As we would expect, these goals and incentives quickly altered the mix of loan types that Countrywide offered. Between 2003 and 2004, subprime loans rose from less than 5 percent to 11 percent of its loan mix. Adjustable rate mortgages (ARMs) soared from 18 percent to nearly half of the company's business. The "especially lucrative" Pay Option ARMs more than tripled from 6 to 19 percent of Countrywide's originations between 2004 and 2005; Countrywide made 4 percent profit on these loans—twice the rate earned on FHA-backed, less risky loans.[30] The company was now rolling in high-risk loans—and reaping a tidy bundle.

Addicted to success, behaviors turned from aggressive to shady as Countrywide pressed employees to meet the strategic goals and rewarded them for questionable behaviors—that no one questioned. As profits grew, unethical acts (such as pushing complex loans onto unsuspecting and trusting borrowers) became more frequent. One advocate for consumer protection thought "that Countrywide was targeting immigrants and unsophisticated borrowers with incomprehensible loan documents."[31]

Its "House America" goals pressed the company to take on more risk, almost with eyes closed. By July 2007 "Countrywide sales representatives were approved to lend $400,000 to borrowers rated C-minus, the second-riskiest grade, and with credit scores as low as 500."[32] Late mortgage payments, personal bankruptcies, foreclosures, and default notices didn't deter Countrywide from making a loan. Its tactics were clear.

But Countrywide was not alone. Most lenders increased their risk levels: competition for the subprime niche was intense. Underwriting standards all but disappeared under the guise of "special circumstances" when loan volume started to slump. Rather than strictly enforcing the standard that "mortgage payments should be no more than 28% of. . . income, and all debt payments should be no more than 36% of. . . income," lenders looked for excuses to make exceptions and often interpreted the rules in ways that didn't make much sense.[33] For example, some lenders would sell ARMs whose initially low monthly payments just barely fit the 28 percent

---

29. For statistics and quotations in this paragraph, see Morgenson, 2007.
30. For statistics in this paragraph, see Morgenson and Fabrikant, 2007.
31. Robert Gnaizda, general counsel at Greenlining Institute, wrote accusatory emails to Countrywide. These emails went to the SEC which sued Mozila for insider trading (see Morgenson and Rosner, 2011).
32. Morgenson and Fabrikant, 2007.
33. Shiller, 2005.

guideline. They ignored the probability that monthly payments would go far above this threshold when the terms on these loans reset, particularly if mortgage interest rates increased. Had they considered this factor, they would have disqualified these borrowers in the first place.

Behaviors then grew more unscrupulous—even illegal. Insider stories of ethics breaches are jaw droppers. At Countrywide, some brokers who made loans with doctored applications "had a time-tested system for making sure they progressed smoothly.... Envelopes stuffed with thousands of dollars in cash would be hand delivered by some brokers each month to the account managers for seeing that the loans actually closed."[34]

Other lenders' tactics also hurt borrowers. To compete for loan brokers' business, lenders rewarded brokers for making more mortgage loans. Countrywide incentivized brokers "to maximize fees and costs to borrowers"[35] and on occasion, to sell loans to borrowers who could neither understand nor afford them. Elevated goals were prevalent at other corporations as well. In 1998, shortly after becoming CEO at Fannie Mae, Frank Raines set an extraordinarily high goal to double his company's earnings per share within five years. The goal was so ingrained in employees' minds that it "became a kind of mantra." In tactics similar to Countrywide's "the only way Fannie Mae could continue its rapid growth was to keep expanding its controversial mortgage portfolio."[36]

* * * * * * * *

The combination of corporate strategy, addiction to success, intense competition, and potential for personal gain provoked a glut of subprime loans that finally destroyed many mortgage lenders. When the U.S. economy slowed and when housing prices decreased and interest rates rose, people could not make their payments. Many households faced foreclosure.

Countrywide felt their pain in its fat portfolio of subprime loans. "By 2008, the company had accrued over $8 billion in subprime loans with 7 percent delinquent. The industry average was 4.67 percent delinquency. That year foreclosures doubled, and the firm planned to lay off" thousands of employees.[37] After nearly 40 years in business, Countrywide had failed miserably. Bank of America swallowed it up in July 2008. Ill-considered and often unethical practices, coupled with the poor state of the economy, had been its undoing.

Just months before the U.S. government took over the failed Fannie Mae and Freddie Mac in September 2008, an analysis team found that together these GSEs "could lose as much as $50 billion" from their high risk loan

34. Morgenson and Rosner, 2011.
35. Belsky et al., 2008.
36. McLean and Nocera, 2010.
37. Ferrell et al., 2010.

portfolios and risky strategies.[38] In 2011, the government was still paying legal bills of Fannie Mae's former executives as they defended themselves against shareholder lawsuits.[39]

In corporations such as these, the strategy was often put into place by a select few—respected and successful at the time. However, more than a few individuals implement corporate strategies. Even when goals are honorable, tactics can become tainted, especially in the presence of huge incentives. At the corporate level, if individuals' unethical actions are encouraged, really bad things happen. While Countrywide's strategy proved remarkably successful over the short run in terms of profit for the company and commissions for employees, its failure affected tens of thousands of employees and over half a billion consumers.[40] Mozilo now lists among *Time Magazine*'s top 25 people to blame for the financial crisis and is *Portfolio*'s second worst CEOs of all time.[41]

Initially, Fannie Mae's strategy was as successful as Countrywide's; eventually it failed just as severely. The government bailout and take-over of Fannie Mae increased U.S. national debt by $800 billion;[42] shareholder stock was essentially wiped out.[43] Its "double the earnings per share" strategy had obviously not worked well in the long term.

6.4 DECEITFUL DEALINGS

Unethical behaviors grow ponderous as we move up the ladder to financial institutions that regulated, rated, bought, or sold securities. Major players in this market were companies such as Goldman Sachs, Lehman Brothers, Merrill Lynch, and AIG. Others included quasi-government agencies Fannie Mae and Freddie Mac, rating agencies such as Moody's and Standard & Poor's, and government regulators such as HUD, Department of the Treasury, and the Securities and Exchange Commission.

One catalyst for unethical behavior at this level was the financial innovation called *securitization*. As we learned in Chapter 2, financial companies bought large numbers of mortgage loans, packaged them into mortgage-backed securities (MBSs), and sold these securities to investors. MBSs were similarly bundled and sold as collateralized debt obligations (CDOs). These securities turned into big money-makers, especially when the subprime loan market accelerated.

When mortgage companies sold loans to those who packaged MBSs, they received money to make more loans. This profitable niche allured nonbank

38. McLean and Nocera, 2010.
39. Morgenson and Rosner, 2011; by mid-2011, costs had reached $24.2 million.
40. See Ferrell et al., 2010; "In 2008... [the] secretary of... HUD reported that over 500,000 Countrywide consumers were in danger of facing foreclosure."
41. See *www.time.com/time/specials/packages/article/0,28804,1877351_1877350_1877339,00. html* and *www.cnbc.com/id/30502091?slide=20.*
42. Herszenhorn, 2008.
43. McLean and Nocera, 2010.

mortgage companies that didn't operate under strict banking regulations. With formal deregulation of the over-the-counter market for MBSs, CDOs, and credit default swaps (CDSs) in 2000[44] and an ability to increase debt through a 2004 change in the net capital rule,[45] entry into the mortgage securities business was easy. Extra players and few restrictions weakened scrutiny; opportunity for unprincipled acts behind closed doors rose in proportion.

Lack of regulation in the mortgage-related securities industry was not its only appeal. Initially, risks appeared to be lower than for other investments. First, risk of default on the mortgages that comprised MBSs and CDOs was mitigated by risk-hedging credit default swaps. Additionally, those involved expected that people would not default on a *home* loan (see Chapter 5). With this lower perceived risk, corporations had to set aside only half the capital reserves than they did for other types of securities. They could then invest the money that would have been held in reserve. Consequently, banks were inclined to "stuff their balance sheets with mortgage products" and had great "incentive to hold highly rated mortgage-backed securities."[46] Everything appeared to be well situated in the mortgage securities business; it seemed like a win-win effortless way to make money with acceptable risk.

However, just as the potential for profit was so enormous in these security transactions, so was the temptation for *deceitful dealings*. Thousands involved in this market engaged in some sort of unscrupulous activity. From financial advisors to CEOs, and from credit rating agencies to buyers, most sought to fulfill their own self-interest through their companies. Intertwined, collusive, and self-interested behaviors crawled all over one another like a den of hungry snakes looking for the next victim.

Why were behaviors so incredibly unethical? Nobel Prize recipient Stiglitz observes that "bankers are (for the most part) not born any greedier than other people. It is just that they may have more opportunity and stronger incentives to do mischief at others' expense."[47] At this high level of organizational life, goals are lofty and incentives are immense.

Commissions based on sales volume, bonuses dependent on high stock values, and profitability were glittering gems of temptation. Profiting through deceit spread, particularly among executives and account managers. In this environment of extreme competition and lax regulations, and with immense profits dangling like ripe pears, three types of unethical behaviors emerged: corporate fraud, securities fraud, and ego-driven behavior.[48]

---

44. The Financial Crisis Inquiry Commission, 2011.
45. Satow, 2008.
46. McLean and Nocera, 2010.
47. Stiglitz, 2010.
48. Corporate and securities frauds are two corporate criminal activities that the FBI investigates; see U.S. Department of Justice, 2009.

6.4.1 Corporate Fraud

Corporate fraud includes accounting schemes and executive dealings that were "designed to deceive investors, auditors, and analysts about the true financial condition of a corporation."[49] Many corporations altered their accounting records to appear more profitable for Wall Street and for profit-based executive bonuses. The FBI eventually targeted Fannie Mae, Freddie Mac, and other huge financial corporations in its investigations.[50] The mega-corporation AIG was accused several times of mortgage-related accounting flaws. Then, in February 2008 the evidence proved more serious; AIG had understated a $1 billion loss by nearly $4 billion.[51]

However, accounting frauds were relatively mundane compared to more creative examples. Since 2001, Lehman Brothers had been improperly classifying $50 billion of loans as revenue to make "its finances appear less shaky than they really were."[52] Since no U.S. law firm would endorse such a practice, Lehman found a British law firm that considered it legal[53]—at least according to British law.

Nor were government-supported enterprises exempt. In 2003, newly hired accountants found that Freddie Mac had been seriously understating revenues for years to smooth its apparent growth. Its CEO Gregory Parseghian was personally linked to improper accounting that covered declining profits.[54] Later investigations[55] found that "Fannie Mae had overstated its earnings by $9 billion since 2001"; this amount represented a whopping 40 percent of its profit. Between 1998 and 2004, Franklin Raines, Fannie Mae's then-CEO, received over $90 million in compensation including bonuses, "$52 million of which was directly tied to Fannie's meeting its earnings targets."[56] Because executive bonuses at Fannie Mae were based on earnings growth on their stock, keeping profits up was important.[57]

49. U.S. Department of Justice, 2009.
50. Ryan, 2009; corporations included Lehman Brothers, AIG, Bear Stearns, New Century Financial, Washington Mutual, and Countrywide Financial.
51. Dash, 2008.
52. Trumbull, 2010.
53. This accounting gimmick, called Repo 105, allows banks to borrow "money from big companies that have extra cash" by selling the bank a bond, which the bank buys back at the end of the short loan. For example, Lehman didn't want its balance sheet to show borrowed money, so it took less cash for the "bond" it sold than the bond was worth. For accounting purposes the sale appeared real, rather than like a loan. Lehman used the loan to pay down debts so that it looked more profitable (Goldstein, 2010a).
54. Morgenson and Rosner, 2011.
55. As a regulator, the Office of Federal Housing Enterprise Oversight investigated Freddie Mac and Fannie Mae.
56. McLean and Nocera, 2010; Gordon, 2008.
57. Morgenson and Rosner, 2011.

Morgenson and Rosner found that unethical dealings at Fannie Mae went deeper and had gone on longer than realized.[58] In a 2001 deal, Goldman Sachs helped Fannie Mae "manipulate its accounting... to boost the company's earnings.... Goldman received $625,000 in fees" for its part in the transactions. Investigators concluded that the deals were done solely "to achieve desired accounting results." In 2005, investigations discovered accounting fraud that reached as far back as 1998. SEC filed suit, concluding that Fannie Mae's 1998 results were "intentionally manipulated to trigger management bonuses." Fannie Mae's then-CEO James Johnson received $21 million in bonuses that year; if Fannie Mae had done honest accounting, executives would have had no bonuses at all.

Accounting deceptions were not alone among unethical behaviors for Fannie Mae and Goldman Sachs. A relationship that should have flashed *conflict of interest* in red neon lights had existed between Fannie Mae and Goldman Sachs since 1999. Johnson, former Fannie Mae CEO, was on the board of Goldman Sachs and Stephen Friedman, former Goldman Sachs CEO, was on Fannie Mae's board thus assuring "a close and mutually profitable association." Neither CEO was inclined to hold down or cut back executive pay in the other's firm.[59]

Accounting firms that worked for these big institutions were involved in deceptions of their own. Some endorsed "improper and imprudent practices" by allowing mortgage companies to change accounting practices to their own benefit. In one instance, accounting firm KPMG was accused of helping one financial company misrepresent a loss as a profit. The reason given: "the profit was important because it allowed executives to earn bonuses and convince Wall Street that it was in fine shape financially when in fact its business was coming apart."[60]

During the 2008 meltdown, exceptionally good times triggered extremely bad behaviors characterized by personal greed and ambition of corporate leaders who wanted more bonuses, more status, and more power. Wherever big money could be made, unethical behaviors created a feeding frenzy and the unscrupulous actors wolfed down every crumb of profit. Some resorted to accounting fraud or the morally hazardous attitude of "I.B.G.−Y.B.G.... as in I'll Be Gone and You'll Be Gone" if something goes wrong.[61] This frenzy turned into a reinforcing loop of greed. Used to unprecedented success and money, these leaders revved up their unethical behaviors to gain

---

58. For quotations about Fannie Mae in this paragraph see Morgenson and Rosner, 2011.
59. Morgenson and Rosner, 2011; at the end of his tenure, Johnson earned $500,000 a year as a board member.
60. Bajaj, 2008.
61. Dash, 2009. This phrase was coined by Morgan Stanley bankers during the late 1990s stock market boom (Knee, 2006).

more of the same. However, their unreasoned risk-taking and fraud caught up with them when the economy crashed.

6.4.2 Securities Fraud

Those engaged in securities fraud misrepresent risk or other characteristics to sell more securities, such as MBSs or CDOs. Often collusion is a factor. For example, financial institutions conspired with credit rating agencies to make products appear appealing, or they colluded with mortgage agencies to boost sales of high-risk loans.

6.4.2.1 Inappropriate Ratings

Because MBS and CDO investors are far removed from the mortgages contained in their investments they often do not know the securities' "true value or risk." Thus they rely on rating agencies such as Moody's, Standard & Poor's, or Fitch which sometimes modeled risk incorrectly or without appropriate documentation.[62] This trust in third parties exposed investors to being duped.

Added to this potential inaccuracy, the quality and fidelity of credit ratings was often compromised; financial institutions encouraged analysts to rate new securities highly—and quickly—so they could both make money. Bear Stearns, for example, pushed rating analysts to complete analysis for a new security in a few days. To do so, analysts had to concoct credit data such as FICO scores if the lenders who sold bulk loans to them did not respond quickly enough. Rating agencies depended heavily on their computer models to "cram mortgages through the process." Bear Stearns also prepped "rating agencies for what they 'thought' the loans would look like," then would buy a big batch of loans and spend a day adding details so that the group of loans could receive AAA ratings.[63]

Other firms negotiated with rating agencies—often with the allure of money—to ensure high ratings. When Merrill Lynch created enough MBSs from the mortgages it bought from lenders, it would bundle them into a CDO and then "negotiate hard with the rating agencies—and tinker with the CDO's structure—to get most of the security labeled triple-A."[64]

In their extensive exposés, journalists McLean and Nocera found that profit caused some rating agencies to turn "their backs on their own integrity" and to continue granting AAA ratings when they should have stopped. Precursors of this ethics crisis include "an erosion of standards, a willful suspension of skepticism, a hunger for big fees and market share, and an

---

62. Belsky et al., 2008.
63. Information on rating agencies from Buhl, 2010.
64. McLean and Nocera, 2010; emails revealed that Merrill specifically linked its fee to a high rating.

inability to stand up to Wall Street."[65] Email conversations among officials at Standard & Poor's expose their thinking, particularly when a security was unworthy: "We rate every deal. It could be structured by cows and we would rate it."[66]

These behaviors supported the enthralling quest for highly rated securities that could be sold swiftly—to make money for the corporation, for executives, and for sales agents. In this frenetic environment, people unfortunately made huge mistakes and fatally downplayed the risk of default on these securities.

6.4.2.2 Collusion for Volume

In many instances financial institutions incentivized lenders to make more subprime loans so they could buy the loans, bundle them into MBSs and CDOs, and sell them to make money. Merrill Lynch went so far as to buy a 20 percent stake in one lender and pushed it to "make loans with higher yields" (e.g., poorly documented subprime loans).[67] In another example, Lehman Brothers pressed the First Alliance Mortgage Company (Famco) to make as many subprime loans as possible and then helped it sell millions in MBSs. Neither Lehman nor Famco seemed to care about the "shoddy quality of the loans" since they would just be passed along to investors through CDOs. Famco declared bankruptcy in 2000 and "Lehman was found guilty of 'aiding and abetting the fraudulent scheme.' But the firm's punishment—a $5 million fine—was negligible."[68]

Because of their tight interdependence, Fannie Mae and Countrywide often worked together to design loan types. Fannie Mae was happy to support "certain key Mozilo causes, like low down payments" and in return, Countrywide would sell large numbers of loans for Fannie (up to a quarter of Fannie's loans in some years).[69] In another example, to accelerate the mortgage process and sell more loans, Countrywide designed a special product for Fannie Mae called the "Fast-N-Easy loan." This loan "required no documentation of a borrower's income or assets and gave loans to borrowers whose debt-to-income levels were far higher—50 percent—than what was required by other lenders"—who were lax themselves. Fannie also welcomed loans that had been "doctored" by Countrywide. They continued patting each other on the back. "In 2005, Countrywide sold $12.7 billion in subprime loans to Fannie Mae"; by 2006, nearly two thirds of the loans Countrywide had underwritten for Fannie Mae had required no money down.[70]

---

65. McLean and Nocera, 2010.
66. Sorkin, 2008.
67. McLean and Nocera, 2010.
68. McLean and Nocera, 2010.
69. McLean and Nocera, 2010.
70. For this discussion of Countrywide and Fannie Mae, see Morgenson and Rosner, 2011.

Whether accomplished through collusion, incentive, or mutually beneficial relationships, the motive for these behaviors was to increase the volume
of subprime loans that comprised the MBSs and CDOs. Financial institutions
could then sell more of these securities for profit. The push for volume translated into riskier loans, many of which entered the securitization pipeline.

6.4.2.3 Poor and Misleading Information

Examples of financial institutions deliberately misleading investors about the
quality of their securities appeared everywhere. Famco's tactic for selling
subprime loans in the previous example was to recruit high pressure auto
salesmen and teach them to hide information from borrowers, especially
about enormous fees, about the loan's principal amount, or about the teaser
rates that would soon go up. Incentives for these salespeople swelled as fees
to borrowers increased. They received particularly big commissions when
the fees exceeded 15 percent of the mortgage amount.[71] While these shenani-
gans place Famco in the disreputable lender category, its association with
Lehman Brothers guaranteed that high-risk loans would be passed on to
MBS and CDO investors. More deceit.

Evidence of unethical behavior is still surfacing years after the crisis
peaked in 2008. In 2009, the SEC accused three former Countrywide executives of securities fraud for "deliberately misleading investors" by touting
Countrywide as a reputable lender with good underwriting practices and
quality prime mortgages, all while they were "engaging in very risky lending
practices in order to build and maintain market share."[72] In 2011, lawsuits
continued. A judge granted the request made by annuity and retirement fund
investors for a class action suit against Merrill Lynch, now a Bank of
America (BofA) branch; investors argued that Merrill had misled them about
the worth of $16.5 billion in MBS securities.[73] The National Credit
Union Association sued Goldman Sachs for $491 million, making a total of
$2 billion in lawsuits they had filed against companies that allegedly misre-
presented the risk of MBSs.[74] AIG filed suit for $10 billion, contending that
BofA "fraudulently persuaded AIG" to invest in mortgage-backed securities
by providing false data that misrepresented their quality.[75]

Even more imaginative acts make us ponder moral intent. Hedge funds
top this list. These high-risk funds use sophisticated practices to maximize
their return on investment; these "private entity" hedge funds are not regulated and are generally traded by wealthy investors or financial institutions.

---

71. McLean and Nocera, 2010.
72. Luhby, 2009.
73. Van Voris and Weidlich, 2011.
74. NAFCU, 2011.
75. Semuels, 2011a; fraudulent practices were blamed on Countrywide Financial and Merrill
Lynch, which BofA acquired in 2008.

Although hedge funds have long been used to counter losses during market downturns—they "hedge one's bet" so to speak—the way they were implemented crossed an ethical line. Prior to the crisis, some investment groups designed hedge funds that would profit if their underlying mortgage-based assets defaulted. So far, so good—this strategy meets the intent of hedge funds to reap gain when other assets are declining.

However, in some cases their creators paid investment banks to package their worst performing MBSs as CDOs so that the hedge fund creators could buy CDS insurance against these sure losers—never mind the cost to CDO investors or to CDS holders. Dealers could profit by selling these hedge funds to those who wanted to balance their portfolio with high returns. For example, one hedge fund "facilitated the creation of a few of the worst-performing collateralized debt obligations... by buying the riskiest slices of the instruments, which paid returns of around 20%." At the same time, investment banks that sold these CDOs[76] harvested big juicy fees.

In another well-publicized example, John Paulson's investment firm worked with companies such as Goldman Sachs and Bear Stearns to structure high-risk subprime mortgage-based CDOs. His firm would then create a hedge fund to profit if the CDOs failed. At one time Paulson's personal earnings from these transactions were over $10 million a day. One insider at Bear Stearns felt that creating these CDOs for Paulson was inappropriate: "we'd be selling the deals to investors, without telling them that a bearish hedge fund was the impetus for the transaction."[77] These trades became the basis for the SEC's lawsuit that alleged Goldman Sachs did not tell CDO investors that they had conspired with Paulson to create a losing CDO for Paulson's hedge fund.[78]

6.4.3 Ego-Driven Behaviors

Leaders of the new financial organizations are a different breed from the conservative bankers who previously dominated the mortgage market. Top dogs are generally characterized as "hard-charging, entrepreneurial, and intensely ambitious—natural salesmen who found... a way to make their mark in American business. Some of them may have genuinely cared about putting people in homes. All of them cared about getting rich."[79]

Their nicknames speak for them: the godfather of subprimes (Countrywide's Mozilo); the gorilla of Wall Street (Lehman's Fuld); the Wall Street Wiseman (BlackRock's Larry Fink); the perpetual bull (Goldman Sachs' chief strategist Abby Cohen). Comments reveal more about

76. Ng and Mollenkamp, 2008; Magnetar hedge fund is referenced.
77. Zuckerman, 2009.
78. Reisner et al., 2010.
79. McLean and Nocera, 2010.

their character: "these are the trades that make people famous" said Merrill Lynch's Ricciardi as he encouraged CDO sales;[80] "the consumer has to be an idiot to take on one of those loans [option ARMs]" said hedge fund manager John Devaney;[81] for investment banker John Paulson "making money is all about the sport and competition, and has nothing to do with human lives" even though his earnings meant millions of people faced foreclosure;[82] of Larry Fink, friends say he is intense, opinionated, and "definitely motivated to be extraordinarily regarded."[83] Some blamed the failure of Countrywide on Mozilo's character: "His ego sank him.... He had to be first in everything."[84] Indeed, big egos and competitive aggressiveness spelled success— and failure—in these companies.

Ego-driven behaviors, while often not illegal, were also not uncommon given these personality types. Behaviors included protecting one's own interest at the great expense of others or using poor judgment while the corporation is in financial extremis. A well-known example drew substantial criticism. In January 2009, Merrill Lynch CEO John Thain distributed between $3 and $4 billion in executive bonuses "a month ahead of schedule and just days before his struggling Merrill Lynch firm was acquired by BofA." He reportedly had spent $1.2 million to redecorate his office the year before as the firm was dying.[85]

Other examples are just as malodorous. As his company was going under, Lehman Brothers' Dick Fuld sold his interest in his $14 million mansion to his wife for $100, assumedly to protect it in the event he was sued.[86] Fuld's risk-taking leadership style resulted in the largest bankruptcy in history and earned him the title of *Portfolio*'s Worst American CEO of all time.[87] And in 2007 when Mozilo's Countrywide was in its death throes, Mozilo stashed $22.1 million in salary and "tucked away $121.5 million by exercising stock options... [in] a year when the company lost $704 million, its shares slid 79 percent and it cut 11,000 workers."[88]

Even after the crisis, after the failures, and after the bailouts, companies still doled out enormous executive bonuses. Just months after its multibillion dollar bailout, AIG paid hundreds of millions of dollars in retention bonuses to executives, and in 2010 announced it would pay $100 million more,

80. Ng and Mollenkamp, 2007.
81. CNNMoney, 2007.
82. Tasini, 2009.
83. Andrews, 2010.
84. Reckard, 2008; comments of Muolo (editor of *National Mortgage News*).
85. Chuchmach and Rood, 2009.
86. Adegoke, 2009.
87. See *www.cnbc.com/id/30502091?slide=20.*
88. Tasini, 2009; reference to *The New York Times* (April 25, 2008), "A losing year at Countrywide, but not for chief," retrieved from *www.nytimes.com/2008/04/25/business/25pay. html?dlbkandoref=slogin.*

asserting the bonuses were previous contractual obligations. The Federal government declared the bonuses "outrageous, but legal"; however they worked to recoup some of them.[89] In early 2009, after it had repaid its $10 billion in federal bailout funds, Goldman Sachs set aside a record $11.4 billion to pay employee bonuses.[90] Not against the law, but...

In this category, self-interest stands front and center. Individuals did whatever it took to ensure their own security and wealth—even under heavy criticism for questionable behavior and even when they knew others would suffer.

6.5 SYSTEMS THINKING INTERPRETATION

The greater the temptation and possibility for personal gain, the more likely and the more pervasive were the unethical acts. At the highest levels, the scope of effects was broad, touching those who were involved with mortgage-related products. In the still bigger picture, these effects smudged everyone as the economies in the U.S. and in other nations crumbled.

A reinforcing loop is one way to represent the relationship between unethical behavior and personal material gain. In Figure 6.2, when the *economic environment* and *secrecy* encourage *unethical behavior*, small unprincipled acts create *false appearances* of meeting qualifications or goals, which in turn increases the prospect for *material gain*, such as attractive loans or performance rewards. Greater *material gain* causes people to "do mischief" according to Stiglitz,[91] perhaps initially deceiving "just a little" to qualify for a loan, to meet goals, or to make corporate profit seem higher. As more

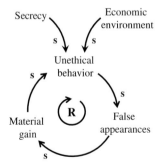

FIGURE 6.2   Reinforcing loop between material gain and unethical behavior.

89. Associated Press, 2010.
90. Harper, 2009.
91. Stiglitz, 2010.

people experience *material gain*, the loop feeds on itself to generate behaviors that grow more unethical. As long as this dishonesty is wrapped in a robe of secrecy, unethical behavior can grow to magnitudes never imagined. We will incorporate these relationships with other influencing factors in chapters that follow.

As we found earlier, reinforcing loops such as this cannot continue forever. Before the financial tower of cards began to fall in 2008, some acts were so bad that they could no longer be hidden. When the housing market crumbled and the toxicity of mortgages and mortgage-related securities was revealed, people and companies were caught in their dishonesties. Reputations were ruined, companies were ruined, and trust in the industry was shattered. Some lost their homes, faced stiff penalties, or were fired. We can see in the previous diagram that when *secrecy* is unmasked or eliminated, *false appearances* evaporate and *material gain* decreases. *Unethical acts* also decrease in this spiral; without secrecy, people have greater fear of repercussions from being caught. However, this result is only true when there *are* repercussions. During the crisis, lack of regulations and lax corporate policies often dulled or eliminated consequences.

6.6 SUMMARY

This chapter categorized unethical behaviors that typified the moral climate in the U.S. housing and financial industries prior to the crisis. The pungent scent of dishonesty permeated that atmosphere in the form of lying, cheating, and other deceitful acts. From the ground level of a single individual to the penthouse of huge financial institutions, behaviors were the same—differing only in degree. Whether fraudulently buying a home or fraudulently selling securities, motives linked directly to personal gain, with a possible side effect of corporate gain. Behaviors were incentivized; from big homes to executive bonuses, everyone sought an appealing reward.

The systems thinking description showed how small acts can become exceedingly unethical as the stakes are raised and the potential for personal gain is heightened. When deception successfully creates a false appearance of value and worthiness, material gain increases. But when secrecy vanishes, the loop that created the gain reveals its origins. Humans are tempted when the potential for gain exceeds their moral thresholds. In an ambiance of plenty, temptations are compelling enough that individuals will step over this threshold, especially when unethical behaviors are condoned by personal justification or corporate strategies, and when secrecy is possible.

Stepping back for a moment for a broader look, these unethical behaviors appear as a surface crisis whose undertow is larger and more lethal than the economic crisis. When you finished reading the compounding list of bad acts, if you felt dismayed, disappointed in humanity, angry, embarrassed, cynical, sick-at-heart, or humbled, you are not alone. As you may have sensed, the roots of this economic crisis are firmly planted in a deeper-reaching ethical crisis—a crisis with human beings and social cultures at its core. Before laying blame or making judgments, we should ask: What lessons can be learned from this destruction? We should say to ourselves, "Wait a minute. I'm a human being with human motives. That could be (or was) me! What can I do about it?"

In the next chapter, we continue our search for ways to transform destructive behaviors into levers of productive actions and small rays of hope. To begin that process, we explore the *why* behind these behaviors and consider the human and environmental factors that intensified unethical behaviors.

Chapter 7

Self Speaks Loudly and Carries a Big Stick: Sources of Unethical Behavior

To fulfill the law of our human nature is what we call the moral law.... The moral law is a law from whose operation we cannot for one instant in our existence escape.

Confucius[1]

Mankind's moral sense is not a strong beacon light, radiating outward to illuminate in sharp outline all that it touches. It is, rather, a small candle flame, casting vague and multiple shadows, flickering and sputtering in the strong winds of power and passion, greed and ideology. But brought close to the heart and cupped in one's hands, it dispels the darkness and warms the soul.

James Q. Wilson[2]

No matter how noble the goals or how honorable the intent, great temptation begets great deception. Whether lying on a loan application, cooking the books, or misrepresenting the characteristics of a loan or security, deception leads to trouble, as we found in the previous chapter. When reviewing the litany of bad behaviors that preceded the economic crisis in the United States, perhaps we shook our heads at the *buy-and-bails*—individuals who duped lenders to get a new home loan then walked away from the old one. We may have felt pangs of impropriety when we heard that executives received hundreds of millions of dollars while their companies lost billions and the individuals on whom they pushed questionable loans lost their homes. We may have been shocked to hear about the magnitude of corruption that occurred under the mantle of a wealth-enhancing environment. Indeed, the lack of ethics was insidious and shocking.

---

1. Confucius, 1994.
2. Wilson, 1993.

Financial Whirlpools.

These abundant examples showed us that all levels, from individual borrowers and lenders to large financial corporations, engaged in four broad types of unethical behaviors. Each of these four (mortgage fraud, disreputable lending, shady corporate strategies, and deceitful dealings) featured dishonesty and self-centered focus. Each transgression caused harm to others. Together they had considerable destructive effects on the economy.

Why didn't more people behave ethically? Were they just bad or immoral? Or were other factors at play? Professor James Wilson's thoughts penetrate the heart of these issues. "The existence of so much immoral behavior," he says, "is not evidence of the weakness of the moral senses. The problem of wrong action arises from the conflict among the several moral senses, the struggle between morality and self-interest, and the corrosive effect of those forces that blunt the moral senses."[3] Because this struggle and these forces relate to unethical behaviors in the economic crisis, Wilson's insights are an appropriate stepping stone from which to explore the roots of these bad acts. To better understand and identify these sources, let us first touch on the concept of ethics itself.

7.1 ETHICS AND ITS PURPOSE

Like describing your dream home after looking at a dozen mediocre options, "I'll know it when I see it" might be a common response to the question "What is ethics?" Simply stated, ethics is "the study and philosophy of human conduct, with an emphasis on determining right and wrong."[4] But what is right and what is wrong? Answers to these questions are the rules of the game, that is, the rules that allow humans to play the game of life successfully. These rules make it possible for us to follow our own self-interest while promoting the well-being of the society in which we live. Major religions and philosophies across the world today share some form of the ancient "Golden Rule," the ethical code that requires reciprocity between one's self and others, namely, treat others as you would like others to treat you.[5]

Many situations require ethical choices, some of which are clear and some of which are painted shades of gray. The most straightforward choices involve known right and known wrong. Ideally in these cases, we expect right to triumph, yet sometimes we may not even know that we are facing an ethical situation, let alone what is right and what is wrong about it. Even

---

3. Wilson, 1993.
4. Ferrell et al., 2010.
5. Principles of the Golden Rule are found in Christianity's Bible, Judaism's Torah, Buddhism's Tripitaka, and Islam's Qur'an. They reach back to ancient Babylon, China (Taoism and Confucianism), Egypt, and Greece.

more difficult to resolve are dilemmas that pit right against right: truth versus loyalty, short term versus long term, justice versus mercy, or individual versus community.[6]

During the crisis, some ethical choices no doubt originated in this last category. One particular choice embodies the built-in dilemma that is a part of human nature: the tension between *self-interest* and *social interest*. For example, individuals might have asked: What harm would it do to tell a little lie that might hurt someone a tiny bit, but would let me take out a loan or score a big bonus? In the crisis, opportunities for self-indulgence were nearly unlimited; little lies became big ones and covered social interests like a great façade of greenery. Awareness that an ethical dilemma existed and concern about others soon fell into the leafy shadows. The primary ethical issue, then, involved extreme self-interest at the expense of others.

7.2 ETHICAL ISSUE: SELF-INTEREST VERSUS SOCIAL INTEREST

Even as they promote their own welfare, humans instinctively band together into collectives intended to promote survival, well-being, and happiness.[7] From the small familial units 10,000 years ago to the huge corporations and nations today, people cluster in groups. In these groups, maintaining a healthy balance between the two human instincts, between self and society, has been a topic of philosophical discussions for millennia, as Huxley and Huxley noted in their review of ethical theories.[8] A basic concern of ethics, they wrote, is "the conflict between man as an individual and man as a social being, the antagonism of selfishness and altruism."[9] But which should weigh heavier, our own well-being or maintaining a healthy society? Must we choose between them? Is choosing our own well-being always unethical?

Self-interest means that we think, believe, and act on behalf of our own personal advantages, whether they are physical, emotional, material, or economic. In some forms, self-interest represents a myopic selfishness to the exclusion or the detriment of others: we form the center of our own universe. Evolutionary biologist Richard Dawkins describes self-interest as part of our DNA: "we are born selfish," he writes.[10] In the late 1700s Adam Smith put a better face on it; in his famed description of the invisible hand of the market, he regarded self-interest as the force behind economic success. He believed that an individual can unintentionally promote society's interest more effectively, "by pursuing his own interest."[11] In contrast, some say that values

6. Kidder, 1995.
7. See Thompson and Hickey, 2008.
8. Huxley and Huxley, 1947.
9. Huxley and Huxley, 1947.
10. Dawkins, 1989.
11. Smith, 1937.

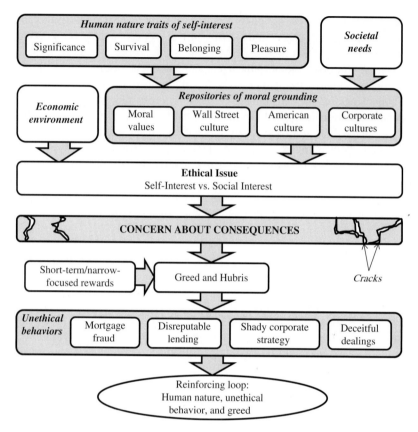

FIGURE 7.1   Genesis of unethical behaviors.

such as concern for others are natural[12] and even part of our genes. At our very core, we hold both self- and other-directed motives.

These questions about balance between self and others are particularly germane for our discussion of the economic crisis in which self-interest had the advantage. In fact, as we saw in Chapter 6, extreme, blinding self-interest was the most glaring foundation for unethical behavior. For example, some participants (particularly high-earning corporate CEOs and hedge fund managers) were so focused on their own material gain that they seemed to operate in an imaginary world. With the spotlight turned inward, they "abandoned any loyalty to their workers, their shareholders or their customers and... even to their country." These players continued to "hand each other multi-million dollar bonuses" even as their businesses crumbled.[13]

---

12. See Smith, 2004; Solomon, 2008.
13. Tasini, 2009.

Using Figure 7.1 as a visual aid, we explore the genesis of this self-interest bias and the weakening of social interest as it applies to individual behaviors and to behaviors of individual employees of organizations. Four primary sources of bias weigh heavily on individuals' ethical choices: (1) human nature traits of self-interest; (2) societal needs; (3) economic environment; and (4) repositories of moral grounding. From the figure, we can imagine that human nature blends with societal needs in the pools and caverns where values and norms are stored—the repositories of moral grounding. Each of us brushes against the colors of right and wrong in our moral values and in the cultures in which we live and work. Permeated with these values and norms, biased by our own human nature, and confronted by countless temptations and opportunities in the economic environment, we face the knotty ethical issue: Should we act only in our own interest or must we be concerned about others? To survive as a species, the answer is, or should be, that we must strike a balance between them.

Our encounter with this ethical issue gets bumpy as we weigh our choices and confront a barrier of *concern about consequences* that can thwart unethical acts. When consequences of our actions are known, considered, and understood, this barrier charges us to care—to keep others in mind with our choices. However, in the economic crisis, the barrier had big cracks and gaping cavities that allowed excessive self-interest to leak through as greed and hubris; these extreme forms of self-interest deposited the sediment of unethical behaviors for others to clean up.

To understand the *whys* behind the unethical behaviors of mortgage fraud, disreputable lending, shady corporate strategy, and deceitful dealings we discussed in Chapter 6, we look to the nature versus nurture argument that has been around for a long while.[14] We can safely say that as we humans adapt, our behaviors are influenced by both environment and nature, and that as a product of both, we make choices and take actions. The remainder of this chapter investigates what it is about our nature, our values, and our economic environment that shaped these behaviors and why self-interest was a common theme in the crisis.

7.3 HUMAN NATURE TRAITS OF SELF-INTEREST

Inherent qualities of human nature help us cope and thrive in the world, but they also create problems, especially when we face moral conflicts. Figure 7.1 shows four of the traits of self-interest that lay at the root of unethical actions: survival, significance, belonging, and pleasure. Each one represents an instinct or need that is deeply embedded in the neuropathways of our brains. In

---

14. See for example, Spencer, 1898: "...moral intuitions are the results of accumulated experiences of utility, gradually organized and inherited, they have come to be quite independent of conscious experience."

moderation, they are neither totally good nor totally bad, however, in excess they turn sour. These self-directed motivations cause us to do whatever it takes—whatever we can get away with—to satisfy them. Worst case, they translate into greed and hubris, and finally become unethical behavior.

7.3.1 Survival

The survival instinct is entwined with self-interest and can overwhelm any latent concern for others. A well-publicized incident off the coast of Italy in early 2012 exemplifies the strength of this instinct. When Captain Schettino tried to abandon his sinking cruise ship and was ordered by the Italian coast guard "to steer his lifeboat to the ship and climb back aboard, he resisted, saying the ship was tipping and it was dark."[15] Such survival-driven behaviors affected economic, emotional, and physical well-being during the crisis. For example, homeowners whose mortgages exceeded what their homes were worth often walked away, seeking to preserve their own well-being regardless of the cost to lenders and stakeholders.

7.3.2 Significance

In its most positive sense, the need for significance—wanting to matter—invigorates our desire to leave our mark on the world; we create, help a worthy cause, aspire to fame, or teach our children. At its most negative, the need for significance taps competitive spirits and causes us to lie, cheat, show off, or use people. Seeking to have more—more money, bigger houses, designer clothes—is one way to satisfy this need. Euphoric in the bountiful environment prior to the crisis, people went on extravagant spending sprees and bought things to feel significant. However, those who could not afford all the buying chose deception to help them gain significance. Through dishonesty they bought new homes or received hefty bonuses, like the $100 million salaries the financial industry's top CEOs received in 2007.[16]

7.3.3 Belonging

In its best light, the need to belong inspires collaboration to accomplish lofty goals; it energizes our compassion and nurturing instincts. At its worst, as an acute emptiness, the need to belong causes us to seek approval by doing what others are doing even when we believe it is wrong. We join gangs or

---

15. Lyman, 2012.
16. Lyon, 2008 and Forbes, 2008; CEO salaries mentioned were: Mozilo of Countrywide ($102M), Blankfein of Goldman Sachs ($73M), and Fuld of Lehman Brothers ($71M). Even if one works 80 hours a week, $100 million a year equals $24,000 an hour or $400 a minute or $6.66 a second. Statistics say that, in 2005, the average CEO in the U.S. was paid 821 times as much as a minimum wage earner (Tasini, 2009).

participate in mob behavior to be accepted, hurting others with our actions. We enlist with the herd of those buying homes and things, even when we must deceive to do so. In the corporate world, the need to be counted among the elite causes some to mislead or be hypercompetitive to display their worthiness. As Wilson notes, "our desire to love and be loved, to please others and to be pleased by them, is a powerful source of sympathy, fairness, and conscience, and, at the same time, a principle by which we exclude others and seek to make ourselves attractive in the eyes of friends and family by justifying our actions."[17] Desire to belong can easily silence our moral sense.

7.3.4 Pleasure

The pleasure-seeking system in the brain compels us to attain coveted goals; research has identified direct connections between brain function and rewards. Dopamine cells, for instance, appear "to cause 'wanting' for hedonic rewards"[18] (rewards that give pleasure). These cells even activate at "the anticipation of reward."[19] Rewards reinforce behaviors as they are being learned and create "an appetite for this behavior after it is learned."[20] Neuroscience also links feelings and emotions (like the pleasure we feel when we receive a reward) to specific areas in the brain.[21] Some go so far as to describe all emotions as states of being that are "elicited by rewards and punishments."[22] Particular rewards, such as money, activate the brain's emotion-related learning area[23] and stimulate "the same reward circuitry as cocaine."[24]

Thus, at an unconscious level, being rewarded is hardwired into us as a pleasurable experience. Rewards are highly addictive and emotionally gratifying. Consider gambling. Not unlike rewards for risky corporate strategies, winning a big jackpot stimulates our brain's pleasure neurons and causes us to gamble away our winnings with the hope of another win—that next high. Rewards make us behave in ways we might normally avoid. With this innate need for pleasure, we can become obsessive about rewards to the exclusion of other concerns, even if it means lying to buy the house we have always wanted or cutting ethical corners to receive that next bonus.

---

17. Wilson, 1993.
18. Berridge, 2007.
19. Oatley et al., 2006; Berridge, 2003; specifically cells in the brain's dopamine-accumbens.
20. Schultz et al., 1997.
21. Damasio, 2010. Damasio and others have traced activity in the brain's insular cortex to "every conceivable kind of feeling" whether elicited by emotion or by pain or pleasure.
22. Rolls, 1999.
23. O'Doherty et al., 2001. The orbitofrontal cortex (OFC) in the brain is associated with emotion and emotion-related learning. Distinct areas of the OFC "were activated by monetary rewards and punishments."
24. Dubner, 2009.

Things that create pleasure, such as money or property, depend not only on their intrinsic value, but also on the context around them; when other people want something, it becomes more valuable to us. Over 80 years ago, economist John Maurice Clark noted, that "to make a man desire a thing... it may be necessary only to keep his attention focused on the idea of getting it. ... pleasure is not absolute but relative to the 'conscious activity at the moment.' "[25] So when advertisements for the good life bombard us and we see that people around us have the latest gadgets or are getting big commissions, we want their same pleasure. We compete to "one-up" them. We might even risk deceit to have the pleasure that they have.

7.4 SOCIETAL NEEDS

Societal needs are echoed in the voices of community all around us—from the taxes that fund common facilities and services, to the charitable organizations that serve public causes; from letters to the editor, to protests and marches. These voices are loudest in their outrage against those who knowingly trample the needs of others. In 2010, for example, the oil spill in the Gulf of Mexico incited cries of indignation charging that Global BP's compromise of safety killed 11 people and countless wildlife, and put hundreds out of a job. The public blamed BP for putting profit ahead of others' welfare;[26] their outcry added to the pressure that caused BP's CEO to resign.[27] In late 2011 after unethical actions in other corporations surfaced, the *Occupy Wall Street* protest in New York City began "with a few hundred people speaking out about corporate greed and inequality."[28] It soon spread across the United States to places such as Madison, Wisconsin and Oakland, California, and to dozens of cities worldwide.

At their most potent, these instances of public conscience are a reminder to maintain balance between self and others. Unfortunately, they often occur in the aftermath of a crisis when conspicuously bad acts surface. Prior to the 2008 meltdown in the U.S., these voices were a soft chorus in the background, drowned out by the energetic shouts of self-interest.

7.5 ECONOMIC ENVIRONMENT

For the crisis, the economic environment was the theater in which the ethical conflict between self-interest and social interest played out. Before the crisis, rapidly increasing housing prices, high demand for subprime loans, and huge appetites for mortgage-backed securities created an ambiance of

---

25. Clark, 1967; citation from Angell, 1905.
26. Associated Press, 2010b.
27. Arnott, 2010. To compensate for their actions, in November 2012 BP agreed to pay a record $4.5 billion in government penalties in addition to $20 billion in damages (see Isidore et al., 2012).
28. Pepitone, 2011.

abundance. Lenders and financial houses were only too happy to embrace innovative but risky products. The profusion of profit-laden opportunities offered a perfect atmosphere for unethical behaviors to become the norm for success, particularly when the excitement of material gain was heightened by secrecy.

This environment provided enough examples of disproportionately high rewards and low risk so that individuals' rational selves could easily engage in risk-reward analysis. In this case, the "apparent increase in the risk-reward ratio" may have been an important reason for fraudulent behavior. When people come to believe that the possibility of getting rich by "cutting corners and bending the rules and deceiving the public" soundly outweighs their risk of getting caught and being fined or embarrassed,[29] they act unethically.

Expectations in such an environment are also important, particularly when they inflate the value of investments and encourage people to invest. Shiller notes that at these boom times, opportunists find ways to profit while pretending, through deception and misrepresentation, to "be the epitome of capitalistic success."[30] What happens when the boom is over and the bubble bursts? Desperate times call for desperate measures, the old proverb says. On the brink of financial disaster, individuals may cheat to avoid bankruptcy or other catastrophe. As "institutions lose liquidity and unsuccessful swindles are about to be revealed, the temptation to take the money and run becomes virtually irresistible."[31] Chapter 6 alluded to typical examples of these behaviors: Fuld sold his mansion to his wife for $100 and Mozilo stashed millions and cashed in stock options as Lehman Brothers and Countrywide went under.

To live as individuals within our social structures and to make these structures flourish, we need guidance, particularly in an environment of countless temptations and opportunities that slant our receptive radars toward self-interest. Part of this guidance comes from our value system and the norms that help us to know right from wrong and to prioritize choices when right and wrong are not so clear.[32] What is this guidance and what happened to it in the crisis? Why didn't moral grounding squelch pleasure-seeking needs or diminish self-serving actions to belong or be significant? Why didn't it overcome temptations in the economic environment? To answer these questions, we consider our moral grounding more closely.

29. Kindleberger and Aliber, 2005.
30. Shiller, 2005.
31. Kindleberger and Aliber, 2005.
32. Over 100 years ago, Thomas Huxley recognized "the existence of a broad general correlation between type of society and type of ethical system" (Huxley and Huxley, 1947).

7.6 REPOSITORIES OF MORAL GROUNDING

Values and norms help us differentiate between good and bad desires or actions.[33] As we discussed in Chapter 4, these values and norms come from many roots and evolve during our lives. Many of them affect our moral choices and constitute the moral grounding that guides our behaviors within society. For our analysis, we consider four repositories of moral grounding: our innate moral values, the American culture in which we live, the corporate cultures in which we work, and finally, specific to the crisis, the Wall Street culture whose ethical values and norms affect certain corporate cultures. All these sources combine with human nature and come into play when we face ethical issues.

At the risk of oversimplifying a complex topic, Figure 7.2 notionally portrays how these components of moral grounding overlap and may sometimes even conflict. The point of this figure is to show that areas of commonality amplify their effects. For example, if all cultures endorse deceit or entitlement, together they can undermine our innate moral values and even overpower our sense of guilt or shame.

In fact this amplifying effect did occur in the crisis when multiple cultures dictated the same message. Chapter 4 described values and norms in the American culture that cultivated self-centered consumption and entitlement. Similarly, culture in the workplace, particularly in lending and finance-related companies, magnified entitlement, self-interest, and risk-taking. In other words, if everyone around you is cheating and reaping positive benefits for doing so, you begin to think that cheating is the right thing to do. The combined power of these values and norms quieted moral values,

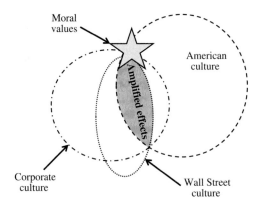

FIGURE 7.2   Repositories of moral grounding and their overlap.

33. Stacey, 2010.

turned self-interest into greed, and tilted the human search for significance, belonging, and pleasure toward self-serving obsessions that ignored, used, or harmed others. We continue this discussion by introducing the first repository of values and norms that accompanies us each and every day: our innate moral values.

7.6.1 Moral Values

Humans have what is called a "moral sense" or moral compass. We refer to this set of intuitive beliefs as *moral values*. We humans feel these values directly; they tell us how not to act, particularly when we are acting voluntarily.[34] Some call them *conscience*, a thought process that takes the form of an emotionally-charged voice in our heads, a wrench in our stomachs, or a pressure on our hearts. As Huxley and Huxley put it, conscience is "the watchman of society, charged to restrain the anti-social tendencies of the natural man within the limits required by social welfare."[35] This internal and regulative knowledge of right intends to resolve conflicts between personal and social interests.[36]

Some psychologists believe our innate moral values are controlled by certain fundamental emotions. Adam Smith in 1790 and Charles Darwin in 1874 both believed that sympathy had "a foundational role in generating our ethical systems."[37] Behavioral physiologists suggest that in addition to "culturally determined norms, tested in practice and arrived at by reasoning," we humans have "innate norms for our ethical behavior."[38] Psychologist Carroll Izard finds that many social emotions including guilt, fear, anger, and shame or "excitement and joy in caring for and helping others" facilitate the development of our conscience and morality.[39] Along with the other "moral emotions" of shame, embarrassment, and pride, guilt in particular reminds us how we should and should not behave, thus helping us attain social status and prevent rejection by a group. These emotions are all "linked to the welfare of others and society as a whole."[40]

---

34. Wilson, 1993.
35. Huxley and Huxley (1947) attribute the original idea of conscience to Lord Shaftesbury's discussion of moral sense in his 1711 publication *Characteristics of Men, Manners, Opinions, Times*.
36. Albert et al., 1984; from clergyman Joseph Butler's eighteenth-century discussion of conscience.
37. Richerson and Boyd, 2008; see also Solomon, 2008.
38. Eibl-Eibesfeldt, 1972; see also Izard, 1977.
39. Izard, 1977; Izard is known for his "discrete emotions theory."
40. Katchadourian, 2010; see also Tangney et al., 2007.

Guilt and other moral emotions emerge around age three.[41] Researchers connect these emotions both to innate tendencies[42] and to learned behavior. For example, neuroscientists find that specific areas in the brain actually "light up" when a person feels these emotions.[43] They now believe that moral perceptions emanate "from many of the same regions of the brain" as sensual perceptions.[44] Because they create neural pathways, these emotions become automatic and are difficult to suppress.[45] Furthermore, studies conclude that "moral reasoning does not cause moral judgment."[46] All these findings mean that we cannot simply talk someone into being moral.

Other researchers disagree that social emotions come from biology or genetics but believe that they emerge from culture. Ausubel, for example, thinks that guilt is so fundamental and basic "to the development and maintenance of social norms that it will develop in all cultures" even under minimally favorable conditions.[47] Recent research expands the focus on the inherited nature of moral emotions to include cultural and social stimuli. While our moral emotions are partially inborn, they solidify as we experience life. Thus, our moral sense is a mixture of biologic and cultural evolution and the cooperation required for us to live together.[48]

The complex emotions in moral values "require self-awareness—a sense of who we are with respect to others."[49] They speak to us when we realize we have broken a rule or violated standards.[50] Unless we are sociopaths, moral values are our constant companion, whether or not we choose to heed them. They subconsciously maintain a powerful hold on our actions. Even so, our moral values can be compromised.

What factors in the economic crisis were strong enough to alter this moral sense, however robust or feeble it may have been? To answer this question, we consider our day-to-day environment. Like basketball players who constantly assess whether they can elbow one another without hearing the whistle, we survey our surroundings for cues, for rules of the game, and for limits. Many of these cues come from the cultural norms that surround us.

---

41. Katchadourian, 2010.
42. Some believe that these emotions are "unlearned" and inborn through the evolutionary process; see Izard, 1977; Damasio, 2010.
43. Katchadourian, 2010; see also Zak, 2008.
44. Brooks, 2011.
45. Zak, 2008.
46. Haidt, 2001.
47. Ausubel, 1955; see also Izard, 1977.
48. Goodenough, 2008.
49. Katchadourian, 2010; see also Tracy and Robins, 2007.
50. Izard, 1977.

7.6.2 American Culture

Culture adds to moral grounding by determining how our moral senses "are converted into maxims, customs, and rules."[51] Cultural trends in America reveal a pervasive self-interest that has changed our "community-oriented culture to one that. . . believes that self-centeredness is necessary for success in life," and one in which those who feel entitled consider their "needs paramount and others' needs minor."[52] Such values in the American culture are powerful enough to engage human nature in ways that foster unethical behavior. Chapter 4 described how America's focus on a façade of success, coupled with a feeling of entitlement to own a home and a burning desire for material comfort, translated into persistent buying of homes and things. Much of this buying behavior was encouraged by loans with favorable terms and ultra-easy credit requirements.

Even so, sometimes more drastic, unethical methods were needed. When interest rates and housing prices increased and borrowers could not make payments, it became difficult to get the subprime loans needed to fuel the whole machine. So people lied on loan applications to qualify for expensive homes, misrepresented loan terms or securities' risks to get more business, or made fraudulent accounting entries to appear more successful. Unchecked by dampened moral senses and tempted by the economic opportunities in the boom market, American culture encouraged, rather than stifled, values and norms that drove unethical behaviors.

7.6.3 Corporate Cultures

In Chapter 4 we learned that corporate cultures and the leaders who guide them have incredible influence on employees' values and behaviors. Individuals may find that the values they can express in the workplace are constrained by the character[53] or culture of the work environment. Personal preferences and moral values often take a back seat, particularly in a cultural climate of entitlement, risk-seeking, ethical complaisance, and other characteristics described in Chapter 4. In the economic crisis, cultural norms in some corporations did push employees to behave in dubious ways and sometimes shoved them beyond their personal moral boundaries and over the ethical cliff. Chapter 6 cited instance after instance of irrational unethical behaviors. To make more money, many misstated the quality of securities built from subprime loans or ignored risk. Leaders of big-name firms such as Lehman Brothers, Merrill Lynch, and Countrywide modeled behaviors and attitudes that became their firms' way of doing business. Rather than act

---

51. Wilson, 1993.
52. Twenge and Campbell, 2009.
53. Schwartz, 1993.

as a backstop for dishonesty, cultures in these firms promoted unethical behaviors.

Other than leaders' influence, did other factors influence corporate cultures? To this question we must answer a resounding "yes"! Significantly, values and norms embedded in "the Wall Street culture" imprinted themselves on some organizations and their leaders, and even endorsed unethical dealings. For many, this culture is unimportant, but for big financial corporations whose success depends on the market, it matters a great deal. Because the Wall Street culture's influence is inherent in some corporate cultures, we did not specifically identify it in earlier discussions; however it is appropriately included here so that we can better understand the origin of unethical behaviors.

7.6.4 Wall Street Culture

While there are norms in all cultures that characterize success, norms in the Wall Street culture are well-defined and uncompromising. To be successful, organizations that depend on Wall Street, particularly those involved in the securities business, must play by its rules. The Wall Street culture reflects arrogance and a gambling mindset. It has been called "a casino for rich men" where everybody "believed that they were brighter than others."[54] Some talk about it as one of "I'm going to push the rules as far as I can."[55] Others describe it in terms of excessive risk-taking and noted that "never has the 'R' word been such an obsession for the men and women who rule the nation's biggest investment banks."[56] Some refer to Wall Street's culture as "high risk/high reward" and a "culture of smartness" that is "reinforced by... dashing appearance, mental and physical quickness, aggressiveness, and vigor."[57] Lack of long-term orientation and desperation to do deals is also apparent in these firms. Former investment banker and anthropologist Karen Ho observes that "Wall Street approaches to compensation not only solidify job insecurity but also engender a relentless deal-making frenzy with no future orientation" which in turn creates booms and busts in the economy. Certainly, these characteristics influenced leaders of big financial firms, but, as Ho points out, Wall Street culture also imposed its "investment banking models of employee liquidity into corporate America."[58] This type of culture is contagious.

---

54. Stiglitz, 2010.
55. Associated Press, 2009; remarks of R. Edward Freeman of University of Virginia's Darden School.
56. Thornton, 2006.
57. Ho, 2009.
58. Ho, 2009.

Aggressive cultures like these do have a positive side, particularly when some level of risk-taking makes a company competitive. Organizations with these cultures can achieve lofty goals such as being the best, increasing profitability, or having the largest market share. However at the extreme, such cultures become destructive, as they did during the crisis. And when disappointments poke their ugly heads through the ground of success, these types of cultures promote underhanded dealings to mask failure. However, we know from Chapter 4 that corporate cultures don't just happen. Leaders' character and actions, strategies, and especially the goals and rewards they use solidify in a company's culture.

Whether in small brokerages, banks, and lending companies, or in massive financial institutions whose success depends on Wall Street, corporate cultures associated with the economic crisis instilled employees with a sense of entitlement, self-interest, and risk-taking that covered over what they knew was right or fair. By appealing to innate human needs for pleasure, belonging, and significance, corporate cultures joined with the American culture to shush inner moral voices and to encourage rather than restrain self-interest. Yet when all else fails, a final inhibitor may impede self-interest and block corrupt motives—a barrier built from the granite of concern about consequences (see Figure 7.1). Unfortunately, leaks in this barrier allowed the already bloated self-interest to become greed and hubris—a precursor of unethical behavior.

7.7 CONCERN ABOUT CONSEQUENCES

At the conclusion of my graduate course in ethics, I ask "what was your greatest lesson?" The most frequent response is: "the need to consider consequences." Students say, "I never thought about the bigger picture, or how my actions might affect others" or "the effects just didn't occur to me." Since the economic crisis hit the United States, I have often wondered whether the results would have been the same if those who behaved in less-than-ethical ways had considered consequences. My conclusion is that some things may have been different. I believe, as Wilson does, that for most of us, moral choices are "powerfully shaped by particular circumstances and our rough guess as to the consequences of a given act."[59] So, what was it about the economic crisis that eroded this barrier of concern about consequences? Where did the cracks originate? Of all the ways to fracture this barrier, secrecy and disregard were the most common.

---

59. Wilson, 1993.

7.7.1 Secrecy

Secrecy in an organization can result from the nature of the business, from lack of communication, or from the complexity or technical intricacy of a product; it can also be a form of intentional silence that occurs when people are belittled for pointing out flaws. In the crisis, two prevalent forms of secrecy—organizational silence and complexity—compromised concern about consequences.

Many failed leaders cultivated high levels of organizational silence through what is called "groupthink." Groupthink allows those in leadership positions to "denigrate or belittle those who tell them they are wrong... and keep those who tell them they are wrong at a distance.... Loyal dissenters self-censor to avoid being thought of as somehow not 'on the team' or 'with the program'."[60] Because nobody wanted to tell the emperor he had no clothes, risk and its consequences remained hidden.

The complexity of loans and securities introduced their own type of secrecy, making these products opaque to buyers and allowing lenders and sellers to mask their risk. Those who sold these "inherently fuzzy" financial products could easily "reshape reality in a way that was comfortable for them."[61] Because these products were too difficult to explain or to understand, agents kept concerns to themselves and set aside social interests in favor of the commissions they would receive. Another form of complexity also encouraged secrecy: the sheer volume of transactions. With stacks of loan applications on their desks or directives to push loan ratings through quickly, lenders, underwriters, and rating agencies simply had no time to nitpick or investigate. In fact, many were paid *not* to look.

7.7.2 Disregard

Disregarding consequences was easily done during the crisis. For example, because it was twice-removed from the quality of individual loans, the process of buying and selling MBSs and CDOs covered underlying risk. Home buyers turned into faceless securities and risk was spread so thin that responsibility for one's actions diluted into nothingness.

In addition to this lack of accountability, people believed that there was nothing to worry about and ignored consequences with an "it'll never happen" attitude. Trusting those who rated securities or those who provided loans offered a certain refuge: "they're experts; they know what they're doing so I don't have to." Expectations of continued prosperity muted any inclination to consider consequences. When people believed that housing prices would continue to rise, or that interest rates would remain low, or that

---

60. Gandz et al., 2010.
61. Ariely, 2009.

subprime loans were safe because no one wanted to lose a home, it wasn't important to think about the "what ifs."

Finally, there is a natural tendency for humans to disregard the future. Neuroscientists find that human decision making tends to discount the future and seek immediate rather than delayed rewards.[62] When faced with instant gratification versus waiting until some future time, people *want it now*. In doing so, they ignore future conditions and consequences.

In the economic crisis, as cracks in the concern about consequences expanded, so did greed and hubris. Nothing emerged to repair the cracks—no inner voices, no rules or regulations, no public outcries, no reminders of who might be hurt, and no cultural norms.

7.8 GREED AND HUBRIS

Greed, grown from excessive self-interest, creates a compulsive desire to possess more than we need. Greed has been labeled many things—from a social emotion, to a trait, to a habit built from repetition, to one of the seven deadly sins. Even the word is ugly; our mouths sneer when we say it. In pursuit of wealth, status, or power, greedy people can become unethical through overindulgence and lack of concern for others. Greed multiplies in times of prosperity. History shows that "swindles are a response to the greedy appetite for wealth stimulated by the boom."[63] Greed is most frequently referenced as a cause of the economic crisis in the United States, even by President Obama.[64] Its opposite occurs when we behave selflessly or with generosity—a rare condition in the crisis.

Similarly, hubris evolves from another aspect of self-interest: self-love. To eighteenth-century clergyman Joseph Butler, self-love "operates when individuals organize their desires to promote their own best interests."[65] Self-love also reveals positive and negative sides. On its positive side, when expressed as respect and appreciation, it has been called an emotion[66] and a virtue of positive pride derived from a big heart or greatness of soul.[67] On its negative side, excessive self-love turns into hubris where we find inflated self-importance and the feeling of being better than others. Even the huffy-puffy sound of the word hubris echoes the bluster that this human trait embodies. Hubris takes effort to contain, for, as Butler notes, to become benevolent and further the public good, individuals must control their

---

62. Harari et al., 2006.
63. Kindleberger and Aliber, 2005.
64. UPI, 2009.
65. Albert et al., 1984.
66. See Plutchik's (2003) discussion of theories from R.S. Lazarus (1991).
67. Aristotle, 1999; to describe this type of pride, Aristotle uses the word magnanimity meaning "a certain greatness of soul."

self-love appetites.[68] At its negative extreme, hubris causes disregard or even contempt for others. In the economic crisis, this most serious of the seven deadly sins presented itself as an "I'm above it all" conceit and a competitiveness that flattened others with the weight of self-importance.

This prideful emotion was conspicuously epitomized by some executives who felt their companies were "'too big to fail'—that is, too big for the public to let fail."[69] The record-breaking bankruptcy of Lehman Brothers was called "a tale of hubris," with the excessive pride and arrogance of its CEO Fuld at its heart.[70] When Fannie Mae's CEO Raines set his unprecedented goal to double the company's earnings per share in five years, it was hard to see this action "as anything but hubris" with "a lot of money riding on it."[71] As we described earlier, leaders help shape cultures; in these cases cultures prone to arrogance, hubris, and risk-taking set the bar for employees' unethical behaviors.

7.9 SHORT-TERM NARROW-FOCUSED REWARDS

Earlier we recognized that incentive systems encouraged the risk-taking, arrogant, and competitive cultures seen during the economic crisis. These systems rewarded employees for meeting the narrowly-focused and short-term goals of lofty loan quotas, massive securities sales, and superficial assessment of risk. More sales generated more bonuses. To reap the huge rewards that came with achieving these goals, individuals in many mortgage loan and financial securities businesses often resorted to unethical behaviors. So what happened? Did all the greedy people gravitate to these types of businesses?

Not really. These ordinary individuals were doing what human nature compelled—seeking rewards. Rewards, we found, are powerful drugs linked to pleasure. The reward/pleasure mechanism built into our brains motivated those who knew they could not afford a home to pursue subprime loans "because the prospects of living large and benefiting from home-price appreciation were too tempting to pass up." Those who made the loans felt the temptations of tantalizing rewards. Those who invested in mortgage-backed securities and knew that the AAA ratings were overstated "purchased these securities anyway."[72] Again these returns were just too attractive. Sellers of securities had similar thoughts. Although bankers may have wanted to play fairly and make good investments for clients, they were

---

68. Albert et al., 1984.
69. Woods, 2009. Says Woods "The argument is that the failure of a large firm that is significantly connected to other firms could send ripple effects throughout the economy, and a great many other firms could wind up toppling as well."
70. Plumb and Wilchins, 2008.
71. McLean and Nocera, 2010; Raines set the goal in 1998.
72. This and previous citation from Dubner, 2009.

incentivized to consider mortgage-backed securities as godsends. Behavioral economist Dan Ariely suggests that we put ourselves in their shoes: "If you could make $10 million simply by getting all your clients to buy mortgage-backed securities, wouldn't you soon convince yourself that such investments were truly wonderful?"[73]

Even when we know that a reward is too good to be true, it may be so appealing that we can't help ourselves; we biologically crave it and we want it *now*. Thus, it is not surprising that the mega-million-dollar profit-driven incentives to CEOs or the inflated commissions to mortgage brokers for selling subprime loans were addictive. Nor is it surprising that desire for and expectation of rewards crept into corporate cultures. However, this expectation promotes risk-taking as the way to do business. Some argue, for instance, that to meet Countrywide's goal of increased market share, its salespeople "were given incentives to undertake riskier transactions in order to continue to grow the company at a rapid rate."[74]

When the reward is greater than the results it elicits and one receives high pay in spite of poor performance, the pressure for dishonesty increases proportionately. An example of this "incentive distortion" is executive stock options. In the crisis, with the promise of these incentives, executives would "do everything they could to get their firms" stock price up—including creative accounting"[75] A final example puts the cherry on top of this bonus sundae. In 2008 when the entire U.S. financial industry was reeling from billions in losses, bonuses were at a near record high of about $33 billion; "Six of the nine banks paid out more in bonuses than they received in profit."[76]

Yet rewards themselves are not necessarily dangerous. The real danger appears when incentive systems allow unethical behaviors to garner rewards and when this behavior insinuates itself into cultural norms. Danger escalates if unethical behaviors become the best way to get quick and substantial rewards, and when employees become callous to their bad effects.

7.10 HISTORIC PRECEDENCE

We have seen how human nature, societal needs, values, and norms pressed heavily on individuals causing them to elevate self far above others during the economic crisis. We identified lack of concern about consequences and followed self-interest as it turned into its most menacing forms of greed and hubris. However, extreme self-interested behavior did not just suddenly appear in the twenty-first century. Historians of financial crises note that while "corrupt behavior is part of virtually every economy," such behavior is

---

73. Ariely, 2009.
74. Quotes in this paragraph from Ferrell et al., 2010.
75. Stiglitz, 2010.
76. Stiglitz, 2010; Craig and Solomon, 2009.

particularly apparent during times of opportunity. The recorded history of booms and busts since the Civil War reveals that when personal wealth increases quickly, there is marked "increase in fraudulent behavior by individuals who want even more rapid increases in their wealth."[77]

Yes, when we humans become used to some good fortune and wealth, we want more. But we cannot justify the dishonesties in the crisis just because they have happened before or because they are part of a market economy or because they are paired with a social disregard that has existed throughout history. We must acknowledge and manage them.

7.11 SYSTEMS THINKING INTERPRETATION

By now we appreciate how the values, norms, and environment that saturate our everyday lives persuade our human nature to reveal its perversions. The more we have and the more we see that others have, the more we want. In these relationships lies a reinforcing dynamic, a spiral that feeds on itself to generate more material gain through more unethical behavior. Figure 7.3 expands the link between material gain and unethical behavior that we introduced in Chapter 6 to describe this dynamic as the greed reinforcing loop, R_{greed}.

In this portrayal, unethical behavior occurs when the *human nature* traits of self-interest (survival, significance, belonging, and pleasure) combine with weakened *moral grounding*, with a permissive *economic environment* full of temptation and opportunity, and with corporate incentive systems that use

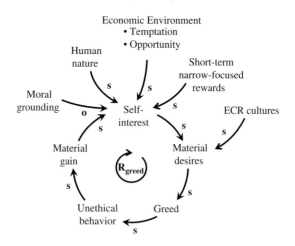

FIGURE 7.3 Greed reinforcing loop and sources of unethical behavior.

77. Kindleberger and Aliber, 2005.

short-term and *narrow-focused (SN) rewards* to promote risk-taking and self-interest. Following this loop, extreme *self-interest* generates *material desires* that are encouraged by the *entitlement, consumption-oriented,* and *risk-seeking (ECR) cultures* in which we live and work. Self-interested needs to satisfy these desires generate *greed* that elicits *unethical behavior*; the result is some sort of *material gain*. When *material gain* is achieved, we want still *more*, magnifying *self-interest* to even higher levels. And so the loop continues.

Earlier we discussed the pervasiveness of hubris in corporate cultures and its significant influence on unethical behaviors. However, because hubris is not necessarily incited by material desires and because its dynamics go beyond the scope of this analysis, we have not included it in this systems depiction. We leave it to the reader to consider other reinforcing loops that include hubris and its possible motivators such as significance, power, or status.

Normally, a *concern about consequences* makes people consider the effects of their actions, weakens the hold of self-interest, and reduces unethical behaviors. However, if the concern is low, self-interest intensifies. Figure 7.4 introduces a new reinforcing loop, R$_{consequences}$, to show how decreased *concern about consequences* not only increases *unethical behaviors*, but further weakens *moral grounding*. When *secrecy* or *disregard* diminishes the *concern about consequences*, more *unethical behaviors* arise. More *unethical behavior* increases *material gain* (at least in the short-term) and greater *material gain* diminishes *concern about consequences* when individuals believe they can just ignore or explain their actions to reap the rewards. Given this double reinforcing pattern, no wonder the crisis

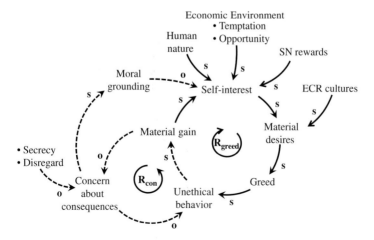

FIGURE 7.4   Consequences reinforcing loop and unethical behavior.

generated so many unethical behaviors; concern about consequences must have been feeble.

Reinforcing loops, however they are composed, cannot continue forever. Once the financial underpinnings crumbled in the economic crisis, individuals and companies faced ruin. When the veil of secrecy disintegrated, unethical dealings were unearthed and material gains disappeared; the loop fell apart. Some of these dealings are still being discovered and prosecuted. At this point, self-interest became self-preservation.

7.11.1 Candidate Leverage Point

Short of total destruction, how can we diminish unethical behaviors? Where is leverage possible? We turn again to *concern about consequences.* If we were so inclined, we could repair the cracks in the consequence barrier and give our moral grounding a voice through a process of "disinterested reflection."[78] In other words, to build our sensitivity to unethical behavior, we must first consider possible outcomes of our acts. We must also feel threatened by penalties; we can't ignore or pass consequences off on others. Thus, part of this repair requires antidotes for secrecy and disregard.

Replacing secrecy with transparency and reducing disregard by increasing regulations, penalties, or social sanctions for wrongdoings can heighten concern for consequences. Figure 7.5 shows how this process might work. Here we enlist the $R_{consequences}$ reinforcing loop where *unethical behavior* generates *material gain,* but we have replaced *secrecy* and *disregard* with increased *transparency* and *penalties* to strengthen concern about consequences. When these factors increase, *concern* grows, the temptation for *unethical behavior* diminishes, and *moral grounding* strengthens. In this environment, the vicious circle has become a virtuous circle. Fewer *unethical acts* reduce ill-gotten *material gain* and increase the need for *concern about consequences* because we want to avoid the penalties. Such an environment could be created through leaders' values and behaviors that influence a corporate culture, or perhaps less effectively through government regulations.

In addition to this leverage around concern for consequences, other actions can have remarkable results. Human reward-seeking tendencies can be motivated to achieve goals that benefit the greater societal good. For example, rather than offering only short-term and narrow-focused rewards, corporate incentive systems can be designed to reward broader long-term goals and to satisfy self-interested behaviors. We describe this potent lever in Chapter 11.

---

78. Wilson, 1993.

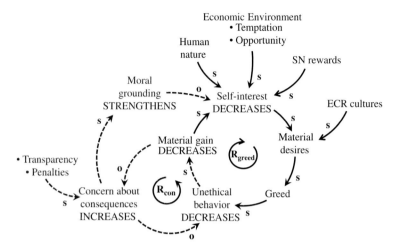

FIGURE 7.5   Transparency and penalties dampen unethical behavior.

7.11.2 Current Activities

These candidate leverage points propose actions that could have improved the situation, but what actually happened? After the economic meltdown hit the U.S., the government attempted to fix systemic problems, some of which involved these very factors. Since it cannot dictate moral sensibility, the government relied on the tools it has, namely regulations to improve transparency and increase penalties. For example, in July 2010, President Obama signed a law to increase regulation of the financial industry with goals of "restoring public confidence in the financial system, preventing another financial crisis, and allowing any future asset bubble to be detected and deflated before another financial crisis ensues." Included are policies for banks, over-the-counter derivatives, and credit rating agencies; a new council to monitor risk; and a requirement for "enhanced disclosure of executive compensation" that allows shareholders to have a "say-on-pay" for executive compensation.[79] We have yet to understand the implications of this legislation, but we know it won't be easy and it won't be cheap.

7.12 SUMMARY

Chapter 6 listed a host of unethical behaviors and extreme examples of fraud and deceit that occurred in the U.S. within the crisis timeline. This chapter explored the *why* behind these excessive behaviors. Our exploration

---

79. Sweet 2010; the full name of the act is the Dodd–Frank Wall Street Reform and Consumer Protection Act.

does not suggest that people are just bad. Instead, it intends to make us look beyond individual actions, sans judgment or blame, to systemic features that encourage corrupt behaviors so that we can identify which causes to tackle.

From our examination, a central ethical issue of the crisis emerged: self-interest versus social interest. Self-interest grew to giant size during the crisis and overpowered social interest at the opposite end of the tug-of-war. To account for this lopsided contest, in this chapter we considered the human nature traits of self-interest and societal needs together with the economic environment and our moral grounding derived from innate moral values and norms in our cultural surroundings. Temptation and opportunity in the economic environment merged with human needs for survival, significance, belonging, and pleasure; the entitlement, consumption-oriented, and risk-seeking cultures intensified material desires and encouraged excessive self-interest. At this point, the last bastion to prevent unethical behaviors, the concern about consequences, was damaged by secrecy and plain old disregard which weakened moral grounding. Finally, inflated self-interest—piqued by narrow-focused and short-term incentives—became greed and hubris beneath the unethical behaviors of mortgage fraud, disreputable lending, shady corporate strategy, and deceitful dealings. This chapter does not conclude our concern with self-interest and social interest; later chapters develop the ethical relationships between them.

Our systems thinking perspective introduced two reinforcing loops, R_{greed} and $R_{consequences}$, which either generate or try to limit bad behaviors. Strong self-interest, material desires, greed, and unethical behaviors together with weak moral grounding and little concern about consequences create a situation that is extremely difficult to surmount. This portrayal recognized potential leverage points that encourage individuals to care about consequences and thus strengthen their moral grounding and decrease their unethical proclivities. Conditions to accomplish these ends include more transparency in lending and securities selling, and more social or regulatory penalties. The U.S. government has already legislated some of these conditions. We also alluded to a potential lever that uses incentive systems to alter the nature of rewards and redirects self-interest toward society-benefitting goals. This variation appears in a later chapter.

We know we cannot justify ethical misdeeds simply because they always happen in an economy, nor can we excuse poor behaviors, but we can conclude that decent people with good intentions and noble motives do bad things, depending on the circumstances. We also know that in the right situation, we might be these decent people. It might be you and I who tell a lie to get the house we've always wanted. It might be you and I who ignore our consciences when we are tempted with a big bonus. So, while we can look to others to fix it and while we appreciate the steps that governments take to repair systemic problems, we must also recognize that the ultimate responsibility is our own.

This chapter completes the section on human behaviors—the yin of the economic crisis. It leaves us with the knowledge that although behaviors that emanate from our values, cultures, and human nature can be productive, they can also destroy. In the following chapters we return to the mechanics of the economy—the yang of the economic crisis—to compose the bigger picture.

Part III

The Yang: Economic Mechanisms

Chapter 8

What Goes Up Must Come Down: The Housing Bubble

The strong rise in home prices since the mid-1990s has raised concerns over a possible bubble in the housing market... [but]market fundamentals are strong enough to explain the recent path of home prices... no bubble exists.

McCarthy and Peach[1]

Just a few days after the Federal Reserve Bank of New York said it found little evidence of a nationwide housing bubble, HSBC said a bubble exists and prices are likely to deflate gradually over a few years.

Reuters[2]

Bulls, bears, booms, busts, and bubbles. Economists use such wonderfully vivid words to describe economic phenomena. The "bursting of the housing bubble" is another dramatic phrase that portrays swiftly deflating housing prices and the exploding mess that energized the economic crisis. Using statistics and systems thinking, this chapter examines the decade-long housing price bubble in the United States. It characterizes the influence of inflation, income, and monetary policy and translates bubble behavior into a systems depiction of the housing market's fundamental structure. To build an intuitive sense and systems understanding of the bubble, we will compare various economic factors in the charts and graphs that follow, so if you prefer to know where we are headed before delving into details, go to the summary and return here later. Throughout the chapter we will endeavor to answer probing questions: Do these behaviors seem unusual? What might have provoked them? Insights into these questions will contribute to the final systems picture at the book's conclusion (Chapter 12).

---

1. McCarthy and Peach, 2004.
2. Reuters, 2004; HSBC is an international bank headquartered in London.

Financial Whirlpools.

8.1 BUBBLE HISTORY

Economic bubbles are real events whose image evokes their description; they are "assets whose prices inflate like air in an expanding balloon and then collapse." Generally, when an asset appreciates for more than a year and faster than the long-term trend, its behavior is interpreted as a *bubble*.[3] Because prices in these bubbles expand above the value that is "warranted by normal returns and demands" they cannot continue to rise.[4] When a bubble does burst, inflated prices drop to levels consistent with market conditions. This bursting is often triggered by small and unpredictable events that simply "change the market's psychology."[5]

Bubbles in an economy are far from new. Before 2008, assets in the world's big 10 bubbles ranged from tulip bulbs to internet-related stock.[6] In the Dutch tulip bubble of the 1630s, the price of certain tulip bulbs exceeded "the value of a furnished luxury house in 17th-century Amsterdam."[7] More recently in the 1980s, the sharp increase in Japan's real estate and stock prices on the upside of a bubble made its economy seem a model of success.[8] However, when that bubble popped in the early 1990s, the value of these assets crashed, ruining many Japanese investors, banks, and financial institutions.

The tenth big bubble hit the United States. After internet technology caught on, speculators and venture capitalists couldn't wait to invest in internet start-up companies.[9] In mid-1995 the technology-heavy NASDAQ stock market, with its many so-called *dot-com* stocks, reached 1000 for the first time. As in other bubbles, investors who helped inflate this internet bubble were "fearful of getting left behind while others grew rich"[10] so they invested—oftentimes irrationally. In March 2000, NASDAQ hit an all-time high of 5048—more than double its value from the year before.[11] However, by December of that year, it had dropped by half, correcting for the speculation that had run it up. In October 2002, NASDAQ hit 1140—lower than it had been in six years. The internet bubble had definitely burst.

At the same time the U.S. economy faced fluctuations brought on by the internet bubble, another situation was brewing. Housing prices had been rising since 1997 when the internet bubble was just forming. Prices still

3. Dreiman, 2001.
4. Foldvary, 2004.
5. Morgenson, 2004.
6. Kindleberger and Aliber, 2005.
7. Thompson, 2007.
8. Kindleberger and Aliber, 2005.
9. Beattie, 2002; there were an estimated 18 million internet users in 1995.
10. Belsky and Gilovich, 2010.
11. NYSE, 2011.

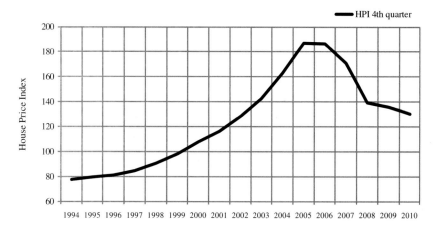

FIGURE 8.1 House Price Index.[12]

climbed in 2000 when the U.S. stock market crashed and in 2001 when terrorist attacks shook the economy. An eleventh bubble perhaps? At that point, no one was concerned about a bubble. It was too soon to tell.

Using what is called the House Price Index, or HPI, Figure 8.1 tells the story of U.S. housing prices during the crisis timeline.[13] Keep the bulging shape in mind—we will see it again many times. Notice how quickly it ascends and descends. Consider its high points in 2005 and 2006. Using a systems perspective, recognize that its behavior over time resembles the *overshoot-and-collapse* contour described in Chapter 1, implying that some combination of reinforcing and balancing feedback loops is involved.

When a bubble is forming, it is difficult to detect whether price increases are based on market principles[14] or whether they represent the ascent of an unrealistic bubble that will soon deflate. After prices drop, it is easier to identify that a bubble has occurred. For example, since 1975 there have been at least two other up-and-down cycles for housing prices.[15] Because other factors explained them, these cycles were not officially declared as bubbles. If we could have predicted the recent housing bubble at its onset, perhaps we could have softened its inevitable effects. No matter—in 2001 housing price growth simply looked good.

---

12. Q4 HPI from Standard & Poors / Case-Shiller (2011).

13. House Price Index (also called Home Price Index), HPI, is a good indicator of housing price fluctuation. It was normalized to 100 in Q1 2000; average housing prices are measured relative to that time.

14. Market principles such as decreasing interest rates, increasing inflation, and increasing income.

15. Data from Dreiman, 2001; using Real HPI (House Price Index), one housing price cycle extended from 1976 to 1982 and another from 1983 to 1995.

8.2 THE RISE AND FALL OF THE HOUSING BUBBLE

By 2004, debates about whether there was a housing bubble were frequent. As others' opinions clashed, some analysts looked at interest rates, mortgage debt trends, and home equity, and caught a disturbing whiff of something rotten. "It's always tricky," they said "to call the top of an overheated market.... But this time something important is different: Interest rates are inching up.... higher mortgage rates will inevitably make houses less affordable.... mortgage debt has shot up even faster than home values."[16] This type of leverage in which homeowners have high debt and low equity can cause big problems if housing prices fall. If they drop a little, homeowners could lose their equity. Worse yet, prices could fall below what they owe on their home. Either way, homeowners would be sorely disappointed or financially hurt.

In 2005, indicators of a housing bubble were more substantial. Economist Robert Shiller predicted that "the market is in the throes of a bubble of unprecedented proportions that probably will end ugly."[17] Some read the tea leaves left by consumer buying habits and the abundance of adjustable rate mortgage loans. Consumers were spending more than they were earning and their debts were mounting. Adding to this growing debt, in 2007 monthly house payments were about to climb for some $2 trillion of adjustable rate mortgages (about a quarter of all loans); these ARMs were ready to reset to higher interest rates.[18] Like a scorpion, the economy was poised to sting its many players.

Even with this uneasiness, in early 2006 housing prices were still ascending. The cost of a home had nearly doubled over the previous 6 years; the House Price Index reached an all-time high of nearly 190.[19] If this *was* a bubble, how much longer would prices increase and when would the bubble burst? Unlike stock market bubbles that rapidly crash within a matter of days or weeks, "housing bubbles typically do not *pop* like a balloon;... Rather, the air in housing bubbles tends to leak out slowly." Who knows "how long bubbles will last and when they will go bust?"[20]

Indicators in early 2006 did portend change; housing prices were still high, but new home sales had declined 18 percent from the previous year.[21] By the end of 2006, worries had come true. It was a bubble—and that bubble was deflating. In March 2009, average housing prices were down by 30 percent from their 2006 peak.[22]

---

16. Quotes and statistics in this paragraph from Coy et al., 2004; in 2000, average homeowners' equity was 55 percent of housing value, down from 72 percent in 1986.

17. Laing, 2005.

18. Laperriere, 2006.

19. Q4 HPI data from Standard & Poors/ Case-Shiller, 2011.

20. Thornton, 2004.

21. Q4 HPI data from Standard & Poors/ Case-Shiller, 2011; home sales from U.S. Census Bureau, 2011b.

22. Q4 HPI data from Standard & Poors/ Case-Shiller, 2011; HPI dropped ∼61 points from 190 in 2006 to 129 in Q1 2009.

8.3 AFFORDABILITY AND THE HOUSING BUBBLE

What does this housing bubble look like on paper? One way to view it is to observe changes in the affordability of housing relative to income. This metric, called the Housing Affordability Index, measures how many years of income equal the average price of a house.[23] If the affordability index stays constant when housing prices increase, we could conclude there is no bubble but that other factors (such as inflation) caused the increase.[24] On the other hand, we know that a bubble is present if this index rises, meaning that housing prices are increasing faster than income. So what actually happened to the index?

Prior to 1999 and as far back as 1980, the price of an average home was equivalent to just over 3 years of income. In 2006 that price exceeded 4.5 years of income; it had escalated since 1999. Like in the 1600s when tulip bulbs cost as much as a house, in 2006 houses cost too much relative to income: prices had reached a limit and simply had to drop.

Judging from this affordability measure, we suggest that the bubble extended from about 2000 when the index exceeded what it had been in the previous 5 years, until 2010 when the index had nearly returned to its long-term average. To illustrate the bubble, Figure 8.2 compares the affordability index with the House Price Index. As expected, when housing prices were their highest, houses were least affordable relative to annual income.

8.4 SUPPLY, DEMAND, AND THE HOUSING BUBBLE

Because the housing bubble was such a vital part of the crisis, it is crucial to our analysis. We could stop here, recognize its extent, and try to determine its causes, but we will go much deeper. By doing so, we can appreciate which factors are significant and which are not. We will discover that traditional economic forces and monetary policies had little power, whereas unpredictable factors and unexpected events blew air into the bubble, and then poked the big hole that deflated it. This detailed investigation begins with a quick review of supply and demand from Chapter 2.

In a competitive market like the housing market, laws of supply and demand govern the behavior of the price and quantity of goods, services, and other items that are bought and sold. Simply stated, when the price of an item is high, consumers buy fewer items and suppliers want to sell more to make money. When prices are low, the opposite is true: consumers buy more and suppliers sell less of the item. In a relatively stable environment, consumers and suppliers do a sort of dance, gliding toward an equilibrium point at which the quantity that consumers will

---

23. The Housing Affordability Index is the ratio between housing prices and income.
24. Dreiman, 2001.

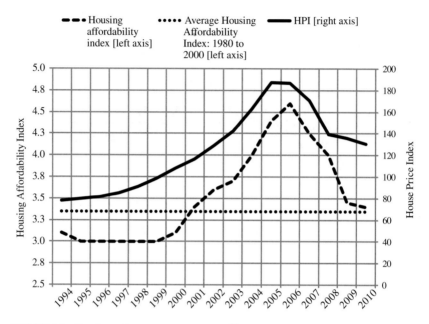

FIGURE 8.2   Housing Affordability Index vs. HPI.[25]

buy approaches the quantity supplied, at a price that satisfies both parties. This equilibrium price and quantity are cornerstones of discussions that follow. Refer to the Appendix for insight into movements and shifts of equilibrium price and quantity.

To investigate the dramatic changes in housing prices between 2000 and 2010, we combine basic concepts of supply and demand with our knowledge of the housing bubble. Tracing aggregate consumer and supplier behaviors allows us to connect price fluctuations to what are called shifts—shifts in demand, shifts in supply, or simultaneous shifts in both. By pushing price and quantity up and down, these shifts created new, temporary equilibrium points and thus generated the housing bubble. Describing equilibrium points as "temporary" will aid our translation of these relationships into systems thinking terms. To begin the analysis, we first look at changes in housing supply and demand during their most active period from 2000 to 2010. The discussion then separates into three distinct time periods, each of which contains different supply and demand shift behaviors.

25. Data from Joint Center for Housing Studies, 2007, 2011. The affordability index is computed using median housing prices and median income; HPI. from Standard & Poors/Case-Shiller, 2011.

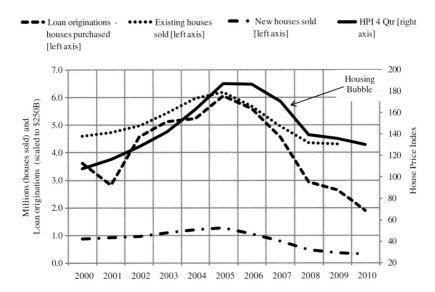

FIGURE 8.3   Housing demand indicators vs. HPI (2000–2010).[26]

8.4.1 Demand Indicators

For a demand-driven bubble, normal market behavior does not apply. Rather than demand decreasing when prices increase, in a bubble, the more people who want an item (and the greater their desire for it), the more they will pay. Here demand shifts and moves up instead of down with rising price. Figure 8.3 shows indicators of demand in the housing market (new houses sold, existing houses sold, and loan originations for houses purchased) relative to housing prices (HPI). As expected, these indicators mimic the shape of the housing bubble; they all increased until 2005 and then began to flatten or decrease.

8.4.2 Supply Indicators

Under normal market conditions or for demand-driven bubbles, if quantity demanded quickly rises to create a shortage, prices increase. When prices are higher, supply should also increase, perhaps after a delay that allows suppliers to respond to consumer behaviors. On the down side of a bubble, when demand reverses and prices decrease, supply should also decrease. This

---

26. Loan origination data from Mortgage Statistics, Feb 13, 2009 for 2001 and 2002 and from U.S. Census Bureau, 2012a for 2000, 2003–2009; HPI from Standard & Poors/Case-Shiller, 2011; new houses sold from U.S. Census Bureau, 2011b; existing homes sold from U.S. Census Bureau, 2011h.

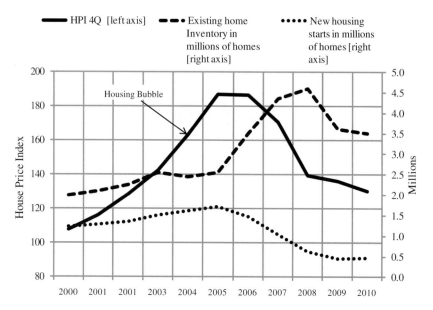

FIGURE 8.4   Housing supply indicators vs. HPI (2000–2010).[27]

relationship between housing prices and supply was mostly true for the housing bubble, with one exception. To illustrate this anomaly, Figure 8.4 compares housing price (HPI) with housing supply indicators that track homes already on the market (existing home inventory) and homes just being built (new housing starts). As we would expect, the trend for *new housing starts* approximates the fluctuation of housing prices. In other words, new housing grew until 2005 and then decreased as prices dropped. By 2007, *new housing starts* barely affected the total supply of housing.

Existing home inventory was a different story. Until 2005, it increased with rising prices as expected. It continued upward until 2006, even though housing prices were relatively flat—perhaps reflecting a lag in suppliers' response to consumers. After 2006 when prices dropped, we would anticipate *existing home inventory* to level off or *decline*. Instead, it *increased* sharply until 2008. Figure 8.5 combines housing prices and indicators of supply and demand on the same chart to show this behavior more clearly.

In this figure, all demand indicators and the *new housing starts* of supply displayed bubble behavior across the entire period, as expected. As demand

27. Existing inventory from Mahoney, 2011; Q2 data extrapolated from a graph based on National Association of Realtors/Haver Analytics (this inventory records what realtors have on the market and does not include sale by owner homes) [unavailable before 2000]; HPI from Standard & Poors/Case-Shiller, 2011; new privately owned housing units started (single family) data from U.S. Census Bureau, 2011g.

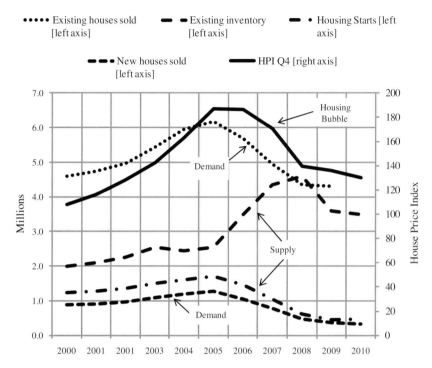

FIGURE 8.5   Supply and demand indicators compared (2000–2010).[28]

went up, prices and supply increased; as demand went down, prices and supply decreased. Clearly, however, the *existing inventory* part of supply climbed for a longer period and was higher than expected. This behavior stimulates questions: Why didn't inventory stop growing and what was its source? Was there just a delay between the decline in demand and the decline in supply or was something else happening? We will soon see. While there are many ways to interpret these supply and demand dynamics, I describe them as shifts in the following sections. We will later translate these shifts into systems thinking terms.

8.4.3 Housing Bubble Behavior: 2000 to 2006

During the six year ascent of the housing bubble, demand, supply, and prices all increased. This concurrent rise indicates that demand pressed the

---

28. New houses sold data from U.S. Census Bureau, 2011b; existing homes sold data from U.S. Census Bureau, 2012a; existing inventory data from Mahoney, 2011; Q2 data extrapolated from a graph based on National Association of Realtors/Haver Analytics (see note in previous footnote); HPI from Standard & Poors/Case-Shiller, 2011; new privately owned housing units started [single family] data from U.S. Census Bureau, 2011g.

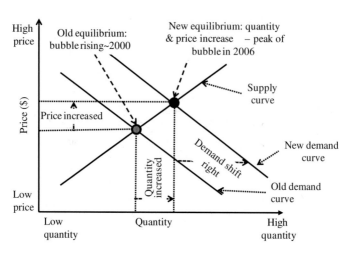

FIGURE 8.6   Demand shift on the upside of the housing bubble (2000–2006).

equilibrium point and caused a right shift in demand (see Appendix). To visualize this shift, compare the two large circles near the center of Figure 8.6. The circle toward the lower left shows the old equilibrium point in 2000. By 2006, this notional equilibrium had shifted up and to the right. As more people demanded homes, buyers were willing to pay higher prices and, in response to rising demand, the supply of homes for sale increased. This depiction tracks our knowledge that the housing bubble peaked in 2006 when housing prices were highest.

8.4.4 Housing Bubble Behavior: 2006 to 2008

Figure 8.5 showed that demand for houses quickly declined between 2006 and 2008 and Figure 8.1 showed that housing prices dropped over the same period. This simultaneous decrease in demand and price suggests that demand had shifted left; decreasing prices no longer attracted buyers. We would anticipate that when demand and price both decrease, supply should also decrease. However, between 2006 and 2008, existing home inventory *increased* over 30 percent to hit a high of 4.6 million houses for sale in 2008, while housing prices *decreased* by 18 percent.[29] Something odd was happening. Apparently the market was in transition; other forces, independent of demand, must have shifted supply to the right (increased quantity and decreased price). Simultaneous and opposite supply and demand shifts shown in Figure 8.7 created a most complex condition.

Note the two large circles in this notional graph. The upper circle marks the 2006 temporary equilibrium at the high point of demand and housing

29. HPI hit 156 in 2008 from its high of nearly 190 in early 2006.

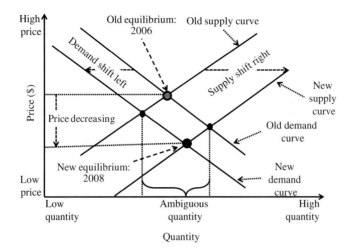

FIGURE 8.7   Demand and supply shifts on the downside of the housing bubble (2006−2008).

prices. The lower one shows that at the new equilibrium point in 2008, prices tumbled. Important conclusions from this graph are: (1) something had suddenly inverted demand in 2006; (2) combined forces of increasing supply and decreasing demand accelerated the drop in housing prices—it wasn't clear how low they would go, and (3) simultaneous and opposite shifts created a disparity between the *quantity demanded* and the *quantity available for sale*. In other words, demand pushed quantity down while supply pushed it up; uncertainty was mounting in the housing market. People were less willing to buy when they didn't know what would happen to their investment. This uncertainty further reduced demand. Was this the beginning of an overshoot-and-collapse condition?

The situation was even more complicated than a simultaneous shift suggests. One underlying factor all but disappeared in this struggle. Monetary policy, intended to stimulate the economy and thus increase demand for houses, reduce surplus inventory, and stabilize prices, was ineffective during this time period. By implementing deep reductions in interest rates, the Fed was arm wrestling other forces that apparently were more powerful. The Fed lost the match. Demand dropped, prices dropped, and increased supply made the price situation worse. No wonder people were insecure with the state of the economy.

8.4.5 Housing Bubble Behavior: 2008 to 2010

After 2008, supply, demand, and prices all traveled downward. Between 2008 and 2010, supply decreased 32 percent and housing prices (HPI) decreased 25 percent. These similar rates of decline indicated that supply

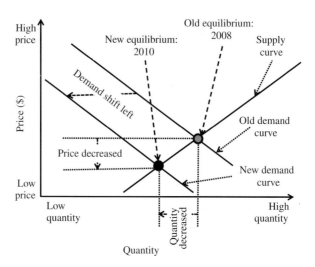

FIGURE 8.8   Demand shift on the downside of the housing bubble (2008–2010).

was now reacting to housing price decreases as expected, unlike in the previous two years. Figure 8.8 shows that demand continued to shift left between 2008 and 2010. Again note that both quantity and price decreased (the equilibrium point moved down and to the left). Supply, demand, price, and quantity were operating more normally.

8.5 REASONS FOR SUPPLY AND DEMAND SHIFTS

Having identified the presence of supply and demand shifts, we now consider economic mechanisms that could have caused these shifts. Generally, broad events such as changes in income, inflation, and interest rates can modify consumer demand and subsequently influence the price of goods and services (demand shift). Factors such as changes in competition and cost of raw materials or transportation can affect housing supply (supply shift). This section explores inflation, income, and monetary policy as possible explanations for housing demand shifts. At the end of the section, we suggest other forces related to the housing industry and to human traits that may have influenced supply and demand.

8.5.1 Inflation

To assess inflation's effects on the housing bubble, consider how prices actually changed relative to how they would have changed with inflation. If inflation were a major contributor to the bubble, price and inflation should

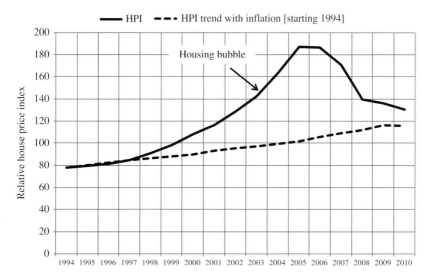

FIGURE 8.9   Housing bubble relative to inflation.[30]

follow the same trend. Figure 8.9 compares actual home prices (HPI) with what they would have been if inflation had been their only influence.[31]

The figure shows the characteristic hump of a bubble starting about 1998 (a couple years earlier than the affordability index indicated) and lasting through 2010: until 2006, housing prices grew much faster than inflation would have predicted. For example, the greatest annual appreciation in home prices (nearly 15 percent) occurred in 2005, a point at which inflation was only 3.4 percent.[32] By 2010, housing prices were slightly above where they would have been if governed solely by inflation. Thus, only a small part of the housing price increase can be attributed to inflation. Between 1994 and when prices peaked in 2006, cumulative inflation contributed about a 36 percent increase in average prices, but the price of homes went up about 140 percent—nearly four times faster than inflation.[33]

8.5.2 Income

Now let's consider whether annual income can explain housing price fluctuation. Ideally, if average incomes increase, more people can afford to buy a

---

30. Q4 HPI from Standard & Poors/Case-Shiller, 2011; inflation data from Historical Inflation, 2012.
31. If you bought a home for $100,000 in 1994 and inflation was 3 percent that year, your home should be worth $103,000 in 1995.
32. Although this level of inflation seems relatively low, it was the highest it had been since 2000.
33. Data used for comparisons were HPI: 77.89 in 1994, 186.44 in 2006; HPI from Standard & Poors/Case-Shiller, 2011; inflation from Historical Inflation, 2012.

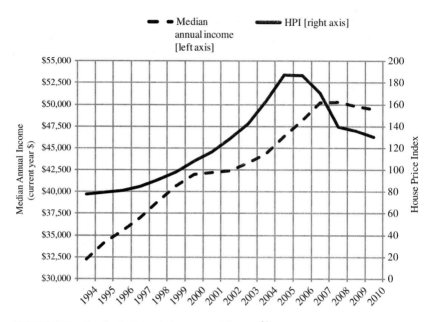

FIGURE 8.10 Housing bubble relative to annual income.[34]

home or upgrade to a bigger one, creating more demand and driving prices upward. Figure 8.10 shows that between 1994 and 2006 at the peak of the housing bubble, median income rose. Thus, we surmise that increased income *partially* explains why HPI ascended during that period: because people had more money to spend, they were willing to pay more for a home. Please note that this graph only depicts trends; it does not relate specific income increases to specific housing prices nor does it normalize the scales.

However, if income were the only reason for the rise in housing prices between 1994 and 2006, income and price should have moved at similar rates, which they did not. During those 13 years, income rose nearly 50 percent, but the price of homes went up about 140 percent—almost three times faster than income.[35] For the bubble's entire ascent, while income rose faster than inflation, it only partially explains the demand shift and subsequent rise in housing prices; other factors joined with income to increase demand and push prices so high.

Simultaneous and opposite shifts in supply and demand occurred between 2006 and 2008. Supply increased dramatically, while demand dropped and prices decreased by 25 percent. If income were the only contributor to this

34. Data from U.S. Census Bureau, 2011a; HPI from Standard & Poors/Case-Shiller, 2011.
35. Data used for comparisons in this section were HPI: 77.89 in 1994, 186.44 in 2006, 139.41 in 2008, and 130.38 in 2010; median income: $32,264 in 1994, $48,201 in 2006, $50,303 in 2008, and $49,445 in 2010. Income from U.S. Census Bureau, 2011a; HPI from Standard & Poors/Case-Shiller, 2011.

decrease in housing prices, income should have *declined* as well. However, during this period, income *rose* about 4 percent—perhaps the result of a lag, but certainly opposite our expectation. Thus, income had little effect during this period; other factors more powerful than income must have pushed housing prices down.

After 2008, housing prices and income both decreased, thus we could deduce that lower income caused housing prices to fall. However, because housing prices (HPI) dropped nearly four times faster than income, we must again conclude that other elements joined with income to push price farther down than income could have done by itself.

To review so far, for the entire duration of the bubble, income and inflation had a small influence on the demand that affected housing prices. More powerful factors caused demand and prices to rise and fall. On the bubble's upside from 2000 to 2006 and on the bubble's downside from 2008 to 2010, supply was mostly responsive to changes in demand. However, from 2006 to 2008 behavior of supply appeared irregular. Conditions that created a large increase in the supply of homes and those that decreased demand masked effects of income and inflation.

8.5.3 Monetary Policy

Chapter 2 described how the Fed uses monetary policy to encourage or discourage spending and to regulate inflation and unemployment.[36] Putting on the brake by increasing interest rates slows the economy and pushing the gas by decreasing interest rates stimulates the economy. In the case of housing, increased interest rates should reduce demand and decrease prices. Lower interest rates should increase demand and increase prices. Let us now consider what actually happened to housing prices when the Fed applied monetary policy.

Figure 8.11 shows the effect of interest rate changes on housing prices. It compares housing price behavior (HPI) with federal funds rates and with rates for long-term fixed rate mortgages (FRM) and 1-year adjustable rate mortgages (ARM). To offset the bursting of the dot-com bubble and the NASDAQ crash, the Fed drastically dropped the federal funds rate from its decade high of 6.5 percent in May 2000 to 1 percent in June 2003.[37] Although not as dramatically, interest rates for 30-year FRMs and 1-year ARMs also decreased during this time. As expected, with low interest rates people found it easier to finance their homes; as they bought more homes, demand increased and the price of housing rose 30 percent between 2000 and 2003 (demand shifted right).[38]

---

36. In this case, the Fed adjusts federal funds rates that determine interest rates on loans.
37. Data from FRBNY, 2011a.
38. HPI went from 100 to 130 between 2000 and 2003.

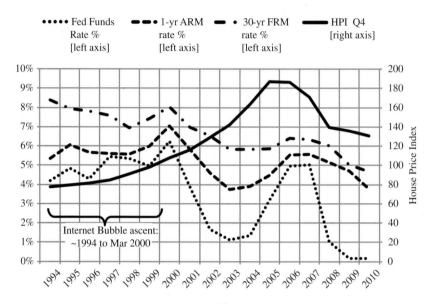

FIGURE 8.11   Interest rates and housing prices.[39]

Pushing the gas did its job for a while—perhaps too well. Low interest rates "sent a strong signal to the economy.... Increased housing demand encouraged home construction, which was already being given a boost by the low interest rates at which developers could borrow."[40] Thus, at least part of the housing price increase between 2000 and 2003 may attribute to lower interest rates.

However, when the Fed tried to cool the economy with higher rates in 2004, housing prices did not respond. In fact, between June 2004 and June 2006 the Fed increased interest rates 17 times[41] (intending to shift demand left). Prices during this 2-year period still climbed. This 2-year delay seems too long to be explained by the time it takes demand to respond to interest rates; other forces opposed monetary policy. Even when the federal funds rate reached 5 percent in 2006 and other mortgage interest rates increased, housing prices didn't drop as expected, but rose to an all-time high. Although monetary policy had placed modest downward pressure on inflation, between 2004 and 2005 it did not work well for housing prices.

In 2007, the Fed again tried monetary policy to counteract economic wounds suffered when housing prices plummeted. Intending to push the gas

---

39. Q4 HPI from Standard & Poors/Case-Shiller, 2011; "effective" federal funds rates from Board of Governors of the Federal Reserve System, Nov 2011b; annual average 1-year ARM rates from Freddie Mac, 2011c; annual average 30-year FRMs from Freddie Mac, Nov 2011b.
40. Rajan, 2010.
41. Data from FRBNY, 2011a.

(shift demand right), it decreased interest rates with the hope that the economy would rebound, and with the expectation that unemployment would stop growing[42] and housing prices would stabilize. Ten adjustments later, by December 2008 the federal funds rate bottomed out below 0.2 percent, 30-year mortgage rates hit 5.3 percent, and 1-year ARMs were just under 5 percent. Even with low interest incentives, fewer people wanted to buy a house. Housing prices tumbled. Pressure from the rising supply and declining consumer demand overpowered monetary policy and forced prices down.

From 2008 to 2010, both demand and supply depressed housing prices, but the Fed was powerless; at just under 0.2 percent, interest rates could go no lower. The Fed's only strategy now was to keep the interest rate steady, at least signaling a persistent intent to stimulate the economy. However, during this period, the *rate* at which housing prices were dropping had slowed, perhaps partially a result of monetary policy.

All these explanations can be easily summarized: except between 2000 and 2003, monetary policy was a weak and impotent tool against greater gorillas. This finding is nothing new. Galbraith's observation about the failure of monetary policy in the 1930s echoes the same message: "There are no cheap and easy inventions involving money alone that will solve all, or any, economic problems."[43]

8.5.4 Other Forces

In previous discussions, we alluded to *other forces* that labored harder than income and inflation, overpowered monetary policy, and shifted supply and demand in the housing market. These forces must have been extremely strong and capricious to cause such fluctuations and unstable conditions, particularly between 2006 and 2010. Now let's see what these mysterious *other forces* might be. We will assess them more fully in subsequent chapters.

8.5.4.1 Shift in Demand: Consumer Expectation

Expectations strongly influence consumer buying decisions and drive demand up or down. They can overwhelm reality, causing irrational behaviors. For example, people are more likely to buy a home if they expect prices to continue rising and are less likely to buy if they expect prices will decline or are uncertain about keeping their jobs in an unstable economy. Speculation, such as property flipping, plays a role in this area, particularly when housing prices are increasing. People purchase homes as an investment if they believe that they will make money by selling it later at a higher price.

---

42. Unemployment in 2006 and 2007 was relatively low at 4.6 percent; by 2008, it had reached 5.8 percent, and by 2010 it hit 9.6 percent (U.S. Bureau of Labor Statistics, 2012a).
43. Galbraith, 1977.

Chapter 5 discusses expectation and the Appendix briefly describes how expectation can cause a demand shift.

8.5.4.2 Shift in Demand: Financial Resources and Availability of Credit

Access to money, whether through income, investment gains, or loans, can drive housing demand up. If money is easily and broadly available, demand increases because more people can buy a home. However, if money is tight, such as during times of unemployment or when fewer people qualify for loans, demand will decrease.

8.5.4.3 Shift in Supply: Expectation of Builders

Supply increases when contractors build homes without a particular customer in mind, believing they can readily sell these homes for a profit. This strategy is an attractive way to make money when interest rates are low.

8.5.4.4 Shift in Supply: Unanticipated Influx of Homes for Sale

During the bubble period a huge number of homes went on the market after owners experienced foreclosure or bankruptcy. This flood of homes caused supply to shift, as we will discover in the next chapter.

8.6 SUPPLY AND DEMAND SHIFT SYNOPSIS

Our discussion of shifts in supply and demand is scattered over several pages, so for clarity, Table 8.1 summarizes these shifts and the behavior of quantity and price. The figure separates the decade between 2000 and 2010 into the three time periods we identified, each of which reflects a change in the direction of the supply and/or demand shift. It further divides these periods into segments in which monetary policy changed. Finally it adds the demand behavior that the Fed *intended* to inspire through monetary policy and describes whether that policy was successful.

Table 8.1 shows that abrupt shifts in demand caused housing prices to increase and decrease rapidly; the housing bubble inflated and burst. We learned earlier that inflation and income played a part in housing price changes, but that their influence was relatively weak. We also saw that since 2003, other dominant forces made monetary policy ineffective. By September 2008, Fed chairman Ben Bernanke must have been frustrated as he recognized that traditional "monetary policy was not working, and only a bailout of the financial system by Congress could stabilize the economy and avert a depression."[44]

---

44. Rajan, 2010.

TABLE 8.1 Summary of Supply and Demand Shifts and the Effects of Monetary Policy

Time Period	Actual Shift of Supply and Demand in the Housing Market				Intended Outcome of Applied Monetary Policy		Success of Monetary Policy
	Supply Shift Direction	Demand Shift Direction	Quantity	Price	Interest Rate Change	Intended Demand Shift	
2000–2003	None	Right	Increase	Increase	Down	Right	Effective
2003–2006	None	Right	Increase	Increase	Up	Left	Ineffective
2006–2007	Right	Left	Ambiguous	Decrease	None	None	No effect intended
2007–2008	Right	Left	Ambiguous	Decrease	Down	Right	Ineffective
2008–2009	None or minimal	Left	Decrease	Decrease	Down	Right	Ineffective
2009–2010	None or minimal	Left	Decrease	Decrease	None	None	No effect intended

8.7 SYSTEMS THINKING INTERPRETATION

Using systems thinking, organizational consultant Dennis Sherwood[45] describes a British railway boom and bust cycle in the late 1990s. He begins with a virtuous reinforcing loop showing that the company made profit and customers were satisfied. Suddenly, the psychological impact of a series of crashes turned this virtuous circle into "the nastiest of vicious circles" in which "exponential growth suddenly became exponential decline." The reason the bust occurred so quickly, he suggests, is that "the *fundamental structure of the system has remained exactly the same.*"

In the 1770s, Adam Smith alluded to this fundamental structure by describing behavior of market price relative to natural or equilibrium price. He noted that "different accidents may sometimes keep them suspended a good deal above it, and sometimes force them down even somewhat below it. But whatever may be the obstacles which hinder them from settling in this center of repose and continuance, they are constantly tending towards it."[46]

Let's pause a moment to understand the importance of this idea of fundamental structure. It is telling us that a system, such as an economic system, can exist in a relatively tranquil state of balance. It suggests that there are limits to this balance and that if we exceed these limits (the capacity of the system) something bad can happen (see Chapter 1). To illustrate this point, compare this fundamental structure to a steel-reinforced foundation of a skyscraper that can support a certain number of floors. As long as the builders do not exceed that number, everything is steady. If they add more floors without augmenting the foundation, the building will flatten from its own weight.

One way to view the housing bubble is to use Sherwood's railway example and the skyscraper analogy. Housing prices quickly ascended, but because the underlying structure of the housing market and the economy did not change, this accelerated growth was an anomaly. Rapid escalation overburdened the capacity of the economic system to support such growth—there were too many floors on this building. Housing prices had to drop to match the underlying structure. The powerful forces that overwhelmed monetary policy, overshadowed income and inflation, and tried to shift housing prices away from this structure ultimately failed.

8.7.1 Stability

The systems depiction of the housing bubble begins with a fundamental structure of stability, like the one Sherwood described. In this case, three forces maintain a stable economy: supply, demand, and monetary policy.

---

45. Sherwood, 2011.
46. Quotes from Smith, 1937.

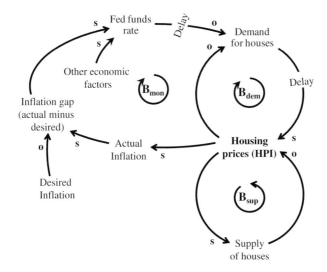

FIGURE 8.12   Stabilizing forces: Supply, demand, and monetary policy balancing feedback loops.

Using systems constructs from Chapter 2, Figure 8.12 combines supply and demand loops for housing with the monetary policy loop. The two balancing loops B_{demand} and B_{supply} move housing prices toward some equilibrium; the balancing feedback loop $B_{monetary}$ alters interest rates to keep inflation within desired bounds and, in doing so, regulates housing prices. A subtle but important change appears in this depiction of supply and demand compared with Figure 2.6. In this case, *actual housing price* (HPI) replaces *equilibrium housing price*. With this alteration, we can follow the dynamic effects of supply and demand as they move and shift actual housing prices toward an unstated temporary equilibrium.

To trace these stabilizing forces, we begin with *actual inflation*. When *actual inflation* is less than *desired inflation*, the Fed drops the *federal funds rate* to stimulate demand (in this case *demand for houses*). Higher *demand for houses* increases *housing prices (HPI)*, which increases *actual inflation*. Although not the only contributor, the cost of housing is a major factor used to calculate inflation.[47] Thus, housing prices have some influence on monetary policy. If *actual inflation* exceeds *desired inflation*, the *federal funds*

---

47. Inflation is calculated from the Consumer Price Index (CPI) that computes a weighted average of seven categories of goods and services, including food, clothing, and housing. Housing accounts for 41 percent of total CPI. The Fed combines sources for inflation to determine monetary policy. Besides CPI, they use a "core price index" that removes volatile elements such as food and energy (see Greenspan, 2000; U.S. Bureau of Labor Statistics, 2001).

rate rises to dampen *demand for houses*, which in turn decreases *housing prices* and reduces *actual inflation*.

Then when the *federal funds rate* drops, *demand for houses* increases in the B_{demand} loop, consumers buy more homes, and *housing prices* increase. When *housing prices* increase, suppliers want to profit, so the *supply of houses* goes up. Greater *supply* pushes *prices* back down. The loops operate continuously as actual housing prices *approach* equilibrium. Note that changes in interest rates shift demand to stimulate or slow the economy. In short, a change to interest rates eventually repositions the housing price equilibrium. As a point of interest, recall from Chapter 2 that the Fed also uses other indicators such as unemployment and GDP to determine when to change interest rate, and that external factors such as foreign investments also affect mortgage loan rates and demand.

Two delays represent the time for interest rate changes to influence the demand for houses, and for housing prices to respond to changing demand. These delays are important. If the Fed reacts before its previous actions have produced results or if it delays taking action, unstable behavior could occur. Here, we simply note the presence and importance of these delays; analyzing them would unduly complicate this simplified systems perspective.

8.7.2 Growth

Although the supply, demand, and monetary loops were active, conditions during the economic crisis were not stable; supply and demand shifts drove the housing market away from its underlying structure. Partial explanations for the shifts involve the expectation that housing prices will rise which was, in part, stimulated by *home buying policies and practices*. The systems representation of these behaviors add the reinforcing feed-forward loop ($R_{expectation}$) from Chapter 5 and a new loop ($B_{contractor}$) built on *contractor speculation* to the three stabilizing loops in Figure 8.12. In this depiction, $R_{expectation}$ increases demand while $B_{contractor}$ adds new houses to supply. Figure 8.13 shows these additional loops with dashed lines.

As we know from Chapter 5, expectation is a potent influence in an economy. If people expect prices to rise, they will want to buy an asset before prices increase further or with the intent to sell later for profit. In either case, these expectations increase demand and raise housing prices, thus creating a demand shift. The loops in this figure reflect this dynamic. *Expectation that housing prices will rise* pushes *demand for houses* upward and ultimately increases *housing prices*. Escalation of *housing prices* amplifies the desire to invest in the housing market, and increased *demand for housing* drives *housing prices* even higher. Slightly increased *financial resources* (income) and easy *availability of credit* add pressure to demand and to price escalation.

When the expectation reinforcing loop overwhelmed the supply, demand, and monetary balancing loops, we saw the upside of a bubble.

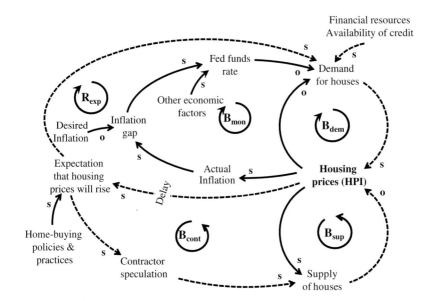

FIGURE 8.13 Expectation and contractor speculation destabilize housing prices.

Because bubbles rely on a "herd mentality" in which prices continue to rise as long as the herd believes that they will, "bubbles survive."[48] Expectation became the self-fulfilling prophecy mentioned in earlier chapters. Inspecting the expectation loop more closely, we most likely witnessed an *irrational exuberance* of confidence that housing prices would continue to rise.

Expectation also affected the supply balancing loop (B$_{supply}$) through another balancing loop (B$_{contractor}$). This new loop strengthened the effects of B$_{supply}$ by adding to the existing supply of houses. Figure 8.4 showed a remarkable 40 percent increase in new housing starts between 2000 and 2005,[49] some of which came from contractor speculation. Tracing the new balancing loop B$_{contractor}$ in Figure 8.13, as the *expectation that housing prices will rise* grows, *contractor speculation* to build new homes increases; new homes raise the *supply of houses*, which tend to reduce *housing prices* and we are back on the path from *prices* to *expectations*. However, especially between 2000 and 2006, expectation increased demand and overshadowed the potential effects of additional supply; prices escalated.

---

48. Haji, 2004.
49. "New privately owned housing units started" from U.S. Census Bureau, 2011g; in 2000, new housing starts were 1.23 million and grew to 1.72 million by 2005, the peak year. By 2007 they decreased to 1.05 million and by 2009, less than 450,000 homes were started.

8.7.3 Decline

Housing prices plunged from 2006 until 2008, and then dropped more slowly through 2010. What caused this sudden reversal? One possibility is that something in the economy touched expectations and turned optimism about housing prices into pessimism. If this occurred, the expectation reinforcing loop $R_{expectation}$ would create an opposite effect and drive demand down. A related possibility is that when demand started to drop and prices declined, the supply balancing loop (B_{supply}) didn't respond normally to reduce supply. The combination of both possibilities would substantially shift housing prices downward and signal the market to expect decreasing prices.

We can trace these behaviors in Figure 8.13 beginning with a change in expectation. In the $R_{expectation}$ loop, when the *expectation that housing prices will rise* turns pessimistic, *demand* decreases. Less *demand* reduces *housing prices*; lower *prices* (over time) diminish the *expectation that housing prices will rise*, and now our virtuous circle will turn into a vicious circle unless it can be stabilized by lower supply in the B_{supply} loop. Normally, lower prices would decrease supply, however, our data show that net supply increased, although contractor speculation (housing starts and new homes sold) declined rapidly. Now the supply balancing loop *contributes* to price decrease (rather than limits it) and further feeds the pessimistic expectation about housing prices.

In fact, statistics support our explanation. Confidence in the economy waned just months after housing prices peaked, dropping nearly 20 percent in 2007, and over 75 percent between January 2007 and early March 2009;[50] aggregate supply increased significantly between 2005 and 2008 (see Figure 8.5). What had happened to change the optimistic expectation and invert supply? I propose they were both affected by the same root cause, namely the fallout from defaulting high-risk loans. In the next chapter we explore this possibility more fully when we introduce debt into our systems picture.

By applying systems thinking to the phenomena we have seen so far, we surmise that the expectation about housing prices had reached its *limit-to-growth* and exhibited the *overshoot-and-collapse* behavior described in Chapter 1. In this case, individuals' ability to feel confident about rising housing prices had eroded and could not be reclaimed even by low interest rates or other positive factors.

8.7.4 Candidate Leverage Points

In the partial systems picture of the crisis in Figure 8.13, two candidate leverage points could have diminished the housing bubble's ascent. These levers do not come from the inflation, income, or monetary policy that we

---

50. Short, 2012; Conference Board Consumer Confidence Index was ~ 110 in early 2007, ~ 90 in early 2008, and fell to ~ 25 the first few months of 2009.

highlighted in this chapter. Instead they originate in consumers' *ability* to buy a home and their *expectation* that buying a home is a good investment. The first involves the demand for houses. Here, reduced *financial resources* or less *availability of credit* causes *demand* to drop in the B_{demand} balancing loop and dampens housing price increases. The second engages the expectation about housing prices. Here less aggressive *policies and practices* that promote home buying would temper beliefs about the future housing market (expectations) and slow the $R_{expectation}$ loop, thus limiting housing price increases. These two leverage points and their underlying constructs are more fully developed in subsequent chapters when we introduce debt and integrate human attributes.

8.8 SUMMARY

Bubbles begin when the price of an asset rises above what can be explained by traditional mechanisms (such as supply and demand, inflation, income, or monetary policy)—above its fundamental structure. They end when price corrects itself, leaving those who bought at the bubble's peak in a bind. This bubble phenomenon was a primary feature of the economic crisis. Affordability data showed that a huge housing price bubble existed between 2000 and 2010. Because the bubble was such a significant component of the economic engine that crashed in 2008, we viewed it from different perspectives. Traditional mechanisms could not explain it. Instead, other factors related to the housing and financial industries and to human behaviors drove consumer and supplier decisions. We summarize our findings as follows:

- At their peak in 2006, housing prices were nearly double what they had been 6 years earlier. Houses were overpriced by nearly 1.5 times relative to historic income levels.
- The effects of inflation and income, while present, were minimal. Except between 2000 to 2003, monetary policy barely touched housing prices.
- On the upside of the bubble, between 2000 and 2006, rising demand fueled by an *expectation that prices would rise* drove prices and the supply of houses up.
- The downhill side of the bubble between 2006 and 2008 revealed instability. Independent forces battled for control, some of which we discuss in the next chapter. In this chapter, monetary policy (which should have slowed the slide of housing prices) struggled with consumers' eroded expectations. Demand was squelched, but supply was unusually high. Uncertainty mounted.
- From 2008 to 2010 at the tail end of the bubble's slide, diminishing demand prodded by fear, dashed hopes, and shattered expectations, was a dominant factor that drove prices downward. Supply finally decreased as

demand and price dropped. Perhaps at this point, monetary policy's small effects slowed the rate at which prices declined.

In the systems interpretation, the center of action was housing prices that were continuously adjusted by the two supply and demand balancing feedback loops and the monetary policy balancing loop. In theory, in a normal economic environment these loops work together to stabilize the housing market and maintain a desired level of inflation. They describe the fundamental structure to which the market may finally return after a bubble bursts.

During the bubble timeframe, other forces also contributed to the rise and fall of housing prices. The predominant influence was a reinforcing loop built upon the *expectation that housing prices will rise*. The systems diagram showed that *home buying policies and practices* increased this expectation and that *financial resources* and *availability of credit* encouraged demand. From these factors, we quickly appreciate how optimistic expectations created a self-fulfilling prophecy around rising prices and generated the upside of the housing bubble. We also saw that during the ascent of housing prices, effects of contractor speculation and increased supply were too weak to counterbalance growing demand.

Less straightforward was how this systems structure operated on the bubble's downside. Here we proposed that the *expectation the housing prices will rise* had reached its limit and that the supply balancing loop didn't do its job, both of which may have been instigated by an external factor related to mortgage loan defaults. In any event, housing prices went quickly back down to their fundamental structure. We will more fully develop our insights into these conditions in the next chapter.

Finally, we looked for leverage that might have taken some pain out of the bubble. None of the major factors from this chapter (income, inflation, and monetary policy) appeared significant. To be thorough, we note here that some economists believe that monetary policy is a negative contributor to the economy and that its simple presence explains boom and bust behavior.[51] Since this perspective has been debated for decades,[52] we leave conjecture about its effectiveness to the experts.

Another view of monetary policy during the economic crisis challenges the Fed's focus on inflation as a trigger to change rates without considering specific asset-price bubbles in their policies.[53] The Fed *dramatically*

51. Woods, 2009; Austrian economic theory, for example, claims that by manipulating interest rates at all, the Fed artificially injects mismatching forces into the economy; this theory proposes that interest rates should be allowed to operate freely based on supply and demand for borrowed funds.
52. For example, building on von Mises' theory (von Mises, 1981), Nobel laureate F.A. Hayek (2007) developed a theory of the business cycle that describes the root of the boom-bust cycle (Woods, 2009). More recently, the Fed has tied monetary policy to unemployment; interest rates will continue to be low as long as unemployment rates are above 6.5 percent (Appelbaum, 2012).
53. Morris, 2008.

decreased interest rates from 2000 to 2002 even though housing prices were rising. Such a policy would not only increase inflation, but would also add to the demand for houses and increase housing prices, further inflating the housing bubble.

Since we concluded that monetary policy as it was implemented was not a strong contributor at this point in our analysis, we set it aside and identified two other candidate leverage points in our partial systems diagram: *financial resources* and *availability of credit* that encouraged demand, and *home buying policies and practices* that fueled the *expectation that housing prices will rise*. We discuss these levers in Chapters 9 and 12 in the context of debt and foreclosures. Chapter 12 examines global repercussions of the U.S. housing bubble.

Chapter 9

On Top of Debt Mountain: High-Risk Loans and Credit

The frenzied lending hit an apex in 2006.... An incredible $250 billion in the riskiest stated-income, no-down-payment subprime loans were originated. In truth, barely anyone expected these loans to be around very long. The expectation was not that they would default, but that they would be refinanced before trouble hit.

Zandi[1]

Even after the bubble had burst, mortgage brokers were still running radio and television ads touting mortgages that could be approved within an hour, with no scrutiny at all, and made available within a week.

Münchau[2]

If you have ever hiked to the top of a high mountain, you know exhilaration. On the way up, your energy sparks, the territory is new, and your goal lies ahead. At the summit, you inhale with a sense of accomplishment and view the world anew. This feeling is especially satisfying if the mountain is one like Telescope Peak in Death Valley, California where the air is clear and the vista is spectacular. Here, you can see as "far as a telescope"—west to the Panamint Valley and Mount Whitney and east to Badwater, an arid, below-sea-level salt basin.

Once you've experienced the highs of attitude and altitude, coming back down can be draining, especially when you're weary and your toes are rubbing the inside of your boots. However, if you feel adventurous, you might choose a different way down. Instead of returning to the trailhead some 7 miles and 3000 feet below, you could take the 21-mile trek to Badwater. This way down, with its drastic drop in elevation, is tough. The terrain is steep. Parts of the hike are unmarked and little-traveled. You might stumble and fall.

---

1. Zandi, 2009.
2. Münchau, 2010.

In some ways, the U.S. economic crisis is like this mountain trek. However, rather than climbing Telescope Peak for the view, people hiked Debt Mountain to experience feelings of well-being and "having arrived." On their way to the summit, they purchased dream homes and satisfied yearnings with whatever borrowed money could buy. Yes, the trip up this mountain was fun, but the journey down—repaying the accumulating debt— was rarely considered. Why bother? After all, rising housing prices made individuals feel wealthy; they could stay up here forever.

However, this wealth had been inflated with the stale air of the housing bubble. Because people had reached such heights without considering nega-tive consequences, their pleasant reveries were disturbed by the thud of past-due bills. For them, the way down the mountain would not be on the benign trail; that path had been washed away by the flood of falling housing prices and rising interest rates. Instead, debtors faced the Badwater route into the territory of loan defaults and bankruptcies.

The debt on this mountain was no ordinary debt. This massive accumula-tion not only stimulated the U.S. housing bubble, it also decimated the finan-cial market (as we will discover in the next chapter). This chapter describes the ascent up Debt Mountain and the slide down the other side into a finan-cial morass. Our journey on this mountain has four segments. The first describes the easy availability of credit, and considers what created the per-missive loan environment and why. The second segment shows how this lax climate incubated subprime and ARM loans. Here we expose the cache of risk in the housing market. In the third segment we find debt that individuals used to buy products other than housing. Finally at the top, we encounter the slippery descent into loan defaults and foreclosures that instigated the U.S. economy's dive and triggered global recession.

Although the journey includes many statistics, don't be side-tracked by the numbers. Concentrate instead on the trends these numbers describe. Note that in all cases, debt, defaults, and foreclosures reached unprecedented heights. Consider also how these factors link to economic policies, interest rates, desires, expectations, and the housing market.

9.1 JOURNEY SEGMENT ONE: EASY AVAILABILITY OF CREDIT

In its discussion of the housing bubble, Chapter 8 showed how expectations and availability of credit elevated demand and prices for houses. The credit gates had opened to those who could never before qualify for a home loan or needed special terms. High-risk loans were more abundant than ever. What was so different this time? Why were risky loans so easy to get? What encouraged them? Figure 9.1 shows three significant reasons for their profu-sion: (1) government and industry home-buying policies and incentives since the 1980s; (2) increased competition in the mortgage market beginning in

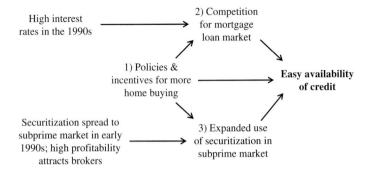

FIGURE 9.1   Origins of the easy availability of credit.

the early 1990s; and (3) expanded use of subprime loan securitization in the early 2000s.

9.1.1 Policies and Incentives for Home Buying

As more Americans confronted stagnant or declining incomes in the late-1980s, the U.S. government introduced "fast-acting measures"[3] to remedy the situation. By allowing income tax deductions for interest on home loans, the Tax Reform Act of 1986 stimulated demand for mortgage loans.[4] Then the 1992 Federal Housing and Enterprise Safety and Soundness Act promoted "affordable housing for low-income groups."[5] Between 1995 and 2004, numerous government and financial industry policies urged the U.S. housing industry and its regulators to help more people buy homes (particularly minority and low-income households).[6] Together, these policies nourished a conviction that more loans to more people were just what America needed.

9.1.2 Competition for Mortgage Loan Market

With an emphasis on home buying that spanned nearly two decades, the era of risky loans flourished. In addition to an ambiance of encouragement, a second condition surfaced. In 1993 when interest rates climbed[7] and the market for prime loans weakened, competition intensified. Struggling to maintain loan volume and meet government mandates, lenders pursued untapped

---

3. Rajan, 2010.
4. Chomsisengphet and Pennington-Cross, 2006.
5. Rajan, 2010.
6. See Chapter 2 for specific policies and regulations.
7. Federal funds rates rose nearly 2 percent from 1993 to 1995, and continued rising until 2000 when they hit over 6 percent (Board of Governors of the Federal Reserve System, Nov 2011b).

markets—particularly the market for subprime and affordability loans.[8] More of these high-risk loans meant more profit for lenders.

9.1.3 Expanded Securitization of Subprime Loans

The entrée of subprime loans into the financial market involved securitization (structuring mortgage loans into securities). In the mid-1990s, high returns on these risky securities attracted more investors.[9] New brokers entered the business and pressed lenders to make more loans, often without concern for borrowers' qualifications. In this case, more high-risk loans meant more profit from high-risk securities.

9.1.4 Convergence of Pressure for Easy Credit

By the early 2000s, pressure to generate home loans had closed in from three sides: government agencies, lenders, and securities agents. All three shared the goal of providing loans to an expanded population. Government agencies wanted more people to own homes; lenders wanted to increase profits; and financial institutions wanted to sell more mortgage-related securities. The pressure was indeed strong and the environment found ways to relieve it. By 2002, more people applied for loans, fewer loans were denied,[10] and risk multiplied.

9.2 JOURNEY SEGMENT TWO: HIGH-RISK LOANS

In decades past, only those with good credit, steady income, and adequate assets qualified for a home loan. Pushed by government goals and pulled by profit, lenders offered loans with adjustable rates or payment options, provided subprime loans to high-risk borrowers, reduced or eliminated loan qualifications, and incentivized employees to increase loan volume.[11]

Besides offering easily available credit, two features of subprime and ARM loans explain their popularity: cost deferral and complexity.[12] Borrowers could finally afford to get into a home and shove the real cost of financing into the future with the hope that their incomes and the value of their homes would grow. Loans were too complex to comparison shop or even to understand long-term ramifications. When they were offered loans that required little qualification, individuals with poor credit rushed in.

---

8. Chomsisengphet and Pennington-Cross, 2006.
9. Chomsisengphet and Pennington-Cross, 2006.
10. Gramlich, 2007 (from Home Mortgage Disclosure Act data, 2005); denial rate dropped in half from just over 30 percent in 1997 to about 15 percent in 2002.
11. In 1992, Countrywide began its "House America" program committed to multibillion dollar goals for high-risk loans. See Ferrell et al., 2010; McLean and Nocera, 2010.
12. Bar-Gill, 2009.

Of course, the higher probability of default on these loans meant greater risk for lenders.

9.2.1 Subprime and ARM Loans

Of the three loan categories (prime, Alt-A, and subprime), subprime loans have the greatest risk of default: subprime borrowers have the lowest credit ratings. And of the two commonly used loan types, adjustable rate mortgages (ARMs) pose more risk than fixed rate mortgages (see Chapter 2). Both Alt-A and subprime loans use ARM loan types. To appreciate how risk multiplied prior to 2008, we will consider statistics on ARMs and on subprimes, recognizing that in some cases these statistics overlap.

Spurred by incentives and policies, the use of subprime loans grew rapidly. In 1995, the *number* of new subprime loans originated rested just above 83,000; by 2003, this number had grown 20 times larger to over 1.6 million.[13] In 2007, there were 7.75 million active subprime loans—about 14 percent of all outstanding mortgage loans in the United States.[14] Annual *market share* of these loan types also grew. Between 2001 and 2006, the share of subprime loans increased from 7 to over 20 percent of all loans.[15] In other words, in 2006 about 1 in every 5 new loans was likely made to someone with low credit ratings and poor repayment history.

ARMs were popular with borrowers whose resources were stretched thin. The percent of ARMs quickly rose from less than a fifth of all mortgage loans in 2003 to over a third in 2005; 1 in every 3 borrowers that year would be vulnerable to rising interest rates when their loans reset. By 2006 there were nearly 10 million ARMs, a large number of which were scheduled to reset in 2007 and 2008.[16] In 1995 about a fourth of all subprime loans originated were ARMs; by 2003, over half were. The *number* of subprime ARMs originated during those years grew 40-fold from around 21,000 to over 866,000.[17] ARMs with interest-only and payment-options[18] went from

---

13. Statistics from Chomsisengphet and Pennington-Cross, 2006; ARM data derived from the LoanPerformance ABS securities database.
14. Kroszner, 2007.
15. FRBSF, 2008; Joint Center for Housing Studies, 2008. These sources are slightly different in 2006; FRBSF notes 25 percent market share for subprimes and the Joint Center for Housing Studies notes nearly 20 percent.
16. Knox, 2006.
17. Chomsisengphet and Pennington-Cross, 2006; ARM data in their discussion came from the extensive LoanPerformance ABS securities database.
18. Option loans payments barely cover or are less than interest; ARM interest rates reset after some term.

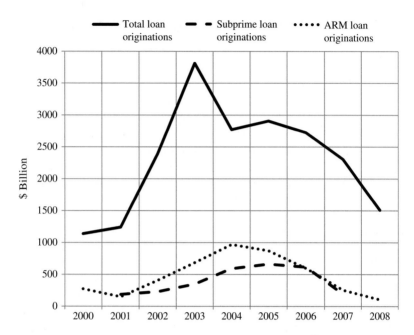

FIGURE 9.2   Subprime and ARM loan types vs. total loan originations.[19]

2 percent of loans originated in 2003 to 20 percent in 2005; in 2006, the less risky prime loans accounted for fewer than half of the loans originated.[20]

These statistics are doubly alarming because the money involved was staggering. Figure 9.2 shows that although total loan originations dropped after their nearly $4 trillion high in 2003, riskier loans raced on.[21] ARM originations grew to about $1 trillion in 2004 and only began to fall when interest rates rose. In 2005 and again in 2006, subprime loan originations reached over $600 billion.[22] Risk was accumulating: fewer prime loans, more subprime, ARM, and affordable option loans. Mortgage lenders were grinding

19. Subprime loan origination data from Joint Center for Housing Studies, 2008, Table A-6 (also see FRBSF, 2008) less nonprime home equity loans; ARM data to compute loan origination from Joint Center for Housing Studies, 2010. Note $B are 2007 $; total loan originations from U.S. Census Bureau, 2012a.

20. Joint Center for Housing Studies, 2008. Alt-A loans grew from 2.5 percent in 2001 to nearly 15 percent in 2006; prime loans accounted for 80 percent of loans in 2001.

21. From 2005 to 2007, Countrywide Financial and Wells Fargo accounted for nearly 30 percent of all originations. Countrywide incentivized high-risk mortgage loans and made 7 percent of all subprime originations and 16.2 percent of all Alt-A loans (Congressional Oversight Panel, 2010).

22. Joint Center for Housing Studies, 2008.

out risky loans like fat sausages and borrowers were only too happy to gobble them up.

9.2.2 Growth of Risk

These statistics speak to the unprecedented acceleration of high-risk-of-default loans in the early 2000s. On the surface, growth was good news for the economy. The housing industry boomed. More houses built meant more jobs for housing-related businesses; more houses sold generated commissions for realtors and profit for speculators. However, beneath the patina of sales and jobs, risk lay in wait. Because subprime loans and ARMs were a foundation for the housing bubble, as loans increased, risk multiplied and piled on the potential for disaster. If something major were to happen with these loans, consequences would reverberate like a shockwave.

And as we know, something major did happen: interest rates increased and ARMs reset. From 2003 to 2006, federal funds rates rose 4 percent and brought ARM interest rates with them. Borrowers whose ARMs had low initial teaser rates were particularly stunned when their payments soared. Higher interest rates not only boosted monthly payments, they also squashed demand for houses. In 2006, the tide of subprime loan originations began to recede. Lower demand and higher interest pushed housing prices down. By then, homeowners couldn't afford their loans, couldn't borrow more money, and couldn't sell without loss—if they could sell at all. Their next step was default. Before exploring the shock of defaulting loans on the mortgage market, let's see what else added to consumers' burdens.

9.3 JOURNEY SEGMENT THREE: ACCUMULATION OF DEBT

Three types of debt shaped the growing mountain: (1) mortgage loans to own a home, including high-risk loans described above; (2) home equity-related loans; and (3) consumer credit.

9.3.1 Home Ownership Loans

With each passing year, the mushrooming number of new loans enlarged homeowners' debt. Of total home loans originated, Figure 9.3 delineates two types: loans to purchase a home and loans to refinance an existing home. Home purchase loans were above $1 trillion each year between 2002 and 2007. Even at this level, when total loan originations peaked in 2003, home purchase loans accounted for only about a third of the total; the dramatic growth that year came from refinancing.

Refinance loans have two uses: one related to home ownership and one related to using equity when a home's price increases. Refinance loans associated with ownership may improve the terms of existing mortgages. In the

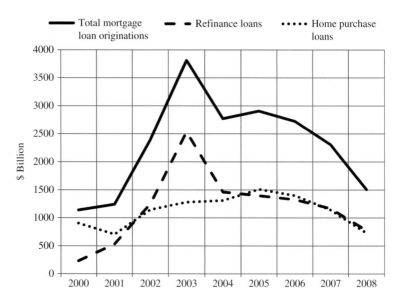

FIGURE 9.3   Home purchase and refinance loans vs. total loan originations.[23]

second case, homeowners refinance larger loans with the appreciated value of their home, *cash out* the equity, and spend the extra money. These loans *increase* total mortgage debt. Thus the mountain of accumulating debt was built on more than buying homes; it included money borrowed to spend on other items.

9.3.2 Home Equity Loans

When housing prices escalated, home equity loans created sudden windfalls for some borrowers. These loans include the equity *cash-out* refinance loans noted above and *new* loans that use equity from the home's higher value as collateral. In either case, households could borrow money to pay other debts, make home improvements, or pay for autos, vacations, education, and medical expenses.[24] Rather than putting money aside, people spent more than they had and gambled that housing prices would continue to rise. Certainly there was no more saving for a rainy day. Savings dropped from 11 percent

---

23. Mortgage loan origination data from U.S. Census Bureau, 2012a; Joint Center for Housing Studies (2008) shows substantially higher numbers from 2001 to 2003; other sources show over $5 trillion in 2003 (see Zandi, 2009; data from HMDA; and Moody's Economy.com).

24. 2001 and 2003 surveys note these uses; see Canner et al., 2002; Kindleberger and Aliber, 2005.

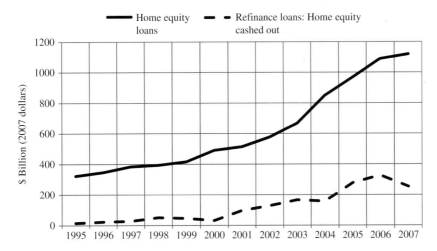

FIGURE 9.4   Debt created by home equity related loans (1995−2007).[25]

of disposable personal income in 1982 to 1.4 percent in 2005; it remained under 2 percent until 2007.[26]

Figure 9.4 shows a steady increase of home equity and cash-out refinance loans between 1995 and 2006. Across the U.S., equity-related debt used for other than buying a home hit over $1.4 trillion in 2007; cash taken from refinance loans alone reached $330 billion in 2006. By then, collateral for these loans was shaky: housing prices and equity were tumbling.

Taking out home equity loans didn't satisfy material desires or soften the country's inclination to consume. The third type of debt, consumer credit, stuffed household pocketbooks so that consumers could keep on buying.

9.3.3 Consumer Credit

Consumer credit contains revolving debt (including credit cards) and nonrevolving debt (for items such as automobiles, education, mobile homes, and boats). Although not directly related to housing, consumer credit was boosted by rising housing prices. Low-income households with subprime loans could now "obtain other forms of nonmortgage credit" based on the growing equity in their

---

25. Joint Center for Housing Studies, 2008, Table A-4 Mortgage, Cash-Out, and Home Equity Loan Volumes: 1995−2007. No data before 1995. Home equity cashed out is the difference between the size of the mortgage after refinance and 105 percent of the balance outstanding on the original mortgage.
26. McCully, 2011; from 1999 to 2007 home owners were net borrowers, i.e., they borrowed rather than saved; before 1999 and after 2007, home owners were savers and provided funds for others to borrow.

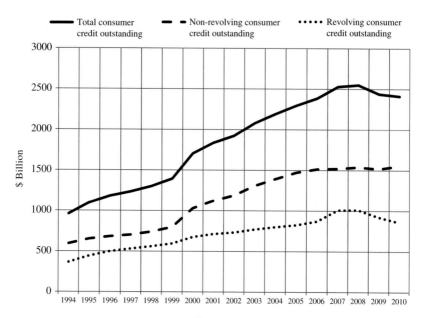

FIGURE 9.5   Consumer credit outstanding.[27]

recently purchased homes.[28] Credit card debt for these households rose nearly 75 percent between 1989 and 2004.[29] This statistic is noteworthy in itself, but when compared with the declining credit card debt for high-income families, we find that "the rapid spread of indebtedness was concentrated in poorer segments of the population."[30] As credit card debt in low-income households mounted up, risk of nonpayment also grew. Figure 9.5 shows over $2.5 trillion total U.S. consumer credit outstanding in 2008.

So what do consumer credit and equity cash-outs have to do with the housing bubble? Simply put, they reduced homeowners' ability to make monthly payments on their home loans and increased the likelihood of default and foreclosure.

9.3.4 Systems Description of Debt Growth

So far we've seen many graphs depicting debt. Their common theme is unparalleled growth over time: new home purchase and refinance loans rose until 2003; subprime and ARM loans grew until 2004; home equity

---

27. Data combined from Federal Reserve Board (1999, 2000, 2005, 2008, 2009, 2011, 2012).
28. Rajan, 2010.
29. Belsky et al., 2008. Data from the Survey of Consumer Finance conducted by the Fed.
30. Rajan, 2010.

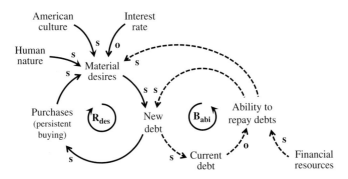

FIGURE 9.6   "Ability to repay" balancing loop limits new debt and material desires.

loans went up until 2006; consumer debt grew until 2008. The reinforcing loop R_{desire} from Chapter 4 illustrates this unrelenting increase in new debt and purchases. In a culture where property and things measure one's worth, consumers ran full speed on the hedonic treadmill depicted by this loop. The more material desires they had, the more purchases they made; the more purchases, the more they desired. Each pass around the loop added new debt which grew unrestrained. The built-in limiter for excessive debt, namely ability to repay, unfortunately had failed to do its job.

To visualize how such a limit could have worked, we rely on the systems thinking limits-to-growth construct from Chapter 1 called S-shaped growth. Figure 9.6 shows how the balancing loop $B_{ability}$ would curtail the growth of debt in the reinforcing loop R_{desire} when debt approached its capacity (i.e., the borrower's ability to repay). In this case, debt would smoothly level off as borrowers realized they could not afford to borrow any more money.

In this diagram, *financial resources* (such as income) are compared with *current debt* to determine consumers' *ability to repay debts*. If they can manage more debt than they have (positive *ability to repay debts*), they can take on *new debt* to make *purchases*. While more *purchases* increase *material desires*, more *new debt* adds to *current debt* and reduces *ability to repay debt* in the $B_{ability}$ loop. As current debt grows to the point that consumers can no longer manage it (zero or negative *ability to repay debts*), they must contain their *material desires* and stop taking on *new debt*. Less *new debt* means fewer *purchases* and stable or lower *current debt*. When current debt drops, consumers can again accumulate *new debt* until they can no longer manage it with their financial resources. Thus, under normal circumstances, $B_{ability}$ limits the growth of new debt to an individual's *realistic* ability to repay it.

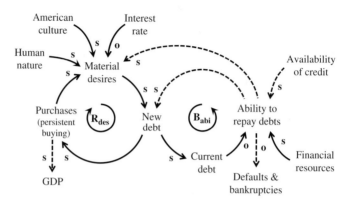

FIGURE 9.7 Availability of credit encourages new debt and material desires.

9.3.5 Weakened Limits for Debt

As we know, circumstances leading up to the crisis were far from normal. Borrowers were inundated with debt well beyond their ability to repay. What created this condition? Why had the balancing loop failed? Figure 9.7 shows that in reality $B_{ability}$ not only relied on existing financial resources to limit new debt, it also depended on easy credit that falsely augmented individuals' ability to repay. This easy-money atmosphere stimulated consumers' material desires in the R_{desire} reinforcing loop, escalated purchases, and drove new debt even higher. Unimpeded by sensible limits, households accrued unreasonable debt that they couldn't possibly afford.

What happened when the burden grew too heavy? What happened when equity cash-outs were spent, credit cards were maxed, and ARM resets made monthly mortgage payments skyrocket? What happened when housing prices dropped and borrowers' homes were worth less than what they owed?[31] In the end, "consumption cannot grow faster than income because there is an upper limit to how much debt households can service, based on their incomes."[32] With unmanageable debt, many households searched for a way to shed their massive loads. The final segment of our journey describes their choices.

9.4 JOURNEY SEGMENT FOUR: DEFAULTS, BANKRUPTCIES, AND FORECLOSURES

When housing prices were rising and anyone could get a loan, everyone was happy. This trend fed demand for homes, encouraged excessive borrowing, and made people comfortable with loans they could barely afford. But once

31. This situation is called negative equity or "being upside down."
32. Glick and Lansing, 2009.

at the top of Debt Mountain, those who had exceeded their ability to repay found only one path down; they descended into arid land where defaults, bankruptcies, and foreclosures popped up like salt crystals in Badwater Basin.

9.4.1 Waves of Loan Defaults

Moody's economist Mark Zandi described three waves of mortgage loan defaults and foreclosures.[33] The first wave between 2005 and 2006 "involved recent buyers who had made only one or two payments—or none—on their loans. Most were 'flippers' who had taken out a mortgage" expecting to sell at a profit and pay off the loan; when these investors could not sell, they defaulted. The second wave occurred in early 2007 when ARMs reset and households faced crushing monthly payments. In the third wave, *lenders* shied away from giving refinance loans to those facing ARM resets; without the ability to refinance and decrease payments, desperate borrowers had few choices. So, "by summer 2007 panic had set in.... The subprime financial shock was in full swing."

From these insights, in addition to recognizing that people had too much debt, we can identify two circumstances that first stimulated defaults and foreclosures: rising interest rates and ARM resets. When ARM loans reset to higher interest rates, borrowers began to default. A few defaults turned into abundant defaults which eventually decimated the housing market. Soon people owed more than their homes were worth. Many were *unable* to make payments; others simply were *not inclined* to do so. Economics professor John Taylor appropriately notes that, "the benefits of holding onto a house, perhaps by working longer hours to make the payments, are higher when the price of the house is rapidly rising. When prices are falling, the incentives to make payments are much less and turn negative if the price of the house falls below the value of the mortgage."[34] Another factor may have contributed to the contagion of defaults. Unlike other nations, in most U.S. states those who cannot pay "can simply hand in the keys to their home to the mortgage lender and be free of further debt service obligations."[35] A lack of good options, declining housing prices, and the ability to get out free and clear compelled many to default on their loans.

---

33. Zandi, 2009.
34. Taylor, 2009.
35. Muellbauer, 2007: "In the U.K., in contrast, borrowers can be pursued for seven years for any debt not covered by the sale of their repossessed home."

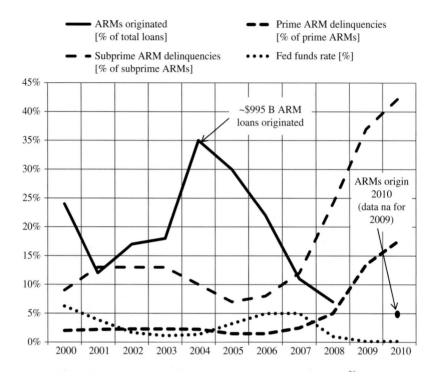

FIGURE 9.8   Subprime ARM loan originations and delinquencies vs. interest.[36]

9.4.2 Transition from Default to Delinquency and Foreclosure

Borrowers are delinquent when they default on their payments for 60 to 90 days. During the crisis, some delinquencies led to foreclosure (particularly subprime ARMs that had reset). People were forced from their homes and lenders were suddenly in the business of selling foreclosed homes. Figure 9.8 shows that by 2010, few who held ARMs were immune to their bite. Nearly 45 percent of all *subprime* ARMs and about 17 percent of all *prime* ARMs were delinquent. Increased interest rates after 2004 and declining housing prices after 2006 amplified the risk of default and foreclosure.

---

36. Subprime and prime ARM delinquencies 2000 to 2007 from FRBSF, 2008 [data from Office of Federal Housing Enterprise Oversight and Mortgage Bankers Association (delinquency is 60 days + past due or in foreclosure)] and from Joint Center for Housing Studies, 2010 (for 2009 and 2010); subprime origination from Joint Center for Housing Studies, 2008; percent of loans with adjustable rates (ARM loans originated) from Joint Center for Housing Studies, 2011, Table A-1 (data not available for 2009); federal funds rate from Board of Governors of the Federal Reserve System, 2011b; also see Bernanke, 2008.

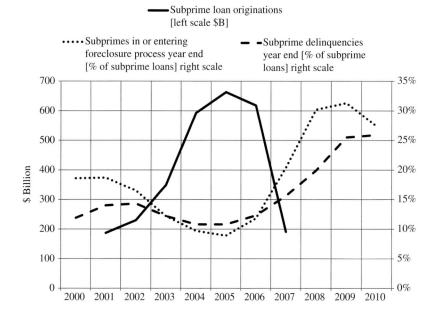

FIGURE 9.9   Subprime loans, delinquencies, and foreclosures (2000−2010).[37]

Total subprime conventional loans[38] (including ARMs) didn't fare much better. As predicted, subprime borrowers were more likely to the take the delinquency-to-foreclosure path; even as early as 2003, "the rate at which foreclosures were begun for subprime loans was more than 10 times that for prime loans."[39]

Figure 9.9 shows that coincident with the 2005 peak of *subprime* origina-tions, the percentage of subprime loan delinquencies and foreclosures were at a low, most likely because these statistics included the flood of subprime loans that were too new to default. However, in 2008, although interest rates were low, it was too late for some: nearly one in five subprime loans and one in four subprime ARMs were delinquent.[40] By the end of 2009 a quarter of all outstanding subprime loans were delinquent and almost a *third* of *all* subprime loans had moved beyond delinquency and were either in foreclo-sure or entering the foreclosure process.

---

37. Subprime loan originations from Joint Center for Housing Studies, 2008, Table A-6; foreclo-sure and delinquency rates from U.S. Census Bureau, 2012a.
38. Conventional loans are those not guaranteed by the VA or FHA.
39. Chomsisengphet and Pennington-Cross, 2006.
40. Subprime and prime ARM delinquency data from FRBSF (2008); subprime and prime delin-quencies from Dunne and Meyer (2007) and Larson (2008); 1 in 25 prime loans and 1 in 20 prime ARMs were delinquent in 2008.

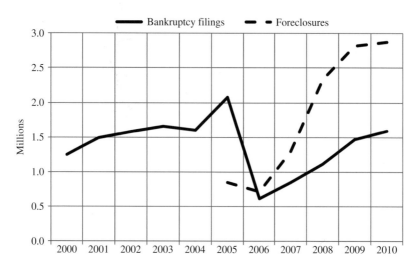

FIGURE 9.10   Trends in bankruptcy filings and foreclosures.[41]

Subprimes and ARMs were not the only troubled loans. In Figure 9.10, total foreclosures, regardless of loan type, jumped from 847,000 to over 2.3 million between 2005 and 2008. By 2005, bankruptcy filings hit a record high of over 2 million[42] and were trending upward when new regulations forced a sudden drop in 2006. Because declaring bankruptcy had been so easy, people filed without trying to meet their obligations and left lenders holding the bag. To slow the swell of bankruptcies and to counteract abuse, in 2005 Congress made the bankruptcy process more complicated, more expensive, and more "daunting for would-be filers."[43] Bankruptcies picked up after 2006 as people began to understand the new regulations.

Consequences were severe when debt exceeded capacity to handle it; defaults, bankruptcies, and foreclosures invaded the sense of well-being in the U.S. Now, using systems thinking, we integrate our knowledge about the housing price bubble and about debt to illustrate some of the dynamics involved in this invasion.

9.5 SYSTEMS THINKING INTERPRETATION

This section describes the effects of debt on the housing market as the economy galloped into crisis. Although there were literally hundreds of

41. Bankruptcy filings from United States Courts, 2011; foreclosures from RealtyTrac, 2007, 2008, 2009, 2011.

42. United States Courts, 2011.

43. Congress passed the Bankruptcy Abuse Prevention and Consumer Protection Act in October 2005. Carey, 2007; see also Cooke, 2006; Abate, 2006.

interactions, 4 balancing loops and 6 reinforcing loops represent the most significant cause and effects over time. These 10 loops portray a fairly complex picture, but don't be daunted. The picture will come together like a puzzle with each piece depicting new relationships. As we proceed, note the tight coupling among the elements. Here it is useful to visualize the loops as heavy intermeshed gears. Imagine you are slowly turning a heavy crank to put all the gears in motion. Because they weigh so ponderously on the economy, the momentum of these gear-like loops keeps them turning; they are difficult to stop.

We begin with previous systems constructs that contributed to the ascent of housing prices; we continue the story with three additional loops that not only stopped housing price growth, but deflated the housing bubble. In these illustrations, the effect of desires, expectations, interest rates, defaults, and foreclosures become obvious and open the way for levers that might have prevented the situation or could have reduced its severity. After digesting the relationships among these loops, we will consider what their interactions portend for the future.

9.5.1 Housing Bubble and Debt Dynamics

To illustrate the close ties between rising housing prices and new debt, Figure 9.11 integrates housing bubble dynamics from Chapter 8 (B_{supply}, B_{demand}, $B_{contractor}$, and $R_{expectation}$) with dynamics related to debt and

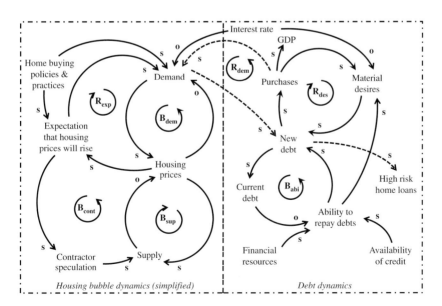

FIGURE 9.11   Housing bubble dynamics affect debt dynamics.

material desires from Figure 9.7 ($B_{ability}$ and R_{desire}). The R_{demand} reinforcing loop from Chapter 5 links the two sets of dynamics through purchases, demand, and new debt.

Beginning on the right side of the figure with debt dynamics, between 2000 and 2004 declining *interest rates* and easy *availability of credit* increased *ability to repay debts,* sparked *material desires,* and bolstered *demand.* With the prospect of low payments, *material desires* increased *new debt,* which led to more *purchases* and energized the first reinforcing loop R_{desire}. More *purchases* and lower *interest rates* crossed into the housing bubble domain to increase *demand.* Accelerating *demand* increased *new debt* and engaged a second reinforcing loop, R_{demand} that further increased *demand.* As we learned in Chapter 8, too many forces pressed on the B_{demand} loop and caused a demand shift. In simpler terms, housing prices rose.

Growth of *new debt* also increased *current debt* and boosted monthly payments in the balancing loop $B_{ability}$. Now, while higher *current debt* should have diminished the appetite for buying and reduced *new debt,* instead easy *availability of credit* caused debt to grow. More *new debt* enabled *purchases* and aroused *material desires* in the third reinforcing loop, R_{desire}. Together interest rates, easy credit, financial resources, and three reinforcing loops inflated the housing price bubble and generated unprecedented *new debt,* particularly for *high risk home loans.* Yet these same relationships existed when prices dropped in 2006. What changed to make these same loops deflate the housing bubble?

9.5.2 Debt, Defaults, Bankruptcies, and Foreclosures

To understand why housing prices spiraled down, consider the right side of Figure 9.12 where we add reinforcing loop $R_{default}$ and show how the *ARM reset rate* affected *current debt.* When *rates* on many ARMs increased after 2005, monthly payments (*current debt*) escalated, inhibiting households' *ability to repay debts.* With diminished *ability to repay,* many households *defaulted* or declared *bankruptcy. Defaults and bankruptcies* decreased *credit ratings* which first reduced the *availability of credit* and eventually limited households' *ability to repay.* After several cycles around the $R_{default}$ loop, results were not pretty: more defaults and less ability to refinance. Some borrowers saw no way out; many walked away, passing debt back to lenders and instigating *foreclosures.*

But the bad news continued. After 2007, falling income and rising unemployment decreased *financial resources* and further diminished *ability to repay debts.* As foreclosures mounted and financial institutions hit hard times, lenders raised *loan qualifications,* which also reduced *availability of credit.* What a sticky web!

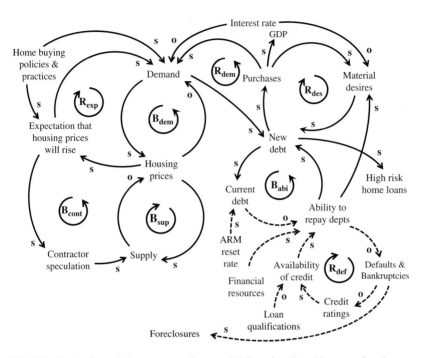

FIGURE 9.12   Default reinforcing loop reduces availability of credit and increases foreclosures.

9.5.3 Foreclosures, Expectations, and Housing Prices

The next puzzle piece captures the effect of foreclosures on expectations, demand, and ultimately on housing prices; foreclosures represent the "other" force we alluded to in Chapter 8. Sometime around 2005 or 2006 expectations about housing prices reversed. Rising *foreclosures* may have deepened awareness of the market's fragility and replaced optimistic expectations with pessimism. Figure 9.13 incorporates this possibility as a new reinforcing loop $R_{\text{foreclosure}}$.

In the $R_{\text{foreclosure}}$ loop, as foreclosures grew, optimistic *expectations* about housing prices diminished and *demand* dropped. Declining *demand* pushed *housing prices* down. From there, decreased *prices* created negative equity for households that were soon either unable or unwilling to repay their loans. As a result, many went into *foreclosure*; thus the decline of *housing prices* increased *foreclosures* to complete this reinforcing loop. For simplicity, the intermediate link to defaults and bankruptcies is not shown.

9.5.4 Foreclosures and Supply

The last puzzle piece illustrates how foreclosures counteracted the smooth operation of supply and demand that normally moves prices toward

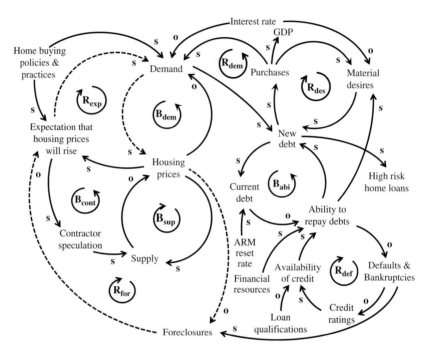

FIGURE 9.13   Foreclosure reinforcing loop affects expectation, demand, and housing prices.

equilibrium. Figure 9.14 shows their influence in reinforcing loop R_{supply}. Increased *foreclosures* raised the *supply* of houses. From there, *supply* flooded the market and *housing prices* decreased. Declining housing *prices* increased *foreclosures*. Now we have returned to the loop's beginning, having once again increased foreclosures. Although *contractor speculation* dwindled, *foreclosures* pumped *supply* up and kept *prices* down.

9.5.5 The Housing Bubble Inflates

Figure 9.15 more clearly traces the rise of housing prices between 2000 and 2006. In simple terms, lower interest rates, availability of credit, and supportive home buying policies initially energized the demand and material desires reinforcing loops, and increased prices and debt. As contractor speculation increased supply, rising housing prices energized the expectation reinforcing loop and vigorously shifted demand. More demand generated new debt and further escalated prices and demand. Then, abundant credit allowed debt to rise unrealistically and pumped air into the housing price bubble. We leave it to the reader to trace paths of interest beginning with any of four external points: (1) decreased loan qualifications; (2) increased financial resources; (3) decreased interest rates; and

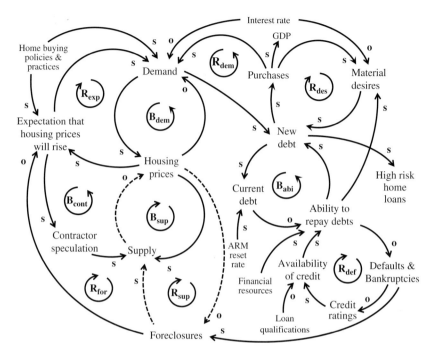

FIGURE 9.14   Supply reinforcing loop bombards supply.

(4) home-buying policies and practices. An important point here is that the combination of three intense reinforcing loops amplified the escalation of housing prices.

9.5.6 The Housing Bubble Bursts

The incredible housing price-growth engine fueled by three reinforcing loops around expectation, desire, and demand hit an inflection point in 2006 and transformed into a decaying spiral. As we suggested in earlier chapters, this rise and fall of housing prices appeared to follow the overshoot-and-collapse behavior described in Chapter 1. Recall that overshoot-and-collapse means that a given factor grows rapidly (exponentially) until it *exceeds* its capacity to sustain growth, then suddenly reverses "to begin an accelerating col-lapse"[44] and erodes its capacity for future growth.

Although this systems phenomenon for housing prices is interesting in itself, its explanation is more fascinating and demonstrates the incredible power of reinforcing loops that function synergistically. As we will see, two other conditions of overshoot-and-collapse (debt and expectation) facilitated

---

44. Senge, 2006 (the limits-to-growth archetype initially appeared in the 1990 edition).

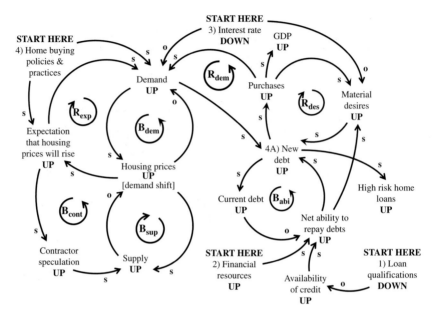

FIGURE 9.15   The housing bubble inflates.

the overshoot-and-collapse of housing prices. These conditions originated from the three decay-generating reinforcing loops related to defaults, bankruptcies, and foreclosures. As we discuss each overshoot-and-collapse condition, refer to Figure 9.16 that adds these decay loops to the growth engine from Figure 9.15. You may also wish to explore this maze of loops from five external starting points: (1) the ARM reset rate that increased monthly payments; (2) fewer financial resources caused by higher unemployment and lower income after 2007; (3) increased loan qualifications; (4) increased interest rate between 2004 and 2007; and (5) economic policies and banking practices whose support for home ownership had waned.

9.5.6.1 Overshoot-and-Collapse of Debt

The addition of $R_{default}$ to the systems picture in Figure 9.16 exposes the full force of the overshoot-and-collapse of debt. By 2006 when interest rates were up and substantial numbers of ARMs were resetting, borrowers could no longer make their house payments. Debt had grown beyond the system's natural capacity to sustain it (i.e., borrowers' ability to repay) and collapsed into *defaults and bankruptcies*. As a result, home owners' credit ratings dropped and their availability of credit contracted, further reducing their *ability to repay debts* because they could not borrow. Poor credit ratings combined with lenders' growing reticence to offer high-risk credit eroded their future ability to take on *new debt*.

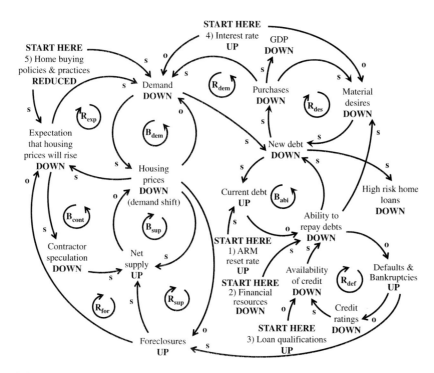

FIGURE 9.16 The housing bubble bursts.

9.5.6.2 Overshoot-and-Collapse of Expectation

The systemic damage from abundant *defaults and bankruptcies* was not confined to debt. Soon, inability to make house payments turned into *foreclosures* which introduced another overshoot-and-collapse condition, this time for expectation. As noted earlier, the reinforcing loop $R_{foreclosure}$ altered the expectation about housing prices and reversed its influence on demand. Now consumers were reticent to buy homes based on this new expectation. Lower demand decreased purchases and triggered lower prices which further diminished expectation of rising housing prices. This spiraling decline of expectation about housing prices is a concern. Once lost, like the cultivation of trust between two people, an expectation that was built on optimism and confidence is not easily restored.

9.5.6.3 Overshoot-and-Collapse of Housing Prices

While the collapse of debt and expectation were enough to force housing prices down, foreclosures added another weight to the heaviness that caused prices to overshoot-and-collapse. Normally as demand drops and prices decline, the supply balancing loop would decrease the supply of houses and push prices upward. But that didn't happen. Just as expectations overexcited demand on the bubble's upside, foreclosures overwhelmed supply on its downside. A deepening flood of foreclosed homes depressed prices further. This dynamic in turn strengthened pessimistic expectations and drove housing prices lower. House Price Index (HPI) statistics corroborate the staying power of this pessimism; after their precipitous decline between 2006 and 2009, housing prices hardly moved for several years.[45] Together, these forces had eroded the system's capacity for growth in the housing market.

9.5.7 Future Forecast

What ruts did the engine of decay dig for our economic future? In addition to the obvious tasks of revitalizing the economy and recovering from the massive loss of wealth, we must be aware of two latent forces that could affect the future: shadow inventory and the erosion of capacity for economic growth. These forces will deter economic recovery and could cause the decay dynamics to resurface.

9.5.7.1 Shadow Inventory

Housing supply data in Chapter 8 included houses that were known to be for sale. However, these statistics do not reveal what was *not* reported: shadow inventory. In fact, the reported inventory of homes was only the "tip of the iceberg."[46] In 2009, an estimated 11 to 30 million homes were *not* listed and were waiting on the sidelines until the market improved. Even so, the 3.5 million houses on the market in 2009 represented about twice the normal supply. If housing prices do begin to recover, this hidden supply could enter the market to keep prices low or to cause their decline.

9.5.7.2 Erosion of Capacity for Economic Growth

Because the decay engine with its three overshoot-and-collapse conditions did considerable permanent damage, economic recovery now faces triple challenges. First, because so many borrowers incurred more debt than they could handle and their ability to borrow eroded, their purchasing power has diminished. Second, economic recovery depends in part on confidence that allows people to feel secure about future prospects. When confident, businesses expand and hire, and consumers buy products and services, thus creating a reinforcing loop of economic growth. Erosion of optimistic expectations about housing prices takes with it confidence in the economy and

---

45. HPI for the 20-city average went from 206 in July 2006 to 139 in April 2009 and ranged between 138 and 148 from April 2009 to July 2011 (Standard & Poors/Case-Shiller, 2012).
46. Discussion on "shadow inventory" excerpted from Noguchi (2009) and Olorunnipa (2011).

decreases purchases and business investments. Third, both these conditions, when combined with the still high supply of foreclosed homes particularly in states such as California, Florida, and Illinois,[47] suggest the likelihood that the housing market will remain in the doldrums. To put a different light on this erosion we can conclude that, although using unrealistic debt to prompt economic growth was a successful short-term strategy, it is a poor long-term strategy.

9.5.8 Candidate Leverage Points

In addition to revealing dependencies and dynamics, another benefit of using a systems perspective is that it allows one to identify the most effective leverage points at which to introduce change. By improving the ability of balancing loops to limit what is intended, slowing the growth of reinforcing loops, and influencing beliefs,[48] leverage could have been applied *prior* to 2008 to dampen growth of housing prices and debt before they got too high, or to soften their exaggerated decline and reduce defaults, bankruptcies, and foreclosures that triggered overshoot-and-collapse conditions.

9.5.8.1 Leverage to Dampen Growth of Housing Prices and Risky Debt

On the upside of economic growth, housing price increases had already out-paced inflation as early as 1998, total loan originations peaked in 2003, and the use of ARMs grew until interest rates rose in 2004 (see Figures 9.3 and 9.8). Around 2001 after the housing bubble began to take shape, leverage could have corrected conditions that encouraged unrestrained growth. Three areas fit this criterion: *home buying policies and practices*; *interest rates*; and *loan qualifications*. Figure 9.17 describes the effects of using these leverage points relative to what actually occurred. Each action by itself can be beneficial, but when actions engage all areas, their effects build on one another to nudge the economy in the same direction.

At leverage point 1, government policies and lenders' practices that pro-moted home ownership for low-income households inundated the economy until 2004 and stimulated housing-related demand and debt. If these *policies and practices* were more moderate, *demand* for homes would rise only grad-ually and *expectations* about housing prices would be more stable. Conservatively managing *interest rates* at leverage point 2 restrains the *desire* and *demand* for homes, allowing them to increase slowly. Early in the

---

47. RealtyTrac, 2012.
48. These are 3 of Meadows' 12 ways to introduce leverage into a system (Meadows, 1999); see Chapter 2.

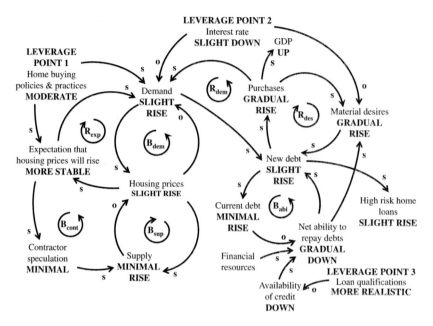

FIGURE 9.17   Leverage slows price growth and reduces debt growth.

growth period, instead of the significant and swift drop in *interest rates* between 2000 and 2003,[49] a smaller decrease would modulate *material desires* and *demand* for homes and contain the increase in *new debt*, *purchases*, and *prices*. Leverage point 3 requires that *loan qualifications* realistically match borrowers' creditworthiness. Actions here reduce *availability of credit* thus decreasing *ability to repay debts* and holding *material desires* and *demand* for homes below crisis levels. These changes directly affect the growth loops $R_{expectation}$, R_{desire}, and R_{demand}, and allow the four balancing loops B_{demand}, B_{supply}, $B_{ability}$, and $B_{contractor}$ to operate effectively. In other words, conservative policies with an eye to future consequences keep expectations, prices, and debt from overinflating.

9.5.8.2 Leverage to Slow Decay

As we know, none of these leveraging actions occurred before the housing bubble inflated. As a result, housing prices grew unrealistically and then fell

---

49. Between 2000 and 2003, federal funds rates dropped 5 percent and 1-year ARM rates dropped 3.25 percent; 1-year ARM rates dropped from 7.04 to 3.76 percent; 30-year fixed rate mortgage rates declined from 8.05 to 5.83 percent; federal funds rates decreased from 6.24 to 1.13 percent (federal funds rates from Board of Governors of the Federal Reserve System, 2011b; annual average 1-year ARM rates from Freddie Mac, 2011c; annual average 30-year FRMs from Freddie Mac, 2011b).

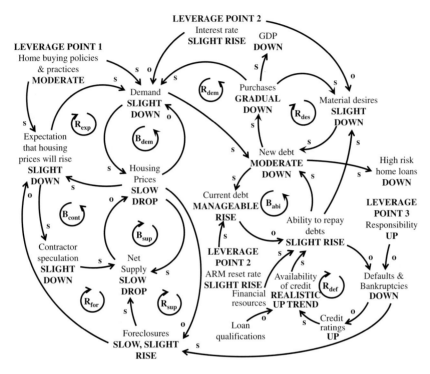

FIGURE 9.18 Leverage slows price decay and reduces defaults, bankruptcies, and foreclosures.

over 30 percent in three short years.[50] Figure 9.18 identifies three leverage points where actions could have reduced this swift decay of prices: *home buying policies and practices*; *interest rate* increases; and *responsibility for defaults and bankruptcies*. The caveat is that actions must be taken when housing prices are on their way up. Leverage here must slow the effects of loops R_{desire}, R_{demand}, and $R_{expectation}$ that have changed from virtuous to vicious, and it must reduce the detrimental effects of loops R_{supply}, $R_{foreclosure}$, and $R_{default}$. In other words, it must mitigate the overshoot-and-collapse conditions. Altering these reinforcing loops allows the four balancing loops B_{demand}, B_{supply}, $B_{contractor}$, and $B_{ability}$ to operate effectively.

More moderate home buying policies and practices would not only slow growth, but could also dampen decay of housing prices. More realistic expectations about housing prices could have discouraged the severely pessimistic expectation about housing prices. Less aggressive policies and

---

50. Data from Standard & Poors/Case-Shiller, 2011; HPI dropped from nearly 190 in 2006 to 129, in 2009.

diminished use of ARMs could also reduce demand, since those who could not afford the debt would not have considered buying a home. Furthermore, rather than counteracting the Fed's monetary policies, these policies would have strengthened the influence of interest rates, particularly after 2004. This leverage point is doubly powerful in that it affects confidence in the economy, which, as economics professor Roger Farmer notes, ultimately stimulates employment by increasing wealth and demand.[51]

The second leverage point requires earlier and more modest changes to *interest rates* prior to the peak of housing prices. For example, in 2003 when the economy heated up, if interest rates had risen gradually and hadn't reached such heights,[52] desires, demand, and new debt would have grown more slowly, ideally translating into a gentler price decline. On the other hand, if interest rates had been lower after 2005 when many ARM loans began to reset, *current debt* would have been more manageable and households would have had greater *ability to repay debts*. Increased *ability to repay* could have lessened *defaults and bankruptcies* and ultimately reduced the *foreclosures* that destabilized housing *supply* and altered *expectation* about housing prices. However, identifying the presence of the bubble prior to 2004 was difficult. Early reaction might have been possible by improving detection, understanding built-in delays, and accounting for the effects of interest rates on high-risk ARMs.

Engaging the third leverage point requires containing *defaults and bankruptcies*. Effective action here means that individuals, banks, and the government assume mutual responsibility: individuals must in good faith try to repay their loans; banks can revise loan terms; the government can offer encouragement or incentives to make this happen.

9.5.9 Current Activities

Our proposed leverage pertains to precrisis actions that slow growth of prices and debt or that slow decay of prices and acceleration of defaults. While this leverage was not used during the crisis, many post-crisis actions to reinvigorate the broken economy touched these levers. At the first leverage point, home-buying policies and practices, the U.S. government has taken steps to build confidence and change expectations. To minimize fear of loss, in October 2008 legislation raised maximum deposit insurance from $100,000

---

51. Farmer, 2010.
52. From 2004 to 2006, federal funds rates rose nearly 4 percent and ARM rates rose nearly 2 percent (1-year ARM rates rose from 3.76 to 5.54 percent; 30-year fixed rate mortgage rates increased from 5.83 to 6.41 percent; federal funds rates increased from 1.13 to 4.97 percent (federal funds rates from Board of Governors of the Federal Reserve System, 2011b; annual average 1-year ARM rates from Freddie Mac, 2011c; annual average 30-year FRMs from Freddie Mac, 2011b).

to $250,000 for accounts at banks and other FDIC-insured organizations; this policy became permanent in July 2010.[53] Policies to modify executive compensation or assure equitable use of bail-out funds have also helped restore confidence. In 2009 executive salaries in companies that accepted bail-out money were limited to $500,000 a year, instead of the millions previously paid.[54] Additional discussions that year (which also touch other leverage areas) implored lenders to make more loans, modify underwater mortgages, control executive compensation, and support additional financial regulations.[55] Results are mixed.

At the second leverage point, in 2009 the Fed reduced interest rates to record low levels and promised to keep them low "until late 2014 to nurture the country's stubbornly slow economic recovery." This promise "reinforced investors' confidence that the Fed was committed to restoring growth" and almost immediately translated to an uptick in world stock markets.[56] Unfortunately, it came too late to avoid most ARM resets. Even several years after the crisis, because negative expectations still deplete consumer confidence, low interest rates are inadequate incentives for borrowers to take out mortgage loans or for lenders to give them.

At the third leverage point where defaults and bankruptcies generate foreclosures, in 2010 the U.S. government forced major banks to slow down foreclosures and repair practices.[57] The government has also led "refinance assistance programs aimed at credit-impaired or underwater borrowers" for those with FHA or GSE backed loans. Some 720,000 FHA borrowers refinanced at lower rates between April 2009 and March 2012 and over a million Freddie Mac and Fannie Mae borrowers had refinanced by the end of 2011.[58] Shadow inventory and the still abundant outstanding ARMs make this leverage relevant for the future.

The government also engaged another leverage point (financial resources) by proposing legislation to "offer more aid for housing" for those who qualify.[59] If Congress accepts this proposal, there may still be systemic effects that could harm "investors in government backed mortgage bonds by more quickly paying off securities."[60]

---

53. FDIC, 2010 and Geffner, 2010; the law was the Dodd–Frank Wall Street Reform and Consumer Protection Act.

54. Mason, 2009.

55. Raum, 2009.

56. Piovano, 2012.

57. Treanor and Kollewe, 2010; these practices are described as the "robo-signing eviction scandal."

58. Joint Center for Housing Studies, 2012. The "Home Affordable Refinance Program" (HARP) for GSE (Fannie Mae and Freddie Mac) borrowers began in 2009.

59. Proposed in President Obama's 2012 State of the Union address.

60. Shenn et al., 2012.

9.6 SUMMARY

This chapter portrays debt dynamics that fueled the economic crisis. It begins with a trek up Debt Mountain when housing prices were ascending and people felt wealthy. Encouraged by policies and practices that promoted home buying and by easily available credit, households went deeply into debt. By the time the trek reached the top of Debt Mountain, debt measured in the multiple trillions of dollars. Seemingly beneficial policies had unintended consequences that devastated rather than stimulated the economy and diminished the quality of life for most everyone.

Down the other side of the mountain, defaults, bankruptcies, and foreclosures were too numerous to sweep under the carpet. By 2007, the good ol' days were gone; the economy was in a ditch and Americans had lost a quarter of their wealth.[61] Higher federal funds rates that bumped up ARM payments finally exposed the risk in subprime and affordability mortgage loans. Housing prices had decreased nearly 9 percent from their 2006 highs and were still dropping;[62] subprime loan originations were down over 70 percent, causing the once robust subprime market to crash; prime loan originations had declined 14 percent. Altogether, in 2007 a quarter of the mortgage market that was so prominent in 2005 had disappeared.[63] Now with less credit and growing defaults and foreclosures, "the whole momentum of the boom was reversed"; demand for houses evaporated.[64] Millions of households declared bankruptcy and/or went into foreclosure. The resulting huge supply of foreclosed homes together with minimal demand literally shoved housing prices down and eroded expectations that housing prices would continue to rise. Instability reigned.

Two conditions harbor a potential for future damage: the shadow inventory of unwanted homes that are waiting to hit the market and an eroded capacity for economic recovery. Other not-so-apparent threats to the future rest with the many homeowners who are still "underwater" and owe more than their homes are worth. These individuals (29 percent of all U.S. homeowners at the end of 2011) are either hoping that housing prices increase or that they will be able to refinance or modify their loans.[65] As they approach foreclosure, some lose this hope. A more subtle effect of these circumstances

---

61. Isidore, 2011; from a peak of $65.8 trillion in 2007, net household worth fell to $49.4 trillion by early 2009.
62. Q4 HPI went from 186.97 in 2005 to 170.75 in 2007; from Standard & Poors/Case-Shiller May, 2011.
63. Statistics from Joint Center for Housing Studies, 2008; in 2005, subprime loans accounted for 20 percent of all loans originated. Between 2005 and 2007, subprime loan originations dropped 71 percent, prime loan originations dropped 14.3 percent, and total loan originations dropped 26 percent.
64. Rajan, 2010.
65. *The Week*, 2011.

is that disposable income is lower for those still making payments on under-water homes; they cannot help revive a sagging economy. The crisis is not yet over.

Using systems thinking, this chapter captured the full dynamics of the housing bubble. Operating on the demand and supply balancing loops, three reinforcing loops built around expectation, material desires, and demand shifted demand for houses and generated a continuous rise in housing prices. Availability of credit and increasing interest rates—intended to benefit the economy—stimulated growth but marginalized the balancing loop that prevents individuals from taking on more debt than they can afford. These forces collaborated until 2006 when housing prices exceeded the capacity of the economic system to sustain them. Their precipitous drop signaled the presence of an overshoot-and-collapse condition. At this point, the system also exhibited two other devastating overshoot-and-collapse conditions that contributed to housing price decline—one for debt and one for expectation about housing prices. These conditions eroded both the ability to take on new debt and the capacity to maintain positive expectations about housing prices. Mechanisms that exacerbated these collapse conditions and unmasked the risk of subprime and ARM home loans come from three reinforcing loops that originated with massive defaults, bankruptcies, and foreclosures. These new loops ultimately tightened credit and diminished ability to repay debts, reversed expectations, and turned price growth into decay, all of which reduced purchases.

Finally, using systems thinking we identified one set of candidate lever-age points that could have curbed the growth of the housing bubble and another set that could have smoothed its decay. This perspective revealed that even if we know where to push the system, we must consider the effects of our actions carefully. Both sets require policy makers to become aware of an impending bubble and to act before it peaks. Growth-limiting actions included less aggressive home buying policies and practices, conservative management of interest rates, and increased rigor of loan qualifications. Decay-reducing actions included these same actions and required individuals, financial organizations, and the government to take greater responsibility for debt. All leverage areas directly affect human behaviors that are stimulated by expectations, demand, and material desires. Remedial actions that engaged these leverage areas to some degree were implemented post-crisis— unfortunately too late to prick the housing bubble as it was inflating and pre-vent economic turmoil.

Although the story in this chapter is bleak, we have yet to discuss the broader effects of the housing market collapse. High-risk loans and defaults (particularly for ARMs and subprime loans) in this chapter are ready to rip-ple through the financial market and hurt multitudes in their wake. These factors appear in the next chapter where we begin the saga of risk and contagion.

Chapter 10

The Risk Tiger Pounces: Financial Market, Risk, and Securitization

Securitization severed the critical link between borrower and lender. Once a lender sold a mortgage to Wall Street, repayment was someone else's problem.

McLean and Nocera[1]

We built this giant machine, and it was making a lot of money—until it didn't. We didn't know why we were making so much money. We didn't have the risk tools to understand that risk.

Larry Fink[2]

Imagine for the moment that you are seated in a darkened auditorium awaiting the spectacular finale of the magic show you had heard so much about. The curtain rises. Hypnotic music, flashing lights, and twirling dancers fill the stage. With dramatic flair, the magician calls your attention to a large cage. The Bengal tiger inside roars and exposes his long teeth. Definitely startling. Definitely dangerous. Definitely something you want to avoid.

The magician gracefully conceals the cage with a big shiny cloth and sends it skyward. More music and lights. More dancing. A few flourishes of a wand. And voilà, the silver fabric slips to the ground. The cage is still there, but where is the tiger? This is awesome, you think. This is magic!

Of course it appears so—the trick was designed to *make* you think so. Truly it was a combination of attention distracters, well-orchestrated moves, and clever props that made the caged animal disappear—not exactly into nothingness, but at least out of view. Now, without its menacing presence, you feel safe and amazed at the same time.

In our story, this magic trick is not performed in an auditorium for an audience who pays to be entertained. Instead, our stage is the economy and

---

1. McLean and Nocera, 2010.
2. Quoted in Andrews, 2010; Larry Fink is current CEO of BlackRock Financial.

our audience is the mass of individuals who are somehow affiliated with mortgage loans. In our show, securitization is the magician who made the dangerous tiger disappear. And the tiger? The tiger is risk—the unprecedented risk of poor-quality loans that bite with the sharp teeth of default. Over and over during the economic crisis, securitization performed the same trick. Again and again, risk vanished from center stage to be passed on in the form of mortgage-backed securities (MBSs), where it once more evaporated, only to be repackaged and sold as collateralized debt obligations (CDOs). Finally, in September 2008, the risk tiger materialized with unprecedented flamboyance. Angry, hungry, and ready to devour the economy, risk finally pounced on the giant financial companies.

This chapter presents the remaining economic mechanisms associated with the economic crisis—the last pieces for the yang of our systems story. In previous chapters we reviewed how policies and interest rates promoted demand for homes and high-risk loans and eventually contributed to a housing price bubble. We saw the housing market quickly go south when interest rates increased, ARMs reset, and borrowers could no longer make their payments. Many people defaulted on their loans or filed for bankruptcy. Homes went into foreclosure. Because the defaults and foreclosures were far beyond what was ever anticipated, they created the "decay engine" described in Chapter 9 that was built from falling housing prices, from the expectation that prices would continue to fall, and from the glut of foreclosed homes on the market. As this engine operated, housing prices tumbled and millions of people were trapped in the ooze. These events were enough to rattle the economy, but the damage didn't stop with housing. Risky loans and resulting defaults were catalysts of destruction in a financial market that thirsted for lofty returns.

So how did defaults jump the fence into the financial market? Quite easily, it turns out. That great financial magician, securitization, captured high-risk loans issued by banks and lending institutions and turned them into investment securities that were sold across the world. This process helped hide risk of these loans and, just as importantly, spread that concealed risk far and wide. To track the risk tiger's path from poor quality mortgage loans to financial securities, this chapter expands the discussion of securitization in Chapter 2 and connects financial market mechanisms to defaults on high-risk loans. And now... the story of the risk tiger and the magician that made it disappear.

10.1 SECURITIZATION, STRUCTURING, AND DERIVATIVES IN THE FINANCIAL MARKET

From Chapter 2 we know that mortgage loans were a keystone of the financial market. Financial institutions bought, bundled, and sold these loans on Wall Street as mortgage-backed securities. Other organizations bought and pooled the MBSs, divided them into bonds (tranches) of collateralized debt obligations at various risk levels, and then sold the CDOs to investors according to their risk and return preferences. Next, to guard against the seemingly unlikely event that the mortgages in these securities might default, CDO investors purchased credit default swaps (CDSs) to hedge against risk.

These innovative financial products appeared to be a win-win for all: lenders funded new loans with earnings made by selling mortgages to those who packaged them into bonds; securities issuers made money by selling these bonds to investors; CDS issuers profited from premiums on the sales; and rating agencies received fees and commissions from assessing risk. Everyone was flying high. But the risk tiger? Although hidden from view, he lay crouched behind the bushes of enthusiasm and self-interest.

10.1.1 The Money-Making Machine

Before long, participants in the financial market realized they had crafted a money-making machine. The grandfather of securitization, Lew Ranieri, was even heard to say that "his mortgage-trading desk 'made more money than all the rest of Wall Street combined'."[3] Figure 10.1 illustrates this

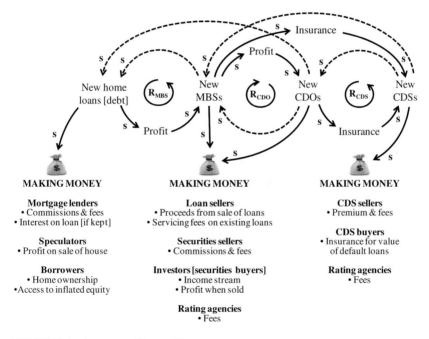

FIGURE 10.1   A money-making machine.

---

3. Time Specials (2011). Ranieri, considered the "godfather of mortgage finance," was former vice chairman of Salomon Brothers.

money-making machine in systems thinking terms; it illustrates how debt (particularly subprime and ARM loans), crossed into financial territory and enticed various entities to participate. The machine begins where we left off in the last chapter—with new home loans. Following the money-making flow (solid lines), as *new home loans* are made, lenders *profit* by keeping these loans for their income or by selling them to firms that convert them into *new MBSs*. These firms *profit* by selling *new MBSs* to investors who gain income, or to other financial organizations that turn them into *new CDOs*. Finally, to cover the growing volume of *new MBSs* and *new CDOs*, securities investors buy *credit default swaps* as protection against loan defaults. In each transaction, whether originating new home loans, issuing securities, or selling default insurance, making money was a gratifying outcome.

Although the linear flow from loans to CDSs shows how everyone profited, the greater power of this machine came from the reinforcing loops (dashed lines) that kept it going. Stimulated by profit, MBS, CDO, and CDS sellers all sought more raw material for their products. Sellers of *new MBSs* encouraged lenders to make more *new loans*, thus completing the reinforcing loop R_{MBS}. Sellers of *new CDOs* encouraged lenders and *MBS* sellers to produce more *new loans* and *new MBSs*, completing the reinforcing loop R_{CDO}. CDS sellers encouraged *new CDOs*, completing reinforcing loop R_{CDS}. Although many other loops are involved, these most significant three illustrate the self-perpetuating concept.

Truly this was an amazing machine. Everyone along the way got a piece of the mortgage pie while spreading the risk of default among a broadening audience. The magic of the financial market had made the risk tiger disappear and reappear elsewhere, only to disappear again. To borrowers, the whole process was transparent. Because the risk tiger was invisible or ignored, lenders felt comfortable making subprime or ARM loans, and financial agents eagerly sold MBS or CDO securities stuffed with them. And since risk was now dispersed among millions of investors, it seemed manageable to CDS sellers. Besides, people don't default on their home loans—do they? However... behind the stage and all the while, stockpiles of high risk home loans, MBSs, CDOs, and CDSs accumulated.

10.1.2 Risk Multipliers

That golden treasure, profit, made securitization contagious. When the money-making machine collapsed, risk stood alone in the spotlight; risk in the form of low quality mortgage loans had not only accrued but had also intensified when the many financial market participants added their own twists. Rating agencies, government, financial organizations in general, securities issuers, and CDS sellers each multiplied risk, as Figure 10.2 shows. Here, a pipeline of risk (three dark arrows) enters the housing market and traverses the financial market, growing wider at each stop.

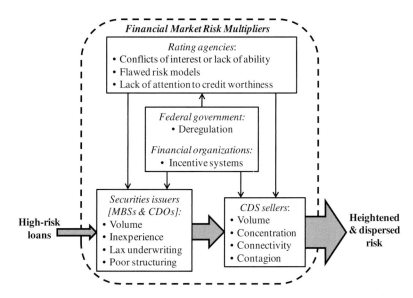

FIGURE 10.2   Risk multipliers in the financial market.

10.1.3 Securities Issuers

Securities issuers who sold mortgage-backed securities and collateralized debt obligations are the heart of this risk-multiplying pipeline. As we learned in Chapter 2, agency (government affiliated) organizations and nonagency (private) corporations popularized the process of turning loans into securities. Beginning in the 1970s with Ginnie Mae's securitization of FHA and VA mortgage loans and continuing into the 1980s when Freddie Mac, Fannie Mae, and some private companies structured qualifying loans as MBSs, securitization became more attractive.

By the 1990s, more private companies joined in. Because government-affiliated GSEs guaranteed their securities, they could only buy loans that met certain criteria.[4] However, private firms did not have these restrictions; they enthusiastically purchased high-risk subprime loans and issued risk-laden securities. Between 1995 and 2005, these less experienced firms expanded the mortgage securitization business by over 16 times (from a modest $80 billion worth of MBSs in 1995, private entity issuance grew to over $1.3 trillion in 2005).[5] Furthermore, risk from these securities was

---

4. For example, Fannie and Freddie could not "buy loans with original loan-to-value ratios greater than 80 percent without a credit enhancement" (Lockhart, 2009).
5. Congressional Budget Office, 2010; data estimated from graph; sources from Securities Industry and Financial Markets Association, Fannie Mae, Freddie Mac, the Federal Housing Finance Agency, Ginnie Mae, and Inside Mortgage Finance mortgage-backed security database.

highly concentrated; in 2006 10 private companies issued the majority of MBSs.[6] Many of these same firms also issued CDOs. At the peak of CDO popularity, four financial institutions issued over half of all CDOs; seven others accounted for an additional third.[7]

Who bought these securities? Buyers ranged from well-heeled individuals, to banks and financial organizations, to other domestic organizations and city governments looking for ways to make money or enlarge retirement funds. Foreign entities seeking big returns on excess capital invested heavily. Potential profits enticed many types of investors, all of whom craved the greater returns of these high-risk securities. Our discussion begins with a look at the first risk multiplier for securities: *volume*.

10.1.3.1 Volume of Mortgage-Backed Securities

Dominated by less-experienced, less-regulated nonagency institutions, the MBS business rose briskly between 2001 and 2003. Increased participation of this private sector multiplied risk of default: more ARMs and subprime loans found their way into securities. Figure 10.3 shows that while mortgage loan originations and agency-issued securities started to drop after 2003, nonagency securities continued upward. In 2005 and 2006, private firms securitized over half of all MBSs[8] surpassing Freddie Mac and Fannie Mae. Further adding to the risk, in 2006 about 70 percent of nonagency MBSs, compared with less than 20 percent of agency MBSs, contained high-risk ARMs.[9]

The securities market grew like ragweed, carrying with it the bitter flavor of risk. If you had a home mortgage in the U.S. in 2008, yours might have been among the seven out of 10 loans that had been bundled, structured, and sold in the secondary market of mortgage-backed securities.[10] You might not know that some stranger was drawing income from your monthly payments or that your original lender was not at all concerned about whether you defaulted.

As risk grew in the financial market, it also became more concentrated. The same GSEs and nonagency firms that *issued* MBSs also *purchased* them as investments, acquiring risk with these purchases. Nonagency MBSs with their many subprime and ARM loans housed the greatest risk. To gauge the enormity of this risk, Figure 10.4 shows that in 2005, investors purchased

---

6. Davidson and Sanders, 2009; these 10 firms issued about 60 percent of all nonagency MBSs in 2006; by 2009, six of them, including Lehman, Bear Stearns, and Countrywide, were out of business or had been acquired.

7. Giannone, 2007. The top four global CDO issuers in Nov 2007 were Merrill Lynch, CitiBank, UBS, and Wachovia. Seven others included Goldman Sachs, Morgan Stanley, and Deutsche Bank.

8. Some sources suggest this number was higher and that the private sector securitized almost two thirds of all U.S. mortgages (see Goldstein and Hall, 2010).

9. Davidson and Sanders, 2009. Over 80 percent of agency issues were built on less-risky fixed rate mortgages.

10. Goldstein and Hall, 2010. Estimates by the Federal Reserve.

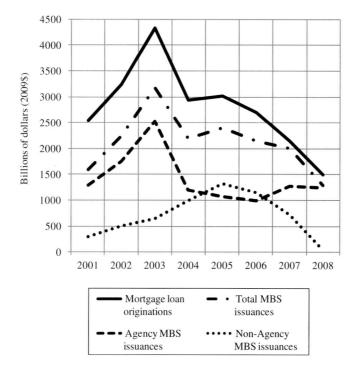

FIGURE 10.3   Mortgage loan originations and mortgage-backed securities issued.[11]

nearly $500 billion of subprime MBSs that were structured by private firms. During that year just over $600 billion of subprime loans were originated, thus most subprime loans left lenders' hands and landed in security investors' laps.

In addition to *selling* these risky securities, nonagency investors also *purchased* over $300 billion of them in 2005 and again in 2006. Because of their "historical focus on prime mortgages," GSEs Freddie and Fannie could not buy enough subprime loans to meet the quotas set by HUD. So to compensate, they invested in nearly $150 billion subprime *MBSs* in those years.[12] Risk had established itself not only within private investors, but also within the traditionally conservative GSEs.

---

11. MBS data from Congressional Budget Office, 2010 [source data from Securities Industry and Financial Markets Association, Fannie Mae, Freddie Mac, The Federal Housing Finance Agency, Ginnie Mae, and the Inside Mortgage Finance mortgage-backed security database]; loan origination data from Joint Center for Housing Studies 2008 (2001−2007) corrected for inflation to 2009 $B and less nonprime home equity loans; loan origination data for 2008 and 2009 from U.S. Census Bureau, 2012a. Note difference in mortgage loan origination data deviates from data presented earlier; data in this chart is in 2009 $ to be comparable to MBS data

12. The Financial Crisis Inquiry Commission, 2011; estimates show that Freddie would have met "affordable housing goals without any purchases of Alt-A or subprime securities, but use(d) the securities to help meet subgoals."; see also Rajan, 2010.

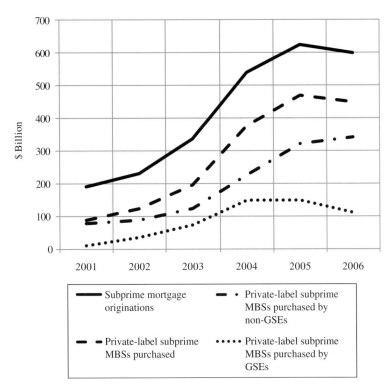

FIGURE 10.4 Estimated purchases of private-label (nonagency) subprime MBSs[13].

When a fourth of the mortgage market disappeared after 2005, the MBS market dwindled. However, although fewer securities and derivatives were traded by 2007, outstanding MBSs (those that were still owned) registered at $6 trillion (see Figure 10.5).[14] Significantly, in that year a third of all outstanding MBSs were nonagency issued, most of which were high risk. However, risk didn't stop with MBSs. From there, we move to the next section of the securities pipeline: collateralized debt obligations.

10.1.3.2 Volume of Collateralized Debt Obligations

Just as mortgage loans and MBSs grew in the decade prior to the crisis, so did the global CDO market. Before 1996, the volume of new CDOs issued

---

13. Subprime MBSs from the Financial Crisis Inquiry Commission, 2011 (data estimates from bar chart); subprime mortgage originations from Gorton, 2008 (Gorton's data sources: Inside Mortgage Finance; the 2007 Mortgage Market Statistical Annual, Key Data, 2006; and Joint Economic Committee, October 2007).
14. Davidson and Sanders, 2009.

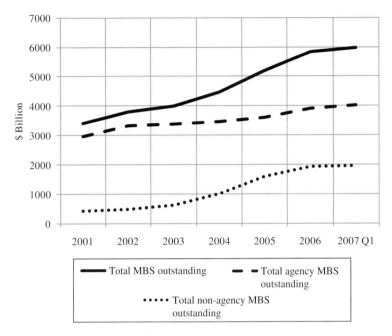

FIGURE 10.5   MBSs outstanding.[15]

across the world was less than $4 billion annually, but by 2005 that number jumped to $165 billion *in the U.S. alone*. Figure 10.6 shows the growth and decline of the global CDO market between 2000 and 2008. CDO sales peaked in 2006 at over half a *trillion* dollars. More disturbing than this number is that by 2005, of *all* outstanding CDOs (those still owned) over 80 percent of their underlying assets were home mortgages (structured finance CDOs). Furthermore, many of these mortgages were high risk subprime and Alt-A loans. In fact, the value of these lethal CDOs jumped from less than $5 billion in 1997 to over $60 billion in 2005.[16] After 2007, the MBS well dried up and the market for CDOs that were backed by risky MBSs died away.[17]

Companies that issued CDOs were also primary buyers of high risk subprime MBSs from which they structured CDOs.[18] For example, a study of 420 CDOs found that between 2003 and 2007, 40 to 50 percent of their

15. Data from Gorton, 2008 (sources: Federal Reserve Board, Inside MBS & ABS, Loan Performance, UBS).

16. Statistics in this paragraph from Vallee, 2006.

17. Deng et al., 2010.

18. Rosen, 2007; see also Shenn, 2007.

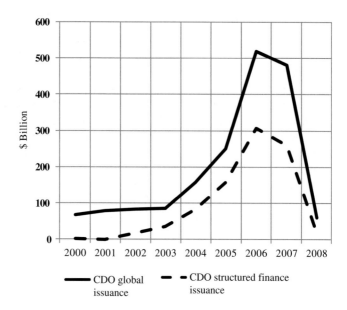

FIGURE 10.6   Worldwide issuance of CDOs.[19]

underlying 4000 mortgages were subprime loans.[20] Overall, many of the risky loans in CDOs were "issued to borrowers with limited or no income and asset verification."[21]

When we add the risk from this high volume of securities into the money-making machine in Figure 10.1, we can appreciate why the Financial Crisis Inquiry Report found that the securitization process "created a pipeline" for risky mortgages. The two reinforcing loops in this figure (R_{MBS} and R_{CDO}) illustrate that this pipeline was a critical factor in "the burgeoning numbers of high-risk mortgages."[22]

10.1.3.3 Other Risk Multipliers from Securities Sellers

In addition to the inherent risk in the sheer volume of subprime MBSs and CDOs, securities sellers multiplied risk in three other ways: *lax underwriting*, *inexperience*, and *poor structuring*.

19. Securities Industry and Financial Markets Association, 2011.
20. Deng et al., 2010; data source for study: UBS, "Mortgage and ABS CDO Losses," December 13, 2007 from Deng et al., 2010, Table I: Residential Mortgage Deals in 420 ABS CDOs.
21. Rosen, 2007.
22. Financial Crisis Inquiry Commission, 2011.

Lax Underwriting

Lax underwriting occurred in both the housing market and the financial market. Goaded by pressure to produce loans for securitization and encouraged by tempting incentives and government policies, lending agencies reduced underwriting standards for high-risk borrowers. This permissiveness piled onto the hazard of default. For example, risk associated with subprime loans issued in 2006 "has been attributed to a decline in underwriting standards and to outright fraud." In fact, over 50 percent of subprime mortgages in both 2005 and 2006 had little or no documentation.[23] MBS issuers accepted badly written loans from lenders based on so-called "reps and warranties" that intend to "protect investors against poor underwriting and loan practices." Unfortunately, when too many defaults caused securities to plunge, this process didn't work; lenders had insufficient capital or declared bankruptcy, making the warrants worthless.[24]

As the appetite for high-risk MBSs outpaced their supply, CDO issuers downplayed or even ignored risk. In many instances, CDO managers who purchased MBS securities used less rigorous risk analysis than previous investors; they "willingly purchased bonds backed by ever-more exotic mortgage loans."[25] Thus CDOs not only *inherited*, but also *caused* "a decline in underwriting quality"; CDO managers relied on rules and ratings rather than taking the time to validate the quality of the underlying assets.[26] When lenders realized that the growing number of those interested in purchasing subprime MBSs wouldn't ask many questions "they rushed to originate loans without checking the borrowers' creditworthiness, and credit quality deteriorated."[27] The threat swelled when the riskiest CDO levels were repackaged into CDO-squared securities. Although not strictly an underwriting issue, this process relabeled some of the worst CDOs as highly desirable (see Chapter 2). By 2003, CDOs "became a dumping ground for bonds that could not be sold on their own—bonds now referred to as 'toxic waste.'"[28]

Inexperience

In the area of *inexperience*, risk increased when new, nonagency MBS originators entered the market in the late 1990s. Some suggest that CDO managers incorporated unreasonably risky mortgage loans because they had less knowledge and experience[29] and that CDO underwriters often had different levels of ability or were "overly aggressive" and took too little time

---

23. Quotation on decline in underwriting standards and lack of documentation from Gorton, 2008.
24. Quotation on reps and warranties and discussion of warrants from Davidson and Sanders, 2009.
25. Barnett-Hart, 2009.
26. Davidson and Sanders, 2009.
27. Rajan, 2010.
28. Barnett-Hart, 2009.
29. Adelson and Jacob, 2008.

on each transaction.[30] With far less skill than the norm, nonagency corporations reduced the "degree of standardization and transparency in the market."[31] Additionally, as Fannie and Freddie invested in the unfamiliar subprime-loan market to meet their HUD-imposed loan goals, their own inexperience led them to disregard the significantly higher risks.[32] New companies entering the securitization business brought a new breed of player who not only lacked knowledge but also was unconstrained by banking regulations and "indifferent to the reputational concerns of banks."[33]

Risk multiplied as inexperienced Wall Street banks grew impatient with loan originators and began "repackaging their own collateral"—their own loans and MBSs—into CDOs.[34] At this point, CDOs became more complex to satisfy the expanding CDO market; this greater complexity hid the poor quality of the CDOs and encouraged "production of even more bad assets to satiate the CDO feeding frenzy."[35]

Poor Structuring

A more complex risk multiplier comes from how MBSs and CDOs were structured. As we learned in Chapter 2, these securities are segmented into tranches or bonds. If defaults occur, highest risk tranches are paid last and form a buffer for lower-risk tranches. Part of this structuring process relies on diversification to spread the risk of default. In other words, the process assumes that not everyone everywhere will default on their loans; when mortgages from different households and different parts of the country are placed into the MBSs and CDOs, the risk should diminish. These so-called "diversification benefits" made it possible for CDOs to "receive an 'A' rating on collateral that would otherwise be rated 'B'."[36]

Unfortunately, several factors erased these diversification benefits and produced false ratings. One factor was that the difference between risk segments (tranches) was too small; they were so similar to one another that the riskier ones didn't protect the less risky ones, making them all vulnerable to loan default. Another factor was the practice of bundling loans from the same geographic area. Securities with clumps of loans from California, Nevada, Florida, and Arizona were most likely to default.[37]

* * * * * * * *

30. Barnett-Hart, 2009.
31. Davidson and Sanders, 2009.
32. Rajan, 2010.
33. McCoy and Renuart, 2008.
34. Barnett-Hart, 2009.
35. Barnett-Hart, 2009.
36. Davidson and Sanders, 2009.
37. See Davidson and Sanders, 2009. These states had the highest number of households in a negative equity position creating more pressure for people to declare bankruptcy or just walk away.

Indeed, securities issuers multiplied risk not only through the volume of subprime and ARM loans they securitized, but also through their failure to account for the poor quality of some loans, their inexperience and low skill, and the lack of diversification in their structuring process. However, they, too, passed risk onward via credit default swaps. Now the risk tiger lay in wait for CDS sellers. At least lenders and securities sellers slept well at night.

10.1.4 CDS Sellers

The risk from mortgage loan defaults finally landed on the shoulders of credit default swaps. CDSs that intended to mitigate risk instead connected the financial industry globally and spread risk worldwide. For investors who had amassed huge portfolios of securities, CDS derivatives were a perfect solution to transfer the risk of mortgage defaults. Securities owners would purchase CDSs in return for which CDS issuers would repay them "in the highly unlikely event of a wave of corporate or bank defaults."[38]

Just as risk in the securities market escalated with the upsurge of MBS and CDOs, so did risk for CDSs. Figure 10.7 shows the popularity of this market. By 2007 an estimated $62 *trillion* CDS contracts were held globally.[39] These CDSs (many high risk) accounted for most of the total $80 trillion outstanding debt securities worldwide.[40] A new market index, the ABX, tracked the large market for subprime CDSs.[41]

Like securities issuers, CDS sellers generated other risk multipliers in addition to *volume*. Derived from the fact that a small group of corporations sold the majority of CDSs, these multipliers involve: (1) *concentration* of risk, (2) *connectivity* of major sellers, and (3) *contagion* of toxic mortgage-related CDSs into the other types of CDSs.

First, only a few major banks and securities houses bought and sold CDSs. In a 2009 survey, five members of this small group accounted for 88 percent of all CDSs.[42] This concentration (particularly for CDSs that insured toxic CDOs) could bring them all down in the event of massive loan defaults. Second, these firms sold MBSs and CDOs to others in their small group, and then bought or sold CDSs within the same group. Because their connectivity was tight, one firm's failure affected the others. Finally, risk from mortgage loan related CDSs was contagious. Failure of these CDSs would contaminate the sellers' nonmortgage CDSs. If too many mortgages defaulted and mortgage-related obligations grew too high, these companies'

---

38. Ferrell et al., 2010.
39. International Swaps and Derivatives Association, 2010.
40. Weistroffer, 2009.
41. Davidson and Sanders, 2009.
42. Weistroffer, 2009.

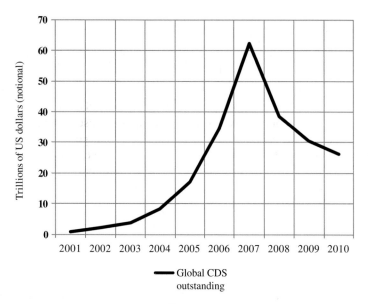

FIGURE 10.7 Global credit default swaps.[43]

resources would be stretched thin, jeopardizing payout on their other CDSs. Too many defaults meant companies had to increase reserves, thus reducing funds available for other investments. This situation affected credit ratings and cost of borrowing to cover obligations. For example, in the last quarter of 2007 after AIG's credit rating was downgraded, the crumbling real estate market and demand for more collateral caused it to lose over $11 billion.[44] Ultimately CDS issuers found themselves with insufficient resources to pay any claims—mortgage or nonmortgage related—which heightened the probability of bankruptcy or buyout.

The high volume of CDSs combined with the concentration, connectedness, and contagion of risk among few participants "fueled concerns that a collapse of a major player would have devastating effects for the financial sector as a whole." Because these players were so entwined, "the potential for contagion played a role in the decision to grant public assistance to AIG."[45] When the CDS market finally sank in 2007, proliferation of new risk diminished. However, the $62 trillion CDSs that investors still held at that time is shocking compared with the $15 trillion U.S. GDP and the nearly $56 trillion world GDP in 2007.[46]

43. International Swaps and Derivatives Association, 2010, 2012 (note 2010 statistics are the last available and were measured at mid-year).
44. Associated Press, 2008b.
45. Weistroffer, 2009.
46. FRED, 2011; International Monetary Fund, 2012.

* * * * * * * *

By now we see how mortgage loans covered the world with an elastic net of risky securities and derivatives. Still, we are left with a question. Since prices for financial products are generally commensurate with risk, why didn't normal financial market mechanisms account for mortgage loan defaults? If high numbers of defaults are expected, the price of MBSs, CDOs, and CDSs should allow issuers to recoup their costs. However, as we will soon see, prices were set too low and government policies did little to monitor risk assessment or regulate the securities market. This lack of guidance, combined with high fees and bonuses that promoted risk-taking, created an inferior rating process that woefully misrepresented the true price of securities and derivatives.

10.1.5 Federal Government

The U.S. Securities and Exchange Commission traditionally provides checks and balances in the financial market.[47] Prior to the crisis, however, oversight for some securities and derivatives markets was lax or missing. For example, after the banking industry was deregulated in 1999, banks could invest depositors' money in high-risk securities.[48] CDSs were formally deregulated in 2000 and sold in over-the-counter trading outside regulatory channels.[49] Lack of oversight caused this market to grow and created an avenue for risky dealings. The self-regulated accountability that the government relied on in this market was ineffective, particularly for untested forms of loans and securities.

As Chapter 2 noted, the government relaxed regulation in other areas as well, including changes to the net capital rule in 2004 which had limited the amount of debt a company could assume.[50] With this change, big financial corporations could take on more debt to buy tainted securities and pump up their risk even further. Finally, lax government involvement took pressure off agencies that rated securities and derivatives.

---

47. U.S. Securities and Exchange Commission, 2011; the SEC oversees "securities exchanges, securities brokers and dealers, investment advisors, and mutual funds" to promote "disclosure of important information, ensure fair dealing and protect against fraud."
48. In 1999, the Gramm−Leach−Bliley Act repealed the 1933 Glass−Steagall Act that reduced risk by separating commercial banking from financial banking. In 2010, the Dodd−Frank Act (the Wall Street Reform and Consumer Protection Act) was enacted; included in this act is the Volcker Rule that prevents banks from trading in securities for profit.
49. Congress passed the DFMA act (the Commodity Futures Modernization Act) in December 2000.
50. Labaton, 2008; see also Chapter 2.

10.1.6 Rating Agencies

Rating agencies such as Moody's, Fitch, and Standard & Poor's notably contributed to the popularity of securities;[51] in fact, their very participation signaled the legitimacy of these securities. However, because rating agencies were not well regulated[52] and had lax processes[53] the quality and accuracy of their ratings suffered. The risk for securities and derivatives was understated, ignored, or purposely misleading. Ongoing debate considers whether the reason for failure was "conflicts of interest at the rating agencies, rating agency incompetence, or unpredicted market forces."[54] Whatever the cause, risk assessments from rating agencies went unchallenged. This laissez-faire environment promoted immense profit-taking with little attention to hazards.

In addition to conflict of interest and lack of ability, faulty risk models and lack of attention to creditworthiness caused poor ratings. For example, Moody's "relied on flawed and outdated models to issue erroneous ratings on mortgage-related securities, failed to perform meaningful due diligence on the assets underlying the securities, and continued to rely on those models even after it became obvious that the models were wrong."[55] Financier Larry Fink suggested that no one understood the risks: "computer systems were inadequate, and so were the programs that measured the impact of key variables such as changes in interest rates."[56] In any event, securitization manufactured attractive securities with bloated AAA ratings. Rating agencies had "extrapolated the past growth in home prices too far into the future"; they severely underestimated the potential for default of subprime loans.[57]

To put the situation into perspective, between a third and a half of the outstanding securities issued between January 2000 and September 2008 were rated AAA.[58] Within 3 years of when they were issued, 1 in 6 of these was "eventually downgraded." The years between 2005 and 2007 were the worst. Over *half* the MBSs rated as investment grade at that time were later downgraded.[59] Of the big three rating agencies, Moody's held

---

51. See McLean and Nocera, 2010.
52. Financial Crisis Inquiry Commission, 2011.
53. U.S. Securities and Exchange Commission, 2008.
54. Davidson and Sanders, 2009.
55. Financial Crisis Inquiry Commission, 2011.
56. Andrews, 2010; Fink's new equity company is called BlackRock, of which he is chairman and CEO. He was the inventor of segmenting bonds according to risk.
57. Barberis, 2011.
58. Data taken in November 2008. Note that ratings differed depending on which agency rated the security.
59. Rating statistics in Barth et al, 2009a. The three major rating agencies are Standard & Poor's, Moody's, and Fitch. Together, these agencies rated about 90 percent of all investment grade securities.

the record for the greatest number of inaccurate ratings. In 2007, it downgraded 83 percent of the nearly $900 billion MBSs that it had rated as AAA the year before.[60]

This downgrading is a hazard for securities owners such as pension funds and other large investors. Corporate-issued bond default rates illustrate its magnitude. For example, from 1970 to 2006 Moody's statistics show that probability of default after 5 years was about 1.9 percent for the lowest investment grade bonds (Baa), while probability of default for the highest below investment grade (Ba) was 10 percent.[61] In other words, for bonds sold as Baa and downgraded to Ba, the probability of default was at least five times greater than investors had originally thought.

Why did investors believe these ratings knowing that the securities were backed by high-risk loans? AIG provides a perfect example of investors' rationale. When it began to offer CDSs in 1998, AIG primarily insured the highest quality, AAA CDOs.[62] These same high ratings hung on after 1998; AIG's rating agencies and investors felt safe because "they believed there was no way hundreds of homeowners would default on their loans at the same time."[63] Rating agencies provided inaccurate ratings—but investors gleefully accepted them.

10.1.7 Financial Organizations

A final risk multiplier loitered in financial sector organizations: short-term narrow-focused (SN) incentive systems that emphasized immediate gain and de-emphasized accountability. Because humans are motivated by goals and promises of reward, their behaviors can be channeled toward personal benefits without concern for broader future consequences. For example, numerous banks and financial houses held large numbers of securities that were backed by subprime loans "because their compensation schemes did not force them to face the consequences of the risks they were taking."[64] Some suggest that the "compensation structure of CDO managers, Wall Street Firms and Rating Agencies" that incentivized more and more new deals reduced the quality of CDO underwriting.[65]

60. Wiseman, 2010; Moody's gave AAA ratings to nearly 43,000 MBSs between 2000 and 2007.
61. Cantor et al., 2007; default for B and Caa to C categories had much higher probability (27 and 52 percent). Note that default rates are used by some banks to define their own rating systems.
62. AIG, 2010.
63. Salmon, 2009.
64. Barberis, 2011; see also Acharya et al., 2009.
65. Davidson and Sanders, 2009.

Financial organizations also increased risk by using incentive systems to remain competitive. For example, a financial institution would give a rating analyst strong financial incentives to give its securities the best AAA rating "even if the rating seemed undeserved." If he did not comply, the analyst might lose the business to another rating agency.[66] Additionally, CDS sellers had unbalanced incentive systems that caused speculative risk-taking. For instance, AIG's culture incorporated a reward system that "placed little responsibility on executives who made very poor decisions"; in 2008 with $40 billion in losses, AIG still gave large bonuses to its managers.[67]

Securities issuers, CDS sellers, and rating agencies alike substantially rewarded agents and executives for boosting sales and offered no counterbalance to assume responsibility for consequences. In some cases, securities and derivatives sellers encouraged lenders to increase subprime loans, and in others they rewarded rating agencies for speeding up their process (with fees or assurance of future business).[68] After the 2008 meltdown, some called for "a change in the compensation structure of rating agencies";[69] the federal government even demanded renegotiation of executive bonuses.[70] In any case, these compensation arrangements emphasized volume, profit, and fees rather than quality; they encouraged poorly underwritten loans, poorly structured and inaccurately rated securities, and poorly researched CDSs.

* * * * * * * *

All participants in Figure 10.2 added their own brand of risk enhancement. The federal government did not regulate the securities or derivatives markets or the rating agencies, thus there were no rules to prevent excessive risk taking. Nonagency securities issuers' lack of experience and push for profitability led to lax underwriting and inferior securities, which concentrated rather than diversified risk. The concentration of CDS holdings and the interconnections among a few large CDS sellers increased their vulnerability to loan defaults and threatened nonmortgage-related CDS holdings. By overrating securities and derivatives, ratings agencies helped hide risk. Finally, incentives encouraged financial organizations to ignore or understate risk and to shun accountability. Beneath these risks was the unspoken assumption that financial markets by nature have all the information necessary to account for risk. This "efficient markets hypothesis" had met its match in the 2008 crisis. Ultimately, the magician made the risk tiger disappear all right, but in the process, the tiger became hungrier. Investors across the world would soon feel its bite.

---

66. Barberis, 2011.
67. Ferrell et al., 2010.
68. See for example Morgenson and Rosner, 2011; Buhl, 2010.
69. Davidson and Sanders, 2009.
70. Andrews and Baker, 2009.

10.2 SYSTEMS THINKING INTERPRETATION

We saw earlier how the system generated money for housing and financial market participants. We now turn to systems thinking to examine the negative aspects of the money-making machine and expose how risk caused economic collapse.

10.2.1 Defaults in the Financial Market

Recall that the money-making phase in the securitization of high risk home loans was early in the game. Low interest rates and easy credit had artificially boosted borrowers' ability to repay debts. During this period, high-risk loans and MBSs grew unchallenged. So, the money-making machine in Figure 10.1 cranked vigorously until one condition turned the money bags into risk tigers: borrowers lost their ability to repay their debts. They defaulted on their loans.

Figure 10.8 inserts the influence of this default factor as two new balancing loops, B$_{loan}$ and B$_{MBS}$, in the money-making machine. (For simplicity, *profit* and *insurance* from Figure 10.1 are removed.) Following the logic of this diagram, more *new high-risk home loans* meant that the more borrowers added to their *current debt*, the greater their danger of losing their *ability to repay debts*. When waves of *ARMs reset* at higher *interest rates*, many couldn't afford the increase in their *current debt*. When borrowers lost their *ability to repay debts*, *defaults* grew dramatically. With more *defaults*, borrower and lender became aware of the risk; *new high-risk home loans* decreased to complete balancing loop B$_{loan}$.

Massive *defaults* not only discouraged new *high-risk home loans*, they also activated the balancing loop B$_{MBS}$ that restrained *new MBSs*. In other words, defaults signaled that risk was too high and reduced the sale of *new*

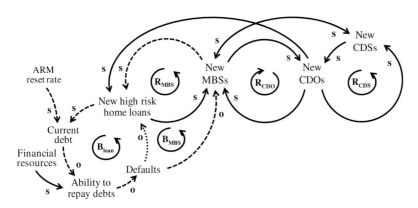

FIGURE 10.8 Defaults affect new loans and invade the financial market.

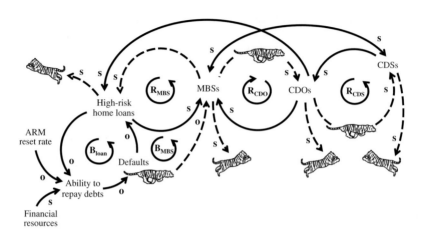

FIGURE 10.9   The risk tiger pounces: Defaults have consequences.

MBSs. With less desire to issue *MBSs* in spite of profit, securities brokers were reluctant to buy *high-risk loans* from lenders. Arrows from *new high-risk home loans* to *current debt* to *ability to repay debts* and to *defaults* complete the B_{MBS} loop.

This systems picture shows how the number of *new* loans, securities, and derivatives declined as defaults rose. However—and this is a *big* however—even though sales were down, outstanding loans, securities, and CDSs were still in the hands of millions of owners, exposing them to ruin if defaults continued. The risk pipeline was still full. Figure 10.9 incorporates these accumulated loans and securities, and illustrates how the risk tiger materialized (for simplicity, *current debt* is removed). When loans defaulted, lenders who had kept them were hurt, owners of the MBSs and CDOs that included these loans were hurt, and firms that had insured these toxic securities against default were hurt. To trace these paths of destruction, follow the risk tiger's dashed lines from *defaults* to *MBSs* to *high risk home loans*, from *MBSs* to *CDOs*, and from *CDOs* to *CDSs*. Eventually the risk tiger pounced on the economy and brought about consequences of spectacular scale and scope.

10.2.2 Consequences

Repercussions took related forms for borrowers and lenders and for securities and derivatives traders. Figure 10.10 lists the consequences these major participants faced. Note that because of their government affiliation, agency investors such as Fannie Mae and Freddie Mac suffered differently than did private lenders or other investors.

CONSEQUENCES OF RISK FOR LOANS	CONSEQUENCES OF RISK FOR SECURITIES	CONSEQUENCES OF RISK FOR DERIVATIVES
Borrowers • Loss = loan amount less sale price • Loss of house & equity • Loss of credit	**Mortgage loan sellers** • Loss of servicing income	**CDS sellers** • Loss = value of default loans • Loss of reserves & costly credit • Corporate bankruptcy
Private mortgage lenders • Loss = loan amount less sale price [if uninsured & loan not sold] • Loss of future income • Bankruptcy & buyouts	**Securities sellers** • Loss of future income **Private investors** [if uninsured] • Loss of income stream • Loss of original investment • Loss of reserves & costly credit • Bankruptcies & buyouts	**Non-agency CDS buyers** • Gain = value of default loans • If CDS seller cannot pay, buyers lose the same as uninsured investors
Agency mortgage lenders **[if loan not sold]** • Loss = loan amount less sale price [if loan not sold] • Loss of future income • Government takeover	**Agency investors** • Loss of income stream • Loss of original investment • Government takeover	**Non-financial/non-housing industry** • Inability to get credit • Sale of goods & services drop • Unemployment • Stock market drop • Economic recession
	Rating agencies • Loss of business	**Rating agencies** • Loss of business

FIGURE 10.10   Consequences of risk for loans, securities, and derivatives.[71]

10.2.3 Systems Integration of Loans, Securities, and Derivatives

Figure 10.11 merges the systems interpretation in Chapter 9 with these new insights to show how high risk home loans influenced the financial market. First, note that this depiction condenses three reinforcing loops, R_{MBS}, R_{CDO}, and R_{CDS}, into a single loop $R_{security}$. From earlier discussions, it should be no surprise that these loops similarly respond to high-risk loans and defaults. Next, look at the spinning gears that kept momentum going: seven reinforcing loops and six balancing loops. On the right side of the diagram, deregulation of the financial industry and corporations' short-term narrow-focused (SN) incentive systems stimulated more high-risk securities and derivatives.

Finally, consider the output of this system: corporate bankruptcies, buyouts, and bailouts. Now we are back to 2008 where this book began: the point at which Fannie Mae and Freddie Mac went into conservatorship; Bank of America bought the failed Countrywide and Merrill Lynch; Lehman Brothers filed the largest bankruptcy in history; Goldman Sachs and Morgan Stanley became traditional bank holding companies under the close supervision of regulators;[72] and the U.S. government authorized an $85 billion bailout for AIG. These are harsh and unintended consequences from a naïve desire to give more people the opportunity to own a home and for a process that issued loans one-by-one.

---

71. For an excellent discussion of expected benefits from MBS and CDO securities, see Levinson, 2010.
72. Dow Jones, 2008; this move ended the rise of securities firms.

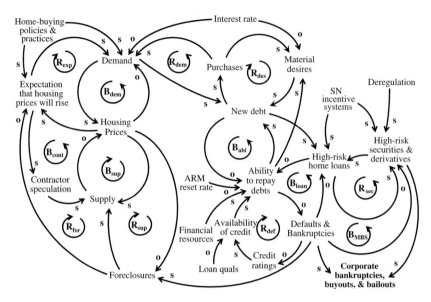

FIGURE 10.11   The integrated system: Housing and financial markets are tightly coupled.

The tail of these consequences reaches beyond 2008. Even in 2012, effects of the defaults circle like buzzards around banking and financial corporations, many of whom are still in the throes of finger-pointing and lawsuits. Bank of America is a prime example of continuing vulnerability. Its purchase of Countrywide in 2008 for a tiny $4 billion is hailed as "the worst deal in history." In addition to business losses of nearly $4 billion in 2009 and nearly $9 billion in 2010, by mid-2011 BofA had settled claims from homeowners, borrowers, securities investors, Fannie Mae and Freddie Mac, and CDO insurers to the tune of nearly $23 billion.[73] As we discovered in Chapter 6, more lawsuits against BofA are pending.

10.2.4 Candidate Leverage Points

From the perspective of the housing market, Chapter 9 identified potential leverage points that could have prevented the economic crisis (restricting credit availability and tempering interest rate changes), and those that might have eased the pain of a fallen economy when the housing bubble burst (low interest rates; fewer foreclosures; greater ability to repay; and restoration of confidence). With the exception of confidence, these levers emphasize formal processes and policies, just as the chapter itself focused on mechanisms that created the housing bubble.

73. Dow Jones, 2011; Gogoi and Pickler, 2011.

Expanding beyond the housing market into the subject of this chapter, Figure 10.11 revealed how securities and derivatives were at the mercy of poor-quality loans. Therefore the same leverage actions to improve loan quality and increase borrowers' ability to repay debt could have reduced the damage for buyers and sellers of securities. Additional levers that may have helped prevent the crisis and avoid a recurrence originate from the risk multipliers (Figure 10.2) and loan defaults. These added levers focus on a single target: reducing risk to diminish massive defaults. Among them are actions that shrink the volume of high-risk securities, actions that raise the standards for loans that are securitized, and actions that improve the accuracy of risk assessments for securities. Specifically these actions would:

- Increase the quality of underwriting for loans that made up the securities.
- Lighten government policies that require GSEs to invest in subprime loans.
- Restructure incentive systems to reward actual performance, balance short-term narrow focus on money-making with longer-term interests, and instill accountability.
- Implement strong, balanced government regulations that require financial corporations and rating agencies to better assess and quantify risk.
- Improve risk models and set securities prices to account for housing downturns and potential changes in interest rates.
- Implement regulations that reduce the conflict of interest and tendency for banks to use "other peoples" money unwisely.

Actions such as these must occur before lingering factors further threaten the economy's frail recovery. Of great concern are loans that rest on the precipice of default or foreclosure. Should these loans fall off the edge, they would energize the detrimental loops in our system and crush those who are still hanging on. The same levers that prevent shaky home loans from defaulting could also inhibit collapse among the securities that are still outstanding.

10.2.5 Current Activities

Chapter 9 highlighted current activities intended to soften economic decay. Among these were maintaining low interest rates and imposing higher limits on deposit insurance to reduce the fear of the loss. Another policy also affects the securities sector: the recent Dodd–Frank act reduces conflict of interest by separating commercial banking from investment banking activities; this policy can diminish future risk.[74] In addition to these actions, there

---

74. The Volcker Rule in the Dodd–Frank Act of 2010, was to go into effect July 2012. However, the rule is contentious; thousands have commented and some believe it will be "impossible" to implement. See earlier footnote and see Torres and Hopkins, 2012.

is evidence of more thoughtful and bigger picture decision-making. For example, in late 2011 BofA tabled its plan to declare bankruptcy for its Countrywide segment, fearing severe repercussions for securities still held by its subsidiaries.[75] Furthermore, researchers such as Mainelli and Giffords persuasively argue that systems thinking could help the financial industry.[76]

* * * * * * * *

This chapter focused on economic mechanisms; its proposed leverage points address formal rules, regulations, and policies. However, these levers are not enough to overturn the damage. Rules, structures, and rewards cannot fully contain human propensities toward self-interest; regulations add inefficiency to any industry and can always be cleverly circumvented. The systems view must also include levers that touch human values, beliefs, and behaviors. In the next chapter, we will integrate these remaining human elements, the yin, into the system.

10.3 SUMMARY

This chapter likened the securitization of poor quality loans to a magic act that makes the tiger of risk temporarily disappear into the financial market. It described unintended effects as financial institutions created mortgage-related securities and sold them on Wall Street, all the while pushing awareness of risk associated with their underlying loans away from those who were in the best position to reduce it. As risky loans wound their way from borrower to lender to securitizing agent to derivatives trader, all participants underplayed or ignored risk instead of spotlighting its presence.

Even before loans left the housing market, borrowers turned a blind eye to whether they could actually afford a loan, and either didn't understand or ignored hazardous terms in these loans. Lenders who could have filtered out questionable borrowers instead made loans to this high-risk market and then sold the loans, along with accountability for them, to financial organizations. Then when financial organizations turned loans into securities, rather than rejecting some of them, they begged for more—regardless of quality. In the pricing and promised returns to investors, these organizations failed to fully account for risk; they were tempted by the expanding housing market and assumed that massive defaults could not happen. Investors, anxious for high returns, were placated by the opinions of rating agencies rather than being alarmed by the actual risk the securities contained. CDS issuers allowed others to quantify the risk of what they insured rather than doing their own digging. Risk rating agencies were mesmerized by customers who wanted immediate turnaround; they rushed to comply, often using inexperienced

75. Davidoff, 2011; Dow Jones, 2011.
76. Mainelli and Giffords, 2009.

raters. And the government deregulated the securities industry, relying instead on personal accountability and the market to contain risk.

One could continue finger pointing. However, a more constructive view is that each participant played a role. Because risk was left unattended, when it finally appeared it had grown to proportions too large to be tamed and had left paw prints in all parts of the housing and financial markets. These two markets had grown hopelessly tangled like a plate of pesto pasta—hard to tease apart and all covered with the same sauce.

Although it is difficult to separate cause from effect, visual depictions in the language of systems thinking allowed us to stand apart from the details and view how the whole system operated. We found three reinforcing loops in the money-making machine of securitization during its early stages and saw how risk moved with profitability. This money-making phase spanned several years, beginning about 2002 (after the stock market crashed and interest rates dropped) and ending about 2007. The first part of the money machine to falter was its front end. Total mortgage loan originations fell dramatically after 2003. Rising interest rates between 2004 and 2006 triggered unmanageably high monthly payments for resetting ARMs.

As huge numbers of defaults finally hit securities, the worst fears and assumed-unlikely consequences attacked the economy like that ravenous risk tiger just out of hiding. The inflection point for this money-making machine occurred in 2005 to 2006, just as defaults swelled and mortgage-related securities waned. The money-making machine collapsed. By 2006 subprime loan originations, MBSs, and CDOs were declining. CDSs dropped drastically in early 2007. By 2008, all except the CDSs (some were nonmortgage related) were below 2001 levels. Figure 10.12 compares peak years for high-risk loans, MBSs, CDOs, and CDSs, with interest rate changes and loan defaults. Although the machine was slowing, its momentum kept some gears moving for a while before it finally stopped. From this depiction we can see lags that span about one year between the various peaks, illustrating the time it took for loans to move along the securitization pipeline.

Yet the collapse of this machine is not the worst of it. While mortgage loans, mortgage-related securities, and CDSs had stopped growing, they left behind a heap of potential defaults. In early 2007, nearly $6 trillion outstanding MBSs were still held by investors somewhere in the world, implying that CDOs and CDSs built from these securities were out there too; all were highly vulnerable to the risk of default even though growth had stopped. At the end of our timeline in 2010—a 3-year lag since the markets disintegrated—over 25 percent of all subprime loans were delinquent and an additional 25 percent had entered or were in the foreclosure process (see Chapter 9). Higher-risk ARMs were in worse shape; nearly 45 percent of subprime ARMs and over 15 percent of prime ARMs were delinquent. In 2012, risk for the remaining toxic loans and securities had not dissipated.

	DEFAULTS CLIMB				
	Fed Funds rate <3% **LOW**		Fed Funds rate >3% **HIGHER**		
	2003	2004	2005	2006	2007
HOME LOANS Total loan originations Peak = $4,330 B	△				
ARM originations Peak = $995 B		△			
Subprime originations Peak = $663 B			△		
MBSs Agency MBSs issued Peak = $2,520 B	△				
Non-agency MBSs issued Peak = $1,320 B			△		
CDOs Total CDOs issued Peak = $520 B				△	
CDSs Total Global CDSs Peak = $62,000 B					△

FIGURE 10.12   Peak years for high-risk loans, securities, and CDSs.

Thirteen loops in the systems depiction in this chapter connect the housing market (with its bubble, high-risk loans, defaults, expectation, and desires) to the financial market (with its high-risk securities). In this portrayal, defaults not only curbed the growth of loans, securities, and CDSs, but also invaded the overflowing storehouses of those already in circulation. Making matters worse, when housing prices dropped 25 percent between 2006 and 2008, defaults soared far above expectations and above the reserves that CDS sellers had set aside; high-risk loans primed the financial industry for bankruptcies, buyouts, and bailouts.

From this systems view, we identified several levers that may help prevent such devastation in the future or clean up its aftermath. Prevention levers in the housing market from the previous chapter could reduce defaults that flattened the financial market; these levers included adjusting interest rates and modifying government policies on home buying and subprime lending, building consumer confidence, and improving borrowers' ability to repay their debts. Levers in this chapter proposed to reduce the volume of securities and derivatives and to tighten thresholds for accepting risk. Further, to mitigate global effects of corporate bankruptcies, buyouts, and bailouts and get the economy back on its feet, other levers added regulations and altered incentive policies. Another important lever was that of systems perspective; any future actions or policies should be assessed in the light of their potential long-term effects.

All these levers seem mundane and imply government intervention and formal rules, which by themselves cannot fix the flagrantly ruinous economic situation. What are we missing? This chapter revealed the most obvious interactions between the housing market and the financial market, and included two fundamental human behaviors: material desires and expectations that fueled growth of demand. However, we did not yet incorporate many of the human attributes from earlier chapters, including the beliefs and values that contribute to desires, and human motivators that feed unethical behaviors. Among these we will find powerful levers which, when combined with the formal actions already mentioned, can strike at the core of what went wrong. The next chapter elaborates on their influence.

Unstated still are the effects of national debt on the American taxpayer, of unemployment and GDP on the economy, of the remaining toxic securities on the many foreign investors, and of the downturn in the American economy on international companies and economies. We expand this global facet in Chapter 12.

Part IV

Yin and Yang: Integration

Chapter 11

Human Roots Are Deep: Yin Meets Yang

Some, in despair of finding meaning and happiness, pursue hedonistic impulses and turn to materialism and consumption.

Richard Ellsworth[1]

By committing ourselves to enterprises that benefit the community, be it our work group or the international community, we reach beyond ourselves and our narrow, personal interests. In the process, we reconcile... self and Other.

Jean Lipman-Blumen[2]

In this book we have popped bubbles, climbed a mountain, tracked a tiger, deplored the state of human ethics, and lamented the loss of wealth and well-being. While these metaphors and concerns enliven descriptions of the economic crisis in the United States, they are just a prelude to the book's finale. We have now reached the point at which all contributing factors come together.

The task of integration is not easily accomplished; interactions are neither isolated nor well-defined. Furthermore, by keeping the human element relatively separate from the mechanics of the crisis, we temporarily side-stepped a greater complexity. Now, having built the story a piece at a time, we are ready to reveal its conclusion. As we do so, keep in mind that like earlier chapters, this chapter uses systems thinking diagrams to illustrate the complexities, dynamics, and interactions in the crisis. And as in earlier chapters, try not to get wrapped up in details. Instead use them to visualize concepts and draw your own conclusions about the story they tell.

This chapter has two themes. First, it elaborates on human influences and combines this Yin of human behavior with the Yang of economic mechanisms. In this merging, humanness makes the crisis more concrete, organic,

---

1. Ellsworth, 2002.
2. Lipman-Blumen, 2000.

and evolving. The significance and deep roots of human influence clearly emerge in the last systems diagram. Second, the chapter demonstrates the unique power of systems thinking, one that "acknowledges the messiness of the world and views a problem in the context of its environment."[3] It helps us appreciate the value of a holistic view in situations where traditional problem-solving and analytic techniques are impotent. Then, by adding human-related levers to our growing list, it re-emphasizes how systems thinking aids in finding solutions whose effects are lasting.

Because understanding the implications of individual behavior in the economic crisis is so vital, we first concentrate on specific human characteristics. Of the traits discussed in earlier chapters, five in particular had the greatest systemic effects: *expectations* (the speculation-driving force in the housing market); *self-interest* and *social interest* (a fundamental source of human tension); *material desires* (the craving for homes and "things"); and finally *greed* (the extreme end of self-interest). These five prevailed during the crisis, while a sixth trait that could have helped ameliorate or prevent the crisis lay dormant. This last trait involves the human search for meaning. All six traits appear in the systems diagram at the end of the chapter and are the origin of our most effective levers.

11.1 EXPECTATIONS

Expectations about the future have a human heritage; they are in part shaped by external sources and in part molded by individual biases and views of the world. Using the tenets of behavioral economics, earlier chapters acknowledged the essential role that expectations play in an economy. Chapter 5 related how consumers' expectations reached a level of irrational exuberance that fueled unrealistic and frantic buying behaviors, and ultimately drove housing prices up. Chapter 8 expressed their importance as part of the $R_{expectation}$ reinforcing loop that raised the demand, supply, and prices of houses. Chapter 9 discovered how the erosion of the expectation about housing prices promoted their collapse and still inhibits economic growth. Expectation and its associated loop appear in the final integration.

11.2 SELF-INTEREST AND SOCIAL INTEREST

Economic journalist William Greider remarked that two ethical systems coexist in our society. These two systems are embodied in *self-interest* and *social interest*. On one hand, at the individual level, self-interest is partly driven by our instinct to survive. And at the societal level, self-interest

---

3. Maani and Cavana, 2007.

allows a capitalist economy to function. In principle, such an economy generates wealth through individuals' self-interested behaviors, implying that we "need not accept responsibility for collateral damage to society." As a result, we tend to push "negative consequences off on someone else."[4] Ethicists Bazerman and Tenbrunsel depict self-interest more candidly. They see it as a "want self" that often behaves "without regard for moral principles."[5]

On the other hand, "society's softer principles" offset pure self-interest and enable individuals to thrive in a society. These principles define "mutual rewards and responsibilities toward life itself... [and create a] happiness that is more central to our lives than material accumulation." Social interest not only obliges us to realize our own potential, but also commits us to "society's common code of right and wrong" and compels us to build "beyond our own needs" for future generations.[6]

These human motivators—one focused on our own needs and the other directed toward living in society—are in constant tension. When self-interest and social interest are balanced, economies, nations, and individuals can function optimally. This chapter explores how balance is maintained or is skewed. It broadens the discussion of *self-interest, social interest, moral grounding,* and *rewards* from Chapter 7 and incorporates *awareness* of consequences and *human defense mechanisms.*

11.2.1 Moral Grounding

Moral grounding helps keep self-interest from overpowering social interest. The "should self"[7] of moral grounding constrains our "want self" and directs us toward what is *right*. Moral grounding varies among individuals and cultures. Chapter 7 described its most significant sources as a combination of innate moral values and ethically relevant norms in the national and work cultures that surround us. When the socially responsible side of human nature weakens and excessive self-interest tempts us, moral grounding appears. It only works, however, when it is strong enough to subdue these temptations *and* when we know that a particular action involves right and wrong.

11.2.2 Awareness

Oftentimes we are so focused on immediate circumstances that we fail to take a long view of our choices. In these cases, we may simply be unaware

---

4. Greider, 2003.
5. Bazerman and Tenbrunsel, 2011.
6. Greider, 2003.
7. Bazerman and Tenbrunsel, 2011.

of how others are involved. When choices are not viewed in the context of right and wrong, or when others are out of sight, individuals may not look beyond their own spheres. An example in the crisis involves the arm's length relationships between those who made and sold risky loans and those who bought securities that contained an indistinct conglomeration of these loans. Lenders couldn't begin to answer (and didn't ask) the question of who would be hurt if loans defaulted. And investors couldn't possibly know whether borrowers would default on their loans. Had lenders or investors been more aware of others, they might have acted differently. Previous chapters noted that this facelessness not only diminished *awareness*, but also encouraged lenders and investors to *disregard* harmful effects, even if they *knew* others were being hurt. Scientific research supports this observation, and finds that the human brain distinguishes between personal and impersonal attributes when making moral judgments: the more personal the consequences, the greater the emotional reaction.[8] Other human traits such as internal defense mechanisms also account for ignoring harm to others.

11.2.3 Human Defense Mechanisms

In contrast with moral grounding, we humans have built-in mechanisms that dull our obligation to take responsible actions. When we experience good feelings or derive material gains from self-interest, we don't want our conscience to spoil the party. Extensive investigation in this area exposes both emotional and rational methods that help individuals either ignore the prickly interruptions of their moral voices or simply alter their tone. In either event, the result is the same: we take no action.

Perhaps the most typical mechanism is rationalizing or justifying the impropriety of an act. Ethicist Saul Gellerman describes three common ways to rationalize: (1) it's not *really* illegal or immoral—everyone else is doing it; (2) it's in my best interest; (3) it's safe because it will never be found out or made public.[9] Other popular rationales during the crisis included reciprocity (the bank treated me poorly, so it's okay to walk away from my loan) and passing the buck (they *made* me do it, it's not *my* fault). Behavioral economist Dan Ariely suggests that we also have a sort of "flexible psychology" that allows us to "cheat 'just by a bit'—benefiting financially from cheating while at the same time managing not to feel bad about ourselves."[10] This technique is one more way to rationalize. A little white lie doesn't seem

---

8. Greene et al., 2001.
9. Gellerman, 1986; Gellerman also identified a fourth rationalization that relates to organizations: "my company will condone it and protect me because it helps them."
10. Ariely, 2009.

so bad; swiping a pack of pencils from the supply room is nothing compared to stealing an iPad or embezzling a million bucks.

Other defense mechanisms divert attention away from moral grounding and toward something more immediate like rewards or current concerns. These mechanisms include "ethical fading" in which rewards and goals make ethical considerations blend into the background; "overly discounting the future" in which individuals or organizations ignore future consequences of their actions; and even "motivated blindness" in which those "who have a vested self-interest in a situation have difficulty approaching the situation without bias."[11] When forces like wanting to belong or seeking external rewards strengthen these defenses, individuals may fail to bring behavior in line with moral grounding.

11.2.4 Short-Term Narrow-Focused Rewards

Rewards are powerful motivators that not only allow us to ignore moral grounding, but also drive us to act without regard for others. Chapter 4 introduced the relationship between short-term rewards used by financial corporations and the risky, self-focused behaviors of employees. Chapter 7 described rewards that incentivize immediate and narrow results so powerfully that they tap our goal-directed and pleasure-seeking human nature and prompt us to behave unethically to receive them. These short-term narrow-focused (SN) rewards significantly influence self-interest and are an important part of our discussion on the tension between self-interest and social interest.

* * * * * * * *

By including moral grounding, awareness, human defense mechanisms, and rewards, we can describe vital interactions between self-interest and social interest in systems thinking terms. While these two interests can be synergistic (such as when other-directed acts also benefit self or when self-directed acts also benefit society), we deliberately contrast them to amplify the point. Figure 11.1 illustrates their relationship in a new balancing loop (B_{ethics}) whose stability comes from moral grounding. In this loop, both self-interest and social interest can exist simultaneously at some intensity, or one can become excessive as the other weakens. I do not suggest that this portrayal is all-encompassing or that it is valid in every instance; nor do I hint that moral grounding is fixed or uniform among individuals. However, the loop does reveal the importance of moral grounding and the continual balancing act between self-interest and social interest. It also shows that individuals must make choices and take action to maintain that balance. In this depiction, balance may be fleeting, particularly when there is little awareness

---

11. Bazerman and Tenbrunsel, 2011. Tenbrunsel and Messick (2004) point out additional interactions between self-interest and unethical behavior and link "ethical fading" with self-interest that causes self-deception, which leads to unethical behavior.

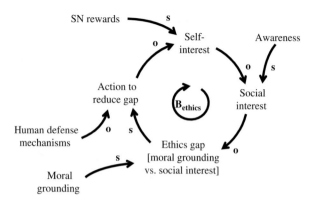

FIGURE 11.1   Self-interest and social interest balanced by moral grounding.

or concern about how others are involved, when human defense mechanisms are strong, or when rewards promote excessive self-interest. During the crisis, these factors powerfully skewed the ethical balancing loop B_{ethics} toward self-interest.

To exaggerate the distinction between the two motives, the B_{ethics} loop puts them in an inverse relationship. Here, when *self-interest* is encouraged by *rewards* and gains undue strength, *social interest* can weaken. If *social interest* dips too far below *moral grounding*, individuals feel the discomfort of an *ethics gap*. As this gap widens, they would try to reduce it by decreasing self-interest or increasing social interest. On the other hand, in theory, if social interest overwhelms self-interest to the point of personal harm or feelings of unfairness, different actions are necessary.

As a trivial example of the ethics loop, suppose you go to dinner with a group and the waiter puts a basket of warm garlic rolls next to you. The delicious aroma entices you to keep them nearby and you surreptitiously eat them. Soon, when your stomach complains and someone asks you to pass the basket, you realize there are no rolls left. In this case, the gap between your mother's lessons on sharing and your gluttony widens. Feeling guilty, you might try to close the gap by apologizing or buying more rolls. However, if your defenses cause you to rationalize, you do nothing; you might tell yourself that you deserve to be rewarded with all the rolls since you hadn't eaten all day.

11.3 MATERIAL DESIRES

Desire for material goods reflects the prominent biases of the American and corporate cultures. Of the cultural attributes introduced in Chapter 4 and discussed in Chapter 7, three have significant effects on material desires: *entitlement* (to own a home and to garner high salaries);

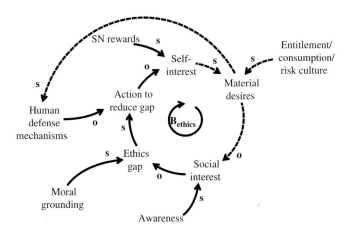

FIGURE 11.2   Culture affects material desires.

consumption (a burning drive for possessions and a willingness to go into debt to get them); and *risk* (consumers' and sellers' propensity toward risk-taking to get rewards). These attributes define an *ECR culture* or entitlement/consumption/risk culture.

Figure 11.2 adds *material desires* to the B_{ethics} loop and shows the influence of *ECR culture* on these desires. When *self-interest* and *culture* both feed *material desires*, these *desires* can blind individuals to a broader *social interest*. Choices that ignore *social interest* trigger an *ethics gap* and signal a need for *action*. However, individuals may fail to act, especially if *material desires* strengthen their *defense mechanisms* and *short-term narrow-focused rewards* stimulate their *self-interest*. For example, to get a fat bonus, lenders may rationalize lying to a borrower about a loan. Lack of corrective action in this case increases self-interest at the expense of social interest.

Culture's influence on material desires and eventually on self-interest is bidirectional. Continued presence of extreme self-interest and materialism embeds these attitudes into organizational or national cultures. Culture also influences moral grounding. If it becomes culturally acceptable to ignore the harmful effects of our actions, some will soon find it personally acceptable. However, because cultural changes occur so slowly and exceed our timeline, neither relationship appears in the diagram.

11.4 GREED

Up to this point, self-interest and social interest functioned in a give-and-take relationship. But what if self-interest overpowers social interest as it did during the crisis? Will other human motivations surface? As earlier chapters described, self-interest was in fact "taken to such an extreme that... [it was]

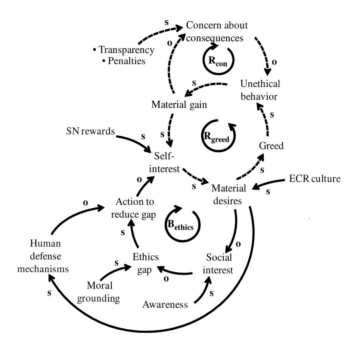

FIGURE 11.3   Interaction of self-interest, unethical behavior, and concern about consequences.

perceived as unacceptable or immoral"[12] and was soon recognized as *greed*. After the crisis, President Obama decried prevalent attitudes "that valued wealth over work, selfishness over sacrifice, and greed over responsibility."[13] Excessive self-interest—greed—engulfed individuals who took on debt without considering consequences. It invaded corporations that legitimized "a push for greater profits."[14] However, self-interest didn't stop at material desires and it didn't stop with greed. Unethical behaviors sprouted when the hardy seeds of greed landed in the fertile soil of secrecy. No one was looking.

To illustrate this progression from *self-interest* to *unethical behavior*, Figure 11.3 merges the B_{ethics} loop with the R_{greed} and $R_{consequences}$ loops from Chapter 7. With little *transparency* and few *penalties*, *concern about consequences* dissipates; lack of concern enables the *unethical behavior* that promotes *material gain* and increases *self-interest*. Now we are squarely in the B_{ethics} loop where extreme *self-interest* elevates *material desires* that can

---

12. This definition of greed is in Wang et al., 2011. The complete definition considers that "extreme" is "based on prevailing social norms regarding the effects of one's behavior on others."
13. Wang et al., 2011; from Obama, September 15, 2009.
14. Wang et al., 2011.

squelch *social interest*. The sequence now follows the path described earlier; individuals must make choices.

11.5 ECONOMIC ENVIRONMENT

Chapter 4 introduced the pre-crisis economic environment and Chapter 7 described it as one of temptation and opportunity that tested individuals' moral grounding. From easy credit and lax loan requirements to the money-making feats of speculators and financial giants, this atmosphere accommodated and even sanctified individual gain. It offered abundant and unimpeded ways to satisfy desires and presented enormous incentives to act in self-interested ways. The sheer magnitudes of gain—like the multimillion dollar bonuses in the securities industry—were too enticing to pass up.

However, temptation and opportunity were not a special privilege of the elite or limited to corporate executives. Ordinary individuals wanting to borrow money discovered that the environment actually promoted their spending habits, in spite of their inability to repay. As early as 2002, Fed chairman Greenspan recognized the unparalleled influence of the environment on greedy behavior, suggesting that "it is not that humans have become any more greedy than in generations past. It is that the avenues to express greed had grown so enormously."[15]

Figure 11.4 shows the effects of the economic environment. In simple terms, it nurtured *self-interest* by providing *opportunity* and *temptation*. This extra boost to *self-interest* joined forces with *rewards*, with the *greed* reinforcing loop R_{greed}, and with the *ECR culture* and worked its way around the loop B_{ethics} to dampen *social interest*. In this depiction, greater *material desires* also strengthened *defense mechanisms* and discouraged any *action* to reduce the *ethics gap*. Ultimately, with no deterrent, *self-interest* grew. In other words, *all* paths exaggerated self-interest and *none* attended to social interest. This shadow side of human nature—excessive self-interest—boldly displayed itself during the economic crisis in the U.S.

We are missing another trait of human nature that can be engaged constructively: the search for meaning. This trait comes from the beneficial side of our need for significance rather than from the detrimental side we discussed in Chapter 7. Although mostly absent during the crisis, the potential of this positive trait belongs in our systems picture for it may be the secret to escaping the grasp of excessive and destructive self-interest.

11.6 SEARCH FOR MEANING

Since the days of the ancient Greeks, human's search for meaning—for significance—has been a topic of intense interest. This yearning is compelling

---

15. Greenspan, 2002.

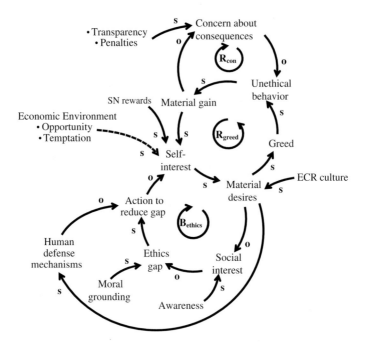

FIGURE 11.4   Economic environment influences self-interest.

and can be dysfunctional if it seeks a myopic fulfillment from monetary rewards, achievement, status, or power as we saw in Chapter 7. Beyond these extrinsic trappings, finding a *meaningful purpose* can pacify our need for significance in beneficial ways and diminish our short-sighted self-interested pursuits. In fact, both ancient and recent findings in psychology and human behavior relate that having a worthy, meaningful purpose expands our happiness and well-being.[16]

For a purpose to be worthwhile and have meaning, it must make us believe in something beyond ourselves; we must feel part of a larger whole (whether family, organization, nation, or society). In systems terms, Figure 11.5 introduces the reinforcing loop $R_{purpose}$ to show how *meaningful purpose* reduces excessive *self-interest*. Although it is not as simple or as clinical as the diagram implies, this reinforcing loop intensifies the power of *meaningful purpose*. It allows us to transcend our small selves and commit to a greater cause—one that focuses our attention on broader *social interests*, strengthens *moral grounding*, and lessens the enticement of *short-term, narrow-focused rewards*. Note the far-reaching influence of meaningful purpose on greed and unethical behavior.

---

16. Meaning is a powerful requisite to individual well-being and organizational success. See Baumeister and Vohs, 2005; Ellsworth, 2002; Frankl, 1985.

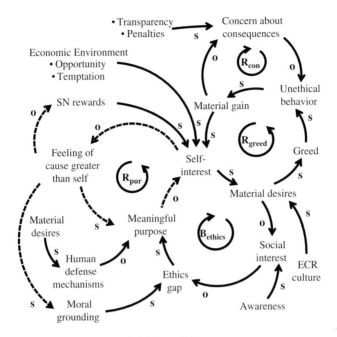

FIGURE 11.5   Meaningful purpose diminishes self-interest.

We know from the well-publicized behaviors of organizations and individuals that the $R_{purpose}$ loop was frail during the crisis—material gain,
rewards, culture, and environment weakened the potential of meaningful purpose. Had it been nurtured, it could have offset other dysfunctions. Later in
the chapter, we will integrate its influences.

11.7 SYSTEMS THINKING INTERPRETATION

Now that we have introduced the final building blocks of human interactions,
we are ready to construct an integrated systems picture of the economic crisis in the U.S. We will assemble it piece by piece, combining human elements with economic relationships from previous chapters. Once the picture
is complete, we will identify candidate leverage points in human-related
areas.

11.7.1 Integrating Self-Interest and Social Interest with Debt Dynamics

The first piece of our systems picture merges self-interest and social interest
with relationships that incorporate debt. Although these relationships apply
to all types of debt, this interpretation concentrates on *high-risk home loans*

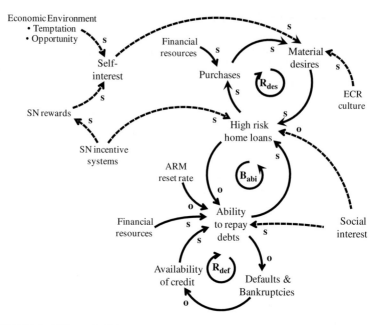

FIGURE 11.6 Effects of self-interest and social interest on debt dynamics.

in particular since they had a primary role in the crisis. We begin with three loops from Chapter 9 that describe debt dynamics, namely R_{desire}, $B_{ability}$, and $R_{default}$. Dashed lines in Figure 11.6 show how *self-interest* and *social interest, economic environment*, corporate *incentive systems* and *rewards*, and the *ECR culture* affected the number of *high risk home loans* and the *ability to repay* these loans.

On the left, *self-interest* that has been elevated by the *economic environment* and by *rewards*, stimulates *material desires* and encourages borrowing (*high risk home loans* in this case) to *purchase* homes in the R_{desire} loop. This loop describes two levels of influence that appeared in the crisis: the behavior of individuals and the aggregated economic behavior of households. First, as discussed in earlier chapters, this loop mimics the hedonic treadmill: the more individuals have, the more they want and the more they borrow to buy what they want. This level applies to all forms of debt used to make purchases, including home loans. In this case, households take on debt that they cannot hope to repay. This excessive debt diminishes ability to make payments on home loans and eventually results in loan defaults and bankruptcies.

Second, the loop in Figure 11.6 purposely describes the cumulative escalation of *high-risk home loans*. In this case, the *ECR culture* stimulates *material desires* of households to own a home. The easy *availability of credit* described in Chapter 9 falsely inflates their *ability to repay debts* and encourages some to take out home loans with "affordability" features even when they normally would not qualify and cannot afford the real cost of the loan. The more borrowers who are in this financially precarious position, the more homes are purchased using *high-risk home loans*. As more of these households buy homes, other prospective home owners want to experience their same success; the ECR culture supports their *material desires* and they too take out a home loan even if they cannot afford it. The R_{desire} loop thus causes escalating growth of *high-risk home loans* and intensifies *material desires* in more households.

On the right of the figure, a sense of *social interest* (and the personal benefits it can have), tends to color choices concerning debt. Greater *social interest* may cause individuals to think twice about taking out a *home loan* they cannot afford when they consider consequences to themselves and to others if they default. For similar reasons, *social interest* may also increase the tendency to repay current debt even if it means personal sacrifice. Both influences can eventually diminish *defaults and bankruptcies* in the $R_{default}$ loop. However, as we noted earlier, self-interest became extreme during the crisis. Individuals were less inclined to limit purchases or repay debt and borrowed more than they could afford to feed their desires, all of which signaled a widespread weakening of *social interest*.

11.7.2 Integrating Greed, Ethics, and Consequences

Figure 11.7 adds the ethics loop B_{ethics}, the greed loop R_{greed}, and the concern about consequences loop $R_{consequences}$ to the growing picture. This depiction shows how *material desires* and low *concern about consequences* boosted *unethical behavior* that further inflated *self-interest* and increased the use of *high risk home loans*. Examples of unethical behavior appeared at every stage: high-risk borrowers lied about their qualifications to get a loan; lenders misled borrowers about risky loan types to make a commission; and those who sold securities that contained these loans ignored their poor quality to increase profit. None of these players considered consequences. More simply put, excessive self-interest and unimpeded material desires evolved into greed and unethical behavior and produced the shaky mountain of debt on which the economy rested—a mountain that exceeded any *ability to repay*. These outcomes initiated the progression toward *defaults* and *bankruptcies*. We already know that the heavy weight of defaults crushed the housing and financial markets.

11.7.3 Integrating the Housing and Financial Markets

The next piece of the picture incorporates housing and financial market dynamics from Chapters 8 and 10. Figure 11.8 joins human-related Yin loops with other mechanistic Yang loops including the $R_{securities}$ loop in the

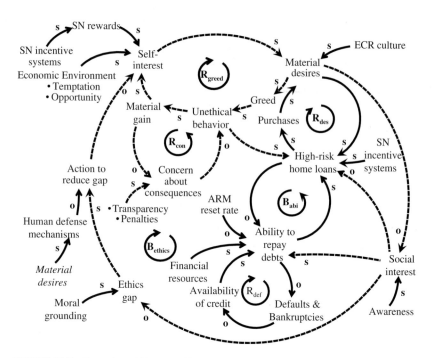

FIGURE 11.7   Excessive self-interest affects debt.

financial market and the R_{demand} loop that linked debt and the housing market. Dashed lines identify three reinforcing loops (R_{desire}, R_{greed}, and
$R_{expectation}$), and one balancing loop (B_{ethics}), which contain five of the six primary human traits we introduced earlier: expectations, self-interest, social
interest, material desires, and greed. You may notice that the previous influence of defaults and bankruptcies on high risk home loans in B_{loan} (from
Chapter 10) now includes social interest. You may also notice that one human
element is missing: meaningful purpose. We will expand on the roles of social
interest and meaningful purpose when we discuss candidate leverage points.

This diagram can be tedious if you faithfully trace each path. So, first
consider the big picture—look at the forest instead of the trees. Hold the diagram a foot or so in front of you. How would you describe the crisis from
this perspective? When I tried this technique on others, responses ranged
from "chaos" to "a multi-armed, multi-eyed monster." Another's reply of
"whirlpools" inspired a mental image of a treacherous ocean where powerful
whirlpools sucked in the nation's wealth; this image inspired the title of the
book. At any rate, one thing is certain: the four primary human-related loops
around material desires, expectations, greed, and ethics (the conflict between
self-interest and social interest) invaded the housing market on the left and
the financial market on the right.

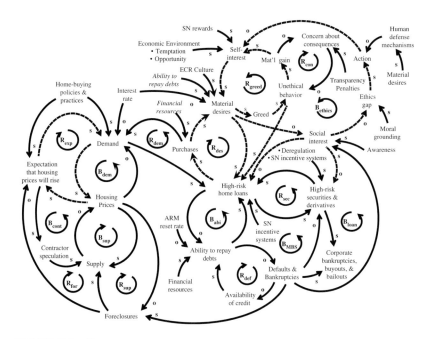

FIGURE 11.8 Yin meets yang.

Rather than plunging directly into the circles and arrows of the diagram, we will tap our right brains again to grasp the difficulty of sweeping up the economic clutter. Imagine that the dashed curves of the human-related loops are roots of noxious weeds that are about to wind around the mechanical gears of the economy. As these weeds grow, their roots inextricably embed themselves into prepared ground—into supply, demand, and housing prices; into debt, defaults, and foreclosures; into the structuring and selling of financial securities. Prior to the crisis, the weedlike tendrils from these loops assailed normal operation of the economy and quickly soaked up its nourishment. Now imagine how time-consuming and damaging it would be to pull the weeds out by their roots once they are established.

Continuing with this analogy, notice the mass of roots that enter the heart of the crisis—into *high risk home loans* and into *high-risk securities and derivatives*. High-risk loans, securities, and derivatives fed on excessive *self-interest, greed,* and *unethical behavior*; they rose through the *expectation* of escalating housing prices; and they climbed without the influence of *social interest* to halt their growth.

We could go on and on with these descriptions, however, once you discover how completely human influences surround loans, derivatives, and securities, you will see that whatever happens to these human elements affects all other paths. In the end, the dynamics lead us to the personal *defaults, bankruptcies* and *foreclosures* that devastated *securities and derivatives* and created the preconditions of *corporate bankruptcies, buyouts,* and *bailouts.* Once the roots of extreme and dysfunctional human behavior grew strong, the economy could no longer survive. While the decay of this little ecosystem was inevitable, we can consider what might have controlled the growth of these human weeds and prevented the subsequent damage.

11.7.4 Candidate Leverage Points

Near the center of the diagram, the area of high risk home loans is an excellent place to look for leverage points. Figure 11.1 with its simple expression of human dynamics and Figure 11.8 with its complex rendering show that strengthening social interest and tempering self-interest could be prime candidates to reduce high-risk debt and at the same time decrease the risk in the securities that contain these loans. Of course, striving to relieve this tension between self and other has been around for ages. Although worthwhile, it is not easily done.[17] Furthermore, effects of actions that touch self-interest or social interest are not immediate for we are dealing with human nature and with beliefs and values.

So exactly how can we produce a healthy balance between self-interest and social interest? We turn to two categories of leveraging actions. In one category, actions can be accomplished by various participants in the economy—individuals, families and friends, corporations, media, and the nation's administrators. The second requires specific actions from corporations involved in the 2008 meltdown.

11.7.4.1 Category 1: Expand Awareness of Consequences

This first category affects social interest. It aims to reduce the growth of high risk home loans (and other debt) and increase the likelihood that individuals will repay their loans. This example gives two ways to bolster social interest: one *after* bad things have happened and the other *before* they can occur.

After Consequences Occur

The mere presence of massive home loan defaults and bankruptcies can increase social interest. Threats from bill collectors or watching neighbors

---

17. Ancient examples are found in Aristotle's virtue of the "golden mean" and Confucius' "doctrine of the golden mean" (Aristotle, 1999, Book II; Confucius, 1994; Solomon, 2005).

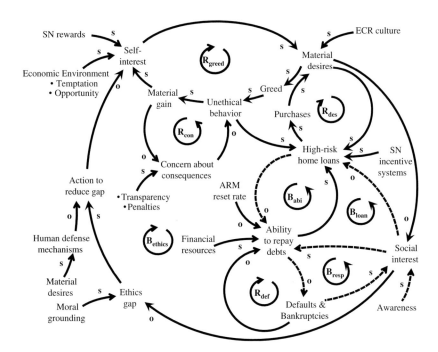

FIGURE 11.9   Awareness affects social interest.

lose their homes can be wake-up calls that cause one to shred credit cards, take on a second job, encourage other family members to work, or make arrangements with the bank. While this approach succeeded for some (there were fewer loan originations after 2003 and consumer debt decreased in 2008), for others it was ineffective. Many people felt trapped. Pushing responsibility onto someone else may have seemed like their only solution (bankruptcy filings peaked in 2005).

Setting bankruptcy aside, Figure 11.9 illustrates the case where pressure from defaults expands social interest, albeit perhaps more from the threat of harm than from a motivation for social good. In this partial systems depiction, two balancing loops (B_{loan} from prior discussions and a new loop $B_{responsibility}$) appear from these dynamics. In the B_{loan} loop, expanded *social interest* reduces the tendency for lenders and borrowers to initiate new *high-risk home loans*; it ultimately reduces *defaults and bankruptcies*. Similarly, in the $B_{responsibility}$ loop, growing *social interest* increases *ability* (or need) *to repay* and again reduces *defaults and bankruptcies*. These balancing loops combine with reinforcing loops R_{desire} and $R_{default}$ to create a limits-to-growth systems construct and put an upper bound on high risk home loans, defaults, and bankruptcies.

Before Consequences Occur

Certain actions can awaken social interest *before* damage happens. For various reasons,[18] individuals simply may not consider others in their decisions or may not view choices through an ethical lens. Perhaps they are too busy. Perhaps they are optimistic or judge risk inaccurately, as did so many in the economic crisis. Perhaps consequences are too far in the future or removed from personal concerns. Regardless of the reason, deliberately considering decisions with *awareness* of consequences to others can increase *social interest* that encourages other-minded behaviors. Through its influence on *social interest*, this awareness engages the two balancing loops B_{loan} and $B_{responsibility}$.

Making side-effects more personal heightens awareness of potential individual and social consequences. Frequent public discussion of the economic damage caused by loan defaults could remind those who are considering new debt or are not repaying current debt that they are at risk and that others are involved. This leverage depends on fear and on the presence or threat of harmful circumstances; it is effective only as long as these conditions exist. When defaults and bankruptcies diminish and no longer trigger responsible behavior, or when there are few reminders of their potential damage, social interest declines and the door to self-interest opens wide. Given these challenges, a second category of levers can have more lasting effects. These levers operate on self-interest and social interest by involving organizations.

11.7.4.2 Category 2: Harness Corporate Influence

This category relies on the human trait we set aside earlier: the search for meaning. Because organizations are essential parts of our lives, they can energize this constructive side of human nature. Individuals spend, will spend, or have spent much of their lives affiliated with some organization or other, whether as a customer, an employee, an investor, or a volunteer. To run smoothly, society depends on their success; as Peter Drucker puts it, organizations "in today's society are increasingly the access to social status, to community, and to individual achievement and satisfaction."[19] What organizations do and how they do it matter to individuals and to society. Thus, with such profound influence and the responsibility this influence imposes, the purpose of an organization "must lie outside of the business itself. In fact, it must lie in society..."[20]

---

18. Messick and Bazerman, 1996. Causes of unethical decision-making include: limiting our assessment of possible consequences, believing we will not be found out or that we are in control, discounting the future, misjudging risk, misperceiving causes, discrimination and bias, and being overly optimistic or overconfident.
19. Drucker, 2008.
20. Drucker, 1986.

If we can motivate organizations to create meaning for individuals and to maintain ethical environments while enhancing organizational success *and* benefitting society, we will have harnessed an enormously powerful lever. Corporate-centered actions, like the three that follow, can increase social interest *and* diminish myopic self-interest that harms others. These actions build on insights described in Chapter 4 about the power of alternate beliefs and long-term-oriented rewards and values.

Strengthen Meaningful Purpose

When a leader defines a *meaningful corporate purpose* from which individuals find significance, that purpose is a powerful precursor for employee well-being and organizational success. It encourages employees to "transcend their own immediate interests to achieve concern for their contributions to their organization and the greater good."[21] Optimally, an organization's purpose would incorporate the needs of society and the growth of its employees as well as its own sustainability and profitability. However, meaningful purpose is not just a bunch of words displayed on a bulletin board. It must touch the heart of human nature; its use involves changing attitudes, values, and beliefs. It will take time.

Restructure Incentives

Keeping the weighty influence of organizations and their leaders in mind, we turn to organizational incentive systems that motivate employees. To be rewarded, individuals must align their efforts with organizational goals. A market economy relies on this alignment with the assumption that profitability goals equate to social good. In the words of economist Joseph Stiglitz, "when private awards are well aligned with social objectives, things work well; when they are not, matters can get ugly..."[22]

This discussion of rewards is germane for the economic crisis, especially because the financial sector was so deeply involved. Incentives here were often grossly distorted; rewarding short-term performance with bonuses engendered huge imbalances that promoted self-interest and demoted social objectives. In this part of the economy, says Stiglitz, "misalignment between social and private returns was clear: financial marketers were amply rewarded but had engaged in such egregious risk-taking that, for the economy as a whole, they had created risk *without reward*" for others in the economy.[23]

Suppose, however, that rewards support a meaningful purpose—one that goes beyond profit and embraces broader interests. By aligning interests of

21. Steger and Dik, 2010.
22. Stiglitz, 2010.
23. Stiglitz, 2010.

three stakeholders (individuals, corporation, and society), leaders amplify the power of rewards. In the systems view, *meaningful corporate purpose* with supportive *incentives* simultaneously reduces *self-interest* and increases *social interest.*

Increase Product Transparency and Penalties

Apart from eliciting positive responses to rewards and purpose, this third action thwarts unethical behaviors. Clear explanations about the benefits and risks of loans and securities, and appropriate penalties for lack of ethics, increase concern about consequences. We met this action earlier in Chapter 7 when trying to increase individuals' concern about consequences.

＊ ＊ ＊ ＊ ＊ ＊ ＊ ＊

The partial systems diagram in Figure 11.10 builds on previously described relationships and incorporates the influence from the three corporate-centered actions: strengthening meaningful purpose, restructuring incentives, and reducing unethical behaviors through transparency and penalties. In this figure, *meaningful corporate purpose* feeds the reinforcing loop, $R_{purpose}$. Individuals who derive meaning from work are less inclined toward excessive *self-interest* that stimulates the R_{greed} loop. As self-interest

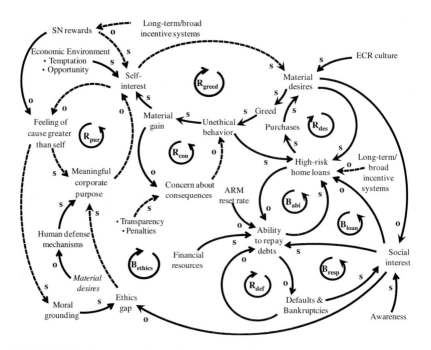

FIGURE 11.10   Corporate actions reduce excessive self-interest.

decreases, the *feeling of a cause greater than self* expands and heightens the importance of that purpose. In addition to defining a meaningful purpose, leaders must also translate that purpose into goals and incentives. Long term, broadly-focused *incentive systems* that replace the *short-term, narrow-focused incentive systems* prevalent during the crisis can encourage individuals to expand their horizons. Finally, when *transparency* replaces secrecy about risk or product flaws, and appropriate *penalties* are applied, *concern about consequences* engages and *unethical behavior* wanes.

When employees' (including executives) self-interest is contained, their *unethical behaviors* diminish because they feel part of something important. As *unethical behaviors* lessen, the number of *high-risk home loans* drops and their quality improves. As a side benefit, when an organization cares about long-term consequences to consumers and to society, consumers find they can trust that organization.

How can we make these actions more concrete? What purpose and what rewards could possibly have this much power? Imagine that the stated purpose of a lending agency is to put the most people successfully into a home rather than to make the most subprime loans. Imagine that success is measured by the number of households who keep these homes for three or four years. Lending behaviors would change; agents would be more interested in ensuring that these households can afford the loan. Then, suppose that the corporate purpose of financial agencies is to build wealth for investors. Suppose that performance is measured three or four years after the sale in terms of how accurately they communicated risk on the securities they sold. These securities agents would try their best to accurately assess risk and clearly describe it. What might happen if executive salaries were based on long-term performance rather than short-term profit? Unethical behaviors should diminish and belief in this type of corporate purpose, when supported by appropriate rewards, should amplify concern about the consequences of short-term behaviors.

11.7.5 Integrating Human-Related Levers

Figure 11.11 combines the human-related levers with all the other relationships we have described to illustrate the complete systems diagram for the economic crisis in the U.S. To make this diagram more universal, *meaningful corporate purpose* became *meaningful purpose*—one that can be derived from other sources as well as from organizations. When all the various levers are applied, particularly those that engage humans' more constructive traits, effects ripple through the system creating greater social interest, less myopic self-interest, and more ethical behavior. In this diagram, we've added the awareness that when meaningful purpose allows individuals to transcend self-interest, *moral grounding* grows and weakens *defense mechanisms* that can cause individuals to stray from a morally grounded path.

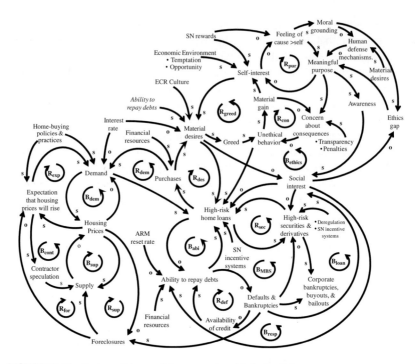

FIGURE 11.11   Systems diagram of the economic crisis in the U.S.

Other insights about the economic crisis and new reinforcing and balancing loops can no doubt be gleaned from this systems depiction. The knowledge that other loops are present underscores both the power of systems thinking and the complexity of the crisis. Furthermore, while this description was specific to the U.S., a tailored version that incorporates specific national issues could most likely apply to other nations as well. These revisions would surely contain similar human behaviors.

11.7.6 Current Activities

Because the crisis had such serious repercussions, solutions have been proposed from all quarters. Let's put a few of the current activities into a systems context and consider how effective they may be. Three types of solutions are significant: those that alter self-interest, those that increase concern about consequences, and those that affect social interest.

11.7.6.1 Self-Interest

The direct path from economic environment to self-interest in Figure 11.11 indicates that less opportunity and lower temptation for material gains can keep excessive self-interest in check. Post-crisis actions that altered the economic environment include changes to home-buying policies and practices and use of monetary policy. These actions reduced credit availability by strengthening loan qualifications, diluted government encouragement of subprime loans, and increased interest rates. However, they also had the unintended consequences of dampening economic growth.

Reducing excessive salaries and ill-conceived bonuses also affects self-interest and decreases motivation to behave unethically. Currently, the government requires disclosure of executive compensation for companies in the financial services industry and allows shareholders to vote on pay increases.[24] For example in April 2012, over half of Citigroup's shareholders surprised the corporation with "a vote of no confidence to the bank's executive compensation plan"; Citigroup's board considered the vote "a serious matter."[25]

11.7.6.2 Concern about Consequences and Social Interest

Greater awareness of damaging consequences from unethical behaviors is a natural fallout of the meltdown. However, more proactive attempts to find, punish, and prevent unethical behaviors have also occurred. Figure 11.11 showed how actions that increase concern about consequences, reduce unethical behavior, and enhance awareness that others are involved can have positive effects.

These types of actions include public humiliation and official investigations. For example, *Time Magazine* pointed a blaming finger at unethical icons such as Angelo Mozilo of Countrywide, Frank Raines of Fannie Mae, Dick Fuld of Lehman Brothers, and Joe Cassano of AIG.[26] Official investigations targeted big corporations such as Countrywide,[27] Merrill Lynch,[28] and Goldman Sachs,[29] and small potatoes such as Argent Mortgage Company in Cleveland.[30] In addition, the Dodd—Frank reform act (see Chapter 2) placed restrictions and consequences on abusers, and required greater transparency and risk assessments for activities in the financial market, thus making it more difficult to behave unethically.

* * * * * * * *

While all these actions were necessary and certainly influenced behaviors, most occurred after the fact. Furthermore each one tried to contain self-interest rather than to nourish the part of human nature that seeks growth

---

24. Sweet, 2010; these conditions are in the Dodd—Frank Wall Street Reform and Consumer Protection Act.
25. Henry and Kerber, 2012.
26. Time Specials, 2011.
27. Clark, 2008.
28. Associated Press, 2008a.
29. McCool and LaCapra, 2012.
30. McLean, 2011.

and societal-driven achievement through meaningful purpose. Their power comes from externally-induced fear, rather than from internal inspiration. Nor are these actions self-perpetuating; continuous efforts to monitor, regulate, and restrict are required. Unlike actions that engage the self-sustaining influence of a reinforcing loop, these actions cannot be left on autopilot. Their leverage is limited, particularly if the economic environment relaxes enough to promote excessive self-interest or if innovative individuals find ways to circumvent the new regulations.

11.8 SUMMARY

Let's stand back for a moment to contemplate what this chapter described and what the loops and arrows in our final diagram are really saying. Basically, there were few forces that encouraged better judgment—no regulations, no moral guidance, no rewards or best practices with an eye on the long-term. On the other hand, everywhere we look, strong forces tempted, prodded, and motivated bad behaviors—environment, culture, incentive systems, greed, and secrecy. Where were the parents at this party? Where were the punishments for poor choices? Should we be surprised at the outcome?

This chapter accomplished one of book's original goals—to view the U.S. economic crisis in its entirety. Built step-by-step, its final systems diagram combined human elements, the Yin of the crisis, with the economic mechanisms, the Yang. Six human traits were most relevant. The first, expectations about housing prices, fueled demand for houses and caused housing prices to escalate. The second and third (self-interest and social interest) not only depicted the continual tension inside individuals, they also described the principles of a market economy. These diverging interests interact in a relationship balanced by moral grounding. During the crisis, however, self-interest overpowered social interest. Self-interest was intensified by tempting opportunities and by national and corporate cultures that promoted entitlement, consumption, and risk-taking. The resulting extreme self-interest fanned the flames of human contributors four and five: material desires and greed. All these human elements ultimately led to unethical behaviors and laid the rotten foundation of lousy loans and poorly structured securities and derivatives. Although it was too weak to contribute during the crisis, a sixth human trait, the search for meaning, inspired a lever that used meaningful purpose to counterbalance self-interest and diminish material desires, greed, and unethical behaviors.

High-risk loans and the high-risk securities and derivatives that harvested these loans like so many vegetables form the hub of the crisis. Four of the eighteen loops in this chapter's final diagram are built around human traits and behaviors: $R_{expectation}$, R_{desire}, B_{ethics}, and R_{greed}. Aided by lack of concern in the $R_{consequences}$ loop, these four loops became lethal for the system. They overpowered the economy and neutered mechanistic forces such as monetary policy and supply and demand. Inevitably, debt grew too high, the risk of default on home loans became extreme, housing prices plummeted, defaults wreaked havoc on securities, and massive corporations went under—we already know this story.

Now to make a point, we digress a moment. Recall that in the introduction, we talked about the ancient Tao philosophy that uses the concept of harmonic balance and continuous flow between Yin and Yang to achieve well-being. If we look at the metaphorical Yin and Yang in our system, we find no harmony or balance between them. Yin simply overpowered Yang. Excessive human behaviors overwhelmed economic mechanisms.

Because these behaviors caused so much damage, we looked for ways to alter them and found two categories of leverage. In the first category, actions bolstered *social interest* either by using bad consequences that had already occurred (such as defaults and bankruptcies) or by pre-emptively making people aware of potential consequences. However, the effects of these actions only last as long as the fear of possible outcomes or the memory of actual consequences lingers. The second category is more sustainable. It proposes that corporations define a meaningful purpose and a corresponding incentive system that allow individuals to grow and take a long view. This type of environment engages human traits that reduce myopic self-interest and broaden social perspectives. To preempt bad behaviors, corporations should also increase transparency and institute appropriate penalties.

In this chapter, we looked at current activities such as increased legislation, punishment of unethical behaviors, and monitoring of incentives. Although these actions have had some immediate benefit, none has staying power. All of them externally restrict bad human behaviors rather than foster good behaviors from individuals' more constructive natures.

From these perspectives on the economic crisis, this book paves the way to understanding any complex situation and to identifying strong, sustainable levers. With systems thinking, individuals, organizations, and government agencies alike can use their own experience and creativity to assess issues and develop solutions. Consistent with our original intent, we will integrate this U.S. crisis into a global system that includes national and international corporate and economic health in the next and final chapter where we open our eyes to the world.

Chapter 12

It's a Small World After All:[1] Global Implications and the Road Ahead

By the late 1970s, policymakers viewed accelerating inflation as signaling the need for restraint in a society that had come to take for granted a continually improving standard of living, and yet state officials were understandably quite reluctant to impose this restraint directly.

Krippner[2]

We are all a part of the global society of minds, and how that society evolves is up to each of us.

Bienhocker[3]

A young man recently asked, "What is your book about?" When I explained that it covered the economic crisis and that the crisis was difficult to characterize, he replied, "Oh, it's really not that hard. People were greedy and spent more money than they had." Well, true. Greed and debt *were* major players, but there are other concerns to investigate. For example, what conditions prompted the crisis? How did it affect the world economy? Can we avoid these circumstances in the future?

These are not easy questions to answer. While the complexity of world issues has mushroomed, the current approach to problem solving is still in the linear age of cause and effect, of problem and solution, primarily in the context of the present. Unfortunately, the world economy functions less like a row of dominos and more like an arena of bumper cars whose collisions cause reactions beyond their immediate paths.

Thus, to analyze the intricate unfolding of the economic crisis, this book deviated from traditional methods and used the holistic lens of systems

---

1. Written by the Sherman brothers for Walt Disney's contribution to the 1964 World's Fair in New York City.
2. Krippner, 2011.
3. Beinhocker, 2006.

Financial Whirlpools.

thinking. By considering data from 1994 to 2010 and events from prior decades, the book exposed how seemingly unrelated decisions, policies, and
behaviors coalesced. This final chapter summarizes findings about the crisis
in the United States and expands the investigation to larger national and
global concerns, one of which is the great global recession that hit the U.S.
in December 2007, spread to nearly 40 other advanced countries by April
2008, and ended in June 2009.[4] From this broad perspective, it identifies
actions that could deflect future crises and examines why current policies
may fall short of success. The chapter concludes with implications for the
future.

12.1 ECONOMIC TRUTHS ABOUT THE CRISIS

In the decade prior to 2006, Americans were riding the crest of a wave that
lifted them to greater wealth and a higher standard of living. When the U.S.
economy crashed in 2008, real-world truths poked their dirty faces out of the
financial rubble. One harsh truth is that Americans' desires exceeded what
they could comfortably afford, even though by past generations' standards,
they already had "unbelievable prosperity."[5] A related truth is that not *everyone* in America can afford to buy a home. Yet those who couldn't afford it
still bought one with the quicksand of risky debt. This impractical pursuit of
desires is one root of the meltdown, which, some believe, reflects our inability as a society to cope with an end to affluence.[6]

At the organizational level, another ugly truth materialized. Amid temptation and opportunity, organizations and their employees had subverted the
financial industry to achieve their own ends.[7] Furthermore, although the
magic bullet of loan securitization enabled greater access to credit and
helped the economy over the past four decades,[8] it also fed the housing bubble and caused the risk-laden securities market to swell. Other realities are
just as bleak. A striking change in America's culture that was suggested in
the 1950s finally surfaced. Americans, it seems, have grown more concerned
with how to spend and enjoy rather than with "how to work and achieve."[9]

A final truth—perhaps the most profound—is that "economies around the
world have never been so tightly linked."[10] Advanced economies and

---

4. NBER, 2010 (U.S. recession). OECD, 2012 (global recession). The OECD (Organisation for
Economic Co-operation and Development) reported the average GDP for most of its 34 member
countries and for 7 others were negative for this one year period. Q4 2008 and Q1 2009 were
the worst; only India and Indonesia had positive GDPs both quarters.
5. Sowell, 2011.
6. Krippner, 2011.
7. Schneier, 2012.
8. Krippner, 2011.
9. Bell, 1996.
10. Wiseman, 2012.

emerging nations alike are connected by a network of consumption and credit. Developing economies "depend on money from Western banks to build factories, buy machinery and export goods to the United States and Europe."[11] The American economy which has "long pulled the global economy out of the slumps" now needs help.[12] Its atrophied ability to buy goods and services threatens other nations' economies. These days we all share hard times.

12.2 SUMMARY OF CRISIS DYNAMICS

At the core of the U.S. crisis rests a massive mountain of high-risk debt that buried the housing and financial markets. As the crisis brewed, insatiable material desires and rising expectations joined with voracious appetites for homes, for mortgage loans, and for high pay-off, high-risk mortgage-related securities. Together with low interest rates and favorable home-buying policies, these human motives inflated the demand for housing, increased housing prices, and magnified risk. Then, rather than restraining excessive behaviors, a temptation-rich environment, permissive practices, and time-honed cultural norms encouraged self-interest, cultivated greed, and overwhelmed moral grounding. Internal forces that normally contain self-interest and muffle material desires were frail and ineffective. Monetary policy and the laws of supply and demand failed to stabilize the economy. Instead, unethical behaviors proliferated, individuals amassed possessions beyond their means, and financial institutions sought not so much to *make* a profit as to *divert* profit into personal wealth for a select few. Once stimulated, behavioral excesses expanded like the population of a rabbit warren whose natural predators are absent. The product of these behaviors—the risk of subprime and ARM loans and loan-related securities—quickly and quietly multiplied unnoticed.

Then when interest rates rose and ARMs reset, behaviors that had created this world of excess turned upside down. No longer supported by a growing economy, expectations and material desires reached the limits of what the economy could sustain and turned the growth engine into a decay engine: housing prices deflated; debt grew beyond consumers' ability to manage it; investments failed; and defaults, bankruptcies, and foreclosures accumulated. Finally, government bailouts of the financial industry were the last resort. The faux affluence that had been fortified with unrealistically high returns on investments and insurmountable debt soon became a mirage for the nation's thirsty population.

A common theme behind these dynamics lies in economist Lionel Robbins' classic insight that humans try to satisfy wants that are limitless

---

11. Landler, 2008.
12. Wiseman, 2012.

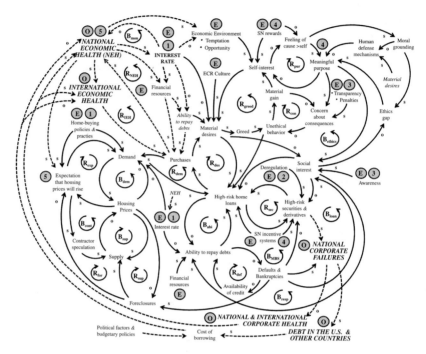

FIGURE 12.1   The global economic system.

with resources that are scarce.[13] This dilemma between boundless and bounded clarifies how the allure of wealth and ever-present materialism generated expectations, high risk, and the self-interested assumptions of plenty that matured into defaults and foreclosures. In the end, the U.S. economy failed to reach its primary goal, namely to enable America's citizens to prosper and pursue their dreams. Other nations' economies then marched to this same tune.

12.3 AN EXPANDED SYSTEMS PERSPECTIVE

To facilitate analysis of the crisis, we originally confined our investigation to the U.S. and to the housing and financial industries that were directly affected. Of course, the U.S. crisis is only a small tree in the economic landscape—a subsystem of a much larger system. To illustrate the crisis in its entirety and understand the world's post-crisis economic conditions, Figure 12.1 adds three loops to U.S. crisis-specific dynamics from

---

13. Robbins, 1932. Robbins' classic definition of an economy is that it "studies human behavior as a relationship between ends and scarce means which have alternative uses."

Chapter 11. Dashed lines highlight the most significant of these new relationships.

In this diagram, 10 distinct external factors (denoted as "E"s) influence the system from outside its boundaries and the system produces five outputs (denoted as "O"s) that feed back into its midst. Circled numbers locate five categories of leverage where changes to system behavior would be most effective. For simplicity, the diagram removes lags (delays) but assumes their importance.

12.3.1 Reinforcing and Balancing Loops

Of the 18 loops in the U.S. crisis subsystem, 10 reinforcing loops accelerated the growth or decay of various factors such as expectations, housing prices, and high risk home loans, securities, and derivatives. Eight balancing loops attempted to keep these factors from moving too rapidly. The three new loops that describe global relationships are: the $B_{monetary}$ balancing loop for monetary policy from Chapter 2 and the reinforcing loops centered on national economic health (R_{NEH}) and international economic health (R_{IEH}). Tables 12.1 and 12.2 summarize these 21 loops.

12.3.2 External Influences

Table 12.3 lists 10 external influences in the global crisis system. For simplicity, this list does not include the early flood of foreign investments in the securities market; however, the effects of loan defaults on these international investments are captured in *national corporate failures*.

12.3.3 Outputs

The major output of the U.S. crisis was *national corporate failures* (corporate bankruptcies, buyouts, and bailouts). Figure 12.1 adds four other outputs: *national and international corporate health*; *debt in the U.S. and other countries*; national economic health; and *international economic health*. Indicators of corporate health include profitability and stock market behavior. National economic health and international economic health contain gross domestic product (GDP), employment, and inflation. Table 12.4 summarizes these outputs.

12.3.4 Global System Interactions

To understand the interaction between the global economy and the U.S. economic crisis we focus on the three new loops: $B_{monetary}$, R_{NEH}, and R_{IEH}.

TABLE 12.1 Summary of Reinforcing Loops (* denotes loops that are external to the U.S. crisis subsystem)

Loop Name	Function	Major Components and Externalities
$R_{consequences}$	Low concern about consequences increases unethical behavior and material gains. With high concern, individuals consider effects of their actions. Companies increase it through transparency and penalties for unethical behavior.	Concern about consequences Unethical behavior Material gain External influences: transparency and penalties
$R_{default}$	Without financial resources, lack of credit causes inability to repay debts that leads to defaults, bankruptcies and lower credit ratings, which diminish availability of credit. Defaults and bankruptcies drive foreclosures, flatten securities and derivatives, and cause corporate failures.	Defaults and bankruptcies Availability of credit Ability to repay debts
R_{demand}	Ever-increasing demand leads to growth of purchases that are enabled by high risk home loans	High-risk home loans Purchases Demand External influences: financial resources and international economic health
R_{desire}	Desire for material goods drives growth of high risk home loans; purchases make consumers hungry to buy more, further increasing desire.	Material desires High-risk home loans Purchases External influences: incentives, financial resources, international economic health, and culture
$R_{expectation}$	The expectation that housing prices will rise that drives demand growth; demand increases prices which operate as a self-fulfilling prophecy to further increase expectations.	Expectation Demand Housing prices External influences: policies and practices
$R_{foreclosure}$	Foreclosures diminish expectations, reduce demand, and push housing prices down. Decreasing housing prices create foreclosures and hurt loan and securities markets.	Foreclosures Expectation Demand Housing prices External influences: policies and practices

(Continued)

TABLE 12.1 (Continued)

Loop Name	Function	Major Components and Externalities
R_{greed}	Excessive self-interest increases material desires; desires becomes greed, encourage unethical behavior to realize material gain, and reinforce self-interest.	Self-interest Material desire Greed Unethical behavior External influences: culture, environment, and rewards
*R_{IEH}	A drop in U.S. national economic health reduces U.S. purchases of foreign products and decreases international economic health; foreign consumers then cannot purchase U.S. products, thus diminishing U.S. national economic health.	International economic health Purchases (of foreign products by U.S. consumers) National economic health
*R_{NEH}	A drop in national economic health decreases financial resources for U.S. consumers, which reduces purchases of U.S. products; fewer purchases affect national economic health.	National economic health Financial resources Purchases (of domestic products by U.S. consumers)
$R_{purpose}$	Meaningful purpose satisfies the human search for meaning and decreases self-interest, generates a feeling of committing to a cause greater than self, and increases social interest.	Meaningful purpose Self-interest Feeling of cause greater than self External influences: rewards
$R_{security}$	This loop combines three financial loops (R_{MBS}, R_{CDO}, and R_{CDS}). High-risk home loans drive sale of high-risk MBS and CDO securities and CDS derivatives.	High-risk home loans High-risk securities and derivatives External influences: deregulation and incentive systems
R_{supply}	Growth of foreclosures increase housing supply. More supply decreases housing prices and creates additional foreclosures.	Foreclosures Supply Housing prices

12.3.4.1 Monetary Policy Balancing Loop

First, note in Figure 12.1 how interest rates are woven into the global system. Previous effects on *ability to repay debts*, *demand*, and *material desires* are now shown as the $B_{monetary}$ balancing loop. We introduced this loop in Chapter 2 and described it in Chapter 8 as one of the economy's stabilizing forces. It illustrates how *national economic health* influences U.S. federal

TABLE 12.2 Summary of Balancing Loops (* denotes loops that are external to the U.S. crisis subsystem)

Loop Name	Function	Major Components and Externalities
$B_{ability}$	Ability to repay debts limits high-risk home loans which affects securities; new high risk home loans increase existing debt and reduce ability to repay. In the aggregate, when ability to repay diminishes, growth of new high-risk home loans declines.	High-risk home loans Ability to repay debts External influences: financial resources, incentive systems, and interest rates
$B_{contractor}$	An increased supply of new homes driven by contractor speculation tends to counteract price increases.	Expectation Contractor speculation Supply Housing prices
B_{demand}	Demand for homes works with supply to move housing prices toward an equilibrium point.	Demand Housing prices External influences: policies and practices
B_{ethics}	Moral grounding tries to limit excessive self-interest, greed and unethical behaviors and increase social interest. Human defense mechanisms oppose actions to balance self-interest with social interest. Social interest affects high-risk loans, securities, and derivatives.	Self-interest Material desire Social interest Ethics gap Action (e.g. meaningful purpose) External influences: rewards, environment, culture, and awareness
B_{loan}	Bad consequences (e.g., defaults and bankruptcies) increase social interest (in a self-interested way) and reduce the inclination to take on new high risk debt.	Defaults and bankruptcies Social interest High-risk home loans Ability to repay debt External influences: awareness, interest rates, financial resources, and incentive systems
B_{MBS}	Defaults limit unbounded growth of high-risk securities and derivatives, which reduces high-risk home loans and increases ability to repay.	Defaults and bankruptcies High-risk securities and derivatives High-risk home loans Ability to repay debt External influences: deregulation, incentive systems, interest rates, and financial resources

(Continued)

TABLE 12.2 (Continued)

Loop Name	Function	Major Components and Externalities
*B_{monetary}	This loop reflects how changes in monetary policy (federal funds rates) are based on inflation, GDP, and employment.	Interest rate National economic health
B_{responsibility}	Bad consequences (defaults and bankruptcies) increase social interest and increase inclination to repay existing debts.	Defaults and bankruptcies Social interest Ability to repay debt External influences: interest rate, financial resources, and awareness.
B_{supply}	Housing supply interacts with demand to limit housing prices. In a normally functioning market economy, these two loops bring prices toward an equilibrium point.	Supply Housing prices

funds rates and vice versa; here a languishing U.S. economy triggers lower *interest rates* to encourage growth while an overheated economy prompts higher *interest rates* to dampen growth.

Interest rates affect purchases through two fundamentally different paths depending on whether individuals use debt or rely on existing resources to make their purchases. On the debt path, *low interest rates* boost temptation and opportunity in the *economic environment* and increase the *ability to repay debts*. With more money available through loans, debt users can make more *purchases*. On the other hand, for those who use savings to fund *purchases*, *high interest rates* generate *financial resources* and motivate similar buying behaviors.

12.3.4.2 National Economic Health Reinforcing Loop

The reinforcing loop R_{NEH} describes interactions among *national economic health, financial resources,* and *purchases*. In a healthy economy, U.S. consumers have more financial resources to make purchases, while, in an ailing economy, they purchase less. When these consumers buy U.S. products, domestic companies can create more jobs and U.S. GDP rises, thus increasing *national economic health*. *National economic health* also influences *interest rates* and *international economic health*.

The U.S. economic boom between 2000 and 2006 exemplifies positive growth from this loop. Using easily available credit and relying on

TABLE 12.3 External Influences on the Crisis

Name	Description	Elements Directly Influenced
Awareness	Awareness is the ability to see one's situation, behavior, or decisions in the context of consequences of actions and ethics.	Social interest
Deregulation	Deregulation in banking and financial industries allowed securities and derivatives risk to grow without oversight. In 1999 the banking industry was deregulated, allowing banks to invest depositors' money in high-risk securities. Derivatives (CDSs) were deregulated in 2000; net capital rule change in 2004 allowed big financial corporations to expand leverage and assume more debt.	High-risk securities and derivatives
Economic environment	The economic environment is the climate in which economic transactions occur. It is shaped by policies, practices, norms, and behaviors. Temptation and opportunity in that environment induce self interest. Temptation was exemplified in the multimillion dollar bonuses, fees, and incentives in the financial industry. Opportunity arose through easily available, cheap credit.	Self-interest
ECR culture	The American culture and corporate cultures particularly in financial organizations have strong embedded norms that promote entitlement, consumption, and risk (ECR). These cultures shape individuals' beliefs and eventually influence behaviors.	Material desires
Financial resources	Financial resources include salaries, bonuses, investments, and other income.	Ability to repay debts Purchases
Home-buying policies and practices	In addition to monetary policies that affect interest rates, economic policies and lending practices encouraged housing purchases for low-income households.	Demand Expectation
Interest rate	U.S. interest rates for short and long-term credit are determined by federal funds rates set by the Fed. Federal funds rates influences reset rate for ARMs.	Ability to repay debts Demand Economic environment Material desires Financial resources

(Continued)

TABLE 12.3 (Continued)

Name	Description	Elements Directly Influenced
SN incentive systems	Short-term, narrow-focused (SN) incentive systems provide rewards (salaries, promotions, bonuses) to motivate employees toward organizational goals.	High-risk home loans High-risk securities and derivatives
SN rewards	Organizations' incentive systems define rewards that motivate employees to accomplish organizational goals. During the crisis, rewards in some housing and financial organizations promoted short-term, narrow-focused (SN) goals.	Self-interest Feeling of cause > self
Transparency and penalties	In financial and lending corporations, transparency and openness about dealings and consequences, and penalties for unethical behaviors will increase concern about consequences.	Concern about consequences

appreciating housing prices, consumer expenditures rose over 27 percent.[14] During the same period, U.S. per capita GDP grew about 9 percent.[15] And after the dot-com shakeup, unemployment dropped 1.4 percent between 2003 and 2006.[16] This positive *national economic health* then contributed to *international economic health*; world GDP grew more than 25 percent between 2000 and 2006.[17]

In addition to *interest rates* and *purchases*, two other elements influence *national economic health*: *national and international corporate health* and the *cost of borrowing*, which depends in part on the level of *debt in the U.S.* The predecessor of both elements is our old acquaintance, *national corporate failures* generated by the U.S. crisis. As we know, corporate failures in the lending and financial industries cut profits for these companies, reduced the

---

14. U.S. Bureau of Labor Statistics, 2012b. Average expenditure was $38,045 in 2000 and $48,398 in 2006.

15. Per capita GDP using 2010 purchasing power parity from FRED, 2011 ($44,081 in 2000 and $48,095 in 2006).

16. Unemployment data from U.S. Bureau of Labor Statistics, 2012a. Unemployment dropped from 6 percent in 2003 to 4.6 percent in 2006 and 2007; it rose to 5.8 percent by the end of 2008.

17. International Monetary Fund, 2012; world GDP growth estimated by adding annual percent change from 2000 through 2006 (constant prices).

TABLE 12.4 Outputs from the Crisis

Name	Description	Predecessors
Debt in U.S. and other countries	Debt measures the money that governments borrow to pay budgetary obligations (e.g., U.S. debt is held by domestic and foreign entities, and by government accounts that hold funds owed to beneficiaries such as social security recipients). Debt plus other political and budgetary policies affect the cost of borrowing to pay expenses.	U.S. national corporate failures that affect international corporations and require governments to provide funding for bail-outs
International economic health	Similar to national economic health metrics, international economic health contains gross domestic product, inflation and employment of foreign countries, particularly the 34 nations that have "advanced economies."	National and international corporate health National economic health Cost of borrowing
National corporate failures	For the crisis, national corporate failures became corporate bankruptcies, buyouts, and bailouts by the U.S. government for companies that could not meet obligations on the high-risk mortgages and mortgage-related security products they had sold. Failures include effects on those foreign entities who had invested heavily in the U.S. financial market.	Failure of securities and derivatives caused by defaults and bankruptcies on risky loans
National and international corporate health	National and international corporate health include: U.S. corporate profit and U.S. stock market; international corporate profit and international stock markets. Poor corporate health pushes U.S. and international stock markets down.	National corporate failures
National economic health	National economic health contains: *Gross domestic product:* A measure of the output of U.S. goods and services, GDP affects unemployment and standard of living	Interest rate National and international corporate health

(Continued)

TABLE 12.4 (Continued)

Name	Description	Predecessors
	Inflation: Changes in the overall prices in an economy (measured by General Price Index). Rising inflation erodes purchasing power. *Employment*: percent of people in the available work force who have jobs.	Cost of borrowing (affected by U.S. debt) Purchases of domestic goods and services by consumers in the U.S. and in other countries

taxes they paid, and harmed investors. These results increased the *U.S. debt* burden. Debt grew from $9.2 trillion in early 2008 to over $14 trillion by the end of 2010.[18] This debt also reflects new heights of global interdependence: international ownership of *U.S. debt* went from 25 to 32 percent between 2006 and 2010.[19]

Many of these failed corporations had global footprints; severe losses also distressed their international divisions. Global stock market responses to these losses reveal how *national corporate failures* affected *national and international corporate health*. Stock market indices like the U.S. Dow Jones Industrial Average, TA in the Middle East, Nikkei in Asia, and ATX in Europe all dropped by over half between the end of 2007 and mid-2009.[20]

Poor *national corporate health*, increasing *debt in the U.S.*, and failing *national economic health* initiated secondary chain "interactions." After rising interest rates, loan defaults and foreclosures, and diminished expectations about housing prices burst the U.S. housing bubble in 2006 (see Chapter 9), *demand* for housing collapsed. The decline in housing purchases bounced back on *national economic health*. From 2006 to 2009, U.S. per capita GDP dropped about 5 percent, unemployment increased nearly 5 percent, annual inflation decreased over 1.5 percent, and median income decreased about

---

18. TreasuryDirect, 2012. In 2008 and again in 2009, U.S. debt grew 15 percent over the prior year.
19. Financial Management Service, 2102.
20. Stock market data from Yahoo!® Finance, 2012. Dow Jones Industrial Average: 14,093 in October 2007 dropped to 6627 in March 2009. TA-100 (Tel Aviv index): about 1150 in July 2007 dropped below 550 in January 2009. ATX (Vienna index): about 5000 in June 2007 dropped below 1500 in March 2009. Japanese Nikkei: 18,239 in July 2007 dropped to 7173 in March 2009.

3 percent.[21] As a result of these losses and the ensuing financial uncertainty, people also purchased fewer goods and services; between 2008 and 2010, consumer expenditures in the U.S. dropped nearly 5 percent.[22] Weak *national corporate health* also hurt *international economic health*. Overseas investors with substantial assets in the stock or securities of failing companies lost huge sums of money. These losses diminished purchasing power in other nations.

12.3.4.3 International Economic Health Reinforcing Loop

Many factors, including *corporate health* already mentioned and the *cost of borrowing*, influence *international economic health*. Another indicator of how failed *corporate health* damaged *international economic health* is the 2008 International Monetary Fund's forecast that corporate failures resulting from a credit crunch would create a $1 trillion loss in the global economy.[23] As an example, in late 2008 when U.S.-based General Motors could not borrow money to cover current expenditures, it closed its Opel car plants in Germany.[24]

Cost of borrowing has a more complex influence on *international economic health*. Like the U.S. government, other national governments instituted stop-gap measures when the financial industry faltered. The European Central Bank cut interest rates and the U.K. initiated £400 billion of bailout assistance to its banks. In October 2008, Germany injected 50 billion euro to save one of its largest banks; by November, China felt the pain and introduced a two-year $586 billion stimulus package.[25] These actions, motivated in part by U.S. *national corporate failures* affected *debt* in other countries, increased their *cost of borrowing*, and eventually damaged *international economic health*. The similarity of these repercussions and reactions, along with comparable movement of global stock markets demonstrate a tight connection between the U.S. and other nations' economies.

The R_{IEH} reinforcing loop describes another major influence. This loop depicts the symbiotic relationship between *national economic health* and *international economic health*. When the U.S. economy booms, U.S. consumers make more *purchases*, including purchases of foreign products that

---

21. Unemployment data from U.S. Bureau of Labor Statistics, 2012a. Unemployment increased from 4.6 percent in 2006 to 9.3 percent in 2009, hit 9.6 percent in 2010, dropped to 8.9 percent in 2011, and was 8.2 percent in May 2012. Inflation data from Historical Inflation, 2012. Average annual inflation dropped from 3.24 percent in 2006 to 1.64 percent in 2010 and increased in 2011 to 3.16 percent. U.S. per capita GDP using 2010 purchasing power parity data from FRED, 2011 ($48,095 in 2006 and $45,854 in 2009—it hit a high of $48,532 in 2007 and rose 3 percent in 2010).Median household income in 2011$ from U.S. Census Bureau, 2011a ($53,768 in 2006 and $52,195 in 2009).
22. U.S. Bureau of Labor Statistics, 2012b. Average expenditure was $50,486 in 2008 and $48,109 in 2010.
23. BBC News, 2009.
24. WideAngle, 2008.
25. Global ramifications in this paragraph from BBC News, 2009.

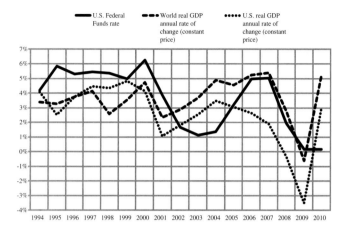

FIGURE 12.2   Annual change in world and U.S. GDP vs. federal funds rate.[26]

improve *international economic health*. Greater *international economic health* means more employment and higher GDP in other economies and enables foreign consumers to *purchase* U.S. goods and services. In turn, these purchases increase *national economic health*. Bottom line: A healthy national economy promotes healthy international economies and vice versa.

Conversely, conditions after the crisis highlight the downside of this relationship. Diminished *national economic health* (lower employment and restricted GDP growth) reduced Americans' ability to purchase foreign products. Fewer purchases meant that the unemployment and GDP of foreign countries also suffered, thus affecting *international economic health*. Figure 12.2 characterizes this correlation. It shows that although U.S. GDP only represented between a fourth and a third of world GDP during our crisis timeline,[27] growth rates of both followed parallel paths between 2000 and 2005. Then when U.S. GDP growth rates plummeted between 2007 and 2009, the growth rate for world GDP behaved similarly. In 2009, GDP growth was negative (indicating a recession) for both U.S. and the world economy.

Next, compare the behavior of U.S. *federal funds rates* with national and world GDP.[28] Recall that U.S. monetary policy intends to stabilize the economy by manipulating interest rates. Just as this policy did not have desired effects on housing prices during some periods (see Chapter 8), it was also ineffective against GDP. For example, when the full force of the crisis hit the U.S. in 2008, the Fed

26. U.S. and world real GDP rates of change from International Monetary Fund, 2012; federal funds rate from Board of Governors of the Federal Reserve System, Nov 2011b.
27. World and U.S. GDP in current price U.S. dollars from International Monetary Fund, 2012. In 2010 and 2011, U.S. GDP had sunk to just over 19 percent of world GDP.
28. Note that there are correlations among global interest rates, but for simplicity, we have not included interest rate data from other countries.

decreased interest rates to stimulate growth. Instead of increasing, the growth rate of national GDP continued its decline; world GDP followed suit. Prolonged low *interest rates* in the U.S. after 2008 may have exacerbated this decay. For example, low rates discouraged retirement and reduced purchasing power for those intending to live on investment income.[29] These circumstances ultimately weakened both *national* and *international economic health.*

* * * * * * * *

Although the most severe repercussions of the crisis persisted through 2009, its effects on the global economy are more enduring. Recent indicators point to continuing struggles in the U.S. and elsewhere—latent effects of the 2008 economic crisis. In July 2012, six of the 17 countries that use the euro were again in recession, and the "economic superstars of the developing world—China, India, and Brazil—are in no position to come to the rescue."[30] Now we see why successful solutions must recognize their larger context.

12.4 CONCLUSIONS FROM THE EXPANDED SYSTEMS VIEW

Having visualized the U.S. crisis as part of the global economy, we can use systems thinking to locate leverage areas where small changes could have helped avoid the crisis or could reduce the likelihood of a future crisis.

12.4.1 Leverage Areas, Potential Pitfalls, and Recommended Actions

Candidate leverage points sprinkled throughout the book recommend various ways to prevent a crisis or to improve economic recovery. The most influential of these fall into four areas that address U.S. crisis-related issues. A fifth area relates to the global economy. These leverage areas, their associated pitfalls, and recommended actions are described in the following subsections. The areas appear as circled numbers in Figure 12.1. While there are many possible levers and actions, these five demonstrate how to use a systems perspective to identify potential solutions.

12.4.1.1 *Area 1: Limit High-Risk Debt*

High-risk debt was a major concern in the U.S. crisis. Heavy traffic around high-risk home loans in Figure 12.1 indicates that by restricting these loan types, we can touch the rest of the system through interest rates and policies that support home buying. This leverage lies on three points in the system, which directly influence other central elements, namely, *demand, material desires,* and *ability to repay debts.* Modulation of key elements will infiltrate

---

29. Hamilton, 2012.
30. Wiseman, 2012.

the rest of the system and eventually reduce the escalation of high-risk loans that intensified economic collapse.

Pitfalls

Political agendas and personal expectations place this leverage area out of favor with some participants. Fewer loans reduce profits in the housing and financial industries and limit agents' rewards for making high-risk home loans. Fewer loans also affect purchases (many can't buy when they can't use debt) which in turn increases unemployment and decreases GDP. Nevertheless, preventing devastation from risky loans far outweighs the pitfalls.

Actions

Two actions involving policies and practices could have limited high-risk debt. These actions must be broadly applied, clearly explained, and their benefits delineated to prevent overreactions from politicians, consumers, and corporations. Government and financial organizations must all participate. Note that some activity in these areas has already occurred or is being considered.

1. Revise monetary policies: Apply monetary policies conservatively (with flatter peaks and valleys) and with concern for long-term global consequences and the actions of other nations. Policies should also address the effects of interest rate on still-active ARMs and associated securities, and on those who use investments for purchases. This action reduces demand for high risk home loans, increases ability to repay debts, makes material desires more realistic, and ultimately limits risk for mortgage-related securities and derivatives. It can, if applied properly, increase purchases that bolster national and global economic health.

2. Tighten economic policies and lending practices: Redefine housing policies and align lending practices with borrower qualifications; institute personal accountability for bad loans; and ensure that borrowers and lenders are well informed about loan terms and risk. These actions limit credit availability and diminish unwitting and uninformed origination of high-risk loans, thus dampening material desires, demand, and expectations. For example, actions would eliminate so-called NINJA loans (no income, no job, no assets) that allowed poorly qualified individuals to borrow large sums with little collateral. Fines or penalties enforce personal accountability for those who sell loans without due diligence; stronger impediments reduce loan defaults and risk in the securities market.

12.4.1.2 Area 2: Reform the Market for Securities and Derivatives

Excessive buying and selling of unregulated mortgage-related securities and derivatives created a gigantic swelling of contaminated investments. Alongside high-risk loans, these investment types hold a central place in Figure 12.1; minimizing and clarifying their risk would permeate the rest of the system. This leverage appears at one point—where deregulation encourages buying and selling of high-risk securities and derivatives.

Pitfalls

This leverage causes loss of income for buyers and sellers of securities and derivatives, and would be unpopular for investors who seek huge returns. Political clout in this area is particularly potent. Some believe that tighter regulation, such as that proposed in the Volker Rule, adds unnecessary complexity, reduces competitiveness, and, of course, affects revenues of major financial firms such as Morgan Stanley and Goldman Sachs.[31]

Actions

Two proposed actions are directed at high-risk securities and derivatives.

1. **Strengthen guidelines for securitization and derivatives:** Enforce higher standards for securitized assets and minimize extreme leveraging. These actions rescind policies that allowed financial companies to take on debt over 33 times their assets[32] and let hedge fund investors leverage investments at ratios of up to 400-to-1.[33] Stringent securitization guidelines will pressure lenders to produce higher-quality loans and reduce risk for securities investors.
2. **Revise risk assessment and improve risk communication:** Revamp risk models to improve accuracy of ratings for securities and derivatives; eliminate conflicts of interest between securities transactions and banking, and between rating agencies and financial firms; ensure that investors are well informed about quality of securities. These actions lower the aggregate risk of MBSs, CDOs, and CDSs and set prices commensurate with risk. Eliminating conflicts of interest allows objective buying or selling of loans and securities.

12.4.1.3 Area 3: Decrease Unethical Behavior

Unethical behaviors produced by extreme self-interest and greed ran rampant during the crisis. These human traits created powerful reinforcing loops that not only fueled material desires, but also stimulated growth of risky loans,

---

31. Touryalai, 2011.
32. Labaton, 2008.
33. Brock, 2012.

securities, and derivatives. Leverage to decrease unethical behavior appears in two locations where transparency and penalties affect concern about consequences and where awareness affects social interest. Strengthening social interest and concern about consequences through fear of repercussion, lack of secrecy, and awareness can reduce bad behavior.

Pitfalls

This leverage area can create a fear-filled environment that reduces innovation and constructive risk-taking. Thus, it can quash individual growth and long-term competitiveness of corporations. Actions should be designed well and implemented wisely.

Actions

Issuing an edict to erase greed or self-interest is idealistic at best. Therefore, the three actions in this area aim at behavior, relying on fear and pain avoidance and on focus of attention. Leverage here strengthens barriers that block unethical behavior.

1. Increase transparency: Promote honesty and instill integrity. To evoke concern about consequences, companies must be honest about product attributes and risks, and make it difficult to keep secrets. Corporate leaders should model this behavior. Corporate transparency makes buyers and sellers think twice before acting unethically.
2. Strengthen penalties: Implement punishments for unethical behavior. Depending on the behavior, penalties would range from criticism and social sanctions, to poor performance evaluations and fewer bonuses, to loss of job, and finally to prosecution. Corporations as well as the government must ferret out and punish those who engage in unethical and unlawful dealings—more than they have done to date.
3. Increase awareness of broad consequences: Make individuals aware of consequences and publicize pitfalls of unethical dealings. These actions diminish material desires, reduce self-interest, and instill social conscience. Institutional, corporate, and government policies, and public media can promote awareness; companies can publically condemn poor behaviors and celebrate positive examples. Increased awareness has a long-term effect and may transform cultural beliefs. As neuroscientist Dan Siegel suggests, "*cultural evolution* may occur by a shift in shared awareness."[34] In this case individual awareness becomes collective awareness as employees communicate with one another every day.

---

34. Siegel, 2012.

12.4.1.4 Area 4: Apply Positive Motivation

Rather than preventative or punitive, this leverage area is motivational. It appears in three locations on the diagram at the places where incentive systems, rewards, and meaningful purpose affect the system. Positive motivation relies on the traits of human nature that drive us to accomplish goals, make us yearn for purpose and inner growth, and encourage us to feel socially accountable. It must be applied at the same time that excessive self-interest is discouraged; humans are too easily lured onto the path of self-interest.

Pitfalls

Because this leverage area is future-looking, its short-term pitfalls are many. Long-term focus means that when participants accept responsibility to build a robust future, the economy will grow very slowly or stay flat until it can recover. There will be few short-term asset bubbles and less hope of "getting rich quick." In fact, there can be no quick anything.

Actions in this category must promote long-term socially-conscious goals rather than short-term results at the expense of the future. These actions will be extremely unpopular unless *widely* used. If few corporations participate, these few would be less competitive and may find it difficult to hire talented executives or attract investors. Such actions run counter to the short-term oriented cultures in America, on Wall Street, and in corporations. Politics and re-election motives oppose these actions since many constituents won't be pleased with flatter pocketbooks.

Furthermore, it is naïve to assume that most humans *freely sacrifice* their own welfare to enhance that of others. If you've ever driven on a busy freeway, you know this reality. Invariably, some aggressive drivers rudely cut others off to move a car length ahead; ironically, if everyone made fewer lane changes, traffic would move faster. However, because this leverage is extremely powerful, even modest results pay high dividends.

Actions

Actions in this area require corporate involvement and rely on individuals' need for significance and fulfilling purpose in life. These actions build on emerging theories in neuroscience, namely that as part of our survival mechanisms, "we are wired to behave in an ethical manner toward others and they toward us"[35] particularly in times of crisis. By nurturing good behaviors, actions here complement those that stifle bad behaviors. These actions are challenging to implement and some may believe that they are naïve; however, any positive shift will have ripple effects.

---

35. Pfaff, 2007.

1. Restructure incentives: Reward long-term oriented behavior. As purposeful beings, humans are motivated by goals and incentives. When bonuses, commissions, and salaries reward achievement of long-term socially responsible goals, employees will adapt to meet the goals and gain the rewards. This action targets success beyond the next quarter and reduces temptation and opportunity for greed and unethical actions. For example, lenders could set goals to keep borrowers in their homes rather than to increase the number of loans they make.

2. Strengthen meaningful purpose: Develop corporate purpose, goals, and strategies that are long-term and which consider societal effects. Companies could also develop outside-of-work programs and recognize socially-interested behaviors to nudge individuals' mindsets beyond their own spheres. This action reduces material desires, self-interest, and unethical behaviors, increases social interest and concern about consequences, and gives individuals a feeling of a cause greater than themselves. In time, it may alter cultural norms, particularly if leaders exhibit desired behaviors.

12.4.1.5 Area 5: Maintain Confidence in the Economy

The previous four leverage areas address U.S. crisis-related issues that eventually spill into the global economy. This fifth area focuses leverage more directly onto national and global economies. Actions appear in two places in the systems diagram where policies affect the national economic health and expectations influence demand.

Pitfalls

This area requires widespread agreement and participation by governments and industries; all must set aside narrow interests to focus on the long-term and greater good of the economy. However, because it is extremely difficult to unite bipartisan politics, industry special interests, and international governments, getting policymakers to agree about the right course of action may be a stumbling block, particularly if they feel a threat to their careers or their nations.

Actions

Although previously proposed actions soften material desires, diminish unethical behavior, decrease high risk home loans, clean up the securities market, and facilitate human growth and moral development, they can also reduce purchases and disturb the global economy. Whereas purchases made with *risky* debt *must* be restrained to avoid future crises, these actions should also promote *normal* and *economically beneficial* buying. Two actions here involve building global consumer confidence through communication and economic policies.

1. Clearly communicate goals and expectations: When people expect positive outcomes, any deviation—however slight—causes disappointment. In an economy, disappointment diminishes confidence and tightens buying behavior. However, when people know what to expect, they can adapt and make purchasing decisions based on affordability rather than on fear-driven expectations. Prior actions hit people in their bank accounts. They depress bonuses and insert accountability. They delay gratification for some and prevent others from buying homes or spending what they don't have. Citizens of all countries must adjust their expectations to accept a standard of living that is not founded on intolerable risk and will not grow for a while. To ease their disappointment, people need the hope of a better tomorrow. Government and industry leaders should devise a comprehensive economic plan, perhaps using the proposed actions as a foundation. They must clearly share the future-oriented intent behind that plan, speak *honestly* about its repercussions, and provide frequent updates on progress. And they must implement it together.

2. Adjust tax, benefits, interest, and budgetary policies: Act as stewards for the future rather than as consumers in the present. It is difficult to judge whether supply-side policies that encourage production or demand-side policies that stimulate demand or a combination of the two would be most effective in today's economies.[36] Though macroeconomic and fiscal policy is beyond the scope of this book, we can deduce that future policies should maintain a *slow-growing* or *level* economy as nations recover from excessive debt. Furthermore, the U.S. must regain its credit standing to exit from the vicious circle of excessive debt that lowers credit ratings and causes it to borrow money at higher rates, thus further increasing debt. Other nations, too, must escape extreme reliance on sovereign debt[37] whose risk depends on their economic health and monetary exchange rates.

12.4.2 Strategic Leverage

Table 12.5 summarizes leveraging actions in each of the five categories and indicates their relative effectiveness and level of difficulty to implement. In

---

36. Supply-side economics focus on production; policies encourage the wealthy to invest by reducing their income and capital gains taxes. Demand-side policies (Keynesian economics) cut taxes or otherwise stimulate consumers to spend more.

37. BusinessDictionary.com, 2012. Sovereign debt refers to debt that is "held in bonds denominated in foreign currencies... the repayment of sovereign debt cannot be forced by the creditors... The only protection available to creditors is threat of the loss of credibility and lowering of the international standing (the sovereign debt rating) of a country, which may make it much more difficult to borrow in the future."

TABLE 12.5 Significant Leverage Areas

Leverage and Actions	Effectiveness	Difficulty
(1) Limit high-risk debt		
Revise monetary policies	Low to moderate	Low
Tighten economic policies and lending practices	Low to moderate	Low
(2) Reform market for securitization and derivatives		
Strengthen guidelines for securitization and derivatives	Moderate	Moderate
Revise risk assessment and improve risk communication	Moderate	Low to moderate
(3) Decrease unethical behaviors		
Increase transparency	Moderate	Moderate
Strengthen penalties	Moderate	Low to moderate
Increase awareness of broad consequences	Moderate to high	High
(4) Apply positive motivation		
Restructure incentives	Moderate to high	Moderate to high
Strengthen meaningful purpose	High	High
(5) Maintain confidence in the economy		
Clearly communicate goals and expectations	Moderate	Moderate to high
Adjust tax, benefit, interest, and budgetary policies	Moderate	High

---

Figure 12.1, these actions are distributed across the system like a military flanking maneuver in battle. Their objective is to weaken the still existing, offensive forces of high-risk debt, securities, and derivatives, and of unethical behaviors, while strengthening positive behavior and confidence in national and international economies.

As you can tell from Figure 12.1, implementing one or two actions cannot achieve desired outcomes since they may oppose ongoing policies and because their power diminishes as their effects become less direct. Optimum leverage requires multiple complementary and concurrent actions. Unlike current policies and actions that seem to be individually orchestrated, such a cohesive strategy requires coordination and unity of intent. A strategy like this is:

- *Integrated and synergistic.* Applying proposed actions as a package requires knowing how each action affects the others and facilitates positive synergies among their effects. This approach lessens the likelihood that one action will undo another or that they will compete with existing policies in other areas to create unintended and negative outcomes.

- *Human growth oriented.* Two ways to motivate human behavior are through fear and through inspiration. The actions proposed here use *both.* First, like most current policies, proposed actions intend to block excessive self-interest through fear of penalty. However, unlike current policies, they generate sustainable constructive outcomes by attending to nobler motives and elevating individuals above extreme self-interest.
- *Slow and deliberate.* Proposed actions translate into a reduced standard of living for many, particularly for those whose apparent wealth was founded on risky debt and greed. They cannot be implemented overnight. Moreover, because it took decades to create this economic morass, recovery cannot occur quickly, certainly not within any 4-year presidential term.
- *Compatible with national and global economies.* While this book concentrates on assessing the crisis within given bounds, it also recognizes that the crisis was a small part of a larger environment. Band-Aid remedies that do not consider larger U.S. and global economic issues may aggravate the very problems they are trying to solve and cause widespread damage in the process. The proposed program of actions intends to avoid such effects.

12.5 SYSTEMS THINKING AS A TOOL

We have used systems thinking to understand the economic crisis and its global implications. Insights from this analysis suggest that the power of systems thinking, with its emphasis on balance, interdependence, lag, and limits, can be used to investigate and offer solutions to other tough issues.

12.5.1 Balance

Social systems (such as an economy) are human collectives whose complex issues are aggravated by human behaviors that are out of balance. Attempts to resolve social issues must not only incorporate actions that prevent or legislate against excessive self-interest, but also must nurture self-growth, collaboration, and meaning over materialism. This approach draws out positive human attributes and builds concern for our societies. When human behaviors reflect this balance, social systems and individuals will function more effectively and successfully.

12.5.2 Lag

Yesterday affects tomorrow in profound and unintended ways. Whether culturally, economically, or ecologically, actions of past generations affect our well-being; what *we* do today will affect future generations. Transgenerational delays like these are one reason we may not recognize the consequences of our decisions. Thus, although our data to analyze the economic crisis began in 1994, certain decisions, behaviors, and policies from the decades before the 1990s were also influential. Consumeritis in the American culture for instance, along with historically-assured rises in housing prices and a preference to borrow rather than to save have been brewing for a while. Furthermore, we are just witnessing post-crisis effects; America's decreased ability to buy is depressing other countries' economic health and will come back to haunt the U.S. economy.

12.5.3 Interdependence

There is no single cause, effect, or solution to a complex problem. Using a systems view of economic trends during the crisis timeline, we concluded that events and contributors were not as solitary or linear as many sources suggest. While some economists identified series of events such as the connection between high risk home loans and failures in the securities market, their insights applied at a subsystem level. Others described the vicious circle between unemployment and consumer demand: businesses won't hire while demand is low, but demand is low because business aren't hiring.[38] Still others called the crisis "a perfect financial storm" and mentioned the simultaneous occurrence of "lax monetary policy, pressure to expand home loan volume, and failure to monitor home lending quality."[39] A few identified a linear chain of events. In their view, as buyers recognized that housing prices could not continue to grow, housing demand dropped; less demand ignited unemployment, decreased business investments, and generated stock market losses and bankruptcies that spilled into the global economy.[40]

What these views miss is that in real life the combined effects of all these elements feed back into the system to inflict more damage. Furthermore, because many events link to multifaceted human behaviors, some influences are difficult to isolate. This interdependence also means that *solutions* to complex issues require insight into potential effects *over time*. Without considering lags and systemwide long-term impacts, solutions can neglect the subtle heart of an issue. For example, while U.S. policies that promoted home ownership seemed magnanimous and were intended to improve the standard of living, they were narrowly composed. They did not recognize one certainty: not everyone can afford to own a home. They also did not predict how deeply home loans would seep into financial securities. Ironically, the very solutions intended to boost home ownership ultimately failed. In the

---

38. Semuels, 2011b.
39. Gokhale, 2008.
40. Farmer, 2010.

decade before 2004, the national average for home ownership rose from 64 to 69 percent, but by early 2012 it had returned to 65 percent. In the hard-hit western U.S., it fell to 60 percent—back to its 1994 level.[41] Home ownership has returned to its foundational level, except that now people are swimming in debt and investors have lost their nest eggs.

12.5.4 Limits

Without adequate balancing mechanisms, reinforcing loops that create growth eventually generate rapid decay. Furthermore, if natural systems exceed their limits and grow beyond their capacity, they will erode their ability to grow in the future. A mundane example illustrates this principle. When weeds grow undisturbed in the yard, they produce seeds; the more seeds they produce, the more weeds there will be—a natural reinforcing loop. Unless this growth is inhibited by something like weed killer, weeds can take over completely. In the natural world, there will be some deterrent, some stabilizing force such as restricted space or lack of water or winter or worse yet, a fungus in the soil that kills weeds, grass, and all.

Systems that involve humans or limited resources such as oil or wealth fall into the category of natural systems. Limits in these systems are subtly insidious; capacity erodes before anyone knows what is happening. The housing bubble illustrates this erosion. As desires, expectations, culture, economic policies, and easy credit encouraged demand for houses, housing prices rose dramatically. Risky debt that funded the sale of these homes and promoted price escalation was the fungus in this system. Resulting defaults from this debt caused demand and housing prices to decay rapidly, and invaded the securities market. This decay indicates that the system had hit a limit. Consumer confidence in the economy eroded and the collective capacity to buy a home had been eaten away; consumers were carrying too much debt.

Another example of this limit principle involves wealth. As economist Thomas Sowell suggests, "there has never been enough to satisfy everyone completely." In other words, wealth is not infinite; its limit is based on a scarcity of resources that is exacerbated by ever-expanding human desires. Scarcity has implications for maintaining any level of wealth; it requires "both productive efforts… and personal responsibility in spending."[42] Without responsibility like this during the crisis, apparent wealth grown from risk-laden debt overshot its threshold and collapsed. Now the economy struggles to rebuild it.

---

41. Rajan, 2010; U.S. Census Bureau, 2012b.
42. Sowell, 2011.

12.6 EFFECTIVENESS OF CURRENT ECONOMIC POLICIES

At this point, we have answered the questions posed at the beginning of the chapter. Factors such as culture, environment, interest rates, and policies had an influence on human behaviors relating to material desires, expectations, and excessive self-interest; these interacting elements stimulated rapid economic overgrowth and pruned it just as quickly. By placing this systems understanding into the context of securitization and the global economy, we saw why crisis-related effects were felt worldwide. Finally, we recommended actions in five areas to mitigate future crises.

These answers and our proposed actions reflect a philosophy that integrates multiple aspects of human nature. Actions of using long-term oriented incentives, defining worthy purpose, exercising awareness and penalties, and maintaining positive expectations, reflect the belief that while we humans are indeed self-interested, we also have concern for others and seek meaningful purpose in life. Such a holistic philosophy of human nature is vital for a healthy economy.

Actions taken since the crisis, however, reflect a different philosophy—one that de-emphasizes human development and social interest and relies on self-interest to regulate its own excess. This alternate view aligns with current actions. By considering it in more detail, we can better assess whether current actions will be effective.

12.6.1 Philosophy Behind Current Actions

The philosophy that best explains actions taken to date marries two long-standing theories about how an economy works, namely that self-interest benefits society and that profit is the only acceptable corporate purpose.

The first theory comes from Adam Smith in the 1770s. His classic "invisible hand" proposes that in pursuing their own self-interests, market participants unwittingly promote society's interest by creating wealth that benefits all.[43] Smith also assumes that participants operate in good faith, are ethical and law-abiding in their dealings, and adequately understand the quality, value, and risk of what they are buying or selling. However, these attributes were mostly absent during the crisis, illustrating that Smith's tenets do not apply when individuals pursue their own narrow interests to the grave detriment of others. In the crisis, participants either ignored or kept information about risk to themselves; self-interested behaviors turned to greed and unethical acts that allowed some to get more than their fair share of the pie.

A second theory from Nobel Laureate Milton Friedman extends Smith's ideas. Arguing on the far side of an age-old debate, Friedman advocates that "there is one and only one social responsibility of business—to use its

---

43. Smith, 1937.

resources and engage in activities designed to increase its profits." He further proposes that if corporations pursue ends other than "to make as much money for their stockholders as possible" they "undermine the very foundation of our free society." Taken out of context, his view ignores other stakeholders such as customers and employees, and appears to excuse bad behaviors that could harm these stakeholders. However, like Smith, Friedman believes that a business must increase its profits only "so long as it stays within the rules of the game, which is to say, engages in open and free competition, without deception or fraud."[44]

So what happened during the crisis? Certainly businesses saw opportunity and pursued profits. Individuals who made economic decisions based on self-interest temporarily increased demand and boosted aggregate wealth. However, not everyone played according to the rules. Deception and fraud allowed the self-interest of some to crush the self-interest of others. Businesses turned profit into personal gain instead of reinvesting it in new jobs or new products or greater efficiency. Individuals took little responsibility for buying behaviors or debt. Furthermore, regulations that could have prevented these behaviors had been dismantled.

This alternate philosophy sees the crisis as a big green greed machine in which excessive self-interest and deceptive acts prevented the invisible hand from doing its job. It implies that the crisis could have been averted if unethical dealings were curtailed and self-interested participants had a level playing field. Most post-crisis actions seem to reflect this philosophy. They primarily involve policies, rules, and regulations that barricade against excessive self-interest and unethical dealings. For example, recent laws make it more difficult to file bankruptcy, require financial institutions to be more transparent, and propose to separate lending and investment banks to eliminate conflicts of interest. Legislation is trying to reduce unreasonable compensation and give stockholders a voice in determining executive benefits. Authorities are identifying and prosecuting offenders whose unethical acts were illegal.

To be fair, however, current actions extend a little beyond erecting barriers against self-interest. The government is also keeping interest rates low, extending unemployment benefits, and considering stimuli and tax adjustments to stimulate the economy and restore confidence. But are these actions enough to encourage recovery from the past crisis or prevent a new one?

12.6.2 Are Current Actions Enough?

Extreme self-interest was indeed a major culprit in the crisis and these new policies and penalties can reduce it—but only in the short-term. Moreover, current actions that use incentives, monetary policy, and tax breaks to restore confidence and kick-start the economy are hitting a brick wall; American's confidence level

---

44. See Friedman (1962) for citations in this paragraph.

dropped nearly 70 percent between 2010 and 2011.[45] The news was still not good in June 2012; the Consumer Confidence index fell over 2 points in 1 month.[46] Low confidence means that consumers buy fewer products, and that companies invest less in facilities and create fewer jobs. In fact, to cope with uncertainty, businesses are hoarding their cash. The Federal Reserve estimates that in Q3 of 2011, U.S. corporations held over $2 trillion in cash.[47]

Without positive motivators like meaningful purpose, or incentives that promote long-term performance, or a deepened awareness of effects on others, the system will resist permanent change and retreat into a condition of extreme self-interest. People always find a way around the latest rules and regulations, particularly when temptation grows. Furthermore, using monetary policy or stimulus programs to restore confidence is like rowing a dinghy across the ocean—there just isn't enough horsepower to overcome the swells of uncertainty, stubborn unemployment levels, and perceived unfairness in compensation and bailouts. In other words, current actions are *not* enough. We *are* likely to repeat the crisis—perhaps this time in a realm other than housing and securities such as sovereign debt.

Rather than returning to business as usual, we must rebuild the economy through short-term sacrifice and long-term planning; without a recovery period, it cannot heal. Moreover, while our extensive global connectivity can boost the international economies, it also allows dysfunction to become contagious and self-sustaining. Perhaps it is time to focus on the long-term and consider human development solutions such as meaningful purpose and long-term incentives that we earlier proposed.

12.7 YIN AND YANG REPRISE

At the beginning of the book, we introduced yin and yang as two halves that achieve optimal performance when they operate harmoniously. In the case of the economy, these two halves are represented by human elements (yin) and mechanistic elements (yang)—an economic *outer yin and yang*. Harmony between human behavior and economic mechanisms was missing during the crisis. Excessive behaviors overwhelmed mechanisms such as monetary and housing policies and deregulation that intended to maintain economic harmony.

Beyond this *outer yin and yang*, a more subtle yin and yang emerged from our analysis. These forces reside *inside* us—in the tension between our self-interested and society-interested natures. When *inner yin and yang* operate compatibly, self-interest and social interest flow as the "dynamic play of

45. Newport, 2011. Gallup's Economic Confidence Index was −49 in October 2011 versus −29 in October 2010.
46. Ausick, 2012. The Conference Board's Consumer Confidence Index fell from 64.4 in May to 62.0 in June 2012.
47. Goldstein, 2011.

opposites" in the familiar divided circle of Tao.[48] When a system's environment encourages this equilibrium, that system—individual, family, organization, or economy—will be healthier. During the crisis, self-interest grew too heavy. Balance was absent in both *outer* and *inner* yin and yang. Nothing nourished the positive side of human nature.

12.8 IMPLICATIONS FOR THE FUTURE

So what trends are shaping the future? What effects might we yet see? By design, this book focused on the housing bubble and on high risk home loans and securities built from these loans—all characteristics of the U.S. crisis. It then expanded into the greater economy that included unemployment and GDP on a national level and considered other nations' economies on a global level. Two implications emerge from this broad view.

First, we retain the seeds of past actions. In the U.S., some seeds are still dormant in outstanding subprime loans (especially ARMs), toxic securities and derivatives built from these loans, and shadow inventory for housing where people are waiting for better times to sell. These seeds may threaten the economy if unemployment increases, if confidence wanes and there is another recession, if housing prices drop, or if interest rates rise too far, too fast. Other seeds have begun to sprout. Losses from prior risky investments are still being uncovered. For example, in mid-2012, JPMorgan Chase finally acknowledged a $5.8 billion loss from "bad derivatives bets"; the company had tried to conceal it by making what some call "really stupid decisions."[49] Losses in other companies are undoubtedly still in hiding. Economic decline in the U.S. also planted its seeds in other countries where manufacturing facilities lay empty, major industries are gutted, and GDPs are negative. The fruit from these seeds will boomerang on the U.S. like bad karma—as long as the U.S. can't buy others' goods, they can't buy U.S. goods.

Second, we are sowing new seeds of future crises. Record debt and a downgraded sovereign credit rating[50] place the U.S. in a precarious position nationally and internationally. Alongside the rising cost of financing resulting from these lower ratings, other debt is mounting. Baby boomers who once contributed to social security are now recipients; health-care costs are escalating; student-loan debt has reached an estimated $1 billion.[51]

---

48. Simpkins and Simpkins, 1999.
49. Henry and Horowitz, 2012; Henry, 2012. To cover up its losses, the company sold profitable securities in its investment portfolios.
50. Swann, 2011. Standard & Poor's downgraded the U.S. long-term "sovereign credit rating" from AAA to AA+. The downgrade reflects its view that "effectiveness, stability, and predictability of American policymaking and political institutions have weakened at a time of ongoing fiscal and economic challenges."
51. Evans, 2012; much of this outstanding debt is held by students who won't graduate or by "older Americans, including retirees."

Furthermore, as nations, we are mortgaging our future. Although countries are managing the fiscal residue of the economic crisis, spending is outpacing income. For example, U.S. deficit exceeded $1 trillion in each of the last four years; debt relative to GDP is the highest since 1950.[52]

Global issues are heavy in this bag of new seeds as well. While Eurozone nations are struggling to balance their budgets, their deficits exceed prescribed limits.[53] Japan is working its own deficit crunch and faces possible downgrade of its sovereign debt.[54] Greece's massive debt, propped up by foreign capital and exacerbated by the global financial crisis, seriously threatens other Eurozone nations. Predictions in 2012 indicated that Greece may experience a fifth year of recession and a 4.5 percent drop in GDP as its unemployment approaches 24 percent.[55] Many estimate that it will cost 100 billion euros to keep the Greek economy alive and will force big European banks to "take losses on their holdings of Greek government bonds."[56] Linked to Greece's concerns, the sovereign debt issue in Europe is so significant that some believe it has become "the new subprime" problem whose implications are just as extensive.[57] Whatever happens, consequences will ripple. These global factors provide the precise ingredients for another reinforcing loop of escalating international debt and eventual economic decay—a legacy to the future unless we manage our debt.

12.9 CONCLUDING REMARKS

So what now? These trends and implications for the future seem overwhelming and discouraging. Do we just give up because the problem is too hard? Do we throw up our hands because we know that strong forces are out there waiting to hurt the world economy? Just the opposite, I think. We must calm the storm and still the financial whirlpools that are consuming our wealth. To do so, our solutions must consider three certainties.

First, we are globally connected. Some have likened the economic crisis to "a power blackout" through which failures cascade; they suggest that policymakers are too focused on small "individual nodes" and are not considering systemic effects.[58] Tweaking small subsystems that touch only one side of human nature or consider only parts of a global economy is inadequate over the long-term. Policies such as altering interest rates in one country are a drop in the bucket in light of world economic conditions.

---

52. Faler, 2012.
53. BBC News, 2012.
54. Otsuma, 2012.
55. AFP, 2012.
56. Strupczewski et al., 2012.
57. Alderman and Craig, 2011.
58. Sachs, 2008.

The system is too complex, too large, too interconnected, and too riddled with delays to adequately predict outcomes of narrow fixes. Before any nation is tempted to cut taxes or provide fiscal stimuli and bailouts, it must take a systems look to understand current and possible future states of the global economy. Policymakers should ensure that expenditures will not negate hoped-for benefits and put their nations further into debt. They must consider what the *combined* effects of these policies will be on national and global GDP, inflation, and unemployment. These policies *cannot* be implemented in isolation.

Using a wide lens means that nations in the global economy must strengthen their alliances to view the problem from all perspectives and implement solutions with caution. Analysts of global fiscal policy agree that "what is needed in these challenging times for fiscal policy is a steady hand, not erratic changes... to sustain the adjustment over time and reverse the long-term fiscal trends that are currently not sustainable."[59]

Second, our economy is out of balance. By recognizing the need for initiatives that balance the *inner yin and yang* (self-interest with social interest), we can balance the *outer yin and yang* (economic policies, rules, and regulations with the human element). Solutions that attend to *growth* of human character, temper excessive behaviors, and move the economy toward slow and steady expansion will prevail long-term. This philosophy along with the systems thinking principles of balance, lag, interdependence, and limits can help us identify initiatives and spark insight into our most complex social issues. These can also help us discern potential unintended consequences early on so that mid-course adjustments are possible.

Third, changing an economy requires altering behavior. Governments and organizations can influence some behaviors through the actions of their leaders. As Peter Drucker recognized more than 50 years ago, managers have a "public responsibility to *make* whatever is genuinely in the public good *become* the enterprise's own self-interest."[60] Yet, organizations and governments can only do so much. The true solution to socioeconomic issues lies in taking *personal* responsibility and being *personally* accountable. It is time to recognize that *each* of us *individually* is a part of the aggregate. In the timeless wisdom of Mahatma Gandhi: "We but mirror the world.... If we could change ourselves, the tendencies in the world would also change.... We need not wait to see what others do."[61] Yes, it is indeed a small world after all: that world begins with me and with you.

---

59. Cottarelli and Schaechter, 2010.
60. Drucker, 1986.
61. Gandhi, 1919. This quotation is more commonly paraphrased as "You must be the change you want to see in the world." It appeared in Gandhi's newspaper, *Harijan*, on September 8, 1913.

In a competitive market, the interaction between supply and demand governs the price and quantity of goods, services, commodities, or other items that are bought and sold. This Appendix describes how supply and demand operate together and translates that relationship into systems thinking terms. Their interaction in the housing market is a fundamental aspect of our systems perspective for the economic crisis.

A.1 RELATIONSHIP BETWEEN SUPPLY AND DEMAND

Two features of a competitive market allow the supply and demand model to function. First "there are many buyers and sellers of the same good or service" and second, "no individual's actions have a noticeable effect on the price at which the good or service is sold."[1] Both criteria are true for the housing market.

A.1.1 Basic Behavior

There are many versions of supply and demand behaviors, all of which represent the same phenomena. In the simplest terms, one way to understand these behaviors is relative to the price of a good or service, as follows:[2]

- *Law of demand*: At a higher price, people tend to demand a smaller quantity.
- *Law of supply*: At a higher price, producers tend to supply more of a good or service.
- *Market equilibrium*: A competitive market is in equilibrium when price has moved to a level at which the quantity of a good or service demanded equals the quantity supplied. This price is called the *equilibrium price*. The quantity bought and sold at that price is the *equilibrium quantity*.

The graph of quantity versus price for a given item in Figure A.1 illustrates supply and demand behaviors. On the supply curve, as the quantity supplied increases (moves left to right), price also increases (moves bottom to top). On the demand curve, as quantity demanded goes up, price goes down. Equilibrium is the point at which both buyer and seller are satisfied with the price of an item and with the quantity at which it is bought and sold. The buyer won't buy if it is priced too high and the supplier won't sell

---

1. Krugman and Wells, 2010.
2. For excellent discussions of the laws of supply and demand, see Krugman and Wells (2010) and Gwartney and Stroup (1990).

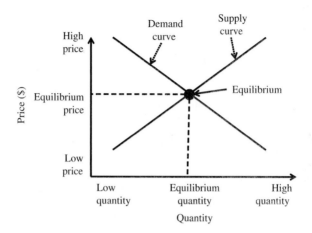

FIGURE A.1 Relationship between supply and demand.

if it is priced too low, so they compromise. The small circle in the center of the graph denotes equilibrium (for price and quantity), the point at which the demand and supply curves cross.

For the purposes of systems thinking, another way to view this relationship is to consider price and quantity under conditions of surplus and shortage. Decades ago economist Hubert Henderson described these conditions as follows.[3]

- When, for a given market price, demand exceeds supply (shortage), price tends to rise. Conversely when supply exceeds demand (surplus) price tends to fall.
- A rise in price tends to decrease demand and to increase supply. Conversely a fall in price tends to increase demand and to decrease supply.
- Price tends to the level at which demand is equal to supply (equilibrium).

Figures A.2 and A.3 illustrate this push and pull process of approaching equilibrium from a shortage condition.[4] In Figure A.2, when actual price is lower than equilibrium, consumers think it is a good deal. More people want more of the good or service than suppliers will sell at that low price. To resolve the shortage, suppliers realize they can charge more, buyers will pay more, and *price* moves up toward equilibrium price. *Quantity* demanded and *quantity* supplied move toward equilibrium where both buyer and supplier are happy.

---

3. From Henderson, 2010/1922.
4. See other examples of supply and demand in Krugman and Wells (2010) and in Gwartney and Stroup (1990).

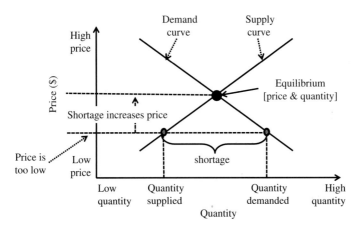

FIGURE A.2 Movement toward equilibrium from a shortage.

Figure A.3 shows that when the actual price of an item is above equilibrium, suppliers want to sell more to make a bigger profit, but buyers think it is too expensive and would rather spend their money elsewhere. Fewer people will buy the item than suppliers want to sell at that price. Thus there will be a surplus (quantity supplied exceeds quantity demanded). To resolve the surplus, producers reduce the price so that people will buy their product. When price decreases, quantities supplied decrease and both move toward equilibrium—a satisfactory level for both consumer and supplier.

A.1.2 Movements and Shifts

To appreciate how supply and demand operated for housing prices in the U.S. prior to the economic crisis, we consider two market trends: movements and shifts. *Movement* occurs when price of a product changes in a relatively stable economic environment. If prices rise, *movement* along the demand curve means consumers will buy more or less of a product and *movement* along the supply curve means that suppliers will make more or less of a product. Earlier discussions of equilibrium described *movements* in supply and demand. Here, supply or demand quantities move back and forth (increase and decrease) to follow price along the supply or demand curve, eventually moving toward equilibrium.

The second trend, a *shift*, is more complex and occurs when the economic environment changes. Using Figure A.1 as a reference, imagine that the entire demand curve travels either to the left (decreased quantity) or to the right (increased quantity) while the supply curve remains stationary. This change is called a *shift*; it alters the equilibrium point. The supply curve can also shift right or left in a similar fashion, while the demand curve stays put.

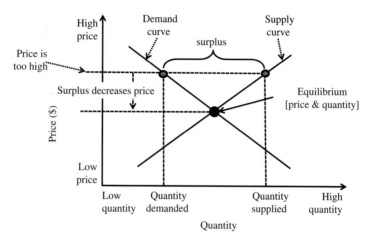

FIGURE A.3 Movement toward equilibrium from a surplus.

One way to tell if a shift has occurred is to look at quantity. "If the quantity sold changes in the *same* direction as the price—for example, if both the price and the quantity rise—this suggests that the demand curve has shifted. If the price and the quantity move in *opposite* directions, the likely cause is a shift of the supply curve."[5]

Figure A.4 shows a right shift in the demand curve; quantity demanded by consumers has increased and price rises as a result. Because the change in demand was not a fleeting occurrence, a new equilibrium point is established at a higher price and quantity.

A right shift of demand can occur, for example, when average income for consumers increases, perhaps with inflation. Higher income means they are less sensitive to price or can afford more, thus increasing demand for an item and pushing the price up. Now, because consumers are *willing* to pay a higher price, increased supply does not push the price down. Demand has essentially shifted equilibrium price and quantity upward.

Changes in consumer expectations also cause demand shifts. In the economic crisis, for example, people expected that housing prices would continue to rise. More people were willing to pay a high price for a home believing they could sell it later for more money (demand shifted right). As demand increased and prices rose, the supply of houses grew. In another crisis-related example, a change in the number of consumers shifted demand. As more people qualified for mortgage loans, the number of home buyers increased and pushed demand and prices up (demand shifted right). The supply of houses to meet this demand then increased.

---

5. Krugman and Wells, 2010.

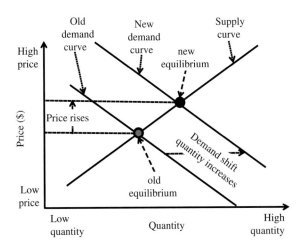

FIGURE A.4　Right shift in demand.

On the other hand a change in preferences could shift demand left. Suppose that a radio-controlled car was popular before Christmas, but lost its appeal afterward. In November, parents paid a premium to get the toy for their children (demand shifted right and price was high), but by February when another toy made the hot list, parents would only buy the car on sale, if at all (demand shifted left and price dropped).

Unlike a demand shift, a supply shift moves price and quantity in opposite directions: if price increases, quantity decreases and vice versa. Figure A.5 depicts a left shift in supply. In this case, if the supplier's costs to produce the good or service increase, he would charge a higher price; higher price means demand drops (price increases and quantity decreases).

An example of a left shift in supply occurs when employees negotiate for higher wages, thus increasing costs for suppliers who pass the increased costs to consumers. For housing, the supply curve might shift left if, for example, the cost of lumber increased. Housing contractors would then charge more causing consumers to buy fewer homes. Technology advances or new materials that reduce suppliers' costs can shift supply to the right where we would expect lower prices and higher quantity demanded at a new equilibrium point. External factors also cause a supply shift to the right. In the case of the crisis, the supply of houses for sale increased dramatically when home loans went into foreclosure. This flood of foreclosed homes pressed prices down.

It is not uncommon that both supply and demand curves shift at the same time in response to a changing economic environment. For these simultaneous shifts, the curve that moves the most (dominates) "has a greater effect

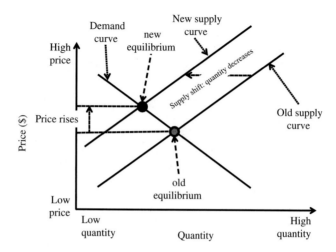

FIGURE A.5 Left shift in supply.

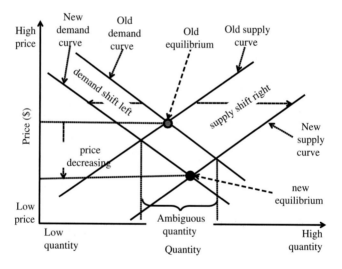

FIGURE A.6 Simultaneous supply shift right and demand shift left.

on the change in equilibrium price and quantity."[6] Figure A.6 illustrates the effects of the supply curve shifting right and the demand curve shifting left. When supply and demand shift in opposite directions, they both push the equilibrium price downward, but they have opposite effects on the quantity bought and sold. Thus it is difficult to tell whether *quantity* will increase or

6. Krugman and Wells, 2010.

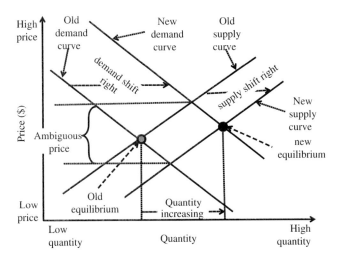

FIGURE A.7 Simultaneous supply shift right and demand shift right.

decrease and by how much. However in this example, one can estimate that quantity increases since supply pushed quantity up more than demand drove it down.

When supply and demand simultaneously shift in the same direction, it is difficult to predict *price*. Figure A.7 shows that simultaneous right shifts of supply and demand increase quantity, however, the supply shift decreases price and the demand shift increases it. Again, we might be able to tell if price increased or decreased relative to the original equilibrium point by considering whether supply or demand moved the most. In this example, demand dominated and we expect prices to be higher rather than lower.

To find your way through this maze of shifts, consult the summary in Table A.1. Shifts to the right mean supply or demand quantities increase; shifts to the left mean supply or demand quantities decrease.

This figure highlights the four areas of ambiguity where supply and demand shift simultaneously. In these areas, we cannot exactly predict the new equilibrium, but we can estimate that the ambiguous price or quantity moves in the general direction of the larger shift.

A.2 SYSTEMS THINKING INTERPRETATION

With this insight, we can now illustrate the interaction of supply and demand in systems thinking terms. Throughout the book we rely on these depictions to build an integrated picture of the crisis.

	Shift direction		New Equilibrium		Other conditions
			Price	Quantity	
Supply	Right	supply increases	down	up	Demand remains the same
	Left	supply decreases	up	down	
Demand	Right	demand increases	up	up	Supply remains the same
	Left	demand decreases	down	down	
Supply/Demand	Right/Right	supply increases/ demand increases	ambiguous	up	Supply and demand move simultaneously
	Right/Left	supply increases/ demand decreases	down	ambiguous	
	Left/Right	supply decreases/ demand increases	up	ambiguous	
	Left/Left	supply decreases/ demand decreases	ambiguous	down	

TABLE A.1 Effects of shifts in supply and demand.

A.2.1 Supply and Demand

To understand how supply and demand move toward an agreed-on equilibrium point using systems thinking constructs, think of them as repetitive processes, or loops that continue to operate until suppliers and consumers are both satisfied. This interpretation of supply and demand is not new. In 1777, long before systems thinking became a formal discipline, Adam Smith used his famous "invisible hand" metaphor to describe how a market economy operates as a balancing feedback system. He "realized that a free market creates powerful negative feedback loops that cause prices and profits to be self-regulating."[7] What we call equilibrium price today he described as the "natural price" of an item at which suppliers adequately recover costs of production and consumers find greater value in that item than they do from alternate ways of spending their money.[8]

Smith also alluded to "market price," or the "actual price at which any commodity is commonly sold." In his philosophical feedback loop, he recognized that market price settles toward the natural (equilibrium) price, noting that "the natural price... is the central price, to which the prices of all commodities are continually gravitating."[9] Figure A.8 notionally depicts the behavior of price as it approaches a goal of equilibrium. The top curve shows how market price that is too high reaches equilibrium and the bottom curve shows how market price that is too low reaches equilibrium.

The systems representation of the supply and demand process is a pair of balancing feedback loops that together seek the goal of *equilibrium price* at

7. Sterman, 2000; see also Smith, 1937.
8. Smith, 1937.
9. Smith, 1937.

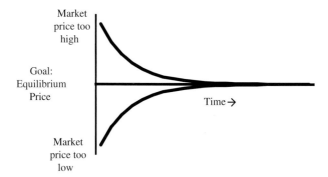

FIGURE A.8 Market price as it moves toward equilibrium price.

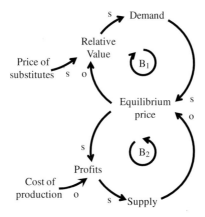

FIGURE A.9 Balancing feedback loops of supply and demand. *Source: Adapted from Sterman (2000). Reproduced with permission of The McGraw-Hill Companies.*

which both supplier and consumer are satisfied. Interacting loops B_1 and B_2 in Figure A.9 reflect the normal behavior of prices for housing or other assets that are bought and sold.[10] To read the diagram, recall from Chapter 1 that an "s" means the factors move in the *same* direction and an "o" says the factors move *opposite* one another.

Beginning with the upper loop, when consumers value an item more than they value potential substitutes (the price of substitutes is too high) they will buy that item and demand for it will rise. Substitutes can include similar products or other alternate uses of money. Increased demand creates a shortage and raises the price that the consumer will agree to pay (equilibrium price).

---

10. See also Morris (2002) for the feedback control theory diagram of the supply and demand relationship.

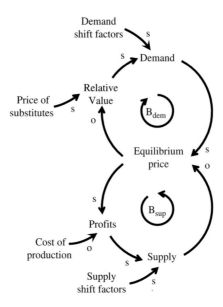

FIGURE A.10 Supply and demand shift factors affect equilibrium price.

In the lower loop, a higher price increases profits (price relative to cost of production). At this point existing producers increase supply to make more money and new producers may enter the market. Increased supply drives price down and a surplus lowers prices to attract customers. In a stable environment, these loops continue to move market price *toward* the equilibrium price goal at which consumer and supplier agree to do business.

A.2.2 Supply or Demand Shifts

On the occasions when factors in the economic environment cause supply and/or demand quantities to shift, equilibrium price will shift, as previously shown. In Figure A.10, these shift factors influence the demand and supply balancing loops (now labeled B_{demand} and B_{supply}) from Figure A.9. Shifts that increase quantity demanded eventually increase equilibrium price; shifts that decrease demand decrease price. In contrast, shifts that increase quantity supplied eventually decrease equilibrium price; decreased quantity has the opposite effects.

In any market economy, there are conditions under which supply, demand, or price exhibit continuous and exponential growth or decay (see Chapter 1). In these cases, a reinforcing loop generates a shift in supply or demand. This condition is important for our systems story. For example, demand shifts created by

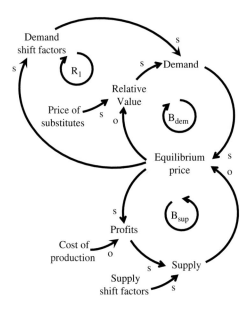

FIGURE A.11   Demand shifts created by a reinforcing loop.

reinforcing loops in a speculative environment[11] can generate asset bubbles like the housing price bubble seen in the U.S. during the economic crisis.

Figure A.11 replaces the demand shift factor from Figure A.10 with a reinforcing loop R_1 that directly influences B_{demand}. While supply and demand loops continually try to stabilize price and quantity around an equilibrium point, the reinforcing loop shifts demand and moves this equilibrium point. Examples of a *demand shift factor* could be increased income or a change in expectations mentioned earlier. Although not included in the diagram, supply shifts can also be built around a reinforcing loop that continually alters supply.

A.3 SUMMARY

This Appendix reviewed the behavior of supply and demand in a competitive market. It considered movements and shifts, surpluses and shortages, all of which apply to the emergence of the housing bubble during the economic crisis. Most importantly, the Appendix introduced systems thinking constructs that will become part of the systems story.

---

11. See Richardson, 1999. One can estimate that price or quantity moves in the general direction of the dominant shift as described by John Stuart Mill (1899/1848) in his discussion of speculative behavior based on expectations: "When there is a general impression that the price of some commodity is likely to rise... This disposition tends in itself to produce the effect which it looks forward to, a rise of price..."

References

Abate, T., 2006, April 5. 20-year low for debtor filings/Drop may reflect revisions last year to bankruptcy law. SFGate.com. Retrieved from <http://articles.sfgate.com/2006-04-05/business/17290250_1_filings-lundquist-consulting-american-bankruptcy-institute>.

Acharya, V., Cooley, T., Richardson, M., Walter, I., 2009. Manufacturing tail risk: a perspective on the financial crisis of 2007−2009. Foundations and Trends® in Finance 4 (4), 247−325, Retrieved from <http://pages.stern.nyu.edu/~sternfin/vacharya/public_html/tail_risk.pdf>.

Adams, J.T., 1931. The Epic of America. Little, Brown & Co., Boston.

Adegoke, Y., 2009, January 25. Lehman's Fuld sold Florida mansion to wife for $100. Reuters. Retrieved from <http://www.reuters.com/assets/pring?aid + USTRE50P04A20090126>.

Adelson, M., Jacob, J. 2008, January 8. The sub-prime problem: causes and lessons. Adelson & Jacob Consulting, LLC. Retrieved from <http://www.securitization.net/pdr/Publications/Sub-prime_Problem_8Jan08.pdf>.

AFP, 2012, July 24. Greek recession to be much worse than expected. Agence France-Presse. Retrieved from <http://news.ph.msn.com/business/greek-recession-to-be-much-worse-than-expected-pm>.

AIG, 2010, May 9. American International Group, Inc. Retrieved from <http://www.aigcorporate.com>.

Akerlof, G., Perry, G., Dickens, W., 1996, August. Low inflation or no inflation: should the Federal Reserve pursue complete price stability? Brookings Policy Brief Series #4. The Brookings Institute. Retrieved from <http://www.brookings.edu/papers/1997/08useconomics_akerlof.aspx?p = 1>.

Akerlof, G.A., Shiller, R.J., 2009. Animal Spirits: How Human Psychology Drives the Economy, and Why it Matters for Global Capitalism. Princeton University Press, Princeton.

Albert, E., Denise, T., Peterfreund, S., 1984. Great Traditions in Ethics, fifth ed. Wadsworth Publishing Co., Belmont, CA.

Alderman, L., Craig, S., 2011, November 10. Europe's banks found safety of bonds a costly illusion. The New York Times. Retrieved from <http://www.nytimes.com/2011/11/11/business/global/sovereign-debt-turns-sour-in-euro-zone.html?pagewanted = all>.

Amadeo, K., 2009, May. Mortgage-Backed Securities. Retrieved from <http://useconomy.about.com/od/glossary/g/mortgage_securi.htm>.

Anderson, V., Johnson, L., 1997. Systems Thinking Basics: From Concepts to Causal Loops. Pegasus Communications, Inc., Waltham, MA.

Andrews, E., Baker, P., 2009, March 15. A.I.G. Planning huge bonuses after $170 billion bailout. New York Times. Retrieved from <http://www.nytimes.com/2009/03/15/business/15AIG.html>.

Andrews, S., 2010, April. Larry Fink's $12 trillion shadow. Vanity Fair. Retrieved from <http://www.vanityfair.com/business/features/2010/04/fink-201004>.

Angell, J.R., 1905. Psychology: An Introductory Study of the Structure and Function of Human Consciousness, third. rev Henry Holt & Co., New York.

Appelbaum, B., 2012, December 12. Fed cites unemployment in keeping interest rate low. The Boston Globe. Retrieved from <http://bostonglobe.com/business/2012/12/12/fed-policy-trim-nyt/G8M72Nf3HO7uXAMl8BLccP/story.html>.

Ariely, D., 2009. Predictably Irrational: The Hidden Forces that Shape our Decisions. HarperCollins, New York.

Ariely, D., 2010. The Upside of Irrationality. HarperCollins, New York.

Aristotle, 1999. Nicomachean Ethics, second ed. Hackett Publishing Company, Inc., Indianapolis, Terence Irwin (Trans.).

Arnott, S., 2010, July 28. BP CEO Tony Hayward: in his own words. Bloomsburg Business Week. Retrieved from <http://www.businessweek.com/globalbiz/content/jul2010/gb20100728_556093.htm>.

Arthur, W., 1990. Positive Feedbacks in the economy. Sci. Am. 262, 92−99.

Arthur, W., Holland, J., Blake, L., Palmer, R., Tayler, P., 1996, December 12. Asset pricing under endogenous expectations in an artificial stock market. Retrieved from <http://tuvalu.santafe.edu/~wbarthur/Papers/documents/Arthur-HollandStockMarket.pdf>.

Arthur, W., Durlauf, S., Lane, D. (Eds.), 1997. Introduction: Process and emergence in the economy. The Economy as An Evolving Complex System II. Retrieved from <http://tuvalu.santafe.edu/~wbarthur/Papers/Pdf_files/ADL_Intro.pdf>.

Arthur, W., 2006. Out-of-equilibrium economics and agent-based modeling. In: Judd, K., Tesfatsion, L. (Eds.), Handbook of Computational Economics, vol. 2: Agent-Based Computational Economics. Elsevier/North-Holland, Oxford, U.K., pp. 1551−1564., Retrieved from <http://tuvalu.santafe.edu/~wbarthur/Papers/documents/OutofEquilPaper-SFI.pdf>.

Ashby, W.R., 1958. An Introduction to Cybernetics. Chapman & Hall Ltd., London.

Associated Press, 2008a, February 2. Merrill accused of fraud for risky sub-prime investments. Los Angeles Times. Retrieved from <http://articles.latimes.com/2008/feb/02/business/fi-merrill2>.

Associated Press, 2008b, May 8. AIG loses $7.8 billion on credit swaps, investment charges. USA Today. Retrieved from <http://www.usatoday.com/money/companies/earnings/2008-05-08-aig_N.htm>.

Associated Press, 2009, Jan 23. Wall Street's entitlement culture hard to shake. MSNBC.com.. Retrieved from <http://www.msnbc.msn.com/id/288178000/#>.

Associated Press, 2010a, February 3. AIG bonuses are "outrageous" but legal, pay czar says. Cleveland.com. Retrieved from <http://blog.cleveland.com/business_impact/print.html?entry=/2010/02/aig_bonuses_are_outrageous_but.html>.

Associated Press, 2010b, June 14. BP engineer called doomed rig a "nightmare well." CBSNews.com. Retrieved from <http://www.cbsnews.com/stories/2010/06/14/national/main6581586.shtml>.

Ausick, P., 2012, June 26. Consumer confidence lower, investor confidence higher. 24/7 Wall Street. Retrieved from <http://247wallst.com/2012/06/26/consumer-confidence-lower-investor-confidence-higher>.

Ausubel, D., 1955. Relationships between shame and guilt in the socializing process. Psychol. Rev. 42 (5), 378−390.

Bajaj, V., 2008, March 26. Report assails auditor for work at failed home lender. The New York Times. Retrieved from <http://www.nytimes.com/2008/03/26/business/26cnd-account.html?_r=1&hp>.

Barberis, N., 2011, August. Psychology and the financial crisis of 2007-2008. Manuscript in preparation. Retrieved from <http://faculty.som.yale.edu/nicholasbarberis/cp10.pdf>.

Bar-Gill, O., 2009. The law, economics and psychology of subprime mortgage contracts. Cornell Law Rev. 94, 1073−1152, Retrieved from <http://legalworkshop.org/wp-content/uploads/2009/07/cornell-a200907>.

Barnett-Hart, A. K., 2009, March 19. The story of the CDO market meltdown: An empirical analysis. Presented to the Department of Economics, Harvard College, Cambridge, MA. Retrieved from <http://www.hks.harvard.edu/m-rcbg/students/dunlop/2009-CDOmeltdown.pdf>.

Barth, J., Li, T., Lu, W., Phumiwasana, T., Yago, G., 2009a. The Rise and Fall of the U.S. Mortgage and Credit Markets: A Comprehensive Analysis of the Meltdown. Milkin Institute, Santa Monica, CA, Excerpt from full-length book version, New Jersey: Wiley. Retrieved from <http://milkininstitute.org/pdf/Riseandfailexcerpt.pdf>.

Barth, J., Li, T., Phumiwasana, T., 2009b. The credit crunch and yield spreads. In: Pringle, R., Carver, N. (Eds.), RBS Reserve Management Trends 2009. Central Banking Publications, London, Retrieved from <http://business.auburn.edu/ ~ barthjr/publications/The%20US%20Financial%20Crisis%20Credit%20Crunch%20And%20Yield%20Spreads.pdf>.

Batini, N., Haldane, A., 2001. Forward-looking rules for monetary policy. In: Taylor, J. (Ed.), Monetary Policy Rule. University of Chicago Press, Chicago, pp. 157−192.

Baumeister, R., Vohs, K., 2005. The pursuit of meaningfulness in life. In: Snyder, C.R., Lopez, S.J. (Eds.), Handbook of Positive Psychology. Oxford University Press, New York, pp. 608−618.

Bazerman, M., Tenbrunsel, A., 2011. Blind Spots: Why we Fail to do What's Right and what to do about it. Princeton University Press, Princeton.

BBC News, 2009, August 7. Timeline: Credit crunch to downturn. Retrieved from <http://news.bbc.co.uk/2/hi/business/7521250.stm>.

BBC News, 2012, May 4. In graphics: Eurozone crisis. Data from Eurostat. Retrieved from <http://www.bbc.co.uk/news/business-13366011>.

Beattie, A., 2002, October 9. Market crashes: The dotcom crash. Investopedia®. Retrieved from <http://www.investopedia.com/features/crashes/crashes8.asp>.

Beeghley, L., 2004. The Structure of Social Stratification in the United States, fourth ed. Pearson Education, Inc., New York.

Beinhocker, E., 2006. The Origin of Wealth: Evolution, Complexity, and the Radical Remaking of Economics. Harvard Business School Press, Boston.

Bell, D., 1996. The Cultural Contradictions of Capitalism (twentieth anniversary ed. New York: BasicBooks, a member of Perseus Books Group.

Bellah, R., Madsen, R., Sullivan, W., Swidler, A., Tipton, S., 1996. Habits of the Heart: Individualism and Commitment in American Life. University of California Press, Berkeley.

Belsky, G., Gilovich, T., 2010. Why Smart People Make Big Money Mistakes...and how to Correct them: Lessons from the Life-Changing Science of Behavioral Economics. Simon & Schuster, New York.

Belsky, E., Essene, R., Retsinas, N., 2008. Consumer and mortgage credit at the crossroads. In: Retsinas, N.P., Belsky, E.S. (Eds.), Borrowing to Live: Consumer and Mortgage Credit Revisited. Brookings Institution Press, Cambridge, MA, pp. 5−64. Joint Center for Housing Studies, Harvard University and Washington, D.C.

Bem, D., 1970. Beliefs, Attitudes, and Human Affairs. Brooks/Cole Publishing, Monterey, CA.

Bernanke, B., 2002, October 15. Asset price bubbles and monetary policy. Speech made to New York Chapter of the National Association of Business Economists. Retrieved from <http://www.federalreserve.gov/boarddocs/speeches/2002/20021015/default.htm>.

Bernanke, B., 2003, March 25. A perspective on inflation targeting. Speech made at the Annual Washington Policy Conference of Business Economists, Washington, D.C. Retrieved from <http://www.federalreserve.gov/boarddocs/speeches/2003/20030325/default.htm>.

Bernanke, B., 2007, February 6. The level and distribution of economic well-being. Speech made before the greater Omaha chamber of commerce, Omaha, Nebraska. Retrieved from <http://www.federalreserve.gov/newsevents/speech/bernanke20070206a.htm>.

Bernanke, B., 2008, May 5. Mortgage delinquencies and foreclosures. Speech made at the Columbia Business School's 32nd Annual Dinner, New York. Retrieved from <http://www .federalreserve.gov/newsevents/speech/Bernanke20080505a.htm>.

Berridge, K., 2003. Pleasure, pain, desire, and dread: hidden core processes of emotion. In: Kahneman, D, Diener, E., Schwarz, N. (Eds.), Well-Being: The Foundations of Hedonic Psychology. Russell Sage Foundation, New York, pp. 525−557.

Berridge, K., 2007. The debate over dopamine's role in reward: the case for incentive salience. Psychopharmacology 191, 391−431.

Bertalanffy, L. von, 1968. General System Theory. George Braziller, New York.

Bezemer, D., 2009, June 16.'No one saw this coming': Understanding financial crisis through accounting models (MPRA Paper No. 15892). Munich, GE: Groningen University. Retrieved from <http://mpra.ub.uni-meunchen.de/15892>.

Bhattacharya, A., Fabozzi, F., Chang, S.E., 2001. Overview of the mortgage market. In: Fabozzi, F. (Ed.), The Handbook of Mortgage-Backed Securities, fifth ed. McGraw-Hill, New York, pp. 1−23.

Board of Governors of the Federal Reserve System, 2011a. Federal Open Market Committee. Retrieved from <http://www.federalreserve.gov/monetarypolicy/fomc.htm>.

Board of Governors of the Federal Reserve System, 2011b, November. Federal funds effective rate. Selected Interest Rates (Daily)-H.15. Retrieved from < http://www.federalreserve.gov/ releases/H15/data.htm>.

Board of Governors of the Federal Reserve System, 2011c, November. Market yield on U.S. treasury securities at 10-year constant maturity. Selected Interest Rates (Daily)-H.15. Retrieved from <http://www.federalreserve.gov/releases/H15/data.htm>.

Bocock, R., 1997. Consumption. Routledge, New York.

Bosworth, M., 2008, July 5. Fighting foreclosure: one family's story. ConsumerAffairs.com. Retrieved from <http://www.consumeraffairs.com/news04/2008/07/foreclosure_fighting. html>.

Boulding, K., 1956. General systems theory: the skeleton of science. Manage. Sci. 2 (3), 197−208.

Boyd, E.E., 2011, January 31. How social media accelerated the uprising in Egypt. FastCompany.com. Retrieved from <http://www.fastcompany.com/node/1722492/ print>.

Braithwaite, T., 2011, January 20. US panel's report reflects partisan rift. Financial Times. Retrieved from <http://www.ft.com/cms/s/1d46933a-2ca7-11e0-83bd-00144feab49a, dwp_uuid = ebe33f66-57aa-11dc-8c65-0000779fd2ac,print = yes.html#>.

Brock, H., 2012. American Gridlock: Common Sense 101 Solutions to the Economic Crises. Wiley, Hoboken, New Jersey.

Brooks, D., 2011. The Social Animal: The Hidden Sources of Love, Character, and Achievement. Random House, New York.

Buhl, T., 2010, May. More corruption: Bear Stearns falsified information as raters shrugged. The Atlantic. Retrieved from <http://www.theatlantic.com/business/archive/2010/05/more-corruption-bear-stearns-falsified-information-as-raters-shrugged/56763>.

Busari, S., 2008, November 27. Tweeting the terror: how social media reacted to Mumbai. CNNWorld Social Media. Retrieved from <http://articles.cnn.com/2008-11-27/world/mumbai.twitter_1_twitter-tweet-terror-attacks?_s = PM:WORLD>.

BusinessDictionary.com, 2012, July 31. Sovereign debt. Retrieved from <http://www.businessdictionary.com/definition/sovereign-debt.html>.

Calder, L., 1999. Financing the American Dream: A Cultural History of Consumer Credit. Princeton University Press, Princeton, New Jersey.

Campbell, J.Y., Cocco, J.F., 2004, August. How do house prices affect consumption? Evidence from micro data. Working paper. Department of Economics, Harvard University and London Business School. Retrieved from <http://faculty.london.edu/jcocco/assets/documents/cam>.

Canner, G., Dynan, K., Passmore, W., 2002. Mortgage refinancing in 2001 and early 2002. Fed. Reserve Bull.469–481, Retrieved from <http://www.federalreserve.gov/pubs/bulletin/2002/1202lead.pdf>.

Cantor, R., Hamilton, D., Tennant, J., 2007, April. Corporate Default Rates. Moody's Investors Service. Retrieved from <http://www.moodys.com/sites/products/DefaultResearch/2006600000426807.pdf>.

Capra, F., 1996. The Web of Life: A New Scientific Understanding of Living Systems. Doubleday, New York.

Capra, F., 2010. The Tao of Physics: An Exploration of the Parallels between Modern Physics and Eastern Mysticism, fifth ed. Shambhala, Boston.

Cardtrak.com, 2007, May 31. Credit card debt—What do Americans really owe? Retrieved from <http://www.cardtrak.com/cardfacts/Press_Releases.2007.05-31_What_Do_Americans_Really_Owe>.

Carey, W., 2007, September 12. High Foreclosures but low bankruptcies: why the disconnect? Knowledge @W.P. Carey. Retrieved from <http://knowledge.wpcarey.asu.edu/article.cfm?articleid = 1472#>.

Chomsisengphet, S., Pennington-Cross, A., 2006. The evolution of the subprime mortgage market. Fed. Reserve Bank St. Louis Rev.Retrieved from <http://research.stlouisfed.org/publications/review/0601/ChomPenCross.pdf>.

Christie, L., 2008, October 27. Mortgage fraud: new and improved. CNN Money. Retrieved from <http://money.cnn.com/2008/10/17/real_estate/new_mortgage_fraud/?postversion = 2008101715>.

Chu, K., Acohido, B., 2008, November 14. Why banks are boosting credit card interest rates and fees. USA Today. Retrieved from <http://www.usatoday.com/money/industries/banking/2008-11-09-bank-credit-card-interest-rates_N.htm#>.

Chuchmach, M., Rood, J., 2009, January 22. Report: Merrill Lynch CEO spent over $1M to redecorate office. ABC News. Retrieved from <http://abcnews.go.com/print?id = 6710369>.

Clark, A., 2008, June 25. Countrywide Financial faces unethical business practices prosecution. New York Guardian. Retrieved from <http://www.guardian.co.uk/business/2008/jun/25/countrywide.subprime>.

Clark, J., 1967. Preface to Social Economics: Essays on Economic Theory and Social Problems. Augustus M. Kelley, Publishers, New York (Written in 1936).

CNN.com, 2006, October 18. Poll: 74 percent of Americans say Congress out of touch. CNN.com Retrieved from <http://cnn.com/2006/POLITICS/10/18/congress.poll/index.html>.

CNNMoney.com, 2007, July 30. Fund manager's fun sailing away. CNNMoney.com Retrieved from <http://money.cnn.com/2007/07/30/news/newsmakers/yacht_sale/>.

Cohen, D., 2008, June 3. The Panglossian world of finance. VOX. Retrieved from <http://voxeu.org/index.php?q = node/1197>.

Cohen, L., 2004. A consumers' Republic: The Politics of Mass Consumption in Postwar America. Vintage Books, New York.

Confucius, 1994. The wisdom of Confucius. Lin Yutang (Ed. & Trans.) New York: The Modern Library.

Congressional Budget Office, 1982. The prospects for economic recovery: a report to the Senate and House Committees on Budget, Part 1. Congress of the United States: Congressional Budget Office. U.S. Government Printing Office, Washington, D.C.

Congressional Budget Office, 2010, December. Fannie Mae, Freddie Mac, and the Federal Role in the Secondary Mortgage Market. Congress of the United States: Congressional Budget Office. Retrieved from <http://www.cbo.gov/ftpdocs/120xx/doc12032/12-23-FannieFreddie.pdf>.

Congressional Oversight Panel, 2010, November 16. November oversight report: examining the consequences of mortgage irregularities for financial stability and foreclosure mitigation. Congressional Oversight Panel. Retrieved from <http://bizjournal.com/southflorida/pdf/Congressional%20report%20foreclosures.pdf>.

Consumer Federation of America, 2010, May 10. Your credit scores. Consumer Federation of America, Fair Isaac Corporation. Retrieved from <http://www.pueblo.gsa.gov/cic_text/money/creditscores/your.htm>.

Cooke, S., 2006, November 8. Bankruptcy filings historically low but climbing one year later. Credit Union Times. Retrieved from <http://www.cutimes.com/2006/11/08/bank-ruptcy-filings-historically-low-but-climbing-one-year-later>.

Corning, P., 1998. The synergism hypothesis: on the concept of synergy and its role in the evolution of complex systems. J. Soc. Evol. Syst. 21 (2), 133−172, Retrieved from <http://www.complexsystems.org/publications/synhypo.html>.

Corning, P., 2002. The re-emergence of 'emergence': a venerable concept in search of a theory. Complexity 7, 18−30, Retrieved from <http://www.complexsystems.org/publications/pdf/emergence3.pdf>.

Cottarelli, C., Schaechter, A., 2010, September 1. Long-term trends in public finances in the G-7 economies. IMF Staff Position Note. International Monetary Fund. Retrieved from <http://www.imf.org/external/pubs/ft/spn/2010/spn1013.pdf>.

Coy, P., Miller, R., Young, L., Palmeri, C., 2004, July 19. Is a housing bubble about to burst? Business Week. Retrieved from <http://www.businessweek.com/magazine/content/04_29/b3892064_mz011.htm>.

Craig, S., Solomon, D., 2009, July 31. Bank bonus tab: $33 billion: Nine lenders that got U.S. aid paid at least $1 million each to 5,000 employees. The Wall Street Journal (p. A1). Retrieved from <http://online.wsj.com/article/SB124896891815094085.html>.

Crippen, D., 2001, May 23. CBO testimony: federal subsidies for the housing GSEs. Congressional Budget Office. Retrieved from <http://www.cbo.gov/doc.cfm?index = 2839&type = 0>.

Damasio, A., 1999. The Feeling of what Happens: Body and Emotion in the Making of Consciousness. Harcourt, New York.

Damasio, A., 2010. Self Comes to Mind: Constructing the Conscious Brain. Pantheon Books, New York.

Dash, E., 2009, September 18. What's really wrong with Wall Street pay. The New York Times: Economix. Retrieved from <http://economix.blogs.nytimes.com/2009/09/18/whats-really-wrong-with-wall-street-pay/>.

Dash, E., 2008, February 12. New losses at A.I.G. trouble Wall Street. The New York Times. Retrieved from <http://www.nytimes.com/2008/02/12/business/12aig.html>.

Davidoff, S., 2011, August 11. For Bank of America, Countrywide bankruptcy is still an option. The New York Times DealBook. Retrieved from <http://dealbook.nytimes.com/2011/08/11/for-bank-of-america-countrywide-bankruptcy-is-still-an-option/>.

Davidson, A., Sanders, A.B., 2009, February. Securitization after the fall. Prepared for the Second Annual UCI Mid-Winter Symposium on Urban Research. Retrieved from <http://merage.uci.edu/ResearchAndCenters/CRE/Resources/Documents/Davidson-Sanders.pdf>.

Dawkins, R., 1989. The Selfish Gene. Oxford University Press, Oxford.

Deci, E.L., 1980. The Psychology of Self-Determination. Lexington Books, Lexington, MA.

Deng, Y., Gabriel, S., Sanders, A., 2010, August 28. CDO market implosion and the pricing of subprime mortgage-backed securities. Social Science Research Network. Retrieved from <http://ssrn.com/abstract = 1356630>.

Department of Corporations, 2009. The secure and fair enforcement for mortgage licensing act of 2008 (SAFE). State of California. Retrieved from <http://www.corp.ca.gov/FSD/MLO/SAFE.asp>.

der Hovanesian, M., 2006, September 11. Nightmare mortgages. BusinessWeek. Retrieved from <http://www.businessweek.com>

Descartes, R., 2008. Discourse on the Method. Oxford University Press, New York (First published in 1637).

Digest of Education Statistics, 2011. Table 8: Percentage of persons age 25 and over and of persons 25 to 29 years old with high school completion or higher and a bachelor's or higher degree by race/ethnicity and sex. National Center for Educational Statistics. Retrieved from <http://nces.ed.gov/programs/digest/d11/tables/dt11_008.asp>.

Dow Jones, 2008, September 21. Goldman Sachs, Morgan Stanley to be bank holding companies. The Wall Street Journal. Retrieved from <http://online.wsj.com/article/SB122204751200261685.html>.

Dow Jones, 2011, June 29. Bank of America-Countrywide: Worst deal in history? The Wall Street Journal. Retrieved from <http://blogs.wsj.com/deals/2011/06/29/bank-of-america-countrywide-worst-deal-in-history/>.

Dow Jones, 2011, November 8. Why BofA decided against a Countrywide bankruptcy for now. The Wall Street Journal. Retrieved from <http://blogs.wsj.com/deals/2011/11/08/why-bofa-decided-against-a-countrywide-bankruptcy-for-now/>.

Dreiman, S., 2001, March 1. Using the price to income ratio to determine the presence of housing price bubbles. Office of Federal Housing Enterprise Oversight: House price index, fourth quarter 2000, 7-10. Retrieved from <http://www.fhfa.gov/webfiles/1214/4q00HPIprint.pdf>.

Drucker, P., 1986. The Practice of Management, rev. ed. Harper & Row, New York.

Drucker, P., 2008. Management: Tasks, Responsibilities, Practices, rev. ed. HarperCollins, New York.

Dubner, S., 2009, January 9. This is your brain on prosperity: Andrew Lo on fear, greed, and crisis management. Retrieved from <http://www.freakonomics.com/2009/01/09/this-is-your-brain-on-prosperity-andrew-lo-on-fear-greed-and-crisis-management>.

Dunne, T., Meyer, B., 2007, April 5. Subprime statistics. Federal Reserve Bank of Cleveland. Retrieved from <http://www.clevelandfed.org/research/trends/2007/0407/07ecoact.cfm>.

Economist Intelligence Unit, 2005. The Economist Intelligence Unit's quality-of-life index. Economist Group. Retrieved from <http://www.economist.com/media/pdf/QUALITY_OF_LIFE.pdf>.

Economic Mobility Project, 2009. Opinion poll on economic mobility and the American dream. Retrieved from <http://www.economicmobility.org/poll2009>.

Economics Resource Center, 2006. Policy Debate: Should the Federal Reserve Aim at a Zero Inflation Policy? South-Western College Publishing, Retrieved from <http://swlearning.com/economics/policy_debates/inflation.html>.

Eibl-Eibesfeldt, I., 1972. Love and Hate: The Natural History of Behavior Patterns. Holt, Rinehart, & Winston, New York.

Ellsworth, R., 2002. Leading with Purpose: The New Corporate Realities. Stanford University Press, Stanford, California.

Evans, K., 2012, July 11. Student debt: America's $1 trillion time bomb. CNBC. Retrieved from <http://finance.yahoo.com/news/student-debt-americas-1-trillion-153953849.html>.

Faber, D., 2009, October 27. House of cards (DVD). CNBC.

Fackler, M., 2008, October 23. Financial crisis spreads to emerging nations. The New York Times. Retrieved from <http://www.nytimes.com/2008/10/24/business/worldbusiness/24won.html?_r = 1>.

Faler, B., 2012, August 22. U.S. budget deficit to reach $1.1 trillion in 2012, CBO says. Bloomberg Businessweek. Retrieved from <http://www.businessweek.com/news/2012-08-22/u-dot-s-dot-budget-deficit-to-reach-1-dot-1-trillion-this-year-cbo-says>.

Fama, E., 1970. Efficient capital markets: a review of theory and empirical work. J. Finance 25 (2), 383−417.

Farmer, R., 2010. How the Economy Works: Confidence, Crashes and Self-Fulfilling Prophecies. Oxford University Press, New York.

FDIC, 2001, January 31. Subprime lending. Federal Deposit Insurance Corporation Press Release PR-9-2001. Retrieved from <http://www.fdic.gov/news/news/press/2001/pr0901a.html>.

FDIC, 2010, January 5. Changes in FDIC Deposit Insurance Coverage. Federal Deposit Insurance Corporation. Retrieved from <http://www.fdic.gov/deposit/deposits/dhanges.html>.

Federal Reserve Board, 1999, December 7; 2000; 2005, December 7; 2008, December 5; 2009, March 6; 2009, June 7; 2011, April; 2012, May). Consumer credit. Federal Reserve Statistical Release G.19. Retrieved from <http://federalreserve.gov/releases/G19/hist/cc_hist_sa.html>.

Federal Reserve Board, 2012. Consumer Handbook on Adjustable-Rate Mortgages. Board of Governors of the Federal Reserve System, Washington, D.C., Retrieved from <http://files.consumerfinance.gov/f/201204_CFPB_ARMs-brochure.pdf>.

Ferrell, O., Fraedrich, J., Ferrell, L., 2010. Business Ethics: Ethical Decision Making and Cases-2009 Update, seventh ed. South-Western Cengage Learning, OH.

FICO, 2010. FICO® Score. Retrieved from <http://www.fico.com/en/Products/Scoring/Pages/FICO-score.aspx/>.

Financial Crisis Inquiry Commission, 2011. The Financial Crisis Inquiry Report: Final Report of the National Commission on the Causes of the Financial and Economic Crisis in the United States. U.S. Government Printing Office, Washington D.C.

Financial Management Service, 2012, June. Ownership of federal securities. Treasury Bulletin. Retrieved from <http://fms.treas.gov/bulletin/index.html>.

Foldvary, F., 2004. The real estate bubble. The progress report: Editorial. Retrieved from <http://www.progress.org/2004/fold364.htm>.

Forbes, 2008, April 30. Special report: CEO compensation. Forbes.com Retrieved from <http://www.forbes.com/lists/2008/12/lead_bestbosses08_CEO-Compensation_Rank.html>.

Forrester, J., 1961. Industrial Dynamics. Productivity Press, Portland, OR.

Forrester, J., 1971a. Counterintuitive behavior of social systems. Simulation, 61−76.

Forrester, J., 1971b. World Dynamics. Wright-Allen Press, Inc, Cambridge, MA.

Frank, R., 2007. Richistan: A Journey Through the American Wealth Boom and the Lives of the New Rich. Free Press, New York.

Frankl, V., 1985. Man's Search for Meaning. Washington Square Press, Boston.

FRBNY, 2007, August. Federal Funds. Fedpoint. Retrieved from <http://www.newyorkfed.org/aboutthefed/fedpoint/fed15.html>.

FRBNY, 2011a. Historical changes of the target federal funds and discount rates. Federal Reserve Bank of New York. Retrieved from <http://www.newyorkfed.org/markets/statistics/dlyrates/fedrate.html>.

FRBNY, February 2011b. Quarterly Report on Household Debt and Credit. Federal Reserve Bank of New York. Retrieved from <http://www.newyorkfed.org/research/national_economy/householdcredit/DistrictReport_Q41020.pdf>.

FRBSF, 2008. The subprime mortgage market: National and twelfth district developments. 2007 Annual Report. Federal Reserve Bank of San Francisco. Retrieved from <http://www.frbsf.org/publications/federalreserve/annual/2007/subprime.pdf>.

FRBSL, 2011. The financial crisis: a timeline of events and policy actions. Fed. Reserve Bank St. Louis1−43, Retrieved from <http://timeline.stlouisfed.org/pdf/CrisisTimeline.pdf>.

FRED, 2011, September 1. Real GDP in the United States. FRED Economic Data, St. Louis Federal Reserve Bank. Retrieved from <http://research.stlouisfed.org/fred2/series/USARGDPR/downloaddata?cid = 32267>.

Freddie Mac, 2011a. Emerging fraud trends: types of mortgage fraud. Freddie Mac. Retrieved from <http://www.freddiemac.com/singlefamily/preventfraud/types.html>.

Freddie Mac, November 2011b. 30-year fixed rate mortgages since 1971. Freddie Mac. Retrieved from <http://freddiemac.com/pmms/pmms30.htm>.

Freddie Mac, November 2011c. 1-year adjustable rate mortgages since 1984. Freddie Mac. Retrieved from <http://freddiemac.com/pmms/pmms/>.

Frieden, T., 2004, September 17. FBI warns of mortgage fraud 'epidemic'. CNN Justice. Retrieved from <http://articles.cnn.com/2004-09-17/justice/mortgage.fraud_1_mortgage-fraud-mortgage-industry-s-l-crisis?_s = PM:LAW>.

Friedman, M., 1962. Capitalism & Freedom: A Leading Economist's View of the Proper Role of Competitive Capitalism. University of Chicago Press, Chicago.

Friedman, T., 2012, March 10. Pass the books. Hold the oil. The New York Times. Retrieved from <http://www.nytimes.com/2012/03/11/opinion/sunday/friedman-pass-the-books-hold-the-oil.html?_r = 1>.

Galbraith, J.K., 1977. The Age of Uncertainty. Houghton Mifflin Company, Boston.

Galbraith, J.K., 2008. The Predator State: How Conservatives Abandoned the Free Market and Why Liberals Should Too. Free Press, New York.

Gandhi, M., 1919. General knowledge about health. Collected works of Mahatma Gandhi, vol. 13, March 12, 1919 − December 25, 1920. Retrieved from <http://www.scribd.com/doc/50262503/Collected-Works-of-Mahatma-Gandhi-Vol-013>.

Gandz, J., Crossan, M., Seijts, G., Stephenson, C., 2010. Leadership on Trial: A Manifesto for Leadership Development. Richard Ivey School of Business, Ontario, Canada.

GAO, 2012, February. Unemployment insurance: economic circumstances of individuals who exhausted benefits. Report to the Chairman, Committee on Finance, U.S. Senate, GAO-12-408. Retrieved from <http://www.gao.gov.assets/590/588680.pdf>.

Gatti, D., Gaffeo, E., Gallegati, M., Gianfranco, F., Palestrini, A., 2008. Emergent Macroeconomics: An Agent-Based Approach to Business Fluctuations (New Economic Windows). Springer-Verlag, Milan, Italy.

Geffner, M., 2010, 23 September. FDIC insures bank deposits to $250,000. Bankrate.com. Retrieved from <http://www.bankrate.com/finance/savings/fdic-insures-bank-deposits-to-250-000-1.aspx>.

Gellerman, S., 1986. Why 'good' managers make bad ethical choices. Harv. Bus. Rev., 85–90.

George, B., 2008, November 19. Failed leadership caused the financial crisis. US News and World Report. Retrieved from <http://www.usnews.com/opinion/articles/2008/11/19/failed-leadership-caused-the-financial-crisis>.

Gethard, G., 2010. Falling giant: a case study of AIG. Retrieved from <http://www.investopedia.com/>.

Giannone, J., 2007, November 9. FACTBOX-Top issuers of CDOs. Reuters.com. Retrieved from <http://www.reuters.com/article/2007/11/09/wallstreet-cdos-idUSN0927796020071109>.

Gilbert, D., 2003. The American Class Structure in an Age of Growing Inequality, sixth ed. Thomson-Wadsworth Learning, Belmont, CA.

Gilovich, T., 1991. How we Know What Isn't so: The Fallibility of Human Reason in Everyday Life. The Free Press, New York.

Gleick, J., 2011. The Information: A History, a Theory, a Flood. Pantheon Books, New York.

Glick, R., Lansing, K., 2009, May 15. U.S. Household Deleveraging and Future Consumption Growth. FRSBF Economic Letter (No. 2009-16). San Francisco: Federal Reserve Bank of San Francisco. Retrieved from <http://www.frbsf.org/publications/economics/letter/2005/el2005-30.pdf>.

Gogoi, P., Pickler, N., 2011, December 21. Bank of America Countrywide settlement: Bank to pay $335 million to settle discriminatory lending claims. Retrieved from <http://www.huffingtonpost.com/2011/12/21/bank-of-america-countrywide-settlement_n_1163208.html>.

Gokhale, J., 2008, September 26. The perfect financial storm. Cato Institute. Retrieved from <http://www.cato.org/publications/commentary/perfect-financial-storm>.

Goldfarb, Z, Schneider, H., 2012, February 28. Local, state and foreign officials attack Volcker Rule. The Washington Post. Retrieved from <http://www.washingtonpost.com/business/economy/local-foreign-governments-protest-volcker-rule/2012/02/27/gIQAE0rFgR_story.html>.

Goldiner, D., 2008, October 9. Wheels falling off for general motors. NYDailyNews.com. Retrieved from <http://articles.nydailynews.com/2008-10-09/news/17907516_1_gm-stock-credit-rating-stock-market-crash>.

Goldstein, D., Hall, K., 2010, November. Private sector loans, not Fannie or Freddie, triggered crisis. McClatchy Washington Bureau. Retrieved from <http://www.mcclatchydc.com/2008/10/12/53802/private-sector-loans-not-fannie.html?storylink = MI_emailed>.

Goldstein, J., 12 March 2010a. Repo 105: Lehman's 'accounting gimmick' explained. Planet Money Blog, National Public Radio. Retrieved from <http://www.npr.org/blogs/money/2010/03/repo_105_lehmans_accounting_gi.html>.

Goldstein, J., 16 April 2010b. The SEC's case against Goldman Sachs, explained. Planet Money Blog, National Public Radio. Retrieved from <http://www.npr.org/blogs/money/2010/04/sec_accuses_goldman_sachs_of_f.html>.

Goldstein, J., 2011, September 20. Companies have been holding more cash for decades. Planet Money Blog, National Public Radio. Retrieved from <http://www.npr.org/blogs/money/2011/09/19/140605375/companies-have-been-piling-up-cash-for-decades>.

Goodenough, O., 2008. Values, mechanism design, and fairness. In: Zak, P.J. (Ed.), Moral Markets: The Critical Role of Values in the Economy. Princeton University Press, Princeton, N.J., pp. 228−255.

Gordon, M., 2008, April 18. Franklin Raines to pay $24.7 million to settle Fannie Mae Lawsuit. The Seattle Times. Retrieved from <http://seattletimes.nwsource.com/html/businesstechnology/2004358433_webraines18.html>.

Gorton, G., 2008, August 4. The panic of 2007. Prepared for the Federal Reserve Bank of Kansas City, Jackson Hole conference, August 2008. Retrieved from <http://www.kc.frb.org/publicat/sympos/2008/gorton.08.04.08.pdf>.

Gramlich, E., 2007. Subprime Mortgages: America's Latest Boom and Bust. The Urban Institute Press, Washington, D.C..

Gramm, S.P., 1999, November 4. Gramm closing floor statement on Gramm-Leach-Bliley Act of 1999; and Senate approves Gramm-Leach-Bliley act. Retrieved from <http://banking.senate.gov/prel99/1104sta.htm>.

Greene, J., Sommerville, B., Nystrom, L., Darley, J., Cohen, J., 2001. An fMRI investigation of emotional engagement in moral judgment. Science 293, 2105−2108.

Greenspan, A., 2000, February 17. Monetary policy report to the Congress pursuant to the full employment and balanced growth act of 1978. Board of Governors of the Federal Reserve System. Retrieved from <http://www.federalreserve.gov/boarddocs/hh/2000/February/FullReport.pdf>.

Greenspan, A., 2002, July 16. Testimony of Chairman Alan Greenspan. The Federal Reserve Board's semiannual monetary report to the Congress. The Federal Reserve Board. Retrieved from <http://www.federalreserve.gov/boarddocs/hh/2002/july/testimony.htm>.

Greenspan, A., 2007. The Age of Turbulence: Adventures in a New World. Penguin Group, New York.

Greider, W., 2003. The Soul of Capitalism. Simon & Schuster, New York.

Gwartney, J., Stroup, R., 1990. Microeconomics: Private and Public Sectors, fifth ed. Harcourt Brace Jovanovich, Publishers, San Diego.

Haidt, J., 2001. The emotional dog and its rational tail: a social intuitionist approach to moral judgment. Psychol. Rev. 108 (4), 814−834.

Haji, S., 2004, July 30. Freddie Mac: no housing bubble. The Motley Fool. Retrieved from <http://www.fool.com/personal-finance/home/2004/07/30/freddie-mac-no-housing-bubble.aspx>.

Hamilton, W., 2012, June 10. Low interest rates hampering retirement plans, survey says. Los Angeles Times.

Harari, A., Brown, S., Williamson, D., Flory, J., de Wit, H., Manuck, S., 2006. Preference for immediate over delayed rewards in associated with magnitude of ventral striatal activity. J. Neurosci. 16 (51), 13213−13217.

Harper, C., 2009, July 14. Goldman Sachs first-half compensation climbs to $11.4 billion. Bloomberg. Retrieved from <http://www.bloomberg.com/apps/news?pid = newsarchive&sid = ajxZp9xH8sc8>.

Hayek, F.A., 2007. The Road to Serfdom. The University of Chicago Press, London.

Heakal, R., 2010. What is a corporate credit rating. Investopedia, A Forbes Digital Company. Retrieved from <http://www.investopedia.com/articles/03/102203.asp>.

Hechter, M., 1993. Values research in the social and behavioral sciences. In: Hechter, M., Nadel, L., Michod, R.E. (Eds.), The Origin of Values. Aldine de Gruyter, Hawthorne, New York, pp. 1−28.

Henderson, H., 2010. Supply and Demand. Echo Library. Originally published in 1922 by Harcourt, Brace & Company, Middlesex, England.

Henry, D., 2012, May 29. Analysis: JPMorgan dips into cooking jar to offset 'London Whale' losses. Reuters. Retrieved from <http://www.reuters.com/article/2012/05/29/us-jpmorgan-loss-gains-idUSBRE84S04820120529>.

Henry, D, Horowitz, J., 2012, July 13. JPMorgan loses $5.8 billion on trades; traders may have hidden losses. Reuters. Retrieved from <http://finance.yahoo.com/news/jpmorgan-profit-falls-4-4-110443269.html>.

Henry, D., Kerber, R., 2012, April 17. Citigroup loses advisory vote on executive compensation. Reuters.com. Retrieved from <http://www.reuters.com/article/2012/04/17/us-citi-vote-idUSBRE83G15U20120417>.

Herszenhorn, D., 2008, July 31. Bush signs sweeping housing bill. The New York Times. Retrieved from <http://www.nytimes.com/2008/07/31/business/31housing.html>.

Higgins, K., Rogers, S., 2012, April. Synergies in a positive culture: Nurturing excellence in an organization. Presented at the Society for the Advancement of Management 2012 Conference, Las Vegas, Nevada. Published in 2012 SAM International Business Conference Proceedings. Corpus Christi, TX: Texas A&M University.

Historical Inflation, 2012. Historical inflation. Retrieved from <http://inflationdata.com/inflation/Inflation_Rate/HistoricalInflation.aspx?dsInflation_current>.

Hitchcock, C., 1903. The Psychology of Expectation (1903). The Macmillan Company, New York.

Ho, K., 2009. Liquidated: An Ethnography of Wall Street. Duke University Press, Durham.

Holhut, R., 2011. The house of cards starts to wobble. Am. Rep. 16 (4,226), Retrieved from <http://www.american.reporter.com/4,226/711.html>.

Hoskins, L., 2005, December 5. Zero inflation: goal and target. Remarks to the Shadow Open Market Committee. Retrieved from <http://www.cmc.edu/somc/2005_12/hoskins_1205.pdf>.

Huxley, T.H., Huxley, J., 1947. Evolution and Ethics: 1893–1947. The Pilot Press, London.

International Monetary Fund, 2012, April. World economic outlook database. Retrieved from <http://www.imf.org/external/pubs/ft/weo/2012/01/weodata/index.aspx>.

International Swaps and Derivatives Association, 2010. ISDA market survey: Notional amounts outstanding at year-end, all surveyed contracts 1987-present. Retrieved from <http://www.isda.org/statistics/pdf/ISDA-Market-Survey-annual-data.pdf>.

International Swaps and Derivatives Association, 2012. ISDA 2010 Mid-year market survey. Retrieved from <http://www.isda.org/statistics/recent.html#2010mid>.

Investopedia, 2010. FICO score. Retrieved from <http://www.investopedia.com>.

Isidore, Chris, 2011, June 9. America's lost trillions. CNNMoney.com. Retrieved from <http://money.cnn.com/2011/06/09/news/economy/household_wealth/index.htm>.

Isidore, C., Riley, C., Frieden, T., 2012, Nov 15. BP to pay record penalty for Gulf oil spill. CNNMoney. Retrieved from <http://money.cnn.com/2012/11/15/news/bp-oil-spill-settlement/index.html>.

Izard, C., 1977. Human Emotions. Plenum Press, New York.

Jackson, M., 2000. Systems Approaches to Management. Kluwer Academic/Plenum Publishers, New York.

Jelveh, Z., 2008, June 17. In praise of the wealth effect. Odd Numbers: Portfolio.com. Retrieved from <http://www.portfolio.com/views/blogs/odd-numbers/2008/06/17/in-praise-of-the-wealth-effect>.

Jickling, M., 2008, September 15. Fannie Mae and Freddie Mac conservatorship. CRS Report for Congress. Retrieved from <http://fpc.state.gov/documents/organization/110097.pdf>.

Johnston, D., 2007, March 29. Income gap is widening, data shows. The New York Times. Retrieved from <http://www.nytimes.com/2007/03/29/business/29tax.html>.

Joint Center for Housing Studies, 2007. The State of the Nation's Housing 2007. Harvard Kennedy School, Boston, Retrieved from <http://www.jchs.harvard.edu/publications/markets/son2007/son2007.pdf>.

Joint Center for Housing Studies, 2008. The State of the Nation's Housing 2008. Harvard Kennedy School, Boston, Retrieved from <http://www.jchs.harvard.edu/publications/markets/son2008/son2008.pdf>.

Joint Center for Housing Studies, 2010. The State of the Nation's Housing 2010. Harvard Kennedy School, Boston, Retrieved from <http://www.jchs.harvard.edu/publications/markets/son2010/son2010.pdf>.

Joint Center for Housing Studies, 2011. The State of the Nation's Housing 2011. Harvard Kennedy School, Boston, Retrieved from <http://www.jchs.harvard.edu/publications/markets/son2011/son2011.pdf>.

Joint Center for Housing Studies, 2012. The State of the Nation's Housing 2012. Harvard Kennedy School, Boston, Retrieved from <http://www.jchs.harvard.edu/sites/jchs.harvard.edu/files/son2012_bw.pdf>.

Kamp, D., 2009. The way we were: rethinking the American Dream. Vanity Fair 1, 1–5, Retrieved from <http://www.vanityfair.com/culture/features/2009/04/american-dream200904>.

Karnitschnig, M., Solomon, D., Pleven, L., Hilsenrath, J., 2008, September 16. U.S. to take over AIG in $85 billion bailout; Central banks inject cash as credit dries up. The Wall Street Journal. Retrieved from <http://online.wsj.com/article/SB122156561931242905.html>.

Katchadourian, H., 2010. Guilt: The Bite of Conscience. Stanford University Press, Stanford.

Katona, G., 1960. The Powerful Consumer: Psychological Studies of the American Economy. McGraw-Hill Book Company, Inc., New York.

Kay, J., 2011. Obliquity. Why Our Goals are Best Achieved Indirectly. The Penguin Press, New York.

Keynes, J.M., 1964. The General Theory of Employment, Interest, and Money. Harcourt Brace & Company, New York.

Kidder, R., 1995. How Good People Make Tough Choices: Resolving the Dilemmas of Ethical living. William Morrow & Co., New York.

Kindleberger, C.P., Aliber, R., 2005. Manias, Panics, and Crashes: A History of Financial Crises, fifth ed. Wiley, Hoboken, New Jersey.

Kirchhoff, S., Bagenbaugh, B., 2004, February 23. Greenspan says ARMS might be better deal. USA Today. Retrieved from <http://www.usatoday.com/money/economy/fed/2004-02-23-greenspan-debt_x.htm>.

Kmitch, J.H., 2010. Alternative measures of personal saving. Surv. Curr. Bus.10–13, Retrieved from <http://www.bea.gov/scb/pdf/2010/10%20October/1010_saving.pdf>.

Knee, J, 2006. The Accidental Investment Banker: Inside the Decade that Transformed Wall Street. Oxford University Press, Oxford.

Knox, N., 2006, April 3. Some homeowners struggle to keep up with adjustable rates. USA Today. Retrieved from <http://www.usatoday.com/money/perfi/housing/2006-04-03-arms-cover-usat_x.htm>.

Krippner, G.R., 2011. Capitalizing on Crisis: The Political Origins of the Rise of Finance. Harvard University Press, Cambridge, MA.

Kroszner, R., 2007, November 5. The challenges facing subprime mortgage borrowers. Speech at the Consumer Bankers Association 2007 Fair Lending Conference, Washington, D. C. Retrieved from <http://www.federalreserve.gov/newsevents/speech/kroszner20071105a. htm>.

Krugman, P., Wells, R., 2010. Microeconomics, second ed Worth Publishers, New York.

Labaton, S., 2008, October 3. Agency's '04 rule let banks pile up new debt. The New York Times. Retrieved from <http://www.nytimes.com/2008/10/03/business/03sec.html? adxnnl = 1&adxnnlx = 1342725800-Sc3yxvrsoFSIUVW4d9Cvdw>.

Laing, J.R., 2005, June 20. The bubble's new home. Retrieved from <http://online.barrons.com/ article/SB111905372884363176.html>.

Lal, D., 2010. The great crash of 2008: causes and consequences. Cato J. 30 (2), 265−277.

Landler, M., 2008, October 23. West is in talks on credit to aid poorer nations. The New York Times. Retrieved from <http://www.nytimes.com/2008/10/24/business/worldbusiness/ 24emerge.html?_r = 1&adxnnl = 1&pagewanted = all&adxnnlx = 1343754694- CohNIHK6HIG1nwzcgV0sTQ>.

Lane, R.E., 1995. The Market Experience. Cambridge University Press, Cambridge.

Lansing, K., 2005, November 10. Spendthrift Nation (FRSBF Economic Letter. No. 2005-30). Federal Reserve Bank of San Francisco. Retrieved from <http://www.frbsf.org/publications/ economics/letter/2005/el2005-30.pdf>.

Laperriere, A., 2006, April 10. Housing bubble trouble: have we been living beyond our means? WeeklyStandard.com, 11(28). Retrieved from <http://www.weeklystandard.com>.

Larson, M., 2008, September 5. MBA: Delinquency and foreclosure rates jump. Interest Rate Roundup (2Q 2008 statistics) Retrieved from <http://interestrateroundup.blogspot.com/ 2008/09/mba-delinquency-and-foreclosure-rates.html>.

Latham, G., 2007. Work Motivation: History, Theory, Research, and Practice. Sage, Thousand Oaks, CA.

Lauck, W.J., 1907. The Causes of the Panic of 1893. The Riverside Press, Cambridge (Reprint of Original Boston: Houghton, Mifflin & Company).

Lawrence, P., Nohria, N., 2002. Driven: How Human Nature Shapes Our Choices. Jossey-Bass, San Francisco.

Lazarus, R.S., 1991. Emotion and Adaptation. Oxford University Press, New York.

Leo, A., 2009, September 18. Bryan Berg: Man trying to set record for tallest card tower sees structure crash at last second (video). Huffpost Comedy. Retrieved from <http://www.huffingtonpost.com/2009/09/18/bryan-berg-man-trying-to_n_291422.html?view = screen>

Leonnig, C., 2008, June 10. How HUD mortgage policy fed the crisis. The Washington Post. Retrieved from <http://www.washingtonpost.com/wp-dyn/content/article/2008/06/09/ AR2008060902626.html>.

Lewin, B., 2012, July 23. Three years after the Great Recession ended, global recovery remains fragile. The Canadian Press. Retrieved from <http:/business.financialpost.com/2012/07/23/ three-years-after-the-great-recession-ended-global-recovery-remains-fragile>.

Lewin, K., 1947. Frontiers in group dynamics. Hum. Relat. 1, 5−41.

Lewis, J., 1998. Mastering Project Management: Applying Advanced Concepts of Systems Thinking, Control and Evaluation, Resource Allocation. McGraw-Hill, New York.

Levinson, M., 2010. Guide to Financial Markets, fifth ed. Bloomberg Press, New York.

Lewes, G., 1875. Problems of Life and Mind, vol. 2. James R. Osgood & Co., Boston.

Lipman-Blumen, J., 2000. Connective Leadership: Managing in a Changing World. Oxford University Press, New York.

Livingston, J., 2003. Pygmalion in management. Harv. Bus. Rev. 81 (1), 97−106 (Originally published in 1969).

Locke, J., 2004. Two Treatises of Government. Cambridge University Press, UK (Originally published in 1690).

Lockhart, J. III, 2009, February 9. Speech to American Securitization Forum, Las Vegas, Nevada. Federal Housing Finance Agency. Retrieved from <http://www.fhfa.gov/webfiles/823/ASFSpeech2909.pdf>.

Lowell, L., 2001. Mortgage pass-through securities. In: Fabozzi, F.J. (Ed.), The Handbook of Mortgage-Backed Securities, fifth ed. McGraw-Hill, New York, pp. 25−50.

Luhby, T. 2009, June 5. Countrywide's Mozilo accused of fraud. CNNMoney.com.. Retrieved from < http://money.cnn.com/2009/06/04/news/economy/mozilo_fraud_charges/index.htm>.

Lyman, E., 2012, January 18. Recording suggests captain tried to abandon ship. Special for USA Today. Retrieved from <http://travel.usatoday.com/cruises/story/2012-01-17/Recording-sug-gests-captain-tried-to-abandon-ship/52624526/1>.

Lyon, S., 2008, July 31. CEO salaries: what is the Average Salary of a CEO? PayScale.com Retrieved from <http://blogs.payscale.com/content/2008/07/ceo-salaries−1.html>.

Maani, K., Cavana, R., 2007. Systems Thinking, System Dynamics: Managing Change and Complexity, second ed. Pearson Education, New Zealand.

Mahoney, M., 2011, September 9. Supply of homes: a perspective on inventory from The National Association of Realtors. The Greater Boston Voice: Clarity in Real Estate. Retrieved from <http://greaterbostonvoice.typepad.com/the_greater_boston_voice_/2011/09/supply-of-homes-a-perspective-on-inventory-from-the-national-association-of-realtors.html>.

Mainelli, M., Giffords, B., 2009. The road to long finance: a systems view of the credit scrunch. Centre for the Study of Financial Innovation (Number 87). Heron, Dawson & Sawyer, London, Retrieved from <http://www.zyen.com/PDF/RTLF.pdf>.

Malthus, T., 1798. Population: The First Essay. The University of Michigan Press, Ann Arbor, MI.

Mamudi, S., 2008, September 15. Lehman folds with record $613 billion debt. MarketWatch. Retrieved from <http://www.marketwatch.com/story/lehman-folds-with-record-613-billion-debt>.

Maslow, A., 1970. Motivation and Personality, third ed. HarperCollins Publishers, New York.

Mason, J., 2009, February 4. Obama to set executive pay limits. Business & Financial News, Reuters. Retrieved from <http://www.reuters.com/article/2009/02/04/us-obama-compensa-tion-idUSTRE5130QG20090204>.

McCabe, K., 2003. Neuroeconomics. In: Nadel, L. (Ed.), Encyclopedia of Cognitive Science. Nature Publishing Group, Macmillan Publishing, New York, pp. 294−298. , Retrieved from <https://files.nyu.edu/avs265/public/whatisneuroeconomics.html>.

McCarthy, J., Peach, R., 2004, December. Are home prices the next 'bubble'? FRBNY Economic Policy Review. Retrieved from <http://www.newyorkfed.org/research/epr/forth-coming/mccarthy/html>.

McClelland, D., 1962. Business drive and national achievement. Harv. Bus. Rev., 99−112.

McCool, B., LaCapra, L., 2012, February 29. Goldman manager investigated in insider trade case: source. Reuters Retrieved from <http://www.reuters.com/article/2012/02/29/us-insider-trading-hedgefunds-goldmansach-idUSTRE81S2BN20120229>.

McCoy, P, Renuart, E., 2008. The legal infrastructure of subprime and nontraditional home mortgages. In: Retsinas, N.P., Belsky, E.S. (Eds.), Borrowing to Live: Consumer and Mortgage Credit Revisited. Joint Center for Housing Studies, Harvard University and Washington, D.C.: Brookings Institution Press, Cambridge, MA, pp. 110−137.

McCully, C., 2011. Trends in consumer spending and personal saving, 1959-2009. Surv. Curr. Bus.14−23, Retrieved from <http://www.bea.gov/scb/pdf/2011/06%20June/0611_pce.pdf>.

McDonald., L., 2009. A Colossal Failure of Common Sense: The Inside Story of the Collapse of Lehman Brothers. Three Rivers Press, New York.

McKinley, V., 1994. Community Reinvestment Act: ensuring credit adequacy or enforcing credit allocation. Regulation 4, 25−37, Retrieved from <http://www.cato.org/pubs/regulation/regv17n4/vmck-94.pdf>.

McLean, B., 2005, January 24. The fall of Fannie Mae. Fortune. Retrieved from <http://money.cnn.com/magazines/fortune/fortune_archive/2005/01/24/8234040/index.htm>.

McLean, B., Nocera, J., 2010. All the Devils are Here: The Hidden History of the Financial Crisis. Portfolio/Penguin Group, New York.

McLean, B., 2011, June 29. Subprime prosecutions: why the government hunts small game. Retrieved from <http://www.slate.com/articles/business/moneybox/2011/06/the_man_that_-got_away.html>.

McNamee, M., 2004, November 29. Lewis S. Ranieri: your mortgage was his bond. Business Week. Retrieved from <http://www.businessweek.com/magazine/content/04_48/b3910023_mz072.htm>.

Meadows, D., Meadows, D., Randers, J., Behrens III, W., 1972. The Limits to Growth: A Report for the Club of Rome's Project on the Predicament of Mankind. Universe Books, New York.

Meadows, D., 1999. Leverage Points: Places to Intervene in a System. The Sustainability Institute, Hartland, VT.

Meadows, D., Randers, J., Meadows, D., 2004. Limits to Growth: The 30-Year Update. Chelsea Green Publishing Company, White River Junction, VT.

Meadows, D., 2008. Thinking in Systems: A Primer. Chelsea Green Publishing, White River Junction, VT.

Mellman Group, 2011, May 17. Economic mobility project: analysis of our recent survey. The Mellman Group. Retrieved from <http://www.economicmobility.org/poll2011/Mellman_Poll_document.pdf>.

Merton, R., 1948. The self-fulfilling prophecy. Antioch. Rev. 8 (2), 193−210.

Messick, D., Bazerman, M., 1996. Ethical leadership and the psychology of decision making. Sloan Manage. Rev., 9−22.

Michod, R.E., 1993. Biology and the origin of values. In: Hechter, M., Nadel, L., Michod, R.E. (Eds.), The Origin of Values. Aldine de Gruyter, Hawthorne, New York, pp. 261−271.

Mill, J., 1836, October. Essay V: On the definition of political economy, and on the method of investigation proper to it. London and Westminster Review. In: Essays on Some Unsettled Questions of Political Economy. London: John W. Parker, 1948, pp. 120−164.

Mill, J., 1899/1848. Principles of Political Economy with some of their Applications to Social Philosophy. Book III. from the fifth London edition. D. Appleton and Company, New York.

Morgan, C., 1927. Emergent Evolution, second ed. Williams & Norgate, London.

Morgenson, G., 2004, July 25. Housing bust: it won't be pretty. The New York Times. Retrieved from <http://www.nytimes.com/2004/07/25/business/yourmoney/>.

Morgenson, G., 2007, August 26. Inside the Countrywide lending spree. The New York Times. Retrieved from <http://www.nytimes.com/2007/08/26/business/yourmoney/26country.html>.

Morgenson, G., Fabrikant, G., 2007, November 11. Countrywide's chief salesman and defender. The New York Times. Retrieved from <http://www.nytimes.com/2007/11/11/business/11angelo.html>.

Morgenson, G., Rosner, J., 2011. Reckless Endangerment: How Outsized Ambition, Greed, and Corruption Led to Economic Armageddon. Times Books, Henry Holt & Co., New York.

Morris, K., 2002. Introduction to Feedback Control. Harcourt, Inc., San Diego.

Morris, C., 2008. The Trillion Dollar Meltdown: Easy Money, High Rollers, and the Great Credit Crash. Public Affairs, New York.

Mortgage Statistics, 2009, February 13. 19 years of mortgage origination data 1990-2008. Retrieved from <http://mortgagestats.blogspot.com/2009/02/19-years-of-mortgage-origination-data.html>.

Muellbauer, J., 2007, September 14. Housing, credit and Consumer Expenditure. Prepared for the Kansas Federal Reserve's Jackson Hole Symposium, 31st August − 1st September 2007. Retrieved from <http://www.kc.frb.org/publicat/sympos/2007/PDF/2007.09.17. Muellbauer.pdf>.

Münchau, W., 2010. The Meltdown Years: The Unfolding of the Global Economic Crisis. McGraw-Hill, New York.

NAFCU, 2011, August 10. NCUA sues Goldman Sachs. National Association of Federal Credit Unions. Retrieved from <http://www.nafcu.org/Tertiary.aspx?id = 23654&css = print>.

Nasiripour, S., 2011, April 27. Economic recovery to lose steam as inflation arrives, Federal Reserve said. Huffington Post. Retrieved from <http://www.huffingtonpost.com/2011/04/27/inflation-federal-reserve-bernanke_n_854506.html>.

NBER, 2010. Business Cycle Dating Committee, National Bureau of Economic Research. NBER, Cambridge, Retrieved from < http://www.nber.org/cycles/sept2010.html>.

Newport, F., 2011, October 11. Economic confidence stabilizes at low levels: Three-quarters of Americans continue to say U.S. economy is getting worse. GALLUP® Economy. Retrieved from <http://www.gallup.com/poll/149999/Economic-Confidence-Stabilizes-Low-Levels. aspx>.

Ng, S., Mollenkamp, C., 2007, October 25. Pioneer helped Merrill move into CDOs. The Wall Street Journal. Retrieved from <http://online.wsj.com/article/SB119326927053270580. html>.

Ng, S., Mollenkamp, C., 2008, January 14. A fund behind astronomical losses. The Wall Street Journal. Retrieved from <http://online.wsj.com/article/SB120027155742887331.html>.

Niebuhr, R., 1960. Moral Man and Immoral Society. Charles Scribner's sons, New York.

Noguchi, Y., 2009, July 7. 'Shadow' inventory may slow housing recovery. NPR. Retrieved from <http://www.npr.org/templates/story/story.php?storyId = 106113137>.

NYSE, 2011. History of the NASDAQ composite index. Retrieved from <http://www.nyse.tv/nasdaq-composite-history.htm>.

Oatley, K., Keltner, D., Jenkins, J.M., 2006. Understanding Emotions, second ed. Blackwell Publishing, Malden, MA.

O'Connor, J., McDermott, I., 1997. The Art of Systems Thinking: Essential Skills for Creativity and Problem Solving. HarperCollins, San Francisco.

O'Doherty, J., Kringelbach, M., Rolls, E., Hornak, J., Andrews, C., 2001. Abstract reward and punishment representations in the human orbitofrontal cortex. Nat. Neurosci. 4 (1), 95−102.

OECD, 2012, July 30. Quarterly growth rates of real GDP change over previous quarter. Organisation for economic co-operation and development. Retrieved from <http://stats. oecd.org/Index.aspx?QueryName = &QueryType = View&Lang = en#>.

Office of Management and Budget, 2010. Budget of the U.S. Government: Fiscal Year 2011. U.S. Government Printing Office, Washington D.C., Retrieved from <http://www.gpo.gov/fdsys/pkg/BUDGET-2011-BUD/pdf/BUDGET-2011-BUD.pdf>.

O'Harrow, R., Dennis, B., 2009, January 2. Credit rating downgrade, real estate collapse crippled AIG. Los Angeles Times. Retrieved from <http://articles.latimes.com/2009/jan/02/business/fi-aig2/4>.

Olorunnipa, T., 2011, October 15. 'Shadow inventory' of homes could topple real-estate recovery. The Miami Herald. Retrieved from <http://www.miamiherald.com/2011/10/15/v-fullstory/2456154/shadow-inventory-of-homes-could.html>.

Otsuma, M., 2012, Aug 28. LDP likely to block deficit bond bill as Noda censure looms. Bloomberg. Retrieved from <http://www.bloomberg.com/news/2012-08-28/ldp-likely-to-halt-japan-deficit-bond-bill-as-noda-censure-looms.html>.

Patalon, W. III, 2008, November 11. Federal government grants AIG a new bailout package. Monday Morning. Retrieved from <http://moneymorning.com/2008/11/11/american-international-group-inc/>.

Pepitone, J., 2011, October 6. How occupy Wall Street has evolved. Retrieved from <http://money.cnn.com/2011/10/06/technology/occupy_wall_street/index.htm>.

Pfaff, D., 2007. The Neuroscience of Fair Play: Why we (Usually) Follow the Golden Rule. Dana Press, New York.

Piovano, C., 2012, January 26. Fed's low interest rate pledge boosts markets. ABC News. Retrieved from <http://abcnews.go.com/Business/wireStory/asia-stocks-gain-feds-low-rates-pledge-15444377>.

Plumb, C., Wilchins, D., 2008, September 14. Lehman CEO Fuld's hubris contributed to meltdown. Reuters. Retrieved from <http://www.reuters.com/assets/print?aid = USN134 1059120080914>.

Plutchik, R., 2003. Emotions and Life: Perspectives from Psychology, Biology, and Evolution. American Psychological Association, Washington, DC.

Pressman, A., 2008, September 29. Community Reinvestment Act had nothing to do with subprime crisis. Bloomberg Businessweek. Retrieved from <http://www.businessweek.com/investing/insights/blog/archives/2008/09>.

Quiggin, J., 2010. Zombie Economics: How Dead Ideas Still Walk Among US. Princeton University Press, Princeton.

Rajan, R., 2010. Fault Lines: How Hidden Fractures Still Threaten the World Economy. Princeton University Press, Princeton.

Raum, T., 2009, December 15. Obama: 'We rise and fall together'. Marietta Daily Journal. Retrieved from <http://mdjonline.com/view/full_story/5147202/article-Obama-We-rise-and-fall-together->.

RealtyTrac, 2007, February 9. U.S. Foreclosure decrease 9 percent in December. RealtyTrac. Retrieved from <http://www.realtytrac.com/content/press-releases/us-foreclosures-decrease-9-percent-in-december-2006-2151>.

RealtyTrac, 2008, April 30. U.S. foreclosure activity increases 23 percent in first quarter. RealtyTrac. Retrieved from <http://www.realtytrac.com/content/press-releases/us-foreclosure-activity-increases-23-percent-in-first-quarter-3950>.

RealtyTrac, 2009, January 15. Foreclosure activity increases 81 percent in 2008. RealtyTrac. Retrieved from <http://www.realtytrac.com/content/press-releases/foreclosure-activity-increases-81-percent-in-2008-4551>.

RealtyTrac, 2011, January 12. Record 2.9 million U.S. properties receive foreclosure filings in 2010 despite 30-month low in December. RealtyTrac. Retrieved from <http://www.realtytrac.com/content/foreclosure-market-report/record-29-million-us-properties-receive-foreclosure-filings-in-2010-despite-30-month-low-in-december-6309>.

RealtyTrac, 2012, August. National real estate trends. RealtyTrac. Retrieved from <http://www.realtytrac.com/trendcenter/trend.html>.

Reckard, S., 2008, July 1. Critics blame Countrywide's Angelo Mozilo for housing fiasco. The Seattle Times. Retrieved from <http://seattletimes.nwsource.com/html/businesstechnology/2008026629_countrywide01.html>.

Reisner, L., Lench, K., Muoio, R., 2010, April 16. SEC charges Goldman Sachs with fraud in structuring and marketing CDO tied to subprime mortgages. U.S. Securities and Exchange Commission. Retrieved from <http://www.sec.gov/news/press/2010/2010-59.htm>.

Retsinas, N.P., Belsky, E.S. (Eds.), 2008. Borrowing to Live: Consumer and Mortgage Credit Revisited. Brookings Institution Press, Washington, D.C.

Reuters, 2004, June 24. HSBC, unlike Fed, sees U.S. housing bubble. USA Today, Money. Retrieved from <http://www.usatoday.com/money/economy/housing/2004-06-25-housing-bubble_x.htm>.

Reynolds, A., 2007, January 8. Has U.S. income inequality *really* increased? Policy Analysis No. 586. CATO Institute. Retrieved from <http://www.cato.org/pubs/pas/pa586.pdf>.

Richardson, G., 1986. Problems with causal-loop diagrams (comment by J. Sterman). Syst. Dyn. Rev. 2 (2), 158–170.

Richardson, G., 1999. Feedback Thought in Social Science and Systems Theory. Pegasus Communications, Waltham, MA.

Richerson, P., Boyd, R., 2008. The evolution of free enterprise values. In: P. J. Zak (Ed.), Moral Markets: The Critical Role of Values in the Economy pp. 107–141.

Richmond, B., 1994. System dynamics/systems thinking: let's just get on with it. Presentation delivered at the 1994 International Systems Dynamics Conference in Sterling, Scotland. Retrieved from <http://www.iseesystems.com/resources/Articles/SDSTletsjustgetonwithit.pdf>.

Rizzo, P., 2012, March 14. Goldman Sachs exec Greg Smith quits, saying environment at firm is 'toxic'. MSNBC. Retrieved from <http://bottomline.msnbc.msn.com/_news/2012/03/14/10687987-goldman-sachs-resignation-letter-an-internet-sensation>.

Robbins, L., 1932. An Essay on the Nature and Significance of Economic Science. Macmillan & Co., London (reprint 2007 Auburn, AL: Mises Institute).

Roberts, R., 2008a, October 3. How government stoked the mania. The Wall Street Journal. Retrieved from <http://online.wsj.com/article/SB122298982558700341.html>.

Roberts, R., 2008b, April 1. Mortgage meltdown: let the finger-pointing begin. RealtyTimes. Retrieved from <http://realtytimes.com/printrtpages/20080401_mortgagemeltdown.htm>.

Rokeach, M., 1989. Beliefs, Attitudes, and Values. Jossey-Bass, San Francisco.

Rolls, E.T., 1999. The Brain and Emotion. Oxford University Press, New York.

Rosen, R., 2007. The role of securitization in mortgage lending. Chicago Fed Letter. Federal Reserve Bank of Chicago, Chicago, Retrieved from <http://www.chicagofed.org/digital_assets/publications/chicago_fed_letter/2007/cflnovember2007_244.pdf>.

Ryan, J., 2009, February 11. Fraud 'directly related' to financial crisis probed. ABC News. Retrieved from <http://abcnews.go.com/TheLaw/Economy/story?id = 6855179&page = 1>.

Sachs, J. (Ed.), 2002. Aristotle's Metaphysics. Green Lion Press, Santa Fe.

Sachs, J., 2008, December 22. Blackouts and cascading failures of the global markets: feedbacks in the economic network can turn local crises into global ones. Scientific American. Retrieved from <http://www.scientificamerican.com/article.cfm?id = blackouts-and-cascading-failures>.

Sahadi, J., 2005, October 17. The new bankruptcy law and you: what you should know about the law, which will make it tougher for consumers to clear their debts. CNNMoney. Retrieved from <http://money.cnn.com/2005/10/17/pf/debt/bankruptcy_law/index.htm>.

Salmon, F., 2009, February 23. Recipe for disaster: the formula that killed Wall Street. Wired Magazine. Retrieved from <http://www.wired.com/techbiz/it/magazine/17-03/wp_quant?currentPage = all>.

Samuelson, R., 2012, May 27. It's time to drop the college-for-all crusade. Washington Post. Retrieved from <http://www.washingtonpost.com/opinions/its-time-to-drop-the-college-for-all-crusade/2012/05/27/gJQAzcUGvU_story.html>.

Satow, J., 2008, September 18. Ex-SEC official blames agency for blow-up of broker-dealers. New York Sun. Retrieved from <http://www.nysun.com/business/ex-sec-official-blames-agency-for-blow-up/86130/>.

Sawhill, I., Morton, J., 2008. Economic Mobility: Is the American Dream Alive and Well? Economic Mobility Project, Washington, D.C., Retrieved from <http://www.economicmobility.org/assets/pdfs/PEW_EMP_AMERICAN_DREAM.pdf>.

Sawhill, I., Morton, J., 2009. Economic Mobility: Is the American Dream Alive and Well? Economic Mobility Project, Washington, D.C., Retrieved from <http://www.economicmobility.org/assets/pdf>.

Schein, E., 2010. Organizational Culture and Leadership, fourth ed. Jossey-Bass, San Francisco.

Schelling, T., 2006. Micromotives and Macrobehavior. W. W. Norton & Co., New York.

Schneier, B., 2012. Liars and Outliers: Enabling the Trust that Society Needs to Thrive. John Wiley & Sons, Indianapolis.

Schultz, W., Dayan, P., Montague, P., 1997. A neural substrate of prediction and reward. Science 275, 1593−1599.

Schwartz, B., 1993. On the creation and destruction of values. In: Hechter, M., Nadel, L., Michod, R.E. (Eds.), The Origin of Values. Aldine de Gruyter, Hawthorne, New York, pp. 153−186.

Scott, J., Leonhardt, D., 2005, May 15. Shadowy lines that still divide. The New York Times. Retrieved from <http://www.nytimes.com/2005/05/15/national/class/OVERVIEW-FINAL.html?pagewanted = 2>.

Scruton, R., 2007. Culture Counts: Faith and Feeling in a World Besieged. Encounter Books, New York.

Securities Industry and Financial Markets Association, 2011, November. Global CDO issuance. Retrieved from <http://simfa.org/uploadedfiles/research/statistics/statisticsFiles/SF-global-cdo-issuance-SIMFA.xls>.

Semuels, A., 2011a, August 8. AIG's lawsuit against BofA illustrates more Countrywide woes. Los Angeles Times. Retrieved from <http://latimesblogs.latimes.com/money_co/2011/08/bank-of-america-aig.html>.

Semuels, A., 2011b, August 14. Companies are afraid to hire, even if business is improving. Los Angeles Times. Retrieved from <http://articles.latimes.com/2011/aug/14/business/la-fi-nohiring-20110814>.

Sengupta, R., 2010. Alt-A: the forgotten segment of the mortgage market. Fed. Reserve Bank St. Louis Rev. 92 (1), 55−71, Retrieved from <http://research.stlouisfed.org/publications/review/10/01/sengupta.pdf>.

Senge, P., 2006. The Fifth Discipline: The Art & Practice of the Learning Organization, revised ed. Doubleday, New York.

Shenn, J., 2007, April 4. Overlapping subprime exposure mask risks of CDOs, Moody's says. Bloomberg. Retrieved from <http://www.bloomberg.com/apps/news?pid = newsarchive& sid = aszosOrxVmjk&refer = home>.

Shenn, J. Woellert, L., Gopal, P., 2012, January 25. Obama answers Bernanke housing pleas with refinancing proposal: mortgages. Bloomberg. Retrieved from <http://www.bloomberg.com/news/2012-01-25/obama-answers-bernanke-housing-pleas-with-refinancing-proposal-mortgages.html>.

Sherwood, D., 2011. Seeing the Forest for the Trees: A Manager's Guide to Applying Systems Thinking. Nicholas Brealey Publishing, London.

Shiller, R., 2005. Irrational Exuberance, second ed. Princeton University Press, Princeton.

Short, D., 2012, July 31. July consumer confidence: the mood improves slightly. Advisor Perspectives. Data from Consumer Board Consumer Confidence Index. Retrieved from < http://www.advisorperspectives.com/dshort/updates/Conference-Board-Consumer-Confidence-Index.php>.

Siegel, D., 2012. Pocket Guide to Interpersonal Neurobiology. W. W. Norton, New York.

Simon, H., 1955. A behavioral model of rational choice. Q. J. Econ. 69, 98−118.

Simon, J., 2011, June 7. Consumer credit card debt drops slightly in April. CreditCards.com. Retrieved from <http://www.creditcards.com/credit-card-news/federal-reserve-g19-consumer-credit-april-2011-1276.php>.

Simpkins, C., Simpkins, A., 1999. Simple Taoism: A Guide to Living in Balance. Tuttle Publishing, Rutland, Vermont.

Skidelsky, R., 2009. Keynes: The Return of the Master. Public Affairs, New York.

Slovic, P., 2009. The construction of preference. In: Kahneman, D., Tversky, A. (Eds.), Choices, Values, and Frames. Cambridge University Press, Cambridge, pp. 489−502. (Originally published 1991 in Am. Psychol. 50 (5), 364−372).

Smith, A., 2004. The Theory of Moral Sentiments. Barnes & Noble Books, New York (Originally published in 1759).

Smith, A., 1937. An Inquiry into the Nature and Causes of the Wealth of Nations. The Modern Library, New York (Originally published in 1776).

Smuts, J., 1926. Holism and Evolution. The Macmillan Co, New York.

Solomon, R., 2005. Introducing Philosophy: A Text with Integrated Readings, eigthth ed. Oxford University Press, New York.

Solomon, R., 2008. Free enterprise, sympathy, and virtue. In: Zak, P. (Ed.), Moral Markets: The Critical Role of Values in the Economy. Princeton University Press, Princeton, pp. 16−41.

Sorkin, A. (Ed.), 2008, October 22. Rating agencies draw fire on capitol hill. The New York Times DealBook. Retrieved from < http://dealbook.nytimes.com/2008/10/22/rating-agencies-draw-fire-capitol-hill/>.

Soros, G., 2009. The Crash of 2008 and what it Means: The New Paradigm for Financial Markets. Perseus Books Group, New York.

Sowell, T., 2011. Basic Economics: A Common Sense Guide to the Economy, fourth ed. Basic Books, New York.

Spencer, H., 1890. The development hypothesis. Essays: Scientific, Political, & Speculative. London: G. Norman & Son. Reprint in 2011 by Filiquarian Publishing, LLC, vol. 1, pp. 1−7

Spencer, H., 1898. The Principles of Ethics, vol. 1. D. Appleton & Co., New York.

Stacey, R., 1996. Complexity and Creativity in Organizations. Berrett-Koehler Publishers, Inc., San Francisco.

Stacey, R., 2010. Complexity and Organizational Reality: Uncertainty and the Need to Rethink Management after the Collapse of Investment Capitalism, second ed. Routledge, New York.

Standard & Poors/Case-Shiller, 2011, May 13 & 2012, January 1. U.S. national S&P/Case-Shiller home price indices. Retrieved from <http://www.macromarkets.com/csi_housing/index.asp>.

Steger, M., Dik, B., 2010. Work as meaning: Individual and organizational benefits of engaging in meaningful work. In: Linley, P., Harrington, S., Garcea, N. (Eds.), Oxford Handbook of Positive Psychology and Work. Oxford University Press, Oxford, pp. 131−142.

Sterman, J., 2000. Business Dynamics: Systems Thinking and Modeling for a Complex World. Irwin McGraw-Hill, New York.

Sterman, J., 2001. System dynamics modeling: tools for learning in a complex world. Calif. Manage. Rev. 43 (4), 8−25.

Stern, S., 2008, April 10. Turmoil in the US credit markets: examining proposals to mitigate foreclosures and restore liquidity in the mortgage markets. Hearing before the Senate Banking Committee: Testimony of Scott Stern, Chief Executive Officer, Lenders One. Retrieved from <http://banking.senate.gov/public/_files/SternBankingStatement041008.pdf>.

Stevenson, L., Haberman, D., 1998. Ten Theories of Human Nature, third ed. Oxford University Press, New York.

Stiglitz, J., 2010. Freefall: America, Free Markets, and the Sinking of the World Economy. W. W. Norton & Company, New York.

Stiglitz, J., 2011, May. Inequality: of the 1%, by the 1%, for the 1%. Vanity Fair. Retrieved from <http://www.vanityfair.com/society/features/2011/05/top-one-percent-201105?currentPage = all>.

Strijbos, S., 2010. Systems thinking. In: Frodeman, R., Klein, J., Mitcham, C. (Eds.), Oxford Handbook of Interdisciplinarity. Oxford University Press, New York, pp. 453−470. , Retrieved from <http://ivl.slis.indiana.edu/km/pub/2010-borner-boyack-map-inter.pdf>.

Stringer, D., 2009, January 26. Iceland's government topples amid financial mess. FoxNews.com. Retrieved from <http://www.foxnews.com/printer_friendly_wires/2009Jan26/0,4675, EUIcelandCrisis,00.html>.

Strupczewski, J., O'Donnell, J. & Baker, L., 2012, July 27. Greed debt crisis fix may cost central banks up to 100 billion euros. DailyFinance, Reuters. Retrieved from <http://www.dailyfinance.com/2012/07/27/greek-debt-crisis-european-central-bank-haircut/>.

Swann, N., 2011, August 5. United States of America long-term rating lowered to 'AA + ' on political risks and rising debt burden; outlook negative. Standard & Poor's Global Credit Portal RatingsDirect. Retrieved from <http://www.standardandpoorss.com/ratingsdirect>.

Swanson, J., 2011, August 18. Housing bust provides new openings for mortgage fraud. Mortgage News Daily. Retrieved from <http://www.mortgagenewsdaily.com/08182011_mortgge_fraud.asp>.

Sweet, W., 2010, July 21. Dodd-Frank act becomes law. The Harvard Law School Forum on Corporate Governance and Financial Regulation. Retrieved from <http://blogs.law.harvard.edu/corpgov/2010/07/21/dodd-frank-act-becomes-law/>.

Taibbi, M., 2011. The people vs. Goldman Sachs. Roll. Stone, 40−46.

Tamny, J., 2009, March 19. Weak dollar, tight credit. Forbes.com. Retrieved from <http://www.forbes.com/2009/03/19/weak-dollar-tight-credit-markets-john-tamny.html>.

Tangney, J., Stuewig, J., Mashek, D., 2007. What's moral about the self-conscious emotions? In: Tracy, J., Robins, R., Tangney, J. (Eds.), The Self-Conscious Emotions: Theory and Research. The Guilford Press, New York, pp. 21−38.

Tasini, J., 2009. The Audacity of Greed: Free markets, Corporate Thieves, and the Looting of America. Ig Publishing, Brooklyn.

Taylor, J., 2009. Getting off Track: How Government Actions and Interventions Caused, Prolonged, and Worsened the Financial Crisis. Hoover Institution Press, Stanford, CA.

Temple-Raston, D., 2008, October 3. Bush signs $700 billion financial bailout. NPR. Retrieved from <http://www.npr.org/templates/story/story.php?storyId = 95336601>.

Tenbrunsel, A., Messick, D., 2004. Ethical fading: the role of self-deception in unethical behavior. Soc. Justice Res. 17 (2), 223–236.

The Economist, 2005, June 16. In come the waves. The Economist. Retrieved from <http://www.economist.com/node/4079027>.

Thiessen, M., 2012, June 8. Japan tsunami debris: 5 pieces found on west coast, more predicted to come ashore. HuffPost Green. Retrieved from <http://www.huffingtonpost.com/2012/06/08/japan-apanese-tsunami-debris_n_1579974.html>.

The Week, 2011, December 9. America underwater. The Week. Retrieved from <http://theweek.com/article/index/221962/real-estate-crisis-america-underwater>.

Thompson, E., 2007. The tulipmania: fact or artifact? Public Choice 130 (1-2), 99–114, Retrieved from <http://www.econ.ucla.edu/thompson/Document97.pdf>.

Thompson, W., Hickey, J., 2008. Society in Focus: An Introduction to Sociology, sixth ed. Pearson Education, Inc., New York.

Thornton, E., 2006, June 12. Inside Wall Street's culture of risk. BusinessWeek. Retrieved from <http://www.businessweeki.com/magazine/content/06_24/b3988004.htm>.

Thornton, M., 2004, August. This inflated house. The free market. Mises Institute Monthly. Retrieved from <http://mises.org/freemarket_detain.aspx?control = 500>.

Time Specials, 2011. 25 people to blame for the financial crisis. Time Magazine. Retrieved from <http://www.time.com/time/specials/packages/article/0,28804,1877351_1877350_1877339,00.html>.

Torres, C., Hopkins, C., 2012, April 4. Fed's Lacker says Volker Rule may be 'impossible' to implement. BloombergBusinessweek. Retrieved from <http://www.businessweek.com/news/2012-04-04/fed-s-lacker-says-volcker-rule-may-be-impossible-to-implement>.

Touryalai, H., 2011, October 12. Volker rule is out, how much will it hurt? Forbes Retrieved from <http://www.forbes.com/sites/halahtouryalai/2011/10/12/volcker-rule-is-out-how-much-will-it-hurt/>.

Tracy, J., Robins, R., 2007. The self in self-conscious emotions. In: Tracy, J., Robins, R., Tangney, J. (Eds.), The Self-Conscious Emotions: Theory and Research. The Guilford Press, New York, pp. 3–20.

Treanor, J., Kollewe, J., 2010, October 14. Robo-signing eviction scandal rattles Wall Street. The Guardian. Retrieved from <http://www.guardian.co.uk/business/2010/oct/14/wells-fargo-mortgage-foreclosure-robo-signer>.

TreasuryDirect, 2012, June 12. The debt to the penny and who holds it. U.S. Department of the Treasury, Bureau of the Public Debt. Retrieved from <http://www.treasurydirect.gov/govt/reports/reports.htm>.

Trice, H., Beyer, J., 1993. The Cultures of Work Organizations. Prentice-Hall, Inc., Englewood Hills, New Jersey.

Trumbull, M., 2010, March 10. Lehman Bros. Used accounting trick amid financial crisis - and earlier. The Christian Science Monitor. Retrieved from <http://www.csmonitor.com/USA/2010/0312/Lehman-Bros.-used-accounting-trick-amid-financial-crisis-and-earlier>.

Tseng, N., 2011, April 21. Where's the wealth effect? *Fortune*. CNN Money. <http://finance.fortune.cnn.com/2011/04/21/wheres-the-wealth-effect/>.

Tversky, A., Kahneman, D., 2008. Judgment under uncertainty: Heuristics and biases. In: Kahneman, D., Slovic, P., Tversky, A. (Eds.), Judgment Under Uncertainty: Heuristics and Biases. Cambridge University Press, New York, pp. 3—20.

Twenge, J., Campbell, W., 2009. The Narcissism Epidemic: Living in the Entitlement Age. Free Press, New York.

United Nations Development Programme, 2010. Human development index and its components. Human Development Report: Statistical Annex 2010. Retrieved from <http://hdr.undp.org/en/media/HDR_2010_EN_Table1.pdf>.

United States Courts, 2011. Bankruptcy courts: Bankruptcy cases commenced, terminated and pending. Retrieved from <http://www.uscourts.gov/Statistics/BankruptcyStatistics.aspx>.

UPI, 2009, January 8. Obama: Greed led to economic crisis. United Press International, Inc Retrieved from <http://www.upi.com/Top_News/2009/01/08/Obama-Greed-led-to-economic-crisis/UPI-39941231434123/>.

U.S. Bureau of Economic Analysis, 2012. Current-dollar and 'real' gross domestic product. Retrieved from <http://www.bea.gov/national/>.

U.S. Bureau of Labor Statistics, 2001. Consumer price index: Revision of the CPI housing sample and estimators. Retrieved from <http://www.bls.gov/cpi/cpifp001.htm>.

U.S. Bureau of Labor Statistics, 2012a. Labor force statistics from the current population survey: Unemployment rate. Retrieved from <http://www.bls.gov/cps/prev_yrs.htm>.

U.S. Bureau of Labor Statistics, 9 Aug 2012b. Consumer Expenditure Survey. Retrieved from <http://www.bls.gov/cex/csxreport.htm>.

U.S. Census Bureau, 2011a. Table H-9. Type of household—All races by median and mean income: 1980 to 2010. Retrieved from <http://www.census.gov/hhes/www/income/data/historical/household/>.

U.S. Census Bureau, 2011b. Houses sold by region: Annual data. Retrieved from <http://www.census.gov/const/soldann.pdf>.

U.S. Census Bureau, 2011c. Median and average sales prices of new homes sold in United States. Retrieved from <www.census.gov/const/uspricemon.pdf>.

U.S. Census Bureau, 2011d. Table 1. Employment, work experience, and earnings by age and education. Retrieved from <http://www.census.gov/hhes/www/income/data/earnings/call2us-both.html>.

U.S. Census Bureau, 2011e. Table P-1. CPS population and per capita money income, all races: 1967 to 2009. Retrieved from <http://www.census.gov/hhes/www/income/data/historical/people/index.html>.

U.S. Census Bureau, 2011f. Table H-4. Gini ratios for households, by race and Hispanic origin of householder: 1967 to 2009. Retrieved from <http://www.census.gov/hhes/www/income/data/historical/inequality/index.html>.

U. S. Census Bureau, 2011g. New privately owned housing units started: annual data, single family. Retrieved from <http://www.census.gov/const/compann.pdf>.

U. S. Census Bureau, 2011h. Table 977. Existing one-family homes sold and price by region: 1990 to 2010. Retrieved from <http://www.census.gov/compendia/statab/2012/tables/12s0977.pdf>.

U.S. Census Bureau, 2012a. Table 1194. Mortgage originations and delinquency and foreclosure rates: 1990 to 2010. Retrieved from <http://www.census.gov/compendia/statab/2012/tables/12s1194.pdf> and from <http://www.census.gov/compendia/statab/2011/tables/11s1193.xls>.

U.S. Census Bureau, 2012b. Table 14. Homeownership rates for the US and regions: 1965 to present. Retrieved from <www.census.gov/hhes/www/housing/hvs/historic/index.html>.

U.S. Department of Justice, Federal Bureau of Investigation, 2008. Financial crimes report to the public: Fiscal year 2008. Financial Crimes Section, Criminal Investigative Division. Retrieved from <http://www.fbi.gov/stats-services/publications/fcs_report2008>.

U.S. Department of Justice, Federal Bureau of Investigation, 2009. 2009 Financial crimes report. Financial Crimes Section, Criminal Investigative Division. Retrieved from <http://www.fbi.gov/stats-services/publications/financial-crimes-report-2009>.

U.S. National Debt, 2008, November 2. PerotCharts. Retrieved from <http://perotcharts.com/2008/11/us-national-debt-2008/>.

U.S. Securities and Exchange Commission, 2008, July. Summary report of issues identified in the Commission Staff's examinations of select credit rating agencies. Office of Compliance Inspections and Examinations. Retrieved from <http://www.sec.gov/news/studies/2008/craexamination070808.pdf>.

U.S. Securities and Exchange Commission, 2011, December 3. The investor's advocate: how the SEC protects investors, maintains market integrity, and facilitates capital formation. U.S. Securities and Exchange Commission. Retrieved from <http://www.sec.gov/about/whatwe-do.shtml>.

U.S. Senate Permanent Subcommittee on Investigations, 2011. Wall Street and the Financial Crisis: Anatomy of a Financial Collapse. Permanent Subcommittee on Investigation, Washington. D.C.

Vallee, D., 2006. A new plateau for the U.S. securitization market. FDIC Outlook3−10, Retrieved from <http://www.fdic.gov/bank/analytical/retional/ro20063q/na/2006_fall01.html>.

Van Voris, B., Weidlich, T., 2011, June 20. Merrill must face class action over mortgage securities. Bloomberg. Retrieved from <http://www.bloomberg.com/news/2011-06-20/merrill-must-face-class-action-by-fund-over-mortgage-backed-securities.html?cmpid = yhoo>.

Veblen., T., 1931. The Theory of the Leisure Class: An Economic Study of Institutions. The Modern Library, New York.

von Mises, L., 1981. The Theory of Money and Credit. Liberty Fund, Indianapolis (1934 trans. first published 1912).

Wang, L., Malhotra, D., Murnighan, J., 2011. Economics education and greed. Acad Manage Learn. Educ. 10 (4), 642−660.

Waring, D., 2008, February 19. An explanation of how the Fed moves interest rates. Informed Trades. Retrieved from <http://www.informedtrades.com/13694-explanation-how-fed-moves-interest-rates.html>.

Weckowicz, T., 2000. Ludwig von Bertalanffy (1901−1972): a Pioneer of General Systems Theory (CSR Working Paper No. 89-2). Edmonton, Canada: Center for Systems Research, University of Alberta. Retrieved from <http://www.richardjung.cz/bert1.pdf>

Weintraub, E., 2011. What is wrong with buy and bail? Retrieved from <http://homebuying.about.com/od/foreclosures/f/061808_Buy-Bail.htm>.

Weistroffer, C., 2009, December 21. Credit default swaps: Heading towards a more stable system. Deutsche Bank Research. Retrieved from <http://www.dbresearch.com/PROB/DBR_INTERNET-EN-PROD/PROD0000000000252032.pdf>.

White, L., 2008. Inflation. Library of Economics and Liberty. Retrieved from <http://www.econlib.org/library/Enc/Inflation.html>.

White, L., 2009, August. Housing finance and the 2008 financial crisis. Cato Institute. Retrieved from <http://www.downsizinggovernment.org/hud/housing-finance-2008-financial-crisis>.

WideAngle, 2008, November 21. Economic crisis in a globalized world. PBS. Retrieved from <http://www.pbs.org/wnet/wideangle/uncategorized/how-global-is-the-crisis/3543/>.

Wiener, N., 1948. Cybernetics. The Technology Press, John Wiley & Sons, New York.

Williams Jr., R., 1965. American society: A sociological Interpretation, second ed. rev. Alfred A. Knopf, New York.

Wilson, J., 1993. The Moral Sense. The Free Press, New York.

WIPO, 2010. World intellectual property indicators. World Intellectual Property Organization. Retrieved from <http://www.wipo.int/export/sites/www/ipstats/en/statistics/patents/pdf/941_2010.pdf>.

Wiseman, P., 2010, June 2. Buffett comes to defense of credit-rating agencies. USA Today. Retrieved from <http://www.usatoday.com/MONEY/usaedition/2010-06-02-fcic-ratings-agencies-hearing_NU.htm?csp = 34>.

Wiseman, P., 2012, July 22. Global economy in worst shape since 2009. Bloomberg Businessweek. Retrieved from <http://businessweek.com/ap/2012-07-22/slower-global-growth-reflects-close-economic-links>.

Wolf, R., 2012, January 27. Obama says college costs must be held in check. USA Today. Retrieved from <http://www.usatoday.com/news/washington/story/2012-01-27/Obama-college-costs-auto-industry/52817938/1>.

World Bank, 2011. Gross Domestic Product: GDP in current U.S. dollars. Not adjusted for inflation. Retrieved from <http://www.google.com/publicdata>.

Woods Jr., T., 2009. Meltdown: A Free-Market Look at Why the Stock Market Collapsed, the Economy Tanked, and Government Bailouts will Make Things Worse. Regnery Publishing, Inc, Washington, DC.

Yahoo!® Finance, 2012, June 12. Retrieved from <http://finance.yahoo.com/>.

Zak, P., 2008. Values and value: Moral economics. In: Zak, P.J. (Ed.), Moral Markets: The Critical Role of Values in the Economy. Princeton University Press, Princeton, pp. 261–279.

Zandi, M., 2009. Financial Shock: A 360° Look at the Subprime Mortgage Implosion, and how to Avoid the Next Financial Crisis. Pearson Education, Inc., Upper Saddle River, New Jersey.

Zuckerman, G., 2009, October 31. Profiting from the crash. The Wall Street Journal. Retrieved from <http://online.wsj.com/article/SB10001424052748703574604574499740849179448.html>.

Adjustable Rate Mortgage (ARM) Unlike a fixed rate mortgage where the interest rate stays the same during the life of the loan, the ARM periodically moves interest rates relative to a specified index. The initial rate and payment amount remains for a short period—from a month to 5 + years. Initially, ARMs may offer lower interest rates than fixed rate mortgages, but the borrower assumes the risk that the interest will go up over time.[1] Those looking for short-term ownership with flexible monthly payments (e.g., they want to buy property and fix it up to sell) would find this type of mortgage useful.

Affordability Index This index is the ratio between median housing prices and median income; it measures how many years of income it would take to buy an average house in the current economic environment.

Balancing Feedback Loops Balancing feedback loops are systems thinking constructs that illustrate how a system moves toward a goal or a desired state, or maintains stability. A condition that resists change, such as culture, can be represented by a continuous loop of balancing feedback.

Behavior over Time (BOT) Behavior over time is a graphical representation of how a given variable moves over a period of time.[2] Three fundamental behavior patterns (exponential, goal seeking, and oscillation) and two hybrid patterns (S-shaped growth and overshoot and collapse) are used in this book. Exponential growth or decay illustrates the behavior of a reinforcing feedback loop and a goal-seeking pattern is created by a balancing feedback loop. Oscillation incorporates delay in the loop. Other patterns use a combination of both reinforcing and balancing feedback loops.

Bond Ratings The grade of corporate bond ratings indicates their credit quality. Bond ratings below BBB/Baa are called junk bonds. A triple-A rating for a corporate bond means a favorable cost of borrowing money and is a coveted status that can reduce a corporation's cost of doing business. Triple-A for a bond indicates to potential investors that the risk of loss is low. If risk is inadequately identified, the bonds or other securities such as CDOs could be underpriced, causing potential losses to the issuing organizations. This was especially an issue for financial organizations such as AIG during the crisis. Their traditionally high credit rating and belief that loans in their CDO offerings wouldn't experience massive defaults masked their actual risk.[3] (See also Credit Ratings).

Causal Loop Diagram (CLD) In systems thinking terminology, causal loop diagrams are simplified ways to describe "the essential components and interactions in a system."[4] These diagrams include curved causal link arrows that depict influence from cause to effect, and the polarity of that linkage. An "s" indicates that cause and effect move in the same

---

1. Federal Reserve Board, 2009.
2. See Maani and Cavana, 2007.
3. Heakal, 2010.
4. Richardson, 1986.

direction and an "o" shows that they move in opposite directions (e.g., when cause increases, effect decreases below what it would have been without influence of cause). Causal link arrows combine into circular forms that represent balancing (B) and reinforcing (R) feedback loops and reinforcing feed-forward loops. Delays between cause and effect are also shown in causal loop diagrams.

Collateralized Debt Obligation (CDO) CDOs are a type of security whose value and payments come from underlying fixed income assets. A financial entity may hold a portfolio of assets, including mortgage-backed securities (MBS), commercial real estate bonds, and corporate loans, then sell packages of cash flow from them in the form of CDOs. CDOs have different maturity and risks; the higher the risk, the more the CDO pays. CDO-squared securities make new CDOs from a collection of CDOs, and segment risk in the same way.

CDO use began to rise in 2001 when a new computer model, Li's Gaussian Copula Model, allowed them to be priced more rapidly. This model was not well understood and risk was often underpriced, especially given the increasing proportion of high-risk mortgages in the underlying assets. The model was sensitive to house price appreciation and would "blow up" if the housing market declined nationwide.[5] CDOs were first issued in 1987; they sometimes offered returns 2 to 3 percent higher than corporate bonds with the same rating.

Consumeritis The book introduces this term to describe the inflamed belief that buying material goods will satisfy all desires. It suggests that this condition is part of the American culture and encouraged excessive buying during the recent economic crisis. It incorporates the idea of "conspicuous consumption" first used in 1899 by Thorstein Veblen to describe Americans' enthusiastic pursuit of material comfort.[6]

Consumer Price Index (CPI) CPI computes a weighted average of seven major categories of goods and services including food, clothing, and housing. The housing group includes cost of renting as well as a home owner's equivalent rent or residential rent to incorporate housing prices. The housing group accounts for 41 percent of the total CPI. CPI is one measure of inflation.[7]

Credit Default Swap (CDS) CDSs hedge against particular credit risks. A CDS buyer receives credit protection, and the seller guarantees the creditworthiness of the product. Thus, default is transferred from the holder of the security to the seller of the CDS. CDSs have existed since the early 1990s; at that time they involved mostly corporate debt. Because there was extensive historical data about corporate debt, executives had confidence in using and pricing them. In 2005, financial managers began to increase their use of CDOs that pooled home mortgages, credit card payments, and personal loans.[8]

Credit Ratings A credit rating is an indicator of creditworthiness of corporations' or individuals' ability to repay their debts. For a corporation, it is based on borrowing and repayment history, as well as on the availability of assets and extent of liabilities. Independent rating services such as Standard & Poor's, Moody's, and Fitch provide these evaluations. There are multiple levels of risk ranging from triple-A, the highest credit quality, to D. "A" ratings are safe, "B" ratings are medium safe to speculative,

---

5. Salmon, 2009.
6. Veblen, 1931.
7. See U.S. Bureau of Labor Statistics, 2001.
8. O'Harrow and Dennis, 2009.

"C" ratings indicate high likelihood of bankruptcy or inability to pay, and "D" ratings indicate bankruptcy and inability to make payments. (See also Bond Ratings.)

For individuals, credit scores "rank-order consumers by how likely they are to pay their credit obligations as agreed." They provide a risk indicator used by financial institutions to make lending decisions. The most widely used credit score model in the U.S. was created by Fair Isaac Corporation (FICO). FICO scores are statistically calculated from consumers' credit files.[9] (See also FICO scores).

ECR Culture ECR stands for *entitlement, consumption, and risk*. ECR culture combines primary values and beliefs from the American culture and from corporate cultures for lending and financial organizations that were prominent in the economic crisis. This hybrid culture directly affected material desires in the systems interpretation of the crisis.

Efficient Markets Hypothesis This hypothesis has influenced decision making in the stock market and the securities markets and was an important theory that influenced financial investment decisions prior to the economic crisis. It asserts that prices in financial markets are efficient in that they "fully reflect all available information," that is, prices reflect relevant risk.[10] It was introduced in the 1970s by finance professor Eugene Fama.

Fannie Mae and Freddie Mac Fannie Mae (FNMA or Federal National Mortgage Association) and Freddie Mac (FHLMC or Federal Home Loan Mortgage Corporation) are privately owned, government-sponsored enterprises (GSE) in the U.S. As housing GSEs, they are exempt from state and local taxes and receive federal subsidies. Fannie Mae was created to give low-income families access to mortgages. Beginning as a wholly owned government corporation in 1938, Fannie Mae was converted to a GSE in 1968.[11] Freddie Mac was created in 1970 to expand the secondary market for mortgages. Rather than hold mortgages, Freddie Mac pools them, guarantees the credit risk, and sells interests in the pools to investors, creating mortgage-backed securities (MBSs). This process increases the money available for mortgage lending and reduces the risk for the issuing banks. On 7 September 2008, the U.S. government put Fannie Mae and Freddie Mac into conservatorship, and took over power to control assets and operate the firm; shareholder dividends were suspended. The government now stands behind about $5 trillion of Fannie Mae and Freddie Mac debt; Freddie and Fannie finance about 40 percent of all U.S. mortgages.[12,13,14]

Fed (the Fed) This term refers to the central bank of the U.S., the Board of Governors of the Federal Reserve System. Founded in 1913, the Fed is congressionally mandated to ensure a healthy economy by maintaining maximum employment, stable prices, and a stable financial system.[15]

Federal Deposit Insurance Corporation (FDIC) This independent U.S. government corporation guarantees the safety of deposits in banks up to $250,000 per depositor.

---

9. FICO, 2010; Investopedia, 2010; Consumer Federation of America, 2010.
10. Fama, 1970.
11. Crippen, 2001.
12. Crippen, 2001.
13. Jickling, 2008.
14. Leonnig, 2008.
15. Rajan, 2010.

Feedback Loops There are two basic types of feedback loops: balancing loops that tend to stabilize a system and bring it toward a goal and reinforcing loops that can either grow or decay without bound. Chapter 1 on systems thinking describes these loops in detail.

Feed-Forward Loops Similar to reinforcing feedback loops, feed-forward loops are generally used to described speculation or self-fulfilling prophecies. In these loops the anticipation or expectation of an outcome determines behavior.

FICO Scores FICO scores represent individuals' credit ratings (see credit ratings) that lenders use to determine suitability for a loan. FICO scores range from 300 to 850; 850 is the best score achievable. In U.S. most people score in the 600 s to 700 s; about 13 percent score above 800 and 2 percent score lower than 500. Higher FICO scores may merit better interest rates. Scores below 600 indicate high risk to lenders who then charge higher rates or turn down loan applications.[16] This credit rating was created by Fair Isaac Corporation.

Fixed Rate Mortgage (FRM) Fixed rate mortgages are the traditional form of home and product loans in the U.S. For these loans, interest rate is set when the loan originates and stays the same during the life of the loan.

Gini Index for Income Inequality The Gini index or Gini ratio, named for Italian statistician Corrado Gini, measures the inequality of given variables. For income, it describes the concentration of household income in a country. This index ranges from 0.0 when every household has the same income to 1.0 when one household has all the income. The Gini index for household income inequality was 0.45 in 1995 and grew to 0.466 in 2008. Thus, more income was held by fewer people as income inequality increased by more than 3.5 percent.[17]

Ginnie Mae Ginnie Mae (GNMA Government National Mortgage Association (GNMA/Ginnie Mae) is a U.S. government corporation that promotes affordable housing for families of modest means. It enables private lenders to sell securities that contain government guaranteed loans.

Government Sponsored Enterprise (GSE) These enterprises were created by the U.S. government to enhance credit availability to various sectors of the economy. In addition they create what is called a secondary market by guaranteeing or bonding loans and by securitization. Fannie Mae, Freddie Mac, and Federal Home Loan Banks are GSEs.

Gross Domestic Product (GDP) First developed in 1934, this metric is the output of goods and services produced by all labor and property within a country for some stated period. In 2008, annual GDP for the United States reached $14.291 trillion (current dollars) and world GDP was $61.38 trillion.[18] U.S. GDP dropped in 2009 to $13.939 trillion and increased to $15.094 trillion in 2011.[19] U.S. GDP far exceeds the GDP of other nations (in 2010 China ranked 2nd and Japan ranked 3rd in the world).

House Price Index (HPI) This index gives a measure of single-family house prices that allows one to follow changes to housing prices. One of the primary indices, and the one used in this book, is the Standard & Poors/Case-Shiller (S&P/Case-Shiller) national home price index. This index is updated monthly and aggregates home price

---

16. FICO, 2010; Investopedia, 2010; and Consumer Federation of America, 2010.
17. U.S. Census Bureau, 2011f.
18. World Bank, 2011.
19. U.S. Bureau of Economic Analysis, 2012.

indices for all 9 U.S. Census divisions. It is normalized at 100 for the first quarter of 2000.[20]

Mortgage-Backed Securities (MBS) Banks sell mortgages to financial entities such as Freddie Mac. These entities then bundle the mortgages into mortgage-backed securities and sell interests in the MBS bundles to individual investors. In this way banks can take mortgages off their balance sheets and no longer worry about whether they go into default. (It removes one incentive for banks to make sure loans are made to qualified buyers.)[21]

Reinforcing Feedback Loops Reinforcing feedback loops are systems thinking constructs that reflect continuous, often exponential, growth or decline.

SN Incentive Systems and SN Rewards Used in the systems description of the economic crisis, SN stands for "short-term, narrow focused." It describes the significant attributes of incentive systems that lending and financial firms used to motivate their employees to accomplish organizational goals and the rewards given to employees.

Securitization Financial institutions, such as Fannie Mae, Freddie Mac, and others pool various types of debt such as residential mortgages and credit card debt, into financial bonds, securities, or MBSs (mortgage-backed securities). Investors who buy these securities receive regular payments of principle and interest from their underlying assets. Securitization allows lenders to sell their loans and use the proceeds to make new loans, thus continually refreshing the source of funds so that more people can borrow money. Securitization practices began in the U.S. in the 1970s when Ginnie Mae bought FHA and VA mortgage loans. Freddie Mac and Fannie Mae began to buy qualifying loans and structure them as MBSs in the 1980; by the mid-1980s, private financial agencies were securitizing loans.

Subprime Mortgages Loans are graded according to credit score and other factors relating to a borrower's ability to repay. Some banks offer six or more loan grades ranging from "premier plus" (or equivalent) to C −. These loan grades are further grouped into prime and subprime categories. Prime, or standard loans, carry the most favorable terms and interest rates. Subprime loans are the most risky and offer less favorable terms and interest rates; their probability of default can be at least six times greater than primes. There are several grades of subprime loans, ranging (in this book) from A − to C −. Subprime loans are typically made to individuals with weak credit history and greater risk of default. Subprime loans usually have FICO credit scores below about 640.[22]

System Dynamics System dynamics was derived from systems theory whose concepts originated in the 1700s. System dynamics became popular in the 1950s and 1960s. It uses models and computer simulations to understand behavior of an entire system, and has been applied to the behavior of large and highly complex national issues. It portrays the structures in systems as feedback loops, lags and other descriptors to explain dynamics (i.e., how a system behaves over time). Its quantitative methodology relies on what are called stock-and-flow diagrams that show how levels of specific elements accumulate over time and the rate at which they change. Qualitative system thinking constructs evolved from this quantitative discipline.

---

20. The reference value for HPI is 100 and moves up or down from there.
21. Amadeo, 2009.
22. Chomsisengphet and Pennington-Cross, 2006.

Systems Thinking Systems thinking is a discipline or process that considers how individual elements interact with one another within a whole entity. As an approach to solving problems, systems thinking uses relationships among individual elements and the dynamics of these relationships to explain the behavior of a whole system, such as an ecosystem, a social system, or an organization.

Tranche This term describes a piece or segment (a bond) of a structured security such as a collateralized debt obligation. Tranche come from the French word for slice. Each tranche is associated with some level of risk, reward, or maturity characteristic.

Troubles Asset Relief Program (TARP) This government program was signed into law in October 2008 to purchase assets and equity from troubled financial organizations that were hit by the subprime mortgage crisis. The U.S. Department of Treasury was authorized to purchase or insure up to $700 billion of these assets.

Index

Note: Page numbers followed by "*f*" and "*t*" refer to figures and tables, respectively.